C-123 RESCUE!

Jackson barely had time to set up a landing attitude as the aircraft settled towards the threshold. The debris-strewn runway looked like an obstacle course, with a burning helicopter blocking the way. Jackson stood on the brakes and skidded to a halt just before reaching the gutted helicopter.

The three controllers scrambled from the ditch and dived into the aircraft as the surprised enemy gunners opened fire. In the front of the aircraft Major Campbell spotted a 122mm rocket shell coming towards them.

Also in the Special Warfare Series

NAKED WARRIORS by Cdr. Francis Douglas Fane, USNR
(Ret.) and Don Moore
MOBILE GUERRILLA FORCE by James C. Donahue

AIR COMMANDO

FIFTY YEARS OF THE USAF AIR COMMANDO AND SPECIAL OPERATIONS FORCES, 1944-1994

PHILIP D. CHINNERY

(Published in hardcover as *Any Time, Any Place*)

St. Martin's Paperbacks

Published in hardcover as *Any Time, Any Place*

First published in the UK in 1994 by Airlife Publishing Ltd

Published by arrangement with the Naval Institute Press

AIR COMMANDO

Library of Congress Catalog Card Number: 94-66597

ISBN: 0-312-95881-1

Printed in the United States of America

Naval Institute Press hardcover edition published in 1994
St. Martin's Paperbacks edition/January 1997

St. Martin's Paperbacks are published by St. Martin's Press, 175 Fifth Avenue, New York, NY 10010.

10 9 8 7 6 5 4 3 2 1

CONTENTS

FOREWORD

I have been involved in Special Air Operations most of my military and civilian career; and this book, *Any Time, Any Place*, is the first effort that attempts to document the full story of our Air Commando and Special Operations Units. For more than 50 years, these units have accomplished nearly every type of operation that can be imagined and even some that cannot be imagined. Beginning in the jungles of Burma and the Philippines during the Second World War and thereafter in Korea and South-East Asia, Air Commandos served in many countries, including South America, Africa, Iran, the Middle East, Grenada, Panama, Somalia and the Persian Gulf. No mission was too difficult or dangerous when our country called. Chinnery is the first author to attempt to compile a comprehensive journal of these unique endeavours.

Air Commando operations reached their peak in South-East Asia, including a multitude of overt and covert operations; Forward Air Control, Covert Helicopter in-and ex-filtration, Air Rescue, Close Air Support, Armed visual and photo recce, Psychological Warfare, Night and Day Interdiction, Gunship operations in AC-47s, AC-119s, AC-130s, helicopters and light aircraft such as Porters and Helio Couriers with 20mm gunpods, Flare Support, Movement and resupply of Special Forces and conventional units. No group of aviators has come close to matching the Special Operators' skills and versatility. Although the conventional military have been prone to write these off as peripheral and ineffective (no body count to back up the claims,) these operations had an immense real and psychological impact on our adversaries; vastly exceeding the nominal investment on our part.

Half of the United States Air Force Congressional Medal of Honor winners in Vietnam were Air Commandos, each flying a different aircraft and mission.

Chinnery in this book covers a majority of these missions. No-one else has even attempted to document so many of these operations. I'm sure there will be many people who will read this book and clamour for more. It is a must for all military personnel and other agencies involved in our national security. High on the list is the CIA, State Department officials and the White House personnel, who are now attempting to formulate a national policy for projecting US military power in many threatened areas.

Harry C. 'Heinie' Aderholt
Brigadier-General, USAF, retired
Commando One, Fort Walton Beach, Florida. June 1994

INTRODUCTION

I originally set out to tell the story of the Air Commando and Special Operations Squadrons of the USAF during the long Vietnam war. The air commandos flew the first combat aircraft to South Vietnam in 1961, and their successors, renamed Special Operations Squadrons, flew the last helicopters out in 1975 as South Vietnam, Laos and Cambodia fell to the communists.

It soon became apparent that the air commandos had a history stretching back to the Second World War, when the 1st Air Commando Group was formed to support the British General Orde Wingate and his "Chindit" jungle fighters in Burma. Epitomising the "Can Do" attitude of this élite group, the air commandos carried out the successful Operation Thursday on 5 March 1944, an airborne invasion of Japanese-held Burma which landed thousands of Chindits 200 miles behind enemy lines.

One month earlier the Air Commandos acquired their motto. Following the crash during training of a C-47 towing two gliders, which killed four British and three American troops, the commander of the Chindit unit sent a note to the Air Commandos: "Please be assured that we will go with your boys any place, any time, any where". The phrase stuck, and fifty years later the motto, and variations thereof, are still used by Air Force Special Operations Command and its units.

Two more Air Commando Groups were created before the end of the Second World War, one fighting in Burma, the other in the South West Pacific. With the outbreak of communist-inspired brush-fire wars in 1960, the air commandos were called to arms again. Volunteers with the qualities of courage, leadership and resourcefulness were sought for an outfit called Jungle Jim. Their attitude was such that, when Colonel Harry C. Aderholt, taking command of the 1st Air Commando Wing in March 1964, called a muster of his pilots and introduced himself with the words ''I hear there are a bunch of fighter jocks looking for a place to die, and I have come to lead you to that place . . .,'' His words were drowned as the troops stamped and yelled their approval.

The Air Commando Farm Gate detachment was the first Air Force unit to fight in Vietnam, arriving in 1961. As the war gathered momentum, more air commando squadrons were formed. They flew old propeller-driven aircraft; T-28s, B-26s, C-47s and A-1s. They took on any job that the regular air force, with its fast jets and atomic bombers, did not want or could not do. Soon they expanded to four Wings, one in Florida, two in South Vietnam and one in Thailand. They formed squadrons to fly behind enemy lines, supporting Army Special Forces, and brought into service a new breed of gunships; Spookies, Shadows, Stingers and Spectres. In 1968 they were renamed Special Operations squadrons and wings, to reflect their roles more accurately.

As the war came to an end in 1975, the special ops fleet dwindled to a shadow of its former self. The seizure of the US Embassy in Iran in 1980 and the failure of the rescue mission, highlighted the deficiencies of the force. A decade of struggle and neglect followed, while the dedicated supporters of the special ops mission fought to establish themselves in the air force community. In the meantime, the squadrons took part in the invasion of Grenada in 1983 and of Panama in 1989.

Eventually the day came in 1990 when Air Force Special Operations Command was created. With three Wings at its command, AFSOC was ready when Saddam Hussein's troops invaded neighbouring Kuwait, and when the allies went to war in 1991, special ops were at the point of the spear. A raiding force, led by Pave Low helicopters from the 20th SOS, flew hundreds of miles into Iraq to destroy two enemy radar sites and open a corridor to Baghdad for the allied bombers, as Operation Desert Storm began.

In this book the reader will find first-hand accounts from the glider pilots who landed deep behind Japanese lines in 1944, and from gunship crews who flew over the dark jungles of Laos in 1968, hunting for North Vietnamese trucks sneaking down the Ho Chi Minh Trail. Read the story of the raid to free the American prisoners of war from Son Tay, deep inside North Vietnam in 1970; share the despair of the aircrews at Desert One in 1980 as the mission to rescue the hostages held in the US Embassy ended amongst the maelstrom of burning aircraft and exploding ammunition.

For fifty years the air commandos and special operators have fought for freedom against dictators, communist aggression and terrorists. With the modern world torn by civil war and starvation, and an unsettled Middle East, not to mention the instability in the former Soviet Union, the reader can sleep easier in the knowledge that brave men with the "Can Do" attitude are still out there, ready to fly and fight "Any Time, Any Place".

Philip D. Chinnery
1994

ACKNOWLEDGMENTS

The author would like to thank the following individuals and associations for their kind assistance with the research for this book.

Mr. Guy Aceto, *Air Force Magazine*; Brig.-Gen. Harry C. "Heinie" Aderholt, 56th ACW; Major Doug Armstrong, 20th SOS; Captain O'Dean E. "Stretch" Ballmes, 6th SOS; Robert A. Beck, 2nd FS, 2nd ACG; Major Charles A. Boerschig, Black Spot; Marc L. Bornn, 311th ACS; Major Joseph A. Buebe, 5th ACS; Olin B. Carter, 6th FS(C), 1st ACG; Colonel Bobby Clark, 16th SOS; Gerald S. Collins, 3rd FS, 3rd ACG; Maj.-General Hugh L. Cox, III, 1st SOW; Colonel Eugene P. Deatrick, 1st SOS; Colonel John Denham, 21st SOS; Jack Drummond, 606th ACS; Captain Melvin Elliott, 1st ACS; Lt.-Colonel Ralph C. Evans, Jr., 5th ACS; William A. Gericke, 17th SOS; Sgt. Cyril Hall, Chindit, 3rd West Indian Brigade, Nigerian Regiment; 2nd Lt. Carter Harman, 1st ACG; Sandra A. Henry, AFSOC/PAO; Owen Hitchings, 1st Flight Det.; Maj.-General Jim Hobson, 8th SOS; Major Joe Holden, 6th FS(C); Larry Holzapfel, 155th LS, 2nd ACG; Dr. Charlie L. Jones, CCT; Colonel Robert H. Karre, 6th SOS; Colonel Jim Kyle, author *The Guts to Try*; Sapper Bill Lark, Royal Engineers, Chindit; John L. Larrison, 602nd ACS; Terry M. Love, photographer; Hap Lutz, Project 404; Paul Marshalk, 609th SOS; Patrick Martin, author; Brig.-Gen. James R. McCarthy; 309th ACS; TSgt. Jim McClain, 15th SOS; Clay McCutchan, AFSOC/HO; Bob McGovern, 155th LS, 2nd ACG; Richard L. McKinney, THAI-AM; Sid McNeil, 6th SOS; Colonel Frank B. Merchant, B-25 section, 1st ACG; Lt.-Colonel Bernard V. Moore, 8th SOS; R. Wayne Moorhead, 604th SOS; Colonel Thomas R. Owens, 56th ACW; Colonel John M. Patton, 14th ACW; Lt.-Colonel Harold G. Pierce, 6th SOS; Dr. Jon Pote, photographer; TSgt. Dale K. Robinson, 20th SOS; Pamela A. Rodriguez-Roberson, 71st SOS; Colonel John S. Rogers, 9th SOS; Eugene D. Rossel, Farm Gate; Colonel Mike Russell, 21st SOS; Neal B. Saxon, 166th LS, 1st ACG; Don Schoknecht, Farm Gate; Tom Schornak, 6th FS(C); Lt.-Colonel Earl W. Scott, 71st SOS; Maj.-Gen. Richard V. Secord; Major Mike Shook, 71st SOS; Colonel Tony Skur, 1st SOS; Lew Smith, 602nd FS(C); Colonel Jay M. Strayer, 40th ARRS; Colonel William C Thomas; Waterpump; MSgt. Stephen A. Thornburg, 16th SOS; MSgt. Chuck R. Timms, 15th SOS; Hal E. Voigt, 2nd ACG; MSgt. Anthony R. Walton, 15th SOS; Colonel Louis W. Weber, 604th ACS; A. R. 'Van' Van De Weghe, 1st FS, 1st ACG; Tom Wickstrom, 609th SOS; Jim Woods, 1st ACG; Robert G. Young, 23rd TASS.

The Code of the Air Commando (1965)

1 I will never forget that I am an American fighting man, placing duty, honor, country above all else.

2 I will fervently uphold my pledge of allegiance to the United States Air Force, the 1st Air Commando Wing, my commander and my comrades.

3 I will always wear my uniform as an emblem of my professional pride, at all times reflecting credit upon the Air Commandos.

4 My conduct and military bearing will be one of the highest standards expected of a professional military man, gentleman and a proud citizen of my country "Any Time, Any Place".

CHAPTER 1

THE BIRTH OF THE AIR COMMANDOS: 1ST AIR COMMANDO GROUP

THE WORLD AT WAR

THE FAR EAST, 1942. The world was at war again. Britain and the Commonwealth had been at war with Nazi Germany since 1939, and on 7 December 1941 the Japanese had attacked the American fleet at Pearl Harbor in Hawaii, forcing the sleeping American giant to go to war.

The Japanese had begun to establish an Empire in 1931, when they annexed Manchuria, and in 1937 they began a systematic march on China's major cities of Peking, Tiensin, Shanghai, Nanking and Hankow. By 1941 the Japanese had more or less cut China off from the rest of the world, although supplies could still reach the beleaguered Chinese along the Burma Road which extended from India, through Burma, to the small mountain town of Kunming in the Yunnan province of China. Japanese strategists realised that by occupying Burma they could starve the Chinese of supplies, munitions and equipment and, when China was completely subdued, their troops could continue their conquests elsewhere. In addition, Burma would provide a springboard for the invasion of India, the greatest British colony in Asia. Civil unrest was being stirred by Mohandas K. Gandhi, and Japan anticipated the support of the Indian population in expelling the British from the country. India was also rich and potentially a greater prize than China, with coal, cotton, chemicals, iron, steel, arms and munitions industries. It was also part of Japan's grand strategy to overrun India and link up with a planned German push into Persia, led by General Erwin Rommel.

Burma itself had potential. The mainstay of its economy

was rice, with almost twelve million acres under cultivation. Burma's export crop of three million tons of rice would help feed the overstretched Imperial Army, and its natural resources, especially oil and manganese, were coveted. Moreover the natural defences of the country would provide a barrier between the Allies and the newly conquered Japanese possessions of the Philippines, French Indochina, Thailand, Singapore and the Dutch East Indies. Geographically, the natural elements which comprised Burma—the mountains, rivers, roads and valleys—ran from the north to the south. Travel from east to west was difficult, the mountains, valleys and jungle combining to restrict travel to meagre road or rail systems or the waterways, the largest of which, the Irrawaddy river, flowed down the center of the country and was joined by the next largest in size, the Chindwin, providing over 15,000 miles of navigable waters. Burma's topography meant that "choke points," where rivers, roads or railroads came together, were commonplace. The British believed they could defend the country, any invader having to follow the existing road and rail routes and being channelled into easily defended areas.

The British hoped that the following year's monsoon rains, lasting from mid-May until late October, would be on their side, limiting military operations to the dry season. The responsibility for the defense of Burma fell to General Archibald Wavell, the Commander-in-Chief of British Forces, India, but his forces were ill-equipped and poorly trained, and mobilisation of additional forces had hardly begun in India when the first Japanese aeroplanes attacked the key Burmese port of Rangoon on 23 December 1941.

Soon the Japanese 15th Army began its move on Burma, crossing the southern border from recently conquered Malaya and initially securing airfields along the southeast coast and then attacking Rangoon itself. On 8 March 1942 the city was abandoned and the remaining troops began a chaotic flight back to India. The British were surprised at the speed of the enemy advance, moving through the jungle while the British troops used the roads. Eventually Major-General William J. Slim and the 12,000 survivors of the two divisions of his Burma Corps reached India on 16 May. They left half of their number behind, and had to destroy the oilfields at Yenan-gyaung before they fell into enemy hands.

The American Lt.-General Joseph W. Stilwell, commanding the Chinese forces fighting in Burma, fared little better in the north. Reluctant to fight, the Chinese were soon driven back by the Japanese, and Stilwell reached India himself on 19 May. Then the monsoon season began.

WINGATE'S CHINDITS

While the ignominious retreat from Burma was still going on, a former British artillery officer arrived in India. Colonel Orde C. Wingate quickly began studying Japanese training and tactics, the climate and topography of Burma, and every report on Japanese fighting methods. He eventually put forward the concept of fighting the Japanese with hit-and-run tactics, carried out by Long-Range Penetration (LRP) groups deep behind enemy lines. General Alexander was impressed by Wingate's ideas. The combination of Burma's jungles and mountains and the Japanese defense system ruled out a direct assault to recapture the country, but the Japanese communication and supply lines to the interior were vulnerable and susceptible to harassment by highly mobile troops moving through the cover of the jungle. For obvious reasons the LRP groups would need to be supplied by air and, as they were lightly armed, they would need to rely on aerial firepower in lieu of artillery.

Wingate reasoned that the Japanese troops in the interior were of inferior quality, and that a small force could wreak havoc all out of proportion to its size, being strong enough to cause damage yet small enough to slip through the enemy's net. Such tactics would cause widespread confusion and uncertainty in the enemy rear areas, and weaken and misdirect the enemy main force units. One criteria had to be met, though. The LRP groups must be used in conjunction with a major offensive, or else the groups would merely focus rather than redirect the Japanese forces, and the small units would be destroyed. The size of the LRP units, and the length of time that they could remain in the field, depended on the availability of supplies. Unfortunately the British did not have air superiority over Burma, and there were problems with ground-to-air communications and the accuracy of air drops as well. The only way to find out if the strategy could work was to try it and see.

In June 1942 Wingate was promoted to Brigadier-General and given the 77th Indian Brigade expressly for LRP purposes. Amongst the units in the brigade were a mule transport company, RAF liaison officers and instructors from the Bush Warfare School. Wingate was a hard taskmaster, and his men worked hard, learning to use the jungle to their advantage and toughening themselves to survive the rigours of jungle warfare.

For reasons beyond his control Wingate had to wait until February 1943 to try out his LRP concept, and even then he had to do without a major Allied offensive to occupy the enemy main forces while he carried out his hit-and-run raids. Operation Loincloth began on 8 February, when 3,000 men crossed the Chindwin River into Burma and moved slowly in columns to their target areas, where they were to cut railway lines and harass the Shwebo area. Two columns were ambushed and lost their radios and, unable to communicate, returned to India. Other columns were more successful, blowing up over 75 sections of the railroad with little loss of personnel. However, the Japanese were able to turn their full attention to the raiders, and with casualties mounting and inadequate air supply, Wingate terminated the operation, dispersing his columns into small groups, and returned to India on 27 March. Fighting the Japanese, the jungle, sickness and disease, and lacking food and water, fewer than 2,200 of Wingate's men found their way back to safety.

A number of strengths and weaknesses soon became apparent. The inability to evacuate casualties had a grave effect on morale, and the slow response time to requests for air support was unsatisfactory. However, the operation did prove that confusion and destruction could be wrought behind enemy lines and that British troops could operate in the jungle as well as the Japanese. Wingate's exploits were reported in the press, and his men were given the name of Chindits, after a mythological beast, half lion and half griffin, which guarded Burmese pagodas and symbolised to Wingate the unique co-operation required between ground and air forces.

It was now time for the Allied strategists to appear on the scene. The Americans were continuing to supply China by flying over the "Hump," the Himalayan mountains, from airfields in northern India, across Burma to China. If they could not reopen the Burma Road, China might fall and the twenty Japanese divisions fighting there could be deployed to fight elsewhere in the Pacific. Whereas US President Roosevelt wanted the overland route to China reopened, Britain's Prime Minister, Churchill, was more interested in preserving the British Empire and recapturing Singapore, than in tackling China's supply problems. The United States, in the throes of supplying Britain with much of its war machinery, persuaded Churchill and his planners to increase their efforts to recapture Burma, and a new organisation, Southeast Asia Command (SEAC), was formed. SEAC was tasked with co-ordinating the complex interlocking and overlapping areas of command, geography and operations. In the meantime, Churchill summoned Wingate to London to discuss his LRP operations and to accompany him to the Quadrant Conference in Quebec, Canada. During the conference Wingate proposed that his forces be expanded to eight brigades for the forthcoming 1943–44 dry season offensive. Four brigades would be held in reserve, with four others in combat for a maximum of 90 days before relief. Wingate's LRP brigades would act in co-ordination with other British and Chinese forces, whose overall objective would be the recapture of Burma north of the 23rd Parallel.

General Wingate briefed President Roosevelt on the plan. Roosevelt endorsed it and agreed to supply the aircraft necessary to support the LRP units. Wingate initially asked for sixteen Douglas C-47 Skytrain aircraft to air-drop supplies, one bomber squadron per unit for close air support, and a light aeroplane force to help evacuate wounded men from the field. The request went to US General of the Army Henry H. "Hap" Arnold, who saw an opportunity to put new life in the China, Burma, India (CBI) theatre, because he felt the previous campaigns had sapped the will of the British ground troops. He became determined to build a new air organisation totally dedicated to supporting Wingate's troops on the ground in Burma. In August 1943 General Arnold met with the newly named

Supreme Allied Commander of SEAC, Admiral Lord Louis
Mountbatten, to discuss plans for American air support of British "Commando" expeditions in the CBI theatre of operations. The new unit changed its name five times as it evolved,
from Project 9 to Project CA 281, then to 5318th Provisional
Unit (Air), Number 1 Air Commando Force, and finally the
1st Air Commando Group (ACG). General Arnold allegedly
coined the term "Air Commando" to honor Lord Mountbatten, who earlier commanded British Commandos.

The general's first task was to find men with the American
"can-do" spirit to command the new force. The choice soon
narrowed to two individuals and, unable to choose between
the two, Arnold made them joint leaders. The first was Lieutenant-Colonel Philip G. Cochran, a confident, aggressive and
imaginative officer with a highly distinguished war record as
a fighter pilot in North Africa. (He was also the model for the
character of Flip Corkin in Milton Caniff's "Terry and the
Pirates" comic strip.) The second was Lieutenant-Colonel
John R. Alison, a tactful, well-educated "ace" pilot with a
superb flying record who had flown in US Major-General
Claire L. Chennault's 23rd Fighter Group, known previously
as the American Volunteer Group "Flying Tigers." General
Arnold interviewed both men and ended the session with the
words, "To hell with the paperwork, go out and fight."

General Arnold gave his new commanders *carte blanche* to
gather men and material under the highest authority. The new
unit soon took shape, acquiring thirteen C-47s for transport
missions, 100 CG-4A WACO gliders capable of carrying fifteen troops each and 25 TG-5 training gliders for use in remote
sites. A dozen Canadian Noorduyn UC-64 Norseman "bush"
aeroplanes were selected to bridge the gap between the C-47s
and the light aircraft planned for casualty evacuation. A hundred Vultee L-1 Vigilants were required for the light aeroplane
force, capable of carrying two or three stretchers behind the
pilot and with a short take-off run. However, that number was
not available, so they were augmented with the newer Stinson
L-5 Sentinel, which was faster but could seat only one evacuee
and required a longer 900ft runway. Lastly, Alison persuaded
Wright Field to send a technical representative to India to test
some of the new Sikorsky YR-4 helicopters in combat con-

ditions. The fighter requirement was covered by the allocation of 30 North American P-51A Mustangs. As of September 1943, the organisation comprised 87 officers and 436 enlisted men; roughly a quarter of the personnel usually required for a unit of that size.

Project 9 was organised at Seymour-Johnson Field in North Carolina in October 1943, and then designated the 5318th Provisional Unit (Air) before reporting to its duty station in India. General Arnold carefully defined the purpose of the unit thus: **1** To facilitate the forward movement of the Wingate columns; **2** To facilitate the supply and evacuation of the columns; **3** To provide a small air covering and striking force, and **4** To acquire air experience under the conditions expected to be encountered. Within six months the men and aircraft were in India, ready to begin operations.

By early 1944 General Wingate and his 3rd Indian Division, also known as Special Force, were ready for action. Together with Cochran and Alison he began planning a behind-the-lines operation, using gliders to fly Chindits and engineers to jungle clearings in Burma, deep behind enemy lines. While the Chindits defended the area the engineers would clear a landing strip long enough to allow C-47s to fly in the rest of Wingate's brigades.

Sadly, on 15 February, a tragic night training accident involving a C-47 towing two gliders resulted in the death of four British and three US troops. The following day, to underline their faith and trust in the air commandos, Wingate's unit commander sent a note to the flyers, stating: "Please be assured that we will go with your boys Any Place, Any Time, Any Where." This phrase was adopted as the motto of the 1st Air Commando Group, and variations have been used in the air commando and special operations community ever since.

The 5318th Provisional Unit (Air) expanded once again when the Royal Air Force could not supply the bombers that Wingate requested. Instead, Cochran obtained twelve North American B-25H Mitchell medium bombers destined for the 14th Air Force. In addition to their bomb-carrying cap ability, they were armed with four 0.50-calibre machine-guns and a 75mm cannon, and were ideal for close air support.

OPERATION THURSDAY

"Nothing you've ever done, nothing you're ever going to do, counts now. Only the next few hours. Tonight you are going to find your souls." So spoke Colonel Philip G. Cochran, USAAF, Commander of the 1st Air Commando Group, at the briefing to his pilots on the evening of 5 March 1944, just before the launch of Operation Thursday. General Wingate's Operation Thursday called for the landing by gliders of two columns of Chindits, engineers and air transportable equipment at two jungle clearings codenamed "Broadway" and "Piccadilly." At that time the only Allied troops participating in the invasion of Burma were Wingate's 16th Brigade and General Stilwell's Chinese forces in the north, so, as in the first Chindit operation, Wingate was being sent into Burma without a major offensive or a strategic objective. However, he learned that the Japanese were massing for an invasion of India, Operation U-Go, and that they would provide the frontal action needed while his brigades attacked their rear areas.

In the last hours before the invasion force took off, Cochran ordered an aerial reconnaissance of the landing zones (LZs). It was a fortuitous decision, because the reconnaissance photographs showed that the landing zone at Piccadilly was strewn with logs, a potential death trap for gliders. That LZ was abandoned, and both groups were told to head for Broadway. At 1815 hours on 5 March 1944, the first gliders carrying troops from the 77th Brigade took off for Broadway, each C-47 towing two gliders. However, the C-47s and gliders combined were very heavy, and it was difficult to clear the mountains en route. Nine gliders suffered broken tow ropes or other problems and went down east of the Chindwin River, most landing near three different Japanese headquarters and creating a diversion as the Japanese searched for the survivors. (Seven of the nine crews made it back to India or onto Broadway.) Eight other gliders went down west of the Chindwin River owing to various problems.

The first glider into Broadway carried British Lieutenant-Colonel Mike Scott, whose job was to rake the surrounding

jungle with machine-gun fire. If he received answering fire
from the Japanese he was to fire a red Very flare to warn the
rest of the troops not to land. He announced beforehand that
he had the flare "so deep in my pocket that I doubt if anyone
else could find it if I'm-killed." In other words, the Chindits
were prepared to fight for the airstrip site even if it was surrounded by a Japanese Division.

Captain Bill Taylor piloted the first glider to land at Broadway.

> The moment I cut loose, my glider went into a dive,
> straight down. I pulled hard on the controls to level off
> and found it almost impossible to keep from plunging
> on down into the jungle below. I couldn't imagine what
> was wrong, and it took all my strength to keep a course.
> The lighter ground of the clearing was plainly visible
> against the black of the jungle and I made the run to
> ground, slowing the glider as best I could. But I couldn't
> slow it to anything like normal. That should have been
> at about sixty miles an hour, and I was going ninety. It
> felt as if the glider was dropping out from under me,
> something different, something wrong.
>
> At the level of the tall trees that surrounded the clear-
> ing I went from moonlight into black shadow, and lost
> all sense of horizon. I was unable to see the ground.
> There was a lashing sound of tall grass whipping the
> front of the glider, then I saw a white patch coming up
> in front and pulled back on the controls with all my
> strength. I was just able to get into the air for a hop over
> the watering hole for elephants, big enough to put a
> house in. If the glider had plunged into the elephant hole,
> we would have been smashed to bits. As it was I lost a
> wheel as I bounced down on the other side, coming to
> a stop within fifty yards of the point chosen weeks be-
> fore in planning."

The first man to set foot on Broadway was Jim Woods, now
a retired colonel, who flew in the right seat of the glider, next
to Bill Taylor. He recalls:

"We were on a double tow and were the first to land, closely followed by Colonel John Alison. Since our glider's exit door latching was a bit tricky, it had been arranged that, upon landing, I would rush to the rear and open the door. The troops gave me a clear aisle in the crowded cabin and we deplaned without incident. The British officer was right behind me and we moved off to our allotted tasks.

After landing my mission was to assemble the US crews into a separate fire team and take station under the orders of the British ground commander. This was partially successful given the darkness and confusion, but ever since I have given thanks that there were no Japs waiting to greet our pitifully weak and disorganised initial landing force."

Fortunately the Japs were nowhere to be found, and a week would pass before they eventually took an interest in the landing zone. The gliders released their tow ropes and began to come down. The LZ was not as smooth or flat as had it looked from the air; some gliders struck plowed ground or tree stumps and knocked off their undercarriages. Without wheels the gliders could not be easily manhandled out of the way, and other gliders crashed into the wreckage, or pulled up and tried to land beyond. Lieutenant Seese came in crosswise on the field, and was heading for a crash with Taylor's glider. He was carrying Brigadier "Mad Mike" Calvert and his men, and in the nick of time he cooly pulled back on the controls and jumped Taylor's glider, landing safely on the other side. However, two gliders did crash whilst landing at Broadway, killing all on board, and others had narrow escapes. Many pilots found that their gliders were coming down too fast, and could not understand why. It was later discovered that the weight of the gliders, calculated to the last pound, had been increased by the troops bringing extra food and ammunition with them.

Lieutenant-Colonel J. W. Bellah, an American infantry officer who accompanied the landing force, witnessed a miraculous escape.

"There was a glider with a bulldozer lashed behind the pilot and copilot in the passenger space. When landing, the pilot turned left to avoid wreckage, overshot and crashed into a clump of trees. The fuselage went between the only two trees that were wide enough apart to let it through. As it skidded along at 100 miles an hour both wings were ripped off and the fuselage continued alone with the bulldozer torn loose inside. When the fuselage finally came to a halt, the momentum carried the machinery forward towards the cockpit. Fortunately it had been rigged to elevate the nose section in such an eventuality, and the hinged cockpit was yanked skywards as the bulldozer roared out underneath the pilot's seats, crashing through the jungle for another 50 yards. The nose flipped back into place with the pilot and copilot still in their seats. The Yank pilot looked the crash over for a moment and nodded sagely, 'I planned it just that way'."

As more gliders landed, patrols were sent into the jungle to search for Japanese while engineers began the task of turning the clearing into a landing strip long enough for the C-47s to land with more troops and supplies. Because of the wreckage, the code word "Soyalink" was flashed back to Wingate, to tell him to stop the operation. The radio failed before more details could be sent, and the commanders back at base spent an anxious few hours before the airstrip was ready and the radio repaired. The code words "Pork Sausage" brought sighs of relief at Chindit HQ, and by nightfall the first C-47s were arriving with reinforcements.

Of the 54 gliders tasked to land at Broadway, 37 reached the LZ. Thirty men were killed and 33 injured in the landings, and most of the gliders were damaged or destroyed. However, 539 men and almost 30,00lb of stores were landed at Broadway. By late afternoon a 4,700ft airstrip had been hewn out of the jungle, and 62 C-47 sorties were flown into Broadway that night. A second operation began on 6 March to fly men into a second landing zone named "Chowringhee," after Calcutta's main street. The sorties were flown by a combination of RAF flights, USAAF Troop Carrier Command and the

5318th Provisional Unit (Air). By 11 March 9,000 men had been landed 200 miles behind enemy lines, together with half a million pounds of stores, almost 1,200 mules and 175 ponies. As soon as they landed, the Chindits formed columns and disappeared into the jungle, their mission being to disrupt the enemy supply lines in Northern Burma by establishing strongholds to control choke points in the enemy lines of communication.

Brigadier Fergusson's 16th Brigade trekked into Burma on foot and brought the Chindit's strength up to 12,000 men. Four of Wingate's six brigades had now been deployed. A fifth, Brigadier Perowne's 23rd Brigade, had been sent to the northern flank of IV Corps. Chowringhee was soon abandoned, and all serviceable gliders were recovered by a new snatch technique, whereby a tug aircraft trailing a hook on an elasticated rope flew over a glider equipped with a special harness, enabling it to be caught up and towed straight into the air.

The first stronghold to be established was "Aberdeen," nearly 40 miles north of Indaw and within easy striking distance of the Indaw-Mogaung railway. Fergusson's column arrived there on 19 March and cleared an airstrip so that Brigadier Tom Brodie's 14th Brigade could be flown in. Fergusson's brigade, although exhausted by their long trek across the Chin Hills, was tasked with capturing the enemy supply hub of Indaw before the start of the monsoons, to make use of the two all-weather airfields there.

Brigadier Calvert's 77th Brigade drove west towards the railroad line between Mandalay and the enemy airfield at Myitkyina. The brigade was to establish a road block named "White City" near Mawlu to prevent supplies from reaching General Stilwell's opposition, the Japanese 18th Division in the Hukawng Valley. Brigadier Lentaigne's 111th Brigade was to push west-southwest towards Wuntho to cut off Japanese reinforcements going north by rail and road. They established a block named "Blackpool," hacked out a small airstrip, and fought heroically against everything the Japs threw at them. In addition, Wingate committed his reserve LRP unit, the 3rd West African Brigade, to Broadway for garrison support. Later, the 3rd Brigade would be flown into Aberdeen and experience heavy fighting at White City.

While Wingate's men roamed the jungle they were supported by C-47s dropping supplies into clearings. Their casualties were taken out by the light aeroplanes, or by the UC-64s if a large-enough clearing was available. Sometimes the L-5 Sentinels would carry 75lb parachute packs on their bomb racks to drop emergency supplies to brigades who had missed their C-47 flights. To help establish their blocks, the Chindits were dropped barbed wire, anti-tank weapons and the hundred-and-one things that a brigade needs to survive in the jungle. Sometimes, when the weather was bad, the columns went without resupply for days, and food often took second place to ammunition. Personal accounts from that period lament the poor food supplied to the Chindits, and the trials and tribulations of trekking through the jungle and fighting the enemy whilst on "short rations." The one big morale booster was the possibility of evacuation of the wounded by air, a vast improvement over the first Wingate operation, when wounded were often left behind.

By the third week of March Wingate's brigades were established in four locations and set to work disrupting the enemy logistical network. Overhead, the P-51A and B-25Hs provided close air support or found targets of their own, striking roads, bridges and airfields. One novel idea was pioneered by the air commando fighter section. With a 450ft cable with a weight in the middle attached to the Mustang's bomb racks, so that it hung down like a pendulum in flight, a pilot would dive at a telephone or telegraph pole, pulling up at the last minute and wrapping the cable around the pole like a bola and uprooting it. Some pilots flew for miles before jettisoning the cable and pole.

History was made on 29 March 1944 when the 5318th Provisional Unit (Air) was finally renamed the 1st Air Commando Group. The renaming of the air commandos probably went unnoticed by the Chindits owing to the tragic events of 24 March. That day, General Wingate left Broadway after a conference with his brigade commanders and headed west towards India in a B-25H. He never arrived. On the last leg of the journey the bomber crashed into a hillside, killing all on board. It was a blow from which the Chindits would never recover.

Lord Louis Mountbatten, the Supreme Allied Commander, issued an order of the day which read:

> "General Wingate has been killed in the hour of his triumph. The Allies have lost one of the most forceful and dynamic personalities that this war has produced. You have lost the finest and most inspirational leader a force could have wished for, and I have lost a personal friend and faithful supporter. He has lit the torch. Together we must grasp it and carry it forward. Out of your gallant and hazardous expedition into the heart of Japanese-held territory will grow the final reconquest of Burma and the ultimate defeat of the Japanese."

General Wingate was succeeded by Brigadier Lentaigne, the most orthodox column commander within the division. He did not endorse the LRP theory, nor was he favourably impressed with Wingate. By mid-April he had ordered the lightly armed Chindits to form large formations and defend fortified positions, ignoring the LRP hit-and-run concept. The air commandos continued to support the Chindits to the best of their ability. As the Japanese resistance began to stiffen, the Chindits' problems began to mulitiply. The main Japanese attack of U-Go had burst on IV Corps, and all priorities were being given to the battles at Imphal and Kohima, across the border in India. There were now 30 Chindit columns loose behind the Japanese divisions, and although they had some effect on the fighting in India they proved of vital importance to General Stilwell and his troops, fighting their way down from China. However, attrition, sickness and lack of supplies weakened the Chindit columns daily, and to compound their problems they were not allowed to withdraw, but kept in the jungle until the end of June, far longer than planned. By the end of the month the survivors had been evacuated to India and the Chindit campaign was over. Many men were unfit for further service; the rest were returned to their parent regiments. Wingate's Chindits ceased to exist, and faded into the annals of history as some of the most courageous men ever to wear uniform.

Following Operation Thursday, Colonel Alison was called home to establish more air commando units. During March

1944 the air commando C-47s had flown over 450,000lb of supplies, and the Waco gliders an additional 310,000lb. Almost 1,500 casualties had been evacuated, and 50 enemy aircraft had been destroyed. When the monsoon rains began in May 1944 the air commandos had to remove their aircraft from eastern India to Asansol in Central India, and their part in the war slowly ground to a halt. Once there, many of the Group's personnel began to return to the United States, including Colonel Cochran, who relinquished command of the Group to Colonel Gaty.

Eventually, the Japanese offensive into India was pushed back into Burma and General Slim's troops pursued with a vengeance. Although the monsoon weather curtailed support by the 1st Air Commando Group, at the end of the year they would be joined by the 2nd Air Commando Group, who would continue their sterling service, supporting the British Army as they fought to clear the Japanese from Burma.

JUNGLE TOWN, 1944

One of the more remarkable discoveries made by the author whilst researching this book was the discovery of a story entitled "Jungle Town 1944," written by Chindit Sergeant Cyril Hall five months after his evacuation from the jungle by L-5 and C-47. Serving with the 12th Battalion, 3rd West African Brigade, Nigerian Regiment, Cyril saw first-hand the support given to the ground troops by the newly-formed Air Commandos. He begins his story with the flight to Aberdeen stronghold on 4 April:

"The Chindits came from places far removed from each other. There were regiments of the Beds and Herts, Black Watch, Yorks and Lancs, Queens, Leicesters, Duke of Wellingtons, Essex, Borders, Kings, Lancashire Fusiliers, South Staffs, Kings Own, Cameronians, Gurkhas, Recce Regiment and West Africans, the latter with whom I fought.

Lalaghat airfield was the base of the USAAF No 1 Air Commando, commanded by a young flyer, Colonel

Philip Cochran. We called his pilots 'Cochran's Young Ladies'. On arrival at the airfield, after days of traveling in nothing more than cattle trucks, we found the area festooned with all the ugly panoply of war. Days passed by, for the Japs were very close to the Imphal Borders and it was touch and go as to whether the operations would go ahead at all. The word Go was given, but on the previous evenings our American friends, headed by that great little character Jackie Cogan (the boy film star) a glider pilot officer, laid on film shows in the jungle clearing and, the night before we were taken into Burma, an American band entertained us, in full evening dress. What a send-off!

In the cool of the evening of 4 April, I gathered my group of eight Africans and four mules near the middle of the airfield, waiting for the Dakota pilot. The two-mile strip was lined with gliders, which looked very light and frail beside their Dakota transport planes. Half an hour later, the pilot walked over and said, 'Who's ready for going? Where's it to be boys? White City via Aberdeen?' Several days earlier a similar invasion armada left our airstrip to land at three fields more than 150 miles inside Burma. Ours was the second phase of operations, to take troops, mules and equipment to support the advance guard.

We walked to the Dakota and were instructed, ''Get those mules in first and make 'em happy in those home-made crates and the rest of you, behind the crates, equal numbers either side, to help balance the ship.'' We dumped our great packs by the door and sat on metal seats either side of the belly facing one-another. It was the first time ever that any of the Africans had been inside a plane, and I must admit, also mine.

First one, then the second engine throttled up and roared; the aircraft shook itself and lurched forward and in seconds the small runway lights fused together into a thin golden streak, then suddenly a final thump when we left the ground of Lalaghat. The full moon was rising slowly, showing the dark range of mountains beneath. We could distinguish forest and paddy fields, and not long after, the thin shining path of the Chindwin River.

Two hours later we were over the strip called "Aberdeen" where small lights could be seen shining like peacetime Piccadilly Circus, and the Dakota bumped down on the rough strip. The aircraft creaked and slithered to a stop, engines coughing, then dying. The pilot opened the door and we trooped out, with the muleteers leading their four-legged friends. A quick search for the remaining groups and we all disappeared into the night to make bivouac until the early morning. We did not know where the Japs were, but we were told they are around somewhere.

In the morning, our 300-strong column moved off into the jungle in snake formation (single file), all eyes watching for movements in the thick undergrowth and up in the heavy foliaged trees, expecting the crack of an enemy sniper at every bend in the track. It was Easter Monday, and owing to a terrific battle raging with our advanced elements, we were forced to halt in a defensive position until orders were given by our advanced Battalion Commander, now fighting around Henu.

The next morning the Recce patrol returned with orders for us to move immediately to the road block established at Henu, near Mawlu, which was known as "White City." Situated between Indaw and Myitkyina, White City straddled the Japs' main line of communication. Our task was to help hold this position for an unknown period until the Jap supplies were exhausted north of this point and to stop all supplies and transport from getting to their 18th Army, who were opposing General Stilwell and his American-Chinese push. On one occasion we had to move off the track to let a column of the Yorks and Lancs pass, who had been fighting the Japs for several weeks; they looked terribly weak and sick and wore great beards and their hair was touching their shoulders.

Our objective was a cluster of small hills, by the road and railway, on which were ribboned white and colored parachutes, used previously for dropping supplies. To get to the fortress we had to cross a mile of open paddy, which was covered by Jap machine-guns and mortars on both flanks. As we advanced we heard the drone of approaching aircraft. It was our fighting boys of the Royal Air Force, with six heavy bombers and nine fighters, ordered up by the fortress commander to pound the Jap positions. The bomb aimers were put on their targets by smoke bombs fired from mortars in the fortress and one at a time the fighters went in, letting go their 50-pound eggs, after which the heavies flew low over the enemy positions and dropped parachute retarded Bunker Busters. The incident was a gift from Heaven for all of us, for it kept Johnny Japs head down whilst our column arrived at White City intact, swelling the number of defenders to about 1,300.

White City should have been renamed "Red City" from the blood that flowed there. The Japs brought up tanks to support their infantry, but our gunners replied with 25-pounders and Bofors. Each night ferocious hand-to-hand battles would take place, British troops wading in with bayonet and rifle butt, whilst the Gurkhas and West Africans engaged with their native knives, the Japs with their two-handed swords.

At one crisis of a battle, Cochran's Air Commandos planted a huge load of high explosives on Jap concentrations preparing to move up. The pilots, whom I cannot praise too greatly, were reluctant, for so short was the distance separating our forces that they feared hitting our own men. However, urging column commanders from below insisted that it was necessary, so with deadly precision they unloaded everything they had, killing hundreds.

By early May we received the long-awaited orders to abandon White City, its main purpose fully accomplished. Jap prisoners captured from the rapidly retreating 15th and 31st Divisions talked of dwindling rations and shortages of ammo, and the swift hammer-like blows at his stores and dumps were beginning to tell. The evacuation began on 10 May, when the first of forty Dakotas came in to land on a rough airstrip, within a

mile of the Japs, to take out our heavy guns, crews and
those wounded or too sick to march.

The next day, those of us remaining spent the day
mining or laying booby traps, before pulling out around
dusk. As we formed into fighting groups a message was
received from Pagoda Hill that Jap tanks were advancing
in the direction of the fortress. They were moving into
position to shoot up our planes, which they expected to
arrive to evacuate the remaining troops. However, we
were moving out on foot, now under the command of
General Stilwell and with orders to link up with his
troops further north.

At the same time, another jungle "Tobruk" was raging. The 111th Brigade, comprising men of the Cameronians, Kings Own Royal Regiment and two units of
Gurkhas, had marched 80 miles over the mountain jungle to Hopin, between Mawlu and Mogaung, to establish
another road and rail block until Stilwell's American brigade and two Chinese Divisions reached Mogaung,
when the campaign could be declared over. Their block
was named "Blackpool."

The Japs reacted violently, and for two whole weeks
flung strong forces continuously against the position. On
23 May the Japs brought up 75 and 105mm artillery and
in the space of one hour 300 shells fell inside Blackpool's perimeter. The garrison had to give up the tiny
airstrip which was used by Cochran's L-5 planes for
transporting wounded, after which they prepared to fight
their way out. Fighting prolonged engagements was not
the role of the Long Range Penetration troops, for we
fought usually with only the weapons we carried on our
backs. With their ammunition and rations low and foul
weather preventing resupply drops, the survivors of the
1,500-strong 111th Brigade loaded their wounded on
stretchers and, after sacrificing much, walked out.

Some of our West Africans were sent to meet up with
the withdrawing Brigade, whilst yet another brigade, the
77th under the command of Brigadier Calvert, DSO, was
battling its way towards its final goal—Mogaung. After
a particularly bloody and fierce battle, they penetrated

the town's defences, but much more heavy fighting took place before complete possession was assured.

Our line of march lay up the Valley of the Indaw Chaung, towards the hills around Mogaung. The other enemy had fallen upon us—driving monsoon rains that turned tracks into leech-laden streams and chaungs into treacherous torrents. After very heavy going, killing and attacking the odd Jap patrol on the way, we arrived at our pre-arranged RV, a Burmese village called Mla. Here we were ambushed by the enemy, but we drove them out and continued our march to Pinbaw, a small village eight miles from Mogaung.

Two days previous, the Chinese had beaten the Japs out of this village and we were to RV here to prepare an attack on Jap positions two miles south of this point, called Hill 60. When the ambush took place we were moving along a track through the treacherous monsoon jungle and were approaching Mla. Several shots were fired at our forward element and we halted and moved off the track into the jungle. Sharpened bamboo *panji* sticks had been concealed at the side of the track, and one of them ripped a jagged hole in my thigh.

A field dressing was placed over the wound and we were soon on the move again, passing one dead Jap on the trail. We scouted the village, but the enemy had fled ahead of us and we made contact with them the following day. My wound was dressed frequently, but after several days the area of the wound was very inflamed and sore. I had difficulty in walking but we had to push forward; it was just a case of survival.

At this time, nearly everyone was suffering from some sort of fever or illness, because of the terrible monsoon conditions, and we eventually halted at a village called Pyindaw. There was an "airstrip" here, a rough track about 150-200 yards long, and an L-5 pilot just dropped in on this small strip, picked me up and took off, heading north towards Myitkyina. We were just skimming the jungle top and about 30 minutes later we landed at the airfield at Myitkyina, where I recall American warplanes taking off with sharks' teeth painted on their snouts. I could hear the constant bombing in the town, a short distance away.

I had not only my leg wound, which was by now looking like a piece of raw, stinking meat, but was full of fever, had sores on my feet, and a very painful right ear, where several abscesses had formed. I was taken to a Dakota with several others and flown to the base hospital, where my ailments were taken care of. I was later informed that the attack went in, not once, but thrice, but owing to the weakness of our troops and the Japs' continuous short-range shelling and mortaring, our lads were forced to withdraw. A few days later a new British Division relieved our remaining men, who were flown out in transports from Myitkyina.''

THE FIRST HELICOPTER COMBAT RESCUE

On the whole, the air commandos were unlucky with their helicopters. They were given six Sikorsky YR-4s, and these were shipped out in halves. The nose of the first one arrived, but the fuselage section was lost when the aeroplane carrying it crashed at Cairo. The two parts of the second helicopter arrived in India, but were lost there. The third was assembled and flown, but it hit some telephone lines, crashed and was destroyed, killing one of the two men on board. The fourth was successful and performed at least six evacuation missions, flown by Lieutenant Harman, the first pilot to take a helicopter into combat. The fifth and sixth were flown, but only locally.

The first helicopter combat rescue took place following the crash landing of an L-1 on 21 April 1944, after enemy ground fire had shot away an oil line. The pilot, Technical Sergeant Ed Hladovcak, and his three wounded British soldier passengers, took cover in the jungle as the Japanese arrived and started to search the undergrowth. Hladovcak, nicknamed ''Murphy'' because of his unpronounceable surname, was in an unenviable predicament. There was nowhere nearby where a light aircraft could land to take them out, and the nearest friendly troops were at Aberdeen, sixty miles away. One hundred and fifty miles away in Lalaghat, India, the operations

shack received news of Murphy's situation, and 2nd Lieutenant Carter Harman was told to take his "egg-beater" and fly
to Taro in Burma, 500 miles distant. Because the 9,000ft-high
Arakan Yoma Mountains were between Lalaghat and Murphy's position, Harman would have to fly around them,
stopping to refuel every 100 miles. Wedging four five-gallon
fuel cans into the cramped cockpit, Harman wondered if they
would upset his magnetic compass as he flew the arc to Di-
mapur, Jorhat, Ledo and Taro. The 175 h.p. motor did not like
breathing the thin Burmese air. There was too little lift, too
little oxygen and the engine often stalled when Harman tried
to hover. The rescue would take time. The helicopter had a
one-day delay at Ledo with a dead battery, but at Taro air
commando mechanics fitted an L-5 wing tank above the pilot's
head in the cockpit so that he could fly on to Aberdeen without
refuelling. In the meantime, the Japs continued to search the
jungle.

At midday on 25 April Harman landed at Aberdeen and
worked out a rescue plan. Murphy and the wounded soldiers
would be lifted from a jungle clearing to a British-held sandbar
on the Mesa River, ten miles away, where an L-5 would evacuate them to Aberdeen. However, Harman could take only one
man at a time, and the condition of the wounded was wors-
ening. An L-5 dropped a message to Murphy, telling him to
move to the clearing nearby and hide, and then led the helicopter to the area. Harman eased the egg-beater into the small
clearing and Murphy lifted the first of the wounded aboard.
With its engine screaming and the tachometer past the 300
r.p.m. red line, Harman jumped the loaded machine into the
air. Ten miles later the passenger was transferred to an L-5 on
the sandbar and Harman returned to the clearing and took out
a second soldier. Problems then arose when the overheated
engine refused to start, and a dangerous thunderstorm enveloped the area ending the rescue operations for the day. Murphy
and the last soldier would spend yet another night in the jungle, avoiding the Japanese.

It was a grey, overcast morning on 26 April when Harman
carried the last British soldier out of the clearing, leaving Murphy alone in the jungle. After five days on the ground he was
anxious to leave, and as the helicopter returned Murphy

dashed from the edge of the jungle to climb aboard. As Harman revved the engine for take-off, soldiers streamed out of the jungle, waving a red flag and charging the helicopter, guns held high. The helicopter clawed at the air and lifted off as the troops screamed above the sound of the engine. They were Chindits! They had spent four days trekking through the jungle from Aberdeen to rescue the stranded men, but arrived just in time to see the last man hover out above their heads. They must have been terribly disappointed. Harman remained at Aberdeen for ten days with his YR-4 and pulled more wounded soldiers out of the jungle. He has now passed into the annals of history as the pilot of the first helicopter combat rescue.

JUNGLE COMMANDO

Another Chindit who owes his life to the Air Commando light plane evacuation system is Bill Lark, who was a Royal Engineer Sapper in the Commando Platoon (Demolitions) attached to a Beds and Herts column. The modern-day British Army special forces, the Special Air Service, like to recruit Royal Engineers, particularly those trained in blowing up things. The Chindits were obviously of the same mind fifty years ago.

Bill spent his early days with Number 5 Bomb Disposal Company, Royal Engineers, in London. The Luftwaffe regularly dropped ''dud'' bombs, and someone had the fine job of digging them up and defusing them. One day Bill was sent to dig up an unexploded 500kg bomb that had fallen fifty yards from the River Thames. It was buried 30ft in the ground, and when they finally dug down to it the hole started filling with water. After pumping the hole dry, they got a strop around the bomb to pull it out of the hole, when it started ticking. Needless to say they climbed out of the hole quicker than they climbed in. However, their lieutenant managed to get a clock stopper on it and they were able to empty the explosive and haul it out.

The bombing raids began to taper off in 1943, and one day Bill and his colleagues went to a cinema to see a show and were then asked if they would like to volunteer for a special job abroad. After such excitement, what could be worse? So Bill said "Yes," and found himself in the Chindits. "Brigadier Wingate gave us a pep talk before we went into the jungle and said we were likely to take heavy casualties, but the job would be well worth it! He wasn't far out!," says Bill. He continues:

"After training in Jhansi, Central Provinces, India, we entrained for Sylhette air base in Assam and flew from there to Aberdeen airstrip in a Dakota. Situated between Kathe and Indaw, Central Burma, the Aberdeen stronghold was deep behind enemy lines. We patrolled the jungle, blowing up railway tracks, culverts, bridges, petrol dumps and anything else we came across. We were supplied with rations etc, by air drops by both RAF and American planes.

When a supply drop was due, we lit fires in an L shape and the drop was planned to fall along the long leg of the L. We could generally tell who was doing the job, as the RAF usually came in at tree-top height and often we had to drag the containers out of a fire. The USAF were usually higher up and the parachutes would drift, taking us most of the night and the next morning to recover. The free drops, without parachutes, were usually mule fodder and the mail sack with several ribbons attached. They came down pretty accurately, although we lost one muleteer when a fodder sack scored a direct hit!

We had an RAF officer attached to the column with a wireless set to contact base and the planes, and his language was quite unprintable during some drops. Where the parachutes snagged on trees we were generally able to recruit local tribesmen who got them down for us, being rewarded with the parachute silk or cloth and the nylon ropes, or a sovereign or two out of the bag carried by the column commander.

I remember that we spent an enjoyable hour or two in the hills above Indaw one night, watching some B-25 Mitchells pounding the town. We obviously could not cheer in case the Japs heard us, but it gave us a buzz for a while.

One night we set off through the jungle and about six miles later made our way through a petrol storage dump, with 50-gallon drums stacked about six feet high in a large clearing. We then made our way along a monsoon ditch through a paddy field to an embankment on which ran the main railway line. The moon was up, so we could see enough to lay our charges under the rails and pressure detonators on top, so that the engine wheels would set the whole lot off. The gen was that a Jap troop train was due, so after completion we withdrew along the ditch with a command wire and plunger as a back up to the detonators.

An Infantry Corporal and a private were left halfway across the paddy with a Bren gun and myself in charge of the plunger. Some mortars were set up on a hill overlooking the proposed ambush site and some machineguns on another, and we settled down to wait. About an hour later we heard some voices approaching and stood-to in case of trouble, but luckily the three Japs or whatever crossed the ditch some five or six yards away and everything quietened down.

Then we heard some noise on the line, but whether the Japs had wind of us or not, it was a light handpropelled truck which set off the charges and went about twenty feet in the air. The mortars and guns opened up on what they thought was the troop train and as the tracers went over our heads we scarpered back to the petrol dump and I was almost bayoneted by a sapper sentry before I could get the password out.

Before setting off to march back to the billet in the jungle, one of the officers took a private with a lifebouy on his back (a flame-thrower) and while the officer used his pistol to puncture the bottom drum, the private gave it a squirt and set the whole lot off. I saw the officer the next day and his ginger beard was almost singed off!

Going through a bad area I contracted tick typhus, and after being carried on a pony for several days I was left behind with several others in a similar condition and was later picked up by a West African column who managed to hack out an airstrip on some paddy fields.

A light 'plane piloted by an American came in and we were loaded in by the lads; my position being above the pilot with my legs hanging down beside him, plus two others jammed in behind us. I didn't think we were going to clear the jungle at the end of the strip, but we got just above the trees and later landed at Myitkyina air base. Unfortunately we landed in the middle of an air raid and some Yanks got us out and onto a stretcher, and I spent the next half-hour or so on the ground with a Yank each side of me. After the raid stopped we were loaded onto a larger 'plane and flown to Digboi hospital in Assam.

I came to out of the fever after two or three weeks in the hospital and asked after my other companions. But they had been dead and buried, so I was very lucky. I would like to find the pilot of the ''plane who brought us out, so I could show my appreciation to him for saving my life.''

By May, the worn-out Chindit brigades were back in India, having wreaked havoc behind the three Japanese Divisions trying to invade India, and behind one other fighting against General Stilwell's troops. After the war, the Japanese Imperial Army Generals testified to the success of Wingate's Chindits and their air commando comrades: ''The penetration of the airborne force into Northern Burma caused the failure of the Army plan to complete the Imphal Operations . . . the airborne raiding force . . . eventually became one of the reasons for the total abandonment of Northern Burma.''

SECOND ROUND

After the Chindits were withdrawn from the jungle in the summer of 1944, the 1st Air Commando Group was tasked with supporting the British 14th Army as it advanced through Burma. They would later be joined by the 2nd Air Commando Group, which began to arrive in November. After the summer of 1944 the fighter section of the 1st Air Commando Group was re-formed into the 5th and 6th Fighter Squadrons, Commando, and operated as a part of Eastern Air Command. Their first commanders were Captain Roland Lynn and Captain Olin B. Carter, respectively. Their P-51As were replaced by Republic P-47D Thunderbolts, which in turn would be replaced by the P-51H-model Mustangs. The liaison aircraft were divided into three separate squadrons in August 1944; the 164th, 165th and 166th.

General Slim did not halt the advance of 14th Army when the monsoons began, and when the clearer weather arrived there were new air commandos to continue the fight. Neal Saxon was one of seven P-40 and P-51 pilots who became tired of waiting at Karachi, India, for assignment to Chennault's 14th Air Force in China:

"We volunteered to fly UC-64s for the 1st Air Commando Group at Asansol around October 1944, and were assigned a couple each to the three liaison squadrons. The aircraft was built by Noorduyn Aircraft of Canada as a bush 'plane, capable of operating from short fields (900ft), carrying loads up to 1,500 to 2,00lb. The pilots preferred 1,500ft of runway though, and would take off around 60 m.p.h., climb at about 80 and cruise around 100 or 110. Landings in a strong crosswind could be difficult, though, with the narrow landing gear and large area of the vertical stabiliser.

The UC-64 could also be fitted with the newly developed 'snatch reel' for recovering downed pilots without landing. The man on the ground would erect two wooden poles with a cable strung between them. He would don a harness and then connect it to the horizontal cable, before lying on his back on the ground. The UC-64 would fly down low, snag the cable between the poles with a trailing hook and pull the pilot off the ground and into the air, where he would be reeled in to the side door of the aircraft. It is not known if this method was ever used in combat.

The three light 'plane squadrons, with their three or four UC-64s and 25 L-planes, were tasked to support the drive of the British Army as it pushed its way south down Burma from Imphal toward Rangoon. General Slim's plan was to pass down the Kabaw Valley from Tamu, then split up, with the 33rd Corps moving through the Kalewa Gorge towards the east and the 4th Corps to proceed south towards Sinthe, where they would cross the Irrawaddy River and move towards Meiktila. The two corps would then join up for the push towards Rangoon. The L-squadrons operated close to the front lines, alternating their two squadrons in Burma with the third back in Asansol.

One day I had to fly out five captured Jap soldiers. Four were severely injured, but one was only shot in the foot and still quite belligerent. He had his hands tied securely with a piece of manilla rope about 12ft long. I was flying alone, but our intelligence officer, 'Pappy', decided to come along for the ride and sat in the copilot's seat, holding the end of the prisoner's rope. Every now and then 'Pappy' would jerk the rope and gesture with his 0.45 at the prisoner. When we landed the Jap pulled a grenade from the loin cloth he was wearing, but was immediately overpowered by our guys. 'Pappy' had been jerking the rope to make sure he kept his hands in sight, and I have wondered since, if I had been alone, whether the Jap would have blown us all up in the air.''

The B-25s suffered losses as well, apart from the aircraft that crashed with Wingate on board. One was strafing a riverboat when it blew up and spun into the jungle. The crew of another had to bale out, but were all recovered safely, as were the crew of a B-25 that caught fire after a belly landing at Hailakandi. One had a lucky escape when it tried to land with a bomb hung up in the bomb bay. When the aeroplane landed the bomb jolted free, went through the bay doors and skidded down the field.

Colonel Frank B. Merchant flew B-25s during the Chindit campaign of February to May 1944, and during the ''second round'' of fighting from November 1944 to May 1945. By November 1944 the B-25s had been fitted with four additional 0.50-calibre machine-guns, two on each side of the aircraft in blisters, for a total of eight, plus the 75mm cannon. The fire-power was awesome. He told the author:

"Although we flew some daylight missions after we started up again in November 1944, most of my memories are of the night intruder missions. We would fly eight or nine nights a month when the moon was at its brightest, following the rail lines or roads, hunting for targets. The most lucrative targets were locomotives and we would fly 300 to 500ft above the terrain and to one side of the tracks, looking for them. It seemed that they would spot or hear us about the same time we saw them, because the sparks would start flying from their brakes as they tried to stop the train.

I always carried a load of incendiary bombs, and would drop two or three clusters on my first pass, as close to the locomotive as possible, not so much to do damage, but as a very visible identification to guide me on subsequent passes. My next several passes would be cross-track at the locomotive and all crew members got into the action. With the eight forward-firing 50s and using the incendiaries to guide me, I would 'walk' in to the locomotive. Once I passed over the target, I would pull up steeply and the top turret and tail gunners would open fire with twin 50s. Then I would go into a steep turn and let the waist gunner get in his licks. Usually not more than three passes were needed to make sure that the locomotive was out of commission, with steam coming out of hundreds of bullet holes in the engine.

On one such mission on 29 December 1944 we located a train just south of Toungoo and worked it over, then proceeded south down the rail line almost to Rangoon. We found no more targets, so reversed the course and as we approached Toungoo I made one more pass at the boxcars. As we pulled off the target we were hit by machine-gun fire and one of our two engines was put out of action. Eventually we had to bale out over the British lines, but we all landed safely and were picked up in the morning."

SHOT BY A B-25

In wartime, not all casualties are caused by the other side.
Often there are just as many non-combat casualties as those
caused in combat. A. R. Van De Weghe was one of the unlucky ones:

"It was the morning of 27 December 1944. We were
waiting for our C-47B to be loaded with combat troops,
some 30 Chinese soldiers with all their equipment, for
the flight from Myitkyina, Burma, to Kunming, China.
At that time I was a copilot on temporary duty for a
special airlift with the 319th Troop Carrier Squadron.
This was to be my fourteenth crossing of 'The Hump'
and my fifty-ninth combat mission.

A flight of B-25Js from the 490th Bomb Group,
known as the 'Burma Bridge Busters' had just returned
from a mission and were being refuelled and rearmed
just across the strip from our C-47B. Since I was not
required to be on hand for the loading I wandered over
to watch their operation, standing some 50ft or so away
from *Pistol Packing Momma*. The crew chief proceeded
to fill the wing tank. As the chief walked across the wing
to insert the nozzle into the tank, there was an explosion.
Immediately I felt a sharp sting in my left leg, followed
by a warm feeling. I looked down to see blood, my red
blood, running down my pant leg. What a shock, I had
been shot by a B-25!

What had happened was that the bombardier's nose
gun had one round left in it, and when the crew chief
walked across the wing, the tilting activated the 0.50-
calibre machine-gun to fire the one round. Fortunately it
was an armour-piercing round that went through the gasoline tank truck, where it shed its copper jacket. Only
the steel core went through my leg. The surgeon in the
operating room said it went in between the fibula and
tibia, which are just about half an inch apart. When he
was finished putting a 'drain' in the wound he said:

'Lieutenant, you are the luckiest man in Burma. A frac-
tion of an inch either way and you probably would have
lost that leg.' ''

MORE AIR COMMANDOS WANTED?

There was much more fighting ahead for the British troops
before the Japanese Army withdrew from Burma, but General
Hap Arnold was determined to help them. Four more Air
Commando Groups were planned, but this was cut to two, the
2nd and 3rd Air Commando Groups, each with its own Combat Cargo Group in support. Following Wingate's ideas, the
new air commando groups would be used to seize and defend
landing sites and later provide close air support for ground
troops, while the combat cargo groups provided large-scale
transport of ground troops and their supplies to forward areas
established by the air commando groups. Each Air Commando
Group would consist of two squadrons of P-51 Mustangs, one
squadron of C-47s and CG-4A gliders, three liaison squadrons
flying the L-5 and UC-64, plus various support organisations
such as airborne engineers. The combat cargo groups would
each have four squadrons of C-47 (later C-46) aircraft to keep
the logistic lifeline open once the troops were on the ground
and operating in enemy territory.

Unfortunately, Admiral Mountbatten's South East Asia
Command would only accept one of the new air commando
groups. Both groups formed and trained in Florida, and the
2nd Air Commando Group joined the 1st in India, while the
3rd Air Commando Group was earmarked for the southwest
Pacific.

Sadly, all three Air Commando Groups eventually shared
the same fate, being absorbed by conventional units. Why
Wingate's theories and General Arnold's new airpower strategy did not flourish after the success of the 1st Air Commando
Group was ably summed up by the British military historian
B. H. Liddell Hart, who wrote: ''The only thing harder than
getting a new idea into the military mind, is to get an old one
out.''

CHAPTER 2

2ND AIR COMMANDO GROUP FOR BURMA

ALTHOUGH TWO MORE AIR Commando Groups were organised following the success of the 1st Air Commando Group, only one, the 2nd Air Commando Group, was committed to Burma. The 3rd Air Commando Group was sent to the southwest Pacific, where it supported the Allied "island-hopping" and continued onto the Japanese mainland at the end of the war.

Activated at Lakeland Army Air Field, Florida, on 25 April 1944, the 2nd Air Commando Group comprised the 1st and 2nd Fighter Squadrons, the 127th, 155th and 156th Liaison Squadrons and the 317th Troop Carrier Squadron. Ground support was ably provided by the 327th, 328th, 340th and 342nd Airdrome Squadrons and the 236th Medical Dispensary (Aviation). Colonel Arthur R DeBolt commanded the group during its six-month training period and its first six months of combat in the China-Burma-India theatre. He was recalled to the United States on 15 May 1945 and replaced by Colonel Alfred J Ball, Jr, the group executive officer. The 2nd Group was not actually employed as a unit; rather it was parcelled out in separate squadrons, each with its own role to play in the expulsion of the Japanese from Burma and Siam (Thailand).

The British 14th Army was on the offensive when the 317th Troop Carrier Squadron arrived in India on 10 November 1944. The unit's C-47s were immediately committed to combat, dropping supplies in the Chindwin Valley, ferrying urgently needed Chinese troops from Nan Sin to Kunming and

Chan Yi, and later transporting critical airfield and road materials to Myitkyina. The squadron sustained its only serious casualties during this period of the campaign, four C-47s and three crews being lost in twenty days. The main reason for this was the bad weather encountered while flying over the Hump to China. One aircraft crashed into a mountain with the loss of all on board, and another, flown by the squadron commander, disappeared without trace. A third was destroyed by enemy action at Meiktila airfield, and the fourth crashed on take-off at Tulihal owing to engine failure.

From 27 February to 2 March 1945 the C-47s airlifted the 99th Brigade into Meiktila to reinforce the 17th Division. For weeks the squadron supported the troops in this area, flying a second brigade into the area between 15 and 18 March. On 12 April the C-47s returned to the group's home base at Kalaikunda to prepare for an ambitious paratroop drop near Rangoon. Joint exercises were conducted with the 23rd Gurkha Battalion of the 50th Parachute Brigade, 15th Corps, before the paratroops were moved up to Akyab on 29 April. On 1 May the drop was made on Elephant Point, the Japanese defensive position on the Rangoon River estuary, and the following day an amphibious landing took place to recapture Rangoon. Little resistance was found, however, as the Japanese had abandoned Rangoon and were already retreating eastwards.

Two months after the 317th had begun combat operations, the first of the liaison squadrons arrived. The 127th was committed to the support of the 15th Indian Corps at Akyab on 10 January 1945, and were involved in the battles for Kangaw, Ramree Island, Ru Ywa, An, Letpan and Taungup. The 155th was assigned to the headquarters of the 4th Corps at Sinthe on 21 February. The 156th was committed last, on 8 April 1945, to reinforce the 155th at Myitche. They had been delayed by a typhoon which struck the group's base at Kalaikunda on 12 March, destroying or damaging beyond repair 117 aircraft, including 44 CG-4A gliders, 54 L-5s, 7 UC-64s and 12 P-51s. Both squadrons flew in support of the fighting at Meiktila; at Letse, West of the Irrawaddy River; and at Kyaukpadaung, Chauk, Magwe and various places in the South. They were constantly coming to the relief of small patrols, and land-

ings behind the enemy lines were commonplace. The role of
the three squadrons was the evacuation of wounded, forward
air supply and the flying in of reinforcements. They were also
used as couriers, and to fly observation missions over the jungle with British officers.

Bob McGovern flew L-5s with the 155th Liaison Squadron
into the strategic town of Meiktila, with its airstrip, rail lines
and roads leading to Rangoon. It had been captured in early
March 1945 by 4th Corps, and a month-long siege began as
the Japanese tried to recapture the town. On 16 March Bob
and Kirk Hoover were told to fly tank mechanics and their
heavy tool boxes from Myitche to Meiktila. Hoover took off
and cleared the trees, but struck a pagoda spire and crashed,
destroying his aeroplane and earning himself a stay in hospital.
Bob just managed a difficult turn on take-off to clear the high
trees with his heavy load, and completed his journey, taking
hits from small-arms fire on the way in. He returned to base
with a severely wounded soldier on board who sadly was dead
on arrival.

The 1st and 2nd Fighter Squadrons began combat operations
with their P-51s on 14 February 1945, in support of the 14th
Army's drive on Meiktila. They had arrived at their airfield at
Cox's Bazaar, south of the Maiskhal Channel, India, only two
days earlier, to find that the 327th Airdrome Squadron had
done such a good job preparing the airfield that they could
start combat operations almost immediately. Their first task
was close air support of the 4th Corps as they crossed the
Irrawaddy River at Nyaungu and established a bridgehead on
the other side. The P-51s provided similar support all the way
to Meiktila, and provided fighter cover for RAF and Air Commando C-47s arriving at Meiktila airfield. The weapons used
by the P-51s included 500lb GPTI bombs, 0.50-calibre machine-guns firing incendiary ammunition, and 4.25in rockets,
the last proving effective against fixed installations. The new
napalm, in 110gal tanks, also proved effective and reportedly
led to the demise of some 3,000 enemy troops. As the support
of the bridgehead lessened, the fighters redirected their efforts
against the enemy-held airfields in Burma. However, most of
the enemy aircraft had been moved to Thailand, so on 15
March 40 Mustangs from the group went looking for them.

The story of the Don Muang fighter sweeps will be told later.

The fighters also provided cover for Allied bombers, destroyed many bridges and attacked the enemy wherever they were found. On 29 April the fighters discovered a Japanese concentration at Pegu, 40 miles from Rangoon, preparing for the trek to Moulmein. They destroyed locomotives, trains, AA guns, cars and trucks and a fuel dump. When British troops arrived the next day they found that the Japanese had fled, leaving behind hundreds of destroyed and abandoned vehicles.

With the advent of the monsoon rains, the fighter squadrons provided cover for the amphibious forces which took Rangoon on 4 May 1945, without a struggle. The fighting on the ground had not finished, however, and in a one-month period the 155th Liaison Squadron evacuated 1,110 wounded men, using their 32 L-5s and four UC-64s. The Japanese Burma Area Army was in disarray, with the remnants of the 15th and 33rd Armies, which had suffered heavy casualties at Imphal, Mandalay and Meiktila, and the 28th Army from the Arakan retreating eastwards. When the 28th Army reached the Sittang River and their escape route east into Siam or south into Malaya, they found the British 4th Corps waiting for them. Maps of the crossing points had been captured, and the breakout turned into a gigantic turkey shoot. By the end of July the survivors had crossed the river and were heading for Moulmein, but time was against them. On 15 August Japan surrendered, and within days the fighting had ceased.

During the war, five pilots from the two fighter squadrons were shot down and taken prisoner by the Japanese. Four were returned at the end of the war, and their stories are told elsewhere. Sadly, the fifth man was killed in captivity. He was Doc Lyons, a pilot with the 1st Fighter Squadron, who had flown 50 combat missions and was credited with four enemy aeroplanes destroyed on the ground. On 20 April 1945, while on a strafing mission in the Rangoon area, his P-51 was struck by groundfire and he had to bale out near the Japanese stronghold of Bassein, Burma. An L-5 was sent to try to locate the downed pilot, but could not find him. Doc hid in a native hut overnight, but was turned over to the Japanese the next morning because the natives feared reprisals for harbouring him. After the war it was learned that Doc had been severely beaten

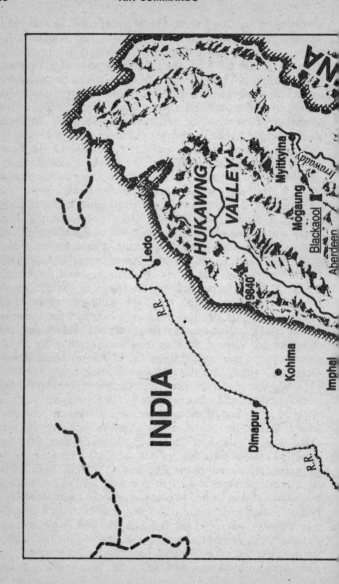

Map of the Chindit Campaign in northern Burma, March–May 1944.

and later beheaded when the Japanese left Bassein and fled towards the East. There is a memorial to Doc, and to other pilots who were killed or missing in action, in the American Cemetery in the Philippines.

Amongst the awards earned by pilots of the group was the Silver Star received by Major Charles M. Gordon, Jr, for his gallantry in attempting to rescue Captain Edward E Atha, who had been forced down behind enemy lines on 25 February 1945. A member of the 1st Fighter Squadron, Major Gordon, now flying an L-5, had already rescued Lieutenant Robert A. Beck from an enemy-held area twenty miles west of Meiktila, and returned after dark to try to find Captain Atha. Attempting to land in a small clearing, he overshot and crashed into a tree, sustaining fractures of the nose, jaw and leg and severe cuts about the head. Both he and Captain Atha were later rescued by British troops. Sadly, Charlie Gordon was killed during a night flight in August 1945.

As the war came to an end the 317th Troop Carrier Squadron was ordered into China to arrange for the repatriation of American military personnel and prisoners of war. In November 1945 the squadron left its aircraft for the Thai Air Force and the personnel were flown to Kalaikunda for shipment home. The 155th Liaison Squadron was withdrawn to Kalaikunda in May, and prepared for the first of many personnel-transfers to other units. In June ten of their L-5s joined twenty others for a long and dangerous flight over the Hump to China. In August the squadron boarded a troopship for transfer to the Pacific Zone of Operations, and was overjoyed to discover en route that Japan had surrendered following the dropping of the atomic bombs on Hiroshima and Nagasaki. They made their final stop at Okinawa, where the squadron was deactivated and the majority of the remaining personnel assigned to the 157th Liaison Squadron in Tokyo.

The 2nd Air Commando Group was officially deactivated on 12 November 1945 and disbanded on 8 October 1948.

BALE-OUT!

There can be few more harrowing experiences than having to bale out of a doomed aeroplane and then finding yourself on the ground in enemy territory, praying that your own side gets to you before the enemy. One pilot who lived through that experience is Robert A. Beck, a P-51 pilot with the 2nd Fighter Squadron of the 2nd Air Commando Group. He had been flying combat missions for only a week or so when the grim reaper passed by him. He told the author:

"During my pilot's training with the P-51 in Florida, we were told there was very little info on how best to parachute from this airplane, other than that of earlier type aircraft. Why? I was afraid to ask. Nevertheless, I was to find out.

Soon after our move from Kalaikunda to Cox's Bazaar, we started flying missions in and about Central Burma. There was considerable activity north and south of the Irrawaddy River where the Yaw River enters into it. Numerous supportive missions were flown in that area to break the counter-attacks made by the Japanese. Many Indian anti-aircraft installations were necessary to protect the river crossing from the strafing Japanese. The strafing had to be stopped. The British needed fighter cover over the area, especially at early-morning hours. Since the 2nd Air Commando Group was ideal for this type of work, we got it!

Captain Atha and his flight were assigned to operate from an advance British airbase near the Irrawaddy River. Our patrol was effective and the flights by the Japanese to the north were stopped. However, our efforts were not without risk, not only from the Japanese fighters but from the Allied Indian anti-aircraft gunners, who fired at us every time we flew near. Thank Heavens they were lousy shots.

After the third day's patrol we received a report that twelve Jap Oscars were flying north with something serious in mind. Captain Atha and I took off at approximately noon to intercept them. Captain Atha determined we should fly low to the town of Chaunggwa, just east of a north/south mountain range, fly east and continue to fly low until we reached Kyaukkyi, a town on the west side of a second north/south mountain range. We would fly between the two points going east and west until the 'planes were sighted.

We flew the first leg of our patrol, turned and started back. About half the distance on this leg I was shaken by a loud explosion from the left front of the airplane. I saw large pieces of cowling flying from the airplane. I immediately turned to a northwest heading and started to climb. The engine was rough, but smoothed out after a few seconds. In about another 15 seconds it started to slow down, meaning it was seizing up and would soon stop.

After a fast look at the terrain, I thought it best to bale out. Putting my head down, I released the canopy, then rolled the elevator trim nose down and released all harness and paraphernalia and prepared to lunge up and to the right. I placed my right hand on the ripcord ring, released my left arm from the stick and pushed up and to the right. The wind slapped me back against the armour plate of my seat and my right arm was forced back, pulling the ripcord and opening the 'chute in the cockpit. My immediate response was 'ah, shit'. That was all I could say when I was yanked out of the cockpit, like nothing I could imagine. I received a second shock like the first. The 'chute, feeding out from the cockpit, caught on the tail, and when I came out my weight ripped it away from whatever part of the tail it was on. I looked up at the chute and saw a tremendous rip in it. I now expressed a second 'ah, shit'.

The 'plane had gone down not far from my descent, exploding into a flash of flame and black clouds. Almost instantly I heard exploding ammunition, tracers were flying every which way and I was floating into it. I knew that to avoid the 'plane I would have to slip the 'chute to get to the ground faster, but what about the rip in the 'chute? I had no choice, I grabbed the rear shroud lines and pulled. I dropped like a rock. Since I wasn't too high to begin with, I was worried about my descent, considering the ripped 'chute. I released the lines, the 'chute opened, causing me to swing forwards. I landed on my buttocks, blacked out and saw white flashes. My crotch hurt like someone had kicked me with a size 12 work shoe. I sat for a second, clearing my head and checking my body for injuries. My left foot hurt badly. I was afraid it was broken, but when I stood up I knew it wasn't. Thank God it could support my weight. My shins were bleeding, but not bad.

Training says when you are down in enemy territory you should remove the backpack from your parachute and bury your 'chute. I concluded that doing that would not help my case, so I tossed the 'chute, kept the backpack and got the hell out of there. Furthermore, the Japanese were near and I wasn't too far from where they shot me down. I started out heading northwest, limping badly on my left leg at first, but ignoring it from then on.

I travelled in ravines or low areas to keep from being spotted. After a short time it became evident that I was becoming disturbed, nervous, possibly from shock. I had a distance to go with no picnic in mind, so I thought I better settle down, rest and clear my head. I found a clump of weeds, crawled in and forced myself to lie still and think of nice things like home in Pittsburgh.

I guess this happens often in life-and-death predicaments, your mind wanders to places like home, family and especially mother. Regardless of how hard life is, it was still good. Here, it's an uncontrollable reality; fight you must, to live, or die. Such was my thinking until I became aware of movement nearby. I heard running and heavy walking. Finding an opening in the brush, I noticed a couple of kids running in the direction of the downed 'plane, followed by three tall Burmese men, draped in long cloaks, each carrying long bamboo spears. Past experience reminded me that the ends of the spears were whittled to needle points.

I recalled the briefing we had concerning the assistance we could expect from the Burmese, should we parachute into enemy territory. The Japanese would kill any native, and everyone living in his village, if he was caught helping Allied soldiers. I continued to lay in the brush for a couple of hours when I decided it was time

to get out and start walking. Once out I gave the landscape a good look. Halfway around my peripheral vision
I noticed a young boy about 200 yards north of me. We
stared at each other for a short time before I pulled out
and showed my small American flag. At this the boy
turned to his right and voiced some fast Burmese and
turned back to me. Almost immediately three Burmese
men came into view, they too stared at me and I waved
the American flag at them. Waving the flag apparently
sparked them into doing something, as it did the boy,
because they started to move towards me. What scared
the hell out me was that they had adjusted the hold on
their spears. I pulled my .45 out of my holster and waved
them off. They stopped and we looked at each other for
about another five or ten seconds, when they ran for the
bushes. I thought 'oh shit, they're going to circle me'. I
then heard at this point what they heard before me; the
drone of a squadron of P-51s. I pulled out my spotting
mirror and did everything I could with it, but was told
later that it wasn't noticed.

An L-5 came up and flew wide circles around my
location. Apparently finding what he was looking for, he
settled the 'plane down about a half mile from me. I
didn't hesitate, I started to run towards him and closed
the distance in short order. Chuck Gordon was the pilot.
He opened the cockpit, said: 'Boy, are you suffering
from shock—jump in—let's go!' He was already in position to take-off, and so he did. He picked a rugged
strip of land between two large rice paddies. I knew it
was short, even though I had given it no more than a
passing glance. He gave the 'plane all it had. He got it
off all right, but hit the top of a tree at the end of his
pull-up. It didn't do enough damage to stop the 'plane
from flying.

We flew back to the British base without incident.
Seeing the base made me feel better than any other time
that day. The British Commandant met us and raved
about the rescue. He gave me a bottle of Four Roses and
bade me have drink. I thanked him and swore I drank

half of it. Most of all I thanked Charles. He did a service I could never repay.

I returned to Cox's Bazaar that night and received medical attention. The other members of our flight also withdrew from the British base in Burma. I want to say here that later that very night the Japanese bombed the same area our airplanes were parked in. It was obvious they weren't sitting on their hands.

I feel I didn't do a bad job under the circumstances. However, holding onto the ripcord from the start was bad. That could have spelled curtains. Thank God for the bubble canopy. I suppose I will never forget that experience, but it's better than being dead like some of my companions who were not as fortunate. Chuck Gordon, God Bless his soul, did not fare as well. He died the same night Japan capitulated. They notified him of this while he was in the air, his home away from home, but he was not heard from again. They found his 'plane the next day. His one love, Elizabeth Short, died several months later in California.''

Bob Beck continued flying missions until May 1945 and returned to the USA in June. He went back as a First Lieutenant, with the Purple Heart, the Air Medal and the Distinguished Flying Cross to his name.

THE DON MUANG FIGHTER SWEEPS

The first hunt for the elusive Japanese air force took place on 15 March 1945, when twenty P-51s from the 1st Fighter Squadron and the same number from the 2nd Fighter Squadron took off from Cox's Bazaar, on the border between India and Burma, and flew a 1,600-mile around trip to Don Muang airport near Bangkok in Thailand to try to destroy the Japanese aircraft based there.

The enemy thought that Don Muang was safe from Allied fighters, and had over a hundred aeroplanes stationed there. Little did they realise that the P-51 Mustangs, with wing tanks, could fly the distance to their field. The 40 Mustangs hit the field at 1330 hours and thoroughly strafed every aeroplane that could be seen, destroying over 50 per cent of the Japanese aircraft in the Burma-Thailand area. Three were shot down from the air, while seventeen were confirmed to have been destroyed on the ground. Twenty-two others were damaged or destroyed. Bob Eason, who related the tale to the author, led the fifth flight of four Mustangs and destroyed two twin-engined bombers, while others in his flight destroyed six more aeroplanes. He recalled:

> "In addition, I was able to strafe a Jap barracks, setting it on fire. The mission was about eight hours long and we were a tired bunch of pilots when we landed, but we were extremely happy for the 'planes destroyed and the record mission we had accomplished. It was the longest fighter sweep of the war up to that time. Unfortunately, one P-51 was shot down and the pilot killed."

On 9 April a second attack was launched on the airport by twenty P-51s from the 1st Fighter Squadron and twelve from the 2nd. As in the first raid, the flight was flown "on the deck" to avoid Japanese radar. This time there were many fires as the raiders destroyed or damaged over 30 aircraft. The anti-aircraft fire was more dense this time, and three pilots were shot down. Captain Albert Abraham of the 2nd Fighter Squadron was hit by enemy ground fire and baled out near the airport. He was taken prisoner by the Thais and held as a prisoner of war together with Lieutenants Mac MacKenzie and Dean Wimer from the 1st Fighter Squadron. MacKenzie was flying Colonel Chase's wing when he was hit, and as he was so close to the ground at the time he made a belly landing. Wimer was hit and baled out, but broke several ribs when he hit the tailplane as he left the cockpit. Both were taken prisoner by the Thais and interrogated by the Japanese, with a Thai officer present. As prisoners of the Thais they received better treatment than the Japanese would have given them, and were returned at the end of the war. All three were awarded the Air Medal, the Distinguished Flying Cross and the Purple Heart.

Bob Eason was again able to bag two Japanese aircraft, bringing his total to four on the two raids. For the two missions the two fighter squadrons were awarded the Distinguished Unit Citation, a Presidential award, for the longest fighter mission of the war. The pilots who participated in the flights received the Distinguished Flying Cross.

THE RESCUE OF COLONEL LEVI CHASE

One incident which typifies the Air Commando attitude was the rescue of Colonel Levi R. Chase, the Commanding Officer of the 1st Fighter Squadron. Bob Eason was again involved:

"On 26 March 1945, after a 3.00 a.m. briefing, our flight of twelve P-51D Mustangs took off from Cox's Bazaar and headed for Rangoon to strafe the airfields nearby, namely Amawbi, Mingaladon and Moulmeim. The first target was Amawbi. Colonel Levi Chase, the 2nd Air Commando Group Operations Officer, and leader of the sweep, led the first four-ship formation, and I led the second four-ship formation. As we got to the field, three Jap Oscars took off and joined in a three-ship formation, at which time Colonel Chase climbed up and blasted the three 'planes with his six 0.50-calibre machine-guns. The other three 'planes in his flight took shots at the three 'planes, and I was behind, hoping that they would miss, but they did not. The three 'planes spun to the ground and hit, still in a V-formation.

I observed that Colonel Chase's 'plane had been hit as coolant was streaming from the underside of the fuselage. Soon he called me and said he was going to 'Belly in.' I saw him land, stop and get out of the 'plane and begin heading for the jungle.

I instructed the other three members of the flight to destroy the downed plane by strafing. They were to go to Ramree Island, a small landing strip west of Rangoon. With my flight of four 'planes, we headed for Ramree and landed.

We soon learned that Major Roger Pryor, the commander of the 2nd Fighter Squadron, had also been shot down and that two rescue 'planes were needed. We attempted to find a Sea Otter and land on a nearby river, but none were available. I saw that there were three or four L-5s at the field, belonging to our Group, and I commandeered two 'planes, much to the objection of the pilots, but I knew where Colonel Chase was down and felt confident that I could pick him up.

Lieutenant Bobby Spann and I took off in the two L-5s and headed for the area where Colonel Chase had landed. It was 200 miles deep in enemy territory and the aircraft did not carry enough internal fuel for the around trip. Therefore we loaded some five-gallon cans of extra fuel and strapped them in the back seat. We took off at about 9.30 a.m. and two P-51s flown by Lieutenants Harold Hettema and James Fishburn flew on to the site to locate Colonel Chase and the downed Major Pryor. They were also to act as top cover for us.

Upon arrival at the clearing I landed and began to fill the gas tanks with the fuel from the extra cans. The field was muddy and full of ruts, and I knew there would be a problem on take-off. Soon Lieutenant Spann landed and we attempted to free the 'plane, but with no success. Colonel Chase then arrived and with the help of natives who appeared, and with rupees from my money belt, the natives helped us get the 'plane free.

With Colonel Chase in the back seat, I began my take-off and had a very difficult time with the impossible field, but finally made it. Lieutenant Spann then took off and headed for the area Major Pryor had gone down in. Later, I found out that he had his maps blown out of the window on take-off. He had to navigate from memory after that, to the area where Major Pryor had landed and then back to Ramree Island.

I headed for Ramree Island, and the fuel was getting very low as we approached the final twenty miles over water to the Island. When I landed, the tailwheel had been jammed up into the fuselage and I ran out of gas on the runway.

Lieutenant Spann had no success finding Major Pryor and soon returned to Ramree, also out of gas. Both of us were very happy to have rescued Colonel Chase, who was given credit for two 'planes shot down, and his wingman received credit for the other. Major Pryor was captured by the Japs, but returned after the war ended.

The natives had been threatened to turn in all Americans by the Japs, and we were lucky that our rescue could have been made. The Japs were on the way, we learned later from Intelligence. I was put in for the Distinguished Service Cross, but as no shots were fired it was reduced to the Silver Star, 'For Gallantry in Action'. I was proud to have it.''

Major Pryor had flown 83 missions with the Flying Tigers of General Claire Chennault's 23rd Fighter Group, and became an ace with five aerial victories to his credit. After capture he was given a difficult time by the Japanese, but survived and was liberated by the Allies when Burma fell. His tour in Burma gave him a total of 114 missions and 240 combat hours in P-40s and P-51s. He retired as a Colonel in 1966, and died in August 1989 after a lengthy illness.

CHAPTER 3

ISLAND-HOPPING TO JAPAN: 3RD AIR COMMANDO GROUP

THE 3RD AIR COMMANDO Group was constituted on 25 April 1944 and activated on 1 May that year. It was ordered to move to the Philippines at the end of the year, where its aircraft would be assigned to the 5th Air Force. Its mission would be to attack Japanese airfields and installations in the Philippines, in Formosa and even as far as the coast of China. The Group would be commanded by Colonel Arvid Olson, one of the glider pilots whose tow broke on the way to Broadway with the 1st Air Commando Group.

The officers and enlisted men of the new group left Alachua Army Air Field, Florida, and arrived at Drew Field, Florida, on 6 October 1944. They departed on 24 October for Camp Stoneman, California, and were settled in five days later. After completing overseas processing they embarked on 7 November for a miserable three-week ocean voyage to Tacloban, Leyte, arriving on 30 November. The men were glad to be ashore, and spent the next five weeks preparing for the arrival of their fighters, which landed at Tanauan airstrip on 7 January 1945. The next day they began flying the first of 6,650 sorties over the seven months of operations that followed, before the Japanese surrendered.

The group comprised a light aeroplane force of three Liaison Squadrons, the 157th, 159th and 160th, flying Stinson L-5 Sentinels. They flew more than 15,000 sorties in three months, and evacuated thousands of casualties to the rear areas where they could receive proper treatment. The air cargo unit of the group was the 318th Troop Carrier Squadron, and their fourteen to seventeen C-47s flew 6,600 sorties before the war came to an end. The 3rd and 4th Fighter Squadrons provided the fighter element of the Group, collecting their P-51D Mustangs which had been shipped to Finschhafen, New Guinea, and flying them back to Nadzab, New Guinea. The fighters provided excellent close air support to the 32nd Infantry Division in their operations against Japanese forces on Luzon. They also flew missions over Formosa and China, and in seven months expended over three million rounds of 0.50-calibre ammunition, 2,210 tons of high explosive bombs and 1,658 napalm bombs. They destroyed 66 enemy aircraft, 78 locomotives, 10 ships and 289 trucks and killed countless enemy troops.

The four Airdrome Squadrons belonging to the Group were the 334th, 335th, 341st and 343rd, and the Medical Detachment was the 237th. There were no special operations requirements for the Group, so they were assigned to 5th Air Force for use in conventional operations. Higher headquarters for the Group was the 308th Bomb Wing, a unit in name only which functioned as a mini Air Force Headquarters and was responsible for the Air Commandos and a number of other fighter organisations. Colonel John Alison was deputy wing commander.

The Group remained on Leyte until 26 January, flying missions throughout the Philippines. They provided fighter escort for light bombers, dive-bombed suspected Japanese installations and strafed enemy air strips. They then moved to Mangalden, Luzon, were they stayed until 19 April. The next move was to Laog, on northern Luzon, which was actually behind Japanese lines. They carried out operations from this base until 1 August, when they moved to Ie Shima in time to fly 57 sorties in the last two days of the war. Their last move was to Chitose, on Hokkaido, the northernmost island of Japan, where they stayed from October 1945 to March 1946.

MUSTANGS FOR THE 3RD

The first North American P-51 Mustangs to operate in the Southwest Pacific Theatre arrived by sea aboard a cargo ship.

They were assembled at Finschhafen, New Guinea, in October and November 1944. These were P-51Ds, together with some F-6Ds, the photo-reconnaissance version assigned to the 82nd Tactical Reconnaissance Squadron, 71st Reconnaissance Group. Most of the P-51Ds were assigned to the 3rd Air Commando Group, soon to be flying combat missions for the Fifth Air Force out of Leyte, Philippine Islands. Whether by intent or by chance, the first pilots to fly the P-51 in the southwest Pacific Theatre were members of the 3rd Fighter Squadron, 3rd Air Commando Group.

The story was told to the author by Jerry Collins, one of the pilots involved in collecting the new aeroplanes. A very capable author himself, Jerry also has the strength of character to tell a good story even if the laugh is eventually on him.

"The pilots were from a group of sixteen brand-spanking new 2nd Lieutenant P-40 pilots, recently based at Nadzab, New Guinea. After completing Overseas Training at Dale Mabry Army Air Field, Tallahassee, Florida, the previous September, each had volunteered to become an Air Commando, was accepted and assigned to the 3rd Air Commando Group, which was preparing to leave Sarasota, Florida, for overseas at that time. Having been transported from the States by air, the new air commandos reached New Guinea months before the main group was to arrive by troopship.

While awaiting the arrival of their parent organisation they came under a local command at Nadzab. It imposed duty assignments upon the leaderless detachment at its pleasure. The most frequent duty involved ferrying war-weary Curtiss P-40 fighters to and from various air bases in Australia, New Guinea and several islands in the Bismark Sea. Normally a C-47 would fly the ferry pilots to the place where the P-40s were to be picked up and then go on its way. However, when the return trip was to be a long over-water flight, the C-47 or one adequately equipped with electronic navigation gear would be available to lead the fighters back to Nadzab. This was because most fighter aircraft had only very basic navigation equipment.

The volunteers for the mission on Sunday 22 October 1944, expected it to be another routine assignment. They were Collins, Kraut, Larson, McNeil, Mangan, Motok, White and Young. It was early morning when the pickup truck carried the eight commandos from their Nadzab encampment to the rendezvous point at the cargo strip. There were three airstrips at Nadzab. One was for fighter aircraft, another for bombers, and one for transient and cargo aircraft. When the truck dropped them off they found themselves quite alone under a rising red-hot sun that promised another day of temperatures well above 100° Fahrenheit. The spot they were dropped at was but a few yards from a large wooden building; a temporary storage facility for foodstuffs. Except for the tropical forest-green Owen-Stanley mountains rising to nearly 16,000ft to the south, the building and a B-25 medium bomber parked about a quarter mile away was all that was in sight. The old Army 'hurry up and wait' factor was alive and well.

The men moved into the shadows of the platform about the base of the storage building to await their transportation to Finschhafen, an airfield on the coast, about 90 miles to the east, where they were to pick up some airplanes and fly them back to the fighter strip. About an hour later a jeep pulled up. Beside the driver, a young Captain, wearing pilot wings above the left pocket of his khaki shirt and a sheepish grin, gave a timid wave before leaping from the vehicle. 'This must be our bus driver,' one of the fighter pilots remarked. The Captain explained that the originally scheduled pilot could not make it for some reason, so he would be our transport pilot to Finschhafen. The transport would be the B-25, but the Captain needed a copilot. Could one of the eight accommodate him? The response was unanimous 'Of course!'. Since none of the young air commandos had ever piloted a twin-engine aircraft, each was eager to do so. An odd-man-out coin toss decided which of the fighter pilots would fly in the right seat of the bomber. Collins won the toss.

After reaching the B-25 and completing an external

inspection of it, the Captain dropped the belly hatch. Seven commandos crawled aboard and packed themselves into the bomber's radio and navigation compartments, just forward of the bomb bay. There were no parachutes, except for the pilot and copilot. Collins and the Captain took their places in the cockpit, cranked up the engines and taxied to the runway.

Over the deafening noise of the two engines, the Captain instructed Collins how to set the wing flaps and to raise and lower the landing gear. Following a quick run-up of the engines and a magneto check, the aircraft was cleared for take-off. On the roll down the perforated steel planking (PSP) reinforced runway, Collins could not help but think about his buddies crowded in the back while he experienced the thrill of getting familiar with a new type of aircraft.

The runway at Finschhafen came into view within 30 minutes. Beyond it, the Huon Gulf and the Pacific Ocean extended to the eastern horizon. Below, in the harbour, many sea-going vessels were being unloaded of their cargoes or loaded with troops being moved Stateside, or to combat units in the Philippines. Attention was directed from the surface activity when Finschhafen airport traffic control tower (code-name 'Harvest') cleared the B-25 for landing.

The Captain manoeuvred the aircraft to the downwind leg, called for ten degrees flaps, then wheels down. As he turned on the base leg, Collins noticed that the Captain had properly set the mixture control to 'Full Rich,' but was now retarding the propeller pitch. The throttle lever remained at the aircraft's cruise setting. 'Not right,' he thought. 'Even operating a twin-engine aircraft should not be so different from that of a single-engine aircraft.' He observed the airspeed begin to fall too rapidly as the turn to final approach was completed, and that the captain was concentrating on visual orientation, paying no attention to the instruments. To get the captain's attention, Collins slapped his hand, which was still slowly retarding the prop pitch. When the captain realised what he was doing, he called for gear up and began a go-around. The aircraft was still half-a-mile from touchdown and not much more than a hundred feet above the sea. Again Collins thought of his buddies in the back and heaved a sigh. For the moment they need not learn to swim.

The second approach was successful and a satisfactory landing was completed . . . after the third bounce. As the aircraft taxied to the ramp, the captain turned to Collins and apologised for his error, adding that he too had never flown a B-25 before in his life. He was a C-47 pilot! He explained that the location of the levers for the prop pitch and the throttle on the two aircraft were exactly reversed.

After bidding the captain farewell, the eight went to Base Operations, which was adjacent to the traffic control tower. They signed for the aircraft they were to ferry back to Nadzab, then jeeps took them to the revetments where newly assembled aircraft were parked. Rounding a clump of bamboo, the airmen beheld their first P-51 Mustang fighters. These were the latest 'D' model with bubble canopy and Packard Merlin 1,695 h.p. engines; about 600 h.p. more than the P-40s they had been flying. A magnificent sight. Things of beauty. Featuring laminar-flow airfoil-section cantilever wings, below the fuselage radiator ducts and four-bladed Hamilton Standard propellers, they stood invitingly with unpainted alclad-covered airframes glistening in the midday sun; tempting any red-blooded pilots to climb aboard for the ride of their lives.

The new air commandos stared unbelievingly at the sight. 'What the hell kind of airplanes are these?,' They muttered among themselves. 'P-51Ds,' said a mechanic, just entering the compound. 'Beautiful,' we replied, 'but do you have any tech manuals or pilot information files on them?' 'Not yet,' came the reply, 'but we expect some with the next shipment of airframes.' 'Oh, Great!' Undeterred by the news, the pilots climbed aboard the aircraft and slid into their cockpits. They sat there for some time, studying the mechanical layout and instrumentation.

Including time at the end of a kite string in the preceding eighteen windy Marches, not one of these airmen had more than 400 hours total flying time. The Curtiss P-40 was the only fighter plane they had mastered. This was their first sight of a P-51; on the very day they were to 'check out' in one. Each of the new airplanes was fully armed with 0.50-calibre ammo for the six machine-guns and a full load of gasoline, including the 50gal fuselage tank behind the pilot's seat. Not an ideal configuration on a first solo in any airplane, and certainly not one for an aircraft encountered for the first time.

All, or nearly all, had to ask a mechanic how to start the engine. Each well knew that to taxi a P-40 with the control stick forward was a recipe for setting the tail-light bird on its nose. What they did not know is that the mass of the P-51 is more evenly distributed, and even at its fully loaded weight of 12,500lb its center of gravity is in balance. The stick in the aft position on a P-51 is designed to lock its tailwheel in a fixed, non-swivel position, to afford greater stability and control for take-off and landing. Therefore, the correct way to taxi a P-51 is with the stick full forward. Because these P-40-trained pilots feared a nose-over, they taxied the P-51s with the stick fully in their laps and, as a result, three blew tailwheel tyres, in fact tore them off, while swinging their aircraft into the taxi queue.

Collins made it to the end of the runway without incident. He was second to be cleared for take-off. Taking the runway, he slipped the throttle forward to 22in of mercury. With that much power a P-40 leapt into the air. No so a P-51. Shortly after starting to roll, the aircraft began sliding diagonally to the left. Unless sufficient speed is quickly gained to acquire rudder control, the engine torque of its 1,695 h.p. engine causes a heavy P-51 to 'fly' sideways. Collins increased the power to 26in of mercury and applied full right rudder and stick. Still the aircraft slipped to the left, coming dangerously close to the runway edge. The control tower loomed closer and closer, its dimension nearly filling the entire area of his windscreen. Just ahead and below the tower

were four cargo aircraft; three C-47s and a C-46, being
loaded and refuelled from supply trucks. Their ground
crews had halted their activity where they stood. As if
frozen in time, they stared goggle-eyed at the fighter
'plane that was screaming directly at them.

For a moment, Collins saw his entire life and a terrible
ending flash before him. He and his aircraft were about
to be spread in a blackened mass across the landscape.
Nonsense, he thought, pushing the throttle to the wire
and simultaneously raising the landing gear. Concentrating on flying the airplane, he barely noticed the crews
that were loading the cargo 'planes taking flying leaps
from wherever they were and striking out towards the
jungle. At the moment, it appeared to them that its den-
izens, while dangerous, seemed safer than the whirling
propeller about to stagger within inches of their airplanes.

As the 'plane finally broke ground, Collins put it into
a wide left turn, pulling up to about 1,500ft above the
ocean, where a number of naval and cargo vessels were
anchored. Gradually he became aware of a voice in his
earphones screeching something like, 'Aircraft on taxiway, hold your position. We may have an emergency'.
'I wonder who's in trouble', he thought. Then, checking
the integrity of his aircraft, he did a double take when
he spotted an aluminium cone with a 4ft base wrapped
around the left stabilizer. It was a runway light. To his
relief, no human had been snared. The runway light was
easily shaken off, and fell into the sea well clear of any
vessel. Then, sighting the first aircraft to take-off, Collins joined up in formation and the two circled until the
others, or most of the others, were airborne. A course
that took them up the fertile Ramu-Markham Valley led
them back to Nadzab.

Scorcher tower, the controlling facility at the Nadzab
fighter strip, having received a message that all of the
P-51s from Finschhafen were airborne, awaited them
with justified nervous anticipation. Larson, then Collins,
were first to land, each making smooth landings. Mangan ground-looped, Motok and Kraut blew main land-

ing-gear tyres. Young was next, and when the runway was cleared he was given an OK to land. As he made the break for his 360° overhead approach, he properly rolled the canopy back. While this was a routine safety precaution intended to preclude a pilot being trapped in the cockpit should a landing accident occur, it also caused any dust or grit that was in the airframe to be sucked out into the slipstream. Young had forgotten to lower his flying goggles over his eyes, and as a consequence he was blinded by a cloud of flying sand and dirt that had accumulated while the airframe was in storage. With eyes watering, he struggled to keep the airport in sight while managing to keep his unfamiliar aircraft in the air. A wide sweeping right turn gave him the distance and time to line-up with the runway and settle down to a tearful but soft landing.

Then came Bob McNeill. When Scorcher cleared him to land, Bob had not yet figured out how to activate the landing gear. Actually it was about the same as a P-40's, except that the lever had to be pulled sideways from its locking notch then cycled to the up or down position. When Bob began his 360° overhead approach to the fighter strip he found himself unable to move the landing gear lever. So, he lowered his head into the cockpit to better see how the mechanism worked. When he had it figured, his 360° turn was completed and he was perfectly lined up on final. He continued his approach and landed. What he didn't realise was that the runway he landed on was not the fighter strip. It was the bomber strip some mile and a half distant. Topline tower was not at all pleased.

White was one of the pilots who had torn a tyre free of his tailwheel at Finschhafen. While he waited for it to be repaired, he went to base operations to refile his flight plan. As he was signing the form, he noticed an obviously disturbed airman being attended to in the corner of the room. White was told that the man was one of the airport traffic controllers who had been on duty only minutes before. He was still in shock, having witnessed a runaway P-51 nearly knock the tower off its stilts, then almost clobber some cargo 'planes. All of the controllers on duty, certain that the wild P-51 would destroy them, had chosen a window from which to leap.

By the end of the following two weeks, all sixteen of the air commandos had checked out in the P-51s. It was about that time that Young and Collins were put aboard a C-47 and transported to Finschhafen again, where they were instructed to pick up two more P-51s. Arriving just before sunset, they made arrangements to remain overnight and get some supper. Learning that a movie was to be shown later, they went to the open-air 'theatre' and took their seats amid the growing audience. Just before the picture was to begin, they heard this conversation between a couple of Majors sitting just behind them: 'Did you hear about the crazy P-51 jockey that was in here a couple of weeks ago?' 'No.' 'Well, the idiot took-off in one of those new P-51s, almost hit the tower, then damn near collided with some cargo 'planes.' 'No kidding?' 'Yeah. Last week they moved the tower another 150ft farther from the runway, just in case he comes back!' Collins and Young remained silent.''

When the 3rd was finally assembled overseas, each pilot was assigned his own aircraft. As far as possible the assigned aircraft's rudder was marked with the first letter of the pilot's last name. Whenever the 26 letters of the English alphabet were insufficient, the Greek Alphabet was employed. The rudder of Jerry's P-51 was marked with a "C" and the aircraft was named *Lady of the sky*.

PEACE AT LAST

Following the detonation of atomic bombs over Hiroshima and Nagasaki, the Japanese surrendered. The men of the 3rd ACG at Ie Shima witnessed a small part of history in the making on 19 August 1945. The event was recorded in the *Ie Shima Daily News* of Monday 20 August 1945, under the headline ''Cornerstone of Peace Laid on Ie Shima'':

''The cornerstone for the world's peace house was set in place here yesterday upon the arrival of Jap peace envoys on 'B' strip at 1230.

A little over one hour prior to the Nip arrival, Brigadier-General Frederic H. Smith, Jr., Commanding Officer 5th Fighter Command, accompanied by Colonel P. H. Greasly and staff, alighted from two C-54s. This party was delegated by General MacArthur to receive Nip emissaries here and carry them to Manila.

At 1230, two Jap Bettys, painted white and bearing green crosses, appeared overhead, flying in formation, flanked on either side by B-25s. Tailing, were P-38s, four flights of four planes each and a B-17, the US rendezvous party with the Nip flight.

The first Betty landed at 12:47 after circling overhead three times. Consternation gripped the waiting thousands; meanwhile word was passed down from the tower that radio contact was momentarily lost. Betty number two landed at 1250. Both planes approached and landed South to North.

They taxied to the south end of the field trailing the 'Follow Me' jeep to the last hard stand, on which was pulled up the waiting official party and their C-54s. There was no demonstration from the waiting thousands who lined the strip behind a border guard. Major Vincent Snyder, the pilot of the second C-54, remarked that he had never seen a Betty land, only shot down!

From the two Bettys alighted the Jap mission—12 men, precisely tailored in green uniforms and large swords. The Nip delegation was headed by Lieutenant-General Tatashiro Kawabe, Vice-Chief of Staff of the Imperial General Staff; Rear-Admiral Ichiro Yokiga, Chief of the Navy General Staff and Mister Schirbi Omnota, the only civilian, in shorts with white socks, the Secretary of Civilian Affairs in Japan.

The Nip representatives, in two rows, faced the US party in the same formation, beside a waiting C-54. A Captain of the US party speaking Japanese acquainted General Kawabe with the facts of the flight to Manila.

There was no bowing by the Nips, no saluting by the US party.

The Jap party was on Ie for one hour and ten minutes, a delay caused by radio failure, precluding the use of one of the transports. A quick transfer of baggage, accessories, briefcases and food was made to the other transport. At 1327 a C-54 piloted by Colonel Earl T. Ricks took off for Manila and General MacArthur, where details were to be completed for the signing of the surrender document.''

On 2 September 1945 General Douglas MacArthur conducted the surrender ceremonies on board USS *Missouri* in Tokyo harbour.

On 10 September 1945, Ty Nelson, an Air Commando C-47 pilot, flew an Allied team of officers into Nagasaki to check into the condition of and provide for the freeing of Allied prisoners of war held near there. Flying from Tokyo, he deliberately veered a little off course toward Hiroshima, where a four-and-a-half-square-mile area had been flattened by the bomb. He later recalled, ''It was hard to tell that there had been a city there. Nagasaki looked similar. There was no city left.'' Buildings more than one mile from the center of the blast were now only skeletons of twisted steel.

Nelson was at Nagasaki airfield for only a few hours while interpreters and Allied officials tried to gather information on the prisoners of war. Eight of the 200 prisoners held in the area were killed by the atomic bomb blast. He estimates that the atomic bomb and resulting Japanese capitulation saved an estimated one million American lives and two million Japanese lives:

''I don't know why anyone would think the Japanese would have surrendered any quicker defending their homeland than they did when they were fighting for the other islands they fought for. They just didn't give up until they, in most cases, were completely wiped out. It would stand to reason that they would fight even more fiercely for their homeland. Millions, not thousands would have died.''

Fortunately, only one pilot from the 3rd Group was taken prisoner by the Japanese. On 31 May 1945 Bernard H. Moncrief was shot down while on a fighter sweep over Formosa. He baled out at very low level and sustained numerous injuries before being captured. His ill-treatment by the Japanese included long periods of time in solitary confinement in a military prison. Moncrief was liberated by the Navy on 6 September 1945 and underwent considerable medical treatment and surgery before being given a disability retirement from the Air Force in July 1947.

As the war came to an end in 1945 the Air Commando units returned home and were disbanded. The unique ''can do'' attitude of the Air Commandos was not required for the next fifteen years, but as the world advanced into the ''swinging sixties'' new enemies took the field and the Air Commandos once again answered their country's call to arms.

SPECIAL OPERATIONS BETWEEN THE WARS

Although the Air Commando squadrons were deactivated at the end of the Second World War and were not reactivated until the start of the communist insurgency in South Vietnam in the early 1960s, other special operations units were in action during the intervening years.

The Office of Strategic Services (OSS) was tasked with special operations outside the China-Burma-India theatre during the Second World War. Using regular Air Force aircraft and specially modified Consolidated B-24 Liberator bombers, they dropped agents and supplies behind enemy lines and recovered downed airmen in Europe.

Between 1946 and 1954 unconventional airpower was used to defeat the Communist Huk insurgency in the Philippines. With US assistance under Major-General Edward G. Lansdale, the Philippine Air Force flew C-47s, P-51s, L-5s, AT-6s and a mixture of liaison aircraft against the Huks. A psychological warfare campaign of leaflets and airborne loudspeaker operations was also initiated. Using a combination of psywar and air and ground attacks, the Philippine armed forces eventually defeated the insurgents.

The United States fought a hard and bitter war against the North Koreans and their Chinese allies between 1950 and 1953, following the North Korean invasion of South Korea. The US Army and the fledgling Central Intelligence Agency (CIA), successor to the OSS, needed to deploy intelligence-gathering teams and drop supplies behind enemy lines in both North and South Korea. Although no Air Commando units were organised for this war, the Air Force did provide special air support using C-47s, C-119s and A-26s. The Air Rescue Service also provided helicopter support.

The Air Force then activated, equipped and trained the 580th, 581st and 582nd Air Resupply and Communication Wings specifically for unconventional warfare and counterinsurgency operations. The wings used a variety of equipment, including C-47s, C-54s, C-118s, C-119s, B-29s, SA-16s and H-19s. The 580th was activated in April 1951 and assigned to USAF Europe from September 1952 to September 1953, based at Wheelus Field in Libya. The 581st was activated in July 1951 and was based at Clark Air Base in the Philippines from July 1952 to September 1953, and conducted limited operations in French Indochina in 1953. The 582nd came into being later, in September 1952, and was based in the United States for the eleven months of its short life-span. Only one of the three wings saw action in Korea, and all were inactivated by late 1953.

Throughout the rest of the 1950s the Air Force had little unconventional warfare capability. Things began to change dramatically as the turbulent decade of the 1960s dawned and Soviet-supported "wars of liberation" in the Third World superseded the Cold War days of direct nuclear confrontation.

CHAPTER 4

UNCONVENTIONAL WARFARE, 1960-'63

VIETNAM

ONLY A FEW MONTHS after the capitulation of Japan in August 1945, the sound of gunfire once again echoed through the jungles of southeast Asia. French Indochina (Vietnam, Laos and Cambodia) had been occupied by the Japanese during the Second World War and a guerrilla movement had evolved, trained and armed by American OSS agents. The guerrillas helped search for shot-down American airmen and tried to cut rail lines used by the Japanese. They were led by a man known as Ho Chi Minh, a Marxist-Leninist who had formed the Indochinese Communist Party in 1930. Although a communist, Ho appeared to have the backing of the Americans and received widespread support for his aims, which were not only to rid his country of the Japanese, but of the colonial French as well.

As the war came to an end and the Japanese were disarmed, Ho and his guerrillas, known as the Viet Minh, marched into Hanoi and formed a provisional government. The Emperor Bao Dai abdicated on 30 August 1945, and two days later Ho Chi Minh's Nationalist forces issued a declaration of independence, establishing the Democratic Republic of Vietnam. However, the American OSS teams were withdrawn in October, following the death of one of their officers at a Viet Minh roadblock. France then sent an expeditionary force of three well-armed Divisions to reclaim their former colony, and when talks broke down in Paris in October 1946, Ho Chi Minh sent his men into the countryside to prepare to fight another guerrilla war.

Fighting broke out between French troops and the Viet Minh in December 1946, and continued until June 1949. Although they had 150,000 troops in the country, the French were unable to defeat the guerrillas, and the situation was at a stalemate. Then the Chinese Nationalists succumbed to Mao Tse Tung's Communists, and the Viet Minh found themselves with an ally on their northern border who was willing to train them and supply arms and ammunition. The tide began to turn.

As the great powers began to take sides in Southeast Asia, the United States decided to give economic and military help to France. President Truman and his advisers concluded "the threat of Communist aggression in Indochina is only one phase of anticipated Communist plans to seize all of Southeast Asia." In the summer of 1950 the United States established a Military Assistance Advisory Group (MAAG) in Saigon, and military advisers began arriving to help the French maintain the first of some 500 aircraft loaned to them.

By 1953 the war was going badly for the French. The Viet Minh had crossed the border into Laos and had set up a revolutionary Pathet Lao government in the capital, Luang Prabang. In their drive towards Laos they had overrun the French garrison and airfield at Dien Bien Phu in northwestern Vietnam, and it was here that the decisive battle of the first Vietnam war was to be fought. On 20 November Operation Castor began when 800 French paratroops jumped into Dien Bien Phu and recaptured the airfield and surrounding area. Soon 10,000 men were dug in around the valley, which was about 180 miles from Hanoi, the nearest French air base. General Navarre, the French commander, wanted to lure the Viet Minh out to a set-piece battle where they could be destroyed by French airpower and artillery. However, he underestimated the enemy, who took up the challenge and dragged their own artillery into the hills surrounding the base. Within a few days the runway was cratered and unusable. Viet Minh anti-aircraft fire shot down 48 aircraft during the 56-day battle, and the French were hard put to supply or reinforce the men in the valley. On 7 May 1954, having suffered 7,000 casualties, the remaining defenders of Dien Bien Phu surrendered and passed into captivity, from which only half would return. The Viet Minh had lost three times as many men as the French, but they had won the battle and indeed the war. A ceasefire was agreed in July, and the French began to go home.

The peace agreement stipulated that Vietnam was to be divided into two countries along the 17th Parallel. The communist North would have Hanoi as its capital, and the non-communist South would have Saigon. There would be a five-mile wide demilitarised zone (DMZ) on either side of the border, and in two years elections would be held to decide the issue of reunification of the whole country.

In February 1955 the US Senate ratified the creation of the Southeast Asia Treaty Organisation (SEATO), whose eight members guaranteed the protection of Laos, Cambodia and ''the free territory under the jurisdiction of the State of Vietnam.'' From now on the United States would provide aid directly to South Vietnam, not through France. Emperor Bao Dai appointed Ngo Dinh Diem Prime Minister in the South, and he set about creating an army and air force. The 342-man US MAAG began training the Army, and in 1957 the US Air Force started training Vietnamese pilots.

The nationwide elections that were due to be held in July 1956 never took place. South Vietnam had not been a party to the French-Viet Minh agreement, and Diem argued that the northerners would not be able to vote freely under Ho Chi Minh's one-party rule. Their block vote would outnumber those cast in the south and, besides, although Ho was a communist, he was a legendary hero to the Vietnamese people and would probably have won a nationwide election. Moreover the wily Ho had taken out insurance for such an eventuality. While 90,000 of his supporters had moved north following the peace agreement, 10,000 more had gone to ground in the South, ready to fight again if needed.

By the end of 1957 these forces, known by the derogatory name of Viet Cong (Vietnamese Communist), had begun to carry out terrorist acts against Diem's regime. The US MAAG in Saigon was bombed on 22 October and eight servicemen were injured. Individual acts of terrorism, such as kidnapping, murder and bombing escalated until, in 1958, the Viet Cong started to form units of 50–200 men and engage government troops in battle. In May 1959 the leaders in the North announced their intention to reunite the country by force. In September a large Viet Cong force decimated a unit of Army of the Republic of Vietnam (ARVN) troops on the marshy Plain of Reeds, southwest of Saigon. According to the Viet Cong this incident marked the official start of their armed struggle.

The Viet Cong insurgency was difficult to contain, and as support grew, mainly due to the dissatisfaction of the populace with Diem's repressive rule, the South requested more American aid. The strength of the MAAG was increased from 342 to 685 men, major airfield construction projects were begun and more modern aircraft and helicopters were delivered to the VNAF. The enemy was far from idle, though, and towards the end of 1959 a North Vietnamese Army (NVA) transportation group began work on the Ho Chi Minh Trail, an infiltration route from North Vietnam, through Laos and Cambodia to the South, avoiding the DMZ. The trail became a vast network of tracks and roads running north and south along the Annamite mountains into Laos and fanning out into the jungles of South Vietnam. Soon the first of a 4,500-man military cadre began to arrive in the South, mostly ethnic southerners who had received indoctrination and training in the North. They established jungle base areas in Tay Ninh province on the border with Cambodia (later designated War Zone C by the Americans), in an area northwest of Saigon known as War Zone D and in the dense U Minh forest area of the Ca Mau peninsula. Dark clouds of war were gathering on the horizon.

THE KINGDOM OF LAOS

Across the western border of Vietnam lay the Kingdom of Laos, with a total land area of some 91,400 square miles, roughly the size of Great Britain or the US State of Idaho. Sixty per cent of Laos, particularly the north, is covered with dense tropical rainforest and mountains, some of which rise to over 7,000ft. Luang Prabang was the Royal capital, and Vientiane the administrative center. Laos became a French protectorate in 1893, and the country was relatively peaceful until the outbreak of the Second World War. When the Japanese took over they did not have to deal with a nationwide resistance movement; the country was divided into three different ethnic groups. The lowland Lao, who made up less than half of the population, worked closely with the French and held most native posts in the administration and military. The Lao Theung tribesmen comprised roughly 25 percent of the population and lived mainly in the southern Laotian panhandle. The Hmong hill tribes comprised only about 5 per cent, having been the last tribe to migrate to Laos from southern China.

The French returned in 1946 and swept aside the small Free Lao nationalist movement, which moved west to Thailand. In 1949 a splinter group led by Prince Souphanouvong crossed into northern Vietnam and made contact with the Viet Minh forces fighting the French. This group became the core of the Communist Laotian forces and were known as the Pathet Lao. They spent the next four years infiltrating the northeast Laotian province of Sam Neua, and were followed in 1953 by a multidivision Viet Minh force, which decimated the French and allowed the Pathet Lao to establish military and political headquarters in the province.

After their defeat across the border at Dien Bien Phu, the French agreed at the Geneva Peace Talks in 1954 to withdraw their forces from Indochina. However, the Armée Nationale de Laos, the armed forces of the independent Kingdom of Laos, continued to fight the Pathet Lao and their North Vietnamese sponsors. Three years passed before all parties signed an agreement for the formation of a coalition government, in November 1957. The political wing of the Pathet Lao was to be recognised as a legitimate party and their fighting units were to be integrated into the Lao Army over the following two years.

Prince Souvanna Phouma tried to maintain a neutral coalition, with Prince Souphanouvong's communist Pathet Lao on one side and Prince Boun Oum's American-supported Royalists on the other. Trouble flared up in 1959 following the arrest of Souphanouvong, the Pathet Lao leader. One of the Pathet Lao battalions scheduled for integration with the Royal Army fled northwards and joined forces with North Vietnamese Army units operating in the country. Together they seized control of the southeastern portion of the Laotian panhandle, thus obtaining a protected corridor along South Vietnam's northwestern border, through which men and material could be infiltrated to the South, bypassing the demilitarised zone.

Skirmishing between Royalist troops and the Pathet Lao continued through 1960, with Captain Kong Le's 2nd parachute battalion emerging as the best government unit. However, on 9 August 1960, while most government dignitaries were in Luang Prabang attending the King's funeral, Kong Le's paratroopers seized Vientiane, the administrative capital of Laos, accused the United States of colonialism and invited both royalists and Pathet Lao to form a truly neutral government. The Pathet Lao quickly moved troops to Vientiane, assisted by Soviet air drops and prepared for the onslaught that they knew must now come.

Royalist forces regrouped in the southern town of Savannakhet, and in December 1960 General Nosavan, the rightwing leader of the Royal Army, led his troops northwards to Vientiane. After a three-day battle, Kong Le and his supporters retreated to the strategic Plaines des Jarres and joined forces with the Pathet Lao and NVA forces operating in north-eastern Laos. The Soviet Union reacted to the crisis by supplying arms to Kong Le and the Pathet Lao. The United States responded by providing the Royal Army, already trained and paid for by the United States, with some old AT-6 Texan trainer aircraft, to be used as fighter-bombers. It was really a token gesture; the Lao had few pilots and the aircraft did not survive long. Soon, American pilots would be flying the skies of Laos on their behalf, and eventually a training organisation would be set up by the Air Commandos to train Lao pilots for the new Lao Air Force.

The United States had actually been giving covert support to the Royal Lao Army since the French began to withdraw in 1955. Because the 1954 Geneva Agreement forbade the United States (or the North Vietnamese) from opening a MAAG in Laos, the CIA established a Program Evaluation Office (PEO) in Vientiane, as a cover for a whole range of clandestine activities against the Pathet Lao and their North Vietnamese sponsors. Originally the PEO just supplied the Royal Army with weapons and equipment, but from July 1959 US Army Special Forces advisers started to arrive. Acting as civilian members of the PEO, they quietly began to take over training the Royal Lao Army, and eventually went into the field with combat units.

On 19 April 1961 the PEO was renamed the US Military Advisory and Assistance Group, Laos. The Special Forces training teams were renamed "White Star" Mobile Training Teams and were officially allowed to wear US military uniforms, including their green berets. It was around this time that the CIA recruited a Hmong leader named Vang Pao, then a major in the Royal Lao Army. Vang Pao was a fearless fighter who had fought with the French since the end of the Second World War, and who now agreed to help create an army of his warlike Hmong tribesmen. Eventually his forces expanded to over 40,000 guerrillas and became the most effective irregular fighting force in Laos.

The necessary support for Vang Pao's guerrillas and the CIA's operations was provided by Air America, the CIA's covert airline. A vast fleet of short take-off and landing aircraft was employed to transport and supply the agency's "customers." Many of the aircraft were provided direct from US military stocks, and most were flown either unmarked or wearing false markings. In addition to the fixed-wing aircraft, Air America was given an initial batch of sixteen former Marine Sikorsky H-34 helicopters. They were painted brown overall and, from a distance, were indistinguishable from the white H-34s operated by the International Control Commission. Compared with South Vietnam, Laos was a more dangerous place in which to fly. Generally, in Laos, a shot-down pilot was on his own. At this early stage of the war there was no established Air Force Air Rescue Service. If you were hit by ground fire and managed to avoid destruction on the sharp-ridged mountains which stretched across the landscape, the only hope of salvation was an Air America H-34.

Apart from enemy ground-fire, there were other problems to contend with. During the early days maps of Laos were very inaccurate, and pilots had to read the ground, watching for landmarks to ensure that they did not get lost. Laos has a unique "manmade season" when the villagers set fire to their fields in preparation for the year's poppy planting. Whirlwinds of flame shoot hundreds of feet into the air and the whole country becomes enveloped in a blue haze of smog. Visibility can be reduced to half a mile or less, and pilots have to rely on dead reckoning—flying time and distance to reach their destination. Despite the weather, Air America usually accomplished the most difficult missions. Their civilian pilots were paid by the flight, whereas the military pilots were paid whether they flew or not.

Following their retreat from Vientiane, Kong Le's forces and the Pathet Lao established themselves on the Plaines des Jarres. In February 1962 they began exerting heavy pressure on the Royal Army garrison at Nam Tha. Despite airborne reinforcements and support from the T-6 aircraft, the garrison fell in early May. Before handing over the reins of power to newly elected President John F. Kennedy, President Eisenhower had expounded his ''domino theory'' that Laos was the key to Southeast Asia, and if it fell to the Communists the rest of the countries in that area would fall as well, one after another. With those words in mind, Kennedy ordered a force of US Marines to nearby Thailand, while the Joint Chiefs of Staff debated whether or not a quarter of a million troops would be enough to keep Laos from the Communists.

As the fighting continued, America and the Soviet Union recognised that they were on a collision course in Laos, and called for a ceasefire while an international conference attempted to negotiate a political solution to the Laotian problem. The Geneva Conference on Laos opened on 16 May 1961 and lasted until 23 July 1962. As a result of the talks another coalition government was formed which lasted until April 1963 when the three Lao factions—Neutralists, Rightists and Pathet Lao—resumed fighting.

In the meantime, North Vietnam continued to build and expand the Ho Chi Minh Trail through Laos to South Vietnam. In those days Laos, a land-locked country, shared a common border with six other nations. To the north of Laos lay the People's Republic of China, to the northwest was neutral Burma and to the southeast, across the Mekong River, lay anticommunist Thailand. The problems in Laos involved the other three frontiers; to the southeast lay South Vietnam, and to the northeast North Vietnam. It was therefore possible for North Vietnamese troops to avoid the DMZ which divided the two Vietnams by trekking into Laos, around the DMZ and thence into the jungles of South Vietnam. The NVA troops could also violate the border that Laos shared in the south with Cambodia and continue their trek southwards on the Cambodian side of the border with South Vietnam, crossing over into the Mekong Delta flatlands in the extreme south of Vietnam.

The United States was forbidden to deploy ground troops or combat aircraft within Laos itself, although North Vietnam treated the country as though it was its own. The war against the communists and the support for the friendlies in Laos was to become the domain of the CIA and the State Department. Air Commandos would eventually fly combat missions over the country and serve with both the aforementioned agencies. They would also act as advisers to the Royal Laotian Air Force, and their stories are told on the following pages.

JUNGLE JIM

The fires of revolution in Laos and South Vietnam were being kindled by China and the Soviet Union, which sought a new path to their aims of global domination. The governments of South Vietnam and Laos was susceptible to the classic weapons of the insurgent: subversion, propaganda, terror and guerrilla warfare. Speaking before the Party Congress in Moscow on 6 January 1961, Nikita S. Khrushchev reaffirmed Soviet determination to support ''wars of liberation'' among the former colonial peoples. President John F. Kennedy took up the challenge, and instructed Secretary of Defense McNamara to study ways of developing counterinsurgency forces. The US armed forces were trained and equipped to fight a major land war on the mainland of Europe, with the air force ready to deliver nuclear weapons into the heart of enemy territory. There was little experience of counterinsurgency. Even the Air Commandos in the Second World War had been used in the opposite role, formed to support Allied guerrilla units operating behind enemy lines. US Army Special Forces were now establishing patrol bases along the South Vietnamese border and training local tribesmen in anti-guerrilla operations. They needed an efficient air supply and support organisation and, the Vietnamese Army needed an experienced close-air-support force. The answer was not long in coming.

On 14 April 1961 the Air Force Tactical Air Command (TAC) activated the 4400th Combat Crew Training Squadron (CCTS) at Hurlburt Field, Florida, also known as Elgin Air Force Base Auxiliary Field Number 9. The unit was to fly operations against guerrillas, either as an overt Air Force operation or in an undefined covert capacity. Known by its nickname "Jungle Jim," the unit was assigned to Ninth Air Force and comprised 124 officers and 228 enlisted personnel. Commanded by Colonel Benjamin H. King, the unit was unique in being staffed entirely by volunteers.

The new unit was to possess its own integral airlift capability, like the original Air Commandos, in the shape of the C-47. While this aircraft was not as versatile as the Fairchild C-123 Provider then equipping TAC's airlift squadrons, many foreign governments used the Skytrain, so it was easier to train and operate with it and carry out covert operations if required. The 4400th CCTS was authorised sixteen C-47s, eight Douglas B-26s and eight North American T-28 Trojans, plus the same number of aircraft in temporary storage. All were old, many recently taken out of desert storage, but they were rugged and more suited to counterinsurgency warfare than the regular Air Force jets. The C-47s were cargo aircraft, configured for supply drops, the B-26s were twin-engined Second World War attack bombers, and the T-28s were training aircraft, modified to carry 0.50-calibre machine guns, 2.75 in rockets and a small quantity of bombs. All aircraft were required to operate from minimal-condition, tactical airstrips, and the C-47s and T-28s from dirt runways.

On 5 May the first aircraft, a T-28A, arrived at Hurlburt Field, and the full complement of aircraft had arrived by 1 July. On 15 August the squadron deployed detachment 1 to Mali, West Africa, under the code name "Sandy Beach 1." This was the first of many overseas assignments, in this case to train Mali paratroopers to jump from SC-47s. By the time they returned to Florida, another detachment had left for Vietnam. From now on, deployments and temporary duties (TDYs) would take them constantly throughout the Continental United States and around the world.

FARM GATE AND THE T-28

On 23 August 1961 the 4400th CCTS was reassigned from Ninth Air Force to Headquarters Tactical Air Command. On 6 November they were tasked by Headquarters Pacific Air Forces Operations Plan 222-61 to send a detachment to Bien Hoa Air Base in South Vietnam, to train South Vietnamese Air Force pilots in offensive operations developed by the squadron at Hurlburt Field.

Detachment 2, code name "Farm Gate," consisted of 41 officers and 115 airmen on a 179-day TDY assignment. They took with them four RB-26s, four SC-47s and eight T-28s. The B-26s carried the RB designation of the reconnaissance version to avoid contravention of the 1955 peace agreement, which stated that bomber aircraft should not be introduced to the area. However, they were not glass-nosed RB-26s; they carried eight 0.50-calibre machine-guns in the nose of the air-craft.

The "official" Farm Gate mission statement said that the aircraft, wearing South Vietnamese Air Force markings, would be used to train local pilots. However, the war was escalating too fast for the aircraft to be used in that role. By November 1961 the first US helicopter units had arrived in Vietnam, to improve the mobility of the Army of the Republic of Vietnam. American advisers were trying hard to motivate the poorly-paid ARVN infantrymen, who generally had no time for the corrupt, oppressive leadership of Saigon. What was needed was Airpower, to give the soldiers of the South an edge over the well organised, highly motivated communist guerrillas who struck without warning and vanished just as quickly.

Farm Gate's main ground attack aircraft was the T-28, de-signed as a tandem two-seat basic trainer for the Air Force. Almost 1,200 were built and the Navy acquired nearly 500 more powerful T-28Bs and 300 tailhook-equipped T-28Cs for aircraft carrier landing training. Almost 400 T-28As and a few T-28Cs were converted to T-28Ds for the Air Force. This var-iant was powered by a 1,425 h.p. Wright R-1820-56S or-86 engine, driving a three-bladed propeller. It also had limited armour plating, a strengthened undercarriage, two gunpods and four bomb racks. The T-28D-5 model had in-wing ammunition storage, two underwing 0.50-calibre machine-gun gondolas and six bomb racks. The ordnance stations could carry napalm, general-purpose and fragmentation bombs, rocket launchers and parachute flares.

Notwithstanding their "official" role of training VNAF aviators, the Farm Gate pilots were soon flying their aircraft in combat, with the proviso that a Vietnamese observer flew in the back seat. Their presence soon reduced the number of Viet Cong attacks on trains and truck convoys. In addition, they escorted flights of helicopters to landing zones, where they remained on call in case of resistance on the ground. The lack of Vietnamese English-speaking observers was a drawback which affected their usefulness for some time. Without clearance to engage targets on the ground, or clear communication with a South Vietnamese Army unit asking for close air support, they often had to return to base with their ordnance still on board. This happened so frequently that the pylon adapters suffered structural damage from landing with unexpended ordnance.

Almost without exception, the T-28's targets were either small boats (sampans), wooden structures or personnel. Owing to the hit-and-run, highly mobile tactics of the Viet Cong, these targets were seldom found in large concentrations. Enemy troop concentrations were rarely more than one or two companies and the structures no more than ten to fifteen small huts; these were ideal-size targets for a flight of two T-28s. Occasionally four or more aircraft would be used against a small enemy supply or ammunition concentration, the size and nature of the target determining the number of aircraft required. The Farm Gate pilots discovered by experience that two 500lb napalm tanks were extremely effective against wooden structures or concealed or dug-in troops, while 120lb fragmentation bomb clusters were very good against scattered troops. The rockets, with their high degree of accuracy were better utilised against spot targets such as sampans, while the 0.50-calibre machine-guns combined with the aircraft's manoeuvrability were better employed against highly mobile ground targets.

ORGANISATION AND CASUALTIES

On 11 February 1962, the first Farm Gate aircraft was lost in
Vietnam. An SC-47 with nine crew and Army advisers on
board left Saigon on a leaflet dropping mission. At 0830 hours
in the morning a province chief reported that a twin-engined
aircraft had crashed in the mountains near his village, 70 miles
northeast of Saigon. There were no survivors. The crew comprised Captain Edward K. Kissam, Jr., First Lieutenants Stan-
ley G. Harrison and Jack D. LeTourneau, Technical Sergeant
Floyd M. Frazier and Airman First Class Robert L. Westfall.

As the months wore on the Viet Cong countermeasures
against the T-28 and B-26 low-level attacks began to take
effect. Their main anti-aircraft weapons at that time were the
12.7mm Soviet or Chinese heavy machine-gun and small-
arms. In the last four months of 1962 the enemy scored 89
hits against Farm Gate and other USAF aircraft, but in the first
four months of 1963 that figure had jumped to 257. Before
the end of the year the Air Force had lost six aircraft to enemy
action.

In March 1962, Headquarters TAC activated the 4400th
Combat Crew Training Group (CCTG) at Hurlburt Field and
Colonel Chester A. Jack was named as commander. A month
later, the Air Force ordered the establishment of the USAF
Special Air Warfare Center (SAWC) at nearby Eglin Air Force
Base under the command of Brigadier-General Gilbert L. Pritchard. The 1st Combat Applications Group was also reassigned from the jurisdiction of HQ TAC to SAWC. They had
the role of developing doctrine, tactics and equipment for field
operations.

Further changes were afoot however and within a few days
the title of the 4400th CCTG was discontinued and replaced
by the 1st Air Commando Group. The new Group had 211
officers and 581 enlisted personnel and comprised the 6th
Fighter Squadron, Commando; the 319th Troop Carrier Squadron, Commando and the 1st Air Material Squadron, Commando. The 4400th CCTS was renamed the 4410th CCTS and
also attached to the new group.

The mission of the resurrected Group was described by Air Force Chief of Staff General Curtis E. LeMay thus;

> "Members of the new Air Commando Group are trained to instruct allied aircrews in all phases of airborne operations, including low-level drop techniques for both personnel and cargo, close air support in daylight or dark for counter-guerrilla forces, rapid deployment to areas of suspected or actual guerrilla activity, the use of flares for night-time detection of guerrilla movements and for reconnaissance, the cutting off of retreat routes by use of anti-personnel weapons, the staking out from the air of areas of suspected enemy activity, interdiction raids, destruction of supply points, and the use of psychological operations such as harassment of counter-information programmes . . ."

Detachment 3 of the 1st ACG was activated at Hurlburt Field on 30 April, under the command of Lieutenant-Colonel Robert L. Gleason. Known as "Bold Venture" the unit had both counterinsurgency training and civic action missions with a number of Latin American countries. One of their first jobs was to fit external wing racks to F-51 Mustangs of the Guatemalan Air Force, so that they could carry 2.75in rockets. By May the unit was established at Howard Air Force Base, Panama with two each of C-46, U-10A, T-28 and B-26 aircraft.

During the summer the Air Commandos at Hurlburt were kept busy. The design and installation of a public address system began, for psychological warfare operations using the C-46, C-47, U-10 and B-26. Hand-to-hand combat training started and the 1st ACG became the first military organisation to receive the new Colt AR-15 rifle, with 150 being sent to Detachment 2 in Vietnam and 670 to Detachment 3 in Panama.

On 28 August, the first Farm Gate T-28 casualty occurred when Captain Robert L. Simpson died in combat. The first U-10 casualties occurred on 15 October when Captain Herbert Willoughby Booth, Jr. and Combat Controller T/Sgt. Richard L. Foxx were killed in action. Less than a month passed before Captain Robert D. Bennett and First Lieutenant William B.

Tully were killed on 5 November in a B-26 crash.

A typical joint arms operation took place on 9 November when a concentration of Viet Cong was discovered on a strip of marsh near the coast, about 50 miles south of Bien Hoa. Vietnamese gunboats blocked the river to the north while helicopters escorted by Farm Gate T-28s moved ground troops into the area. A U-10 flown by Lieutenant Albert A. Wright with a VNAF Forward Air Controller on board, orbited the area while the ARVN began shelling the enemy. A C-47 flown by Captain William F. Brown arrived around 2000 hours and dropped flares at the direction of the FAC, while B-26s dropped their ordnance on the Viet Cong concentration. The ARVN spent the next two days mopping up and although, as usual, exact casualty figures were not known, the operation was claimed a success.

The support of isolated forts and outposts became a key role for the air commandos in these early days. In one such instance on 16 November, Captain Dalton and his navigator Lieutenant Charles Kuczaj were scrambled in their B-26 at 2325 hours and arrived over a besieged ARVN fort near Tra Vinh around midnight. A VNAF flare ship cleared them to drop ordnance to within 200 meters of the fort and they attacked the Viet Cong with napalm, 120lb fragmentation bombs and 0.50-calibre machine-gun fire. As the enemy withdrew along a river, Dalton continued his attack with 100lb general purpose bombs and machine-gun fire. The night belonged to the Viet Cong and many such outposts would have been overrun were it not for the skill and bravery of the Farm Gate pilots. In one week alone, from 18-24 November, Farm Gate crews flew 70 combat support missions, air dropped 9,000lb of cargo and air landed another 7,000lb.

Lieutenant-Colonel Philip O'Dwyer and Major Robert P. Guertz carried out an attack on 23 November on a large building south of Can Tho and then raked the bordering canal, which was obscured by overhanging trees. Friendly ground forces found that the area had been an arms factory with sampans using the canal to transport raw materials in and finished arms out. The crew were credited with 281 enemy casualties, 20 motorised sampans, six smaller boats and a wrecked arms factory.

On the negative side of the account, problems were being encountered with the 0.50-calibre ammunition which had been manufactured in 1945. The ammunition crates were rotten, the cans inside were rusted, the belts fell apart when removed from the cans owing to rusty links, ammunition caps were pushed in by the firing pins and swollen rounds were common. Similar problems were encountered by some types of bombs and the problems would remain until newer ordnance arrived.

By the end of the year the Farm Gate crews had flown 4,040 sorties in support of the Government of South Vietnam. Over a thousand flights were escort duty for trains, convoys and aircraft. During the year, over half a million items of ordnance were used by the crews, who were credited with 3,381 enemy casualties, 4,151 structures and 405 sampans damaged and destroyed. However, as the enemy grew more aggressive and confident, they developed their own tactics to counter air attack. In the meantime, in 1963 the Air Commandos were to suffer more casualties due to their own defective aircraft than to enemy fire.

OPERATION RANCH HAND

In May 1961 President John F. Kennedy had sent his Vice-President, Lyndon B. Johnson, to South Vietnam to discuss the escalating Viet Cong insurgency with President Diem. As a result of the discussions United States military aid was increased. More aircraft were to be supplied, the South Vietnamese Army was to be expanded, and additional training centers would be set up. One of the centers was a joint American/South Vietnamese Combat Development and Test Center, tasked with learning and improving counterinsurgency techniques and tactics.

One of the first ideas put forward by the new center involved the use of air-delivered defoliants to reduce jungle cover along major highways, where the Viet Cong frequently ambushed government convoys. The idea grew within months into Operation Ranch Hand, and the first Fairchild C-123 Provider fitted with the MC-1 Hourglass spray system arrived at Tan Son Nhut Air Base on 7 January 1962. Operations commenced a week later. It is interesting to note that this was a full 30 months before the infamous "Gulf of Tonkin Incident" that brought America into the war, and over three years before the arrival of the first American combat troops.

The unit, known as the Special Aerial Spray Flight, was later attached to the 309th Air Commando Squadron. In October 1966 an expansion of the Ranch Hand program led to the establishment of the flight as a separate squadron, the 12th Air Commando Squadron. On 1 December that year the 12th ACS moved its base of operations from Tan Son Nhut to Bien Hoa.

The herbicide selected for initial use was 24D/245T, proven weed-control chemicals widely used throughout the world and readily available from chemical manufacturers. The most widely used herbicide sprayed by Ranch Hand aircraft was herbicide Orange. The name was derived from the colored bands painted on the 55gal drums, which allowed longshore-men and logistics personnel to identify the different liquid products. Herbicide Orange killed weeds, brush and other foliage of the broadleaf variety. One element of the herbicide is Dioxin, now believed by many to cause birth defects in children fathered by men who have had contact with the chemical. Over the years the program expanded, and by the time it was halted, in 1971, following concern about the chemical's side-effects on humans, 41 percent of the mangrove forests in South Vietnam had been affected, together with 19 percent of the uplands forests and 8 percent of all cultivated land. Eleven million of the nineteen million gallons of chemicals used were of the type known as "Agent Orange." Thousands of Vietnam Veterans subsequently filed disability claims against the US Government, alleging damage to their health caused by the herbicide.

Political, legal, moral and ecological aspects notwithstanding, the defoliation program seemed a good idea at the time, and the first flight took place on 13 January 1962. Three weeks later, on 2 February 1962, one of the Ranch Hand C-123s became the first Air Force aircraft to be lost over South Vietnam, when it crashed, killing the crew of three, Captain Fergus C. Groves, Captain Robert D. Larson and Staff Sergeant Milo B. Coghill. Although the cause of the crash was never determined, from then onward the Thirteenth Air Force requested escorts by Farm Gate aircraft for all defoliation missions.

Being hit by enemy groundfire became almost routine for Ranch Hand aircraft while flying at 150 m.p.h. and 150ft above the cropland and jungle of Vietnam. Ranch Hand aircraft sustained well over 7,000 hits by enemy fire during a ten-year period. That is the equivalent of driving to work every day for a year and having your car hit by a deadly bullet 60 out of 365 days. The most celebrated Ranch Hand aircraft was nicknamed "Patches" after being hit by more than 800 rounds of enemy fire, and is now on display at the Air Force Museum at Wright-Patterson AFB, Ohio. Twenty-five Americans lost their lives flying defoliation missions in Vietnam.

Major Jack Spey, head of the Ranch Hand Association, told the author:

> "The uniqueness of the Ranch Hand mission led to a level of camaraderie, *esprit de corps* and dedication to mission seldom matched in military history. 'Cowboys', the nickname for the men of 'the Ranch', had the well-earned respect of all who knew and worked with the unit in Southeast Asia. During its ten-year history the organisation received five Air Force Outstanding Unit awards, twice with the 'V' for valor. Ranch Hand was also awarded two Presidential Unit Citations, and the government of South Vietnam awarded the Cross of Gallantry on two occasions."

One of the more ambitious operations involving Ranch Hand was the attempt to burn the Boi Loi Woods in Tay Ninh Province in March 1965. This was an area of tropical forest about 25 miles northwest of Saigon and ten miles from the Cambodian border in War Zone C. The ARVN was unable or unwilling to undertake the long and costly job of clearing and holding the woods by mounting a conventional ground operation. In a pattern often repeated during the Vietnam war, Americans sought to substitute technology for manpower, and Operation Sherwood Forest was the result.

The 18,500-acre woods were thought to shelter one Viet Cong Regiment, two village guerrilla units and about 100 acres of crops. It was assumed that the whole area was under Viet Cong control, together with the 6,000 people living there. The Director of Operations at MACV proposed saturating the southeast portion of the woods with fuel and igniting the area through the use of napalm, white phosphorus and incendiaries. The theory was that the wind would then spread the fire throughout the defoliated area, creating a firestorm effect. The woods were sprayed with 83,000gal of herbicides then, on 31 March 1965, twenty-four C-123 sorties dumped 1,200gal each of diesel fuel on the southeast end of the defoliated area. Sky-raiders flew twenty-nine sorties, each delivering thirteen tanks of napalm onto the same ignition point, followed by eight B-57s, each scattering eight M35 incendiary clusters in advance of the primary fire. Shortly after the fires began, a thunderstorm moved through the area, dampening them, and another storm that night put out what was left. There was little fire spreading from the initial ignition points, and although analysts initially blamed the rain for causing the failure, later attempts to burn defoliated jungle proved that the type of vegetation and high moisture content in the air made it impossible to set self-sustaining fires in South Vietnam.

EVALUATIONS AND EXPANSION

During the first six months of 1963 the SAWC continued to test and evaluate new equipment for the counterinsurgency role. Between January and April Fairchild's one-off YC-123H Provider flew 180 missions in South Vietnam, under all types of conditions and on all types of terrain. The aircraft was fitted with a new wide track main landing gear taken from a Lockheed C-130A Hercules transport aircraft. This improved the turning radius of the aircraft and allowed an increase in gross weight. In addition, two underwing mounted jet engines were installed, together with a deceleration parachute system. The parachute would be deployed on landing, enabling the aircraft to make a steep approach to landing zones and reducing the time the aircraft might be exposed to enemy ground fire. The new jets were invaluable for increased safety and the extra thrust allowed an increase in payload to 20,165lb, compared to 10,572 for a normal C-123B and its take-off distance was reduced from 940ft to 750ft. Although the aircraft was destroyed in an accident in the United States in late 1963, the knowledge gained led to the successful introduction of the jet-equipped C-123K in 1966.

Other equipment undergoing testing included a C-123 cargo extraction system, a leaflet dispensing device for the C-46 and C-47, a drop ramp for the U-10, a float equipped U-10, flame suppressors for the C-123 and an in-flight pick-up system on the C-46 and C-47. The new public address system had been installed in the C-47, with four speakers in the jump door and four more if required in the cargo doors, used in conjunction with a tape recorder or direct voice microphone.

On 1 June 1963 the 1st Air Commando Group was renamed the 1st Air Commando Wing (ACW). A week later the Secretary of the Air Force announced that due to air commando success in Vietnam, the strength of the SAWC would increase from 2,665, to 3,000 and the number of flying squadrons increased to six. On 30 June the 1st ACW had under its control the 319th Air Commando Squadron, Troop Carrier and the 6th and 602nd Fighter Squadrons, Commando.

Two of the new squadrons were the 603rd and 604th* Fighter Squadrons, Commando, descendants of the 3rd and 4th Fighter Squadrons of the 3rd ACG, which served in the Southwest Pacific during the Second World War. They each received one of the two A-1E aircraft assigned to the 6th Fighter Squadron, Commando and this left the 6th with an all T-28 force. By October it was confirmed that the 6th would have seven B-26s and twelve T-28s and the 602nd and 603rd nineteen A-1Es each. The sixth new squadron was the 775th Troop Carrier Squadron, renamed soon afterwards as the 317th Air Commando Squadron, Troop Carrier.

Detachment 3 of the 1st ACW in Panama was renamed the 605th Air Commando Squadron, Composite, in November. The squadron was based at Howard Field, and remained assigned to the 1st ACW until it was transferred to USAF South-

---

*The 604th was later designated Reconnaissance Technical and manned to perform an operational and support type photographic function.

ern Command on 1st July 1964. On 8 November 1967 it was reassigned to the 24th Composite Wing, and it was finally deactivated on 30 April 1972. The 605th inherited the lineage of the 5th Fighter Squadron, one of the two fighter squadrons to serve with the original 1st ACG in Burma.

A NEW B-26 REQUIRED

Don Schoknecht, a B-26 maintenance engineer assigned to Farm Gate, arrived at Bien Hoa in August 1963. He recalls:

> "All the B-26s were 1944 models; three of them were painted black and used mostly for convoy escort etc. They were the only B-26s with fourteen 0.50-calibre machine-guns; eight in the nose and six in the wings. Because of their configuration they only had one bomb rack on either wing, inboard of the guns. The other aircraft had three bomb racks on each wing and six 0.50's in the nose. The usual load was six 750-lb napalm canisters on the wings and in the bomb bay a mixture of general-purpose and fragmentation bombs and WP, white phosphorous bombs. The pilots liked a load of napalm and WP.
>
> There were only two things on a '26' that I didn't like working on, and that was replacing oil coolers and installing cockpit canopies. I will never forget my first oil cooler change. The right oil cooler had to be replaced, but as we did not have any, I was sent to Saigon to get one out of a '26' the French left there. This was the day after President Diem was overthrown and killed, and we went right past the bullet-riddled palace.
>
> I had one canopy change after Captain Smith landed at night and in the rain without flaps, due to a broken cable. They went into the grass and mud between the runway and taxiway and jettisoned the canopies. Another incident was when a '26' hit a tree and the left bottom cowling was all torn up and wood was so hard packed in the cooling fins we couldn't get it out with a hammer and chisel!

'Jumping Joe' Kittinger was one of our pilots, and I remember his last mission, when he came in over the flight line and rolled his '26'!''

The pilots of Farm Gate had been given old aircraft to work with, and eventually both the T-28s and B-26s started to crash owing to structural defects. February saw two Farm Gate B-26 aircraft destroyed within days of each other. On the 3rd, Captain John P. Bartley and Captain John F. Shaughnesy, Jr., were killed during a strafing run on a Viet Cong concentration 33 miles west of Soc Trang. Three days later Major James E. O'Neill's aircraft lost both engines whilst on a training flight at 500ft. He ordered the other two crew members, an American navigator and a VNAF observer, to bale out. Major O'Neill held the aircraft steady while they did so, but the aircraft crashed before he himself could escape. The lack of a good ejection system was a hazard on these old types of aircraft, and the B-26 was notoriously difficult to bale out of when flying straight, let alone whilst banking or in a dive. One had to blow the canopy, climb out of the cockpit and then dive off the trailing edge of the wing, taking care not to hit the propeller or the tailplane.

On 8 April Captain Andrew C. Mitchell III, pilot and Captain Jerry A. Campaigne, navigator, and a VNAF observer, were killed when their B-26 crashed on a mountain during a two-aircraft interdiction mission. Those who observed the incident reported that part of a wing broke off during a strafing run.

In the opinion of some pilots, the B-26s should have been withdrawn from Vietnam a lot sooner than they were. It took the crash of a B-26 at Eglin Fields Range 52 on 11 February 1964, during a night demonstration for an invited audience, including nineteen journalists, for the aircraft to be grounded. Captains Stan Moore, pilot, and Larry Lively, navigator, were killed. In April 1964 the surviving B-26s finally left Vietnam and returned to the States. The T-28s were not far behind them, going to the Waterpump detachment in Thailand. The Farm Gate detachment became the 1st Air Commando Squadron, and started to re-equip with the Douglas A-1 Skyraider.

Meanwhile, back in the USA a modified version of the B-

26 was being built, and in February the prototype counterin-surgency (COIN) version of the Invader arrived at the SAWC for evaluation by the 1st Combat Applications Group. Desig-nated YB-26K, the aircraft had been extensively modified by On-Mark Engineering and had improved short-field take-off and landing capabilities and better performance resulting from the installation of Pratt & Whitney R-2800-103W radial en-gines offering 2,500 h.p. for take-off, with water injection. Modifications included the addition of 137 Imp gal wingtip fuel tanks, anti-skid brakes, strengthened wings with modified flaps, and a large rudder. Eight 0.50-calibre machine-guns were mounted in the nose, and eight pylons could carry up to 4,000lb of bombs under each wing. The maximum cruising speed with external stores was 305 m.p.h., and the aircraft had a combat radius of 576 miles, flying at 5,000ft with 8,000lb of ordnance.

Forty-one B-26s were modified by On-Mark, and in June 1966 the first of these would be sent to Thailand for testing in combat under Project Big Eagle.

VOLUNTEERS WANTED

Not everyone could become an Air Commando. In later years pilots would simply be assigned to the Air Commandos, but in the early days you had to volunteer or be invited to join. Joe Holden recalls:

"I originally got involved with the Air Commandos as a result of a tour of duty in Taiwan when the Chinese Communists and Nationalists were going at it. Whilst there I met an old friend who later contacted me while I was an instructor at the Ground Control Intercept School at Tyndall Air Force Base. I did not like the job, and was looking for an opportunity to get out of the assignment, when my friend called me and told me about a new classified organisation over at Hurlburt Field. He told me how to go about applying for a job, and I felt that I was well qualified, having flown quite a number of missions in the guerrilla environment during the Ko-

rean war. Following the breakout from the Pusan perimeter, several thousand North Koreans escaped into the
mountains and it was our job to find them. I learned
how to spot people in places where they shouldn't be.

So I applied and was accepted in September 1962. I
was assigned to the 6th Fighter Squadron, Commando.
At that time there were three areas that the Air Commandos operated in; Central America in the Panama
Canal Zone, West Germany and South Vietnam. We
were not allowed to refer to these places by name, so
the Canal Zone was known as WBF, West Bum Fuck,
and the South Vietnam detachment was known as EBF,
East Bum Fuck.

When I reported to Hurlburt we were evaluated and
tested and had a talk to a psychiatrist. I guess they
wanted to know what kind of goofy people would volunteer for an assignment that they did not really know
much about. I then went to Stead Air Force Base, Nevada, to the Air Force Survival School, where we learnt
escape and evasion tactics, including a lot that had been
learnt during the Korean war. We were held in simulated
captivity and interrogated and a few people actually
broke during the 'activities.' We had been on an outdoor
survival exercise prior to my graduating on Thanksgiving Day 1962; we had not eaten for five days and had
to walk 20 miles through the mountains. We had to
scrounge for food, although I got by just drinking water.
On the way home to Phoenix, Arizona, I ate three separate Thanksgiving dinners in three different towns.

When I got back to Hurlburt, I discovered that my
friend Bob Bennett, who had recently gone to Vietnam
to fly the B-26, had been killed. I think he was only the
second air commando casualty in Vietnam. A fellow
called Foxx was the first, having died when his U-10
was shot down. In fact they told me that I had to fly U-
10 Helio Couriers, but I did not feel that I was cut out
for that. It was a funny airplane and you could slow fly
it about 35–40 m.p.h. into a 35–40 knots headwind
around 5,000ft and from the ground it would look as
though you were going backwards. Every landing was a

controlled crash; the plane was designed to land in 200–300ft, similar to the German Fieseler Storch from the Second World War.

Anyhow, I was soon back with T-28s. We spent a lot of time learning how to deliver ordnance at night and on the gunnery ranges at Hurlburt. We flew the T-28B, which was the model also in use in Vietnam. Compared to the A model, which I first flew in 1951, it was a magnificent machine. It had an R-1820 engine in it, which developed about 1,450 h.p. and had no structural weaknesses that we knew about at that time, unlike the A models that were recalled and modified in 1951. It was built for the Navy and had speed brakes, unlike the later D model, and they came in very handy in South Vietnam. Soc Trang had a 2,000ft runway with a canal at the north end and a Buddhist temple at the south end, and you did not have much room to stop.

When we were training we used to fly from Hurlburt to El Paso, Texas, because in those days you could bring a gallon of cheap booze into the United States from Mexico without paying duty on it. We utilised the cavernous storage compartment behind the cockpit of the T-28, and each brought back five or six gallons of booze, which would last us for a couple or three months. On one of these trips I landed to refuel at a military airfield in Big Springs, Texas, where they flew T-38 jet trainers. Of course we had four ordnance pylons on them and the pods for the 0.50-calibre machine-guns, and a good-looking kid, a Steve Canyon type who was clean-shaven, square-jawed with long wavy hair, came out and asked me how to join us. His name was Condon Terry, and about two months later he showed up at Hurlburt Field. I was assigned to the operations section at Wing Headquarters, and it was my job to assign people to Southeast Asia. We kept twelve B-26s and twelve T-28s in South Vietnam, and it was becoming apparent that we were going to have to go outside the unit to find more pilots. The normal TDY assignment was 179 days; any more than that and it was considered a PCS, a permanent change of station, and you were then lost from that unit.

Replacements were sent out every 90 days, and half of the men in Vietnam would then come home. So I assigned Terry to Vietnam and three months later I went over as detachment commander to Soc Trang, where six of the T-28s were based.

Soc Trang was an airfield built by the Japanese in the Second World War in the Mekong Delta. There were no navigation aids in the Delta, to help you pinpoint where you were. Every bit of your navigation had to be VFR, visual flight rules; you had to be able to read a map and identify landmarks and find your way around. We flew close to the ground, low enough so that the people on the ground did not have the time to track you, and if you were hit it was usually a lucky shot. We flew either 25–40ft off the ground, or above 5,000ft.

On my first mission, on 24 June 1963, I was part of two flights of T-28s that were going to escort the CH-21 helicopters that the Army's 93rd Transportation Company kept at Soc Trang. They had been decimated at Ap Bac in the Plain of Reeds in January 1963 when four of their Shawnees had been shot down whilst landing ARVN troops. Then they only had armed UH-1 Huey helicopters with them, and were subsequently criticised for going ahead with the mission without adequate fixed-wing support.

The first flight had prepped the landing zone, by attacking any tree lines or places where the enemy might be hiding, before the helicopters went in, to minimise the enemy groundfire. I was with the second flight, and we remained on station while the CH-21s landed the ARVN troops and then flew back to Soc Trang. As soon as we landed we were told that one of our aircraft was down, so we refuelled and rearmed and were airborne again within fifteen minutes. The missing T-28 was found lying on its side on the ground and we could see that the pilot and observer were both deceased. When the bodies were recovered it was determined that the pilot had been hit by a bullet and then crashed. Sadly it turned out that it was the same blond pilot who I had met in Texas and who had become the first T-28 casualty in Vietnam. One of the streets at Hurlburt Field is named after him.''

CRASH LANDING

First Lieutenant Tom Schornak was amongst 80 Air Commandos who flew into Vietnam for the June 1963 rotation. It was a mix of officers and enlisted personnel; pilots, navigators, armament and maintenance. Almost all of them were on flying status one way or another. Six months later, thirteen of that group had been killed. Only Tom managed to survive his shoot-down and make it out alive. This is his story.

"Although the Asian monsoon was just getting started, it was an unusually sunny day as Frank Gorski and I sat in the alert trailer. We were scrambled from the trailer at 1130 hours on 10 September to escort two Marine H-34 helicopters on a medevac mission about 40 miles north of Saigon. Our call sign was "Mom Cat" flight of two T-28s. The medevac escort was uneventful and when the choppers neared Saigon, I called Paris Control, the Air Ops Centre, advising we had completed the escort and had not expended any ordnance.

Paris Control said they had been attempting to contact me and we were to proceed South, towards the very tip of the Delta near Ca Mau. They gave me the target coordinates and the call sign of the Forward Air Controller, Idaho Bravo Two.

It would take us a good 45 minutes to get down there and on the way it was obvious there was a lot of activity. Idaho Bravo asked me to relay to Paris Control that he needed at least two more fighters and as many as they could get throughout the day. He also mentioned an RF-101 was shot at by small-arms and machine-gun fire while making a high speed photo pass. One of our B-26s just leaving the area gave me a call on the squadron frequency and said they had taken some hits in the cockpit and wing. His navigator had picked up a few fragments and they were going to shut down an engine. I don't know what Frank was thinking when he heard all this, but I knew damn well it was going to be pretty sporty down there.

We arrived on the scene with Idaho Bravo in an orbit at about 3,000ft, below him I could see some smoke from the B-26s ordnance, but other than that, the area appeared rather serene. Idaho Bravo said that he thought he had located the machine-gun emplacement and dropped two red smoke grenades. As a side note, you might wonder how he did this from 3,000ft? Well you pulled the pins very carefully and placed the live grenades in a jar then threw the jar over the side. When it hit the ground the glass broke and the grenade detonated!

After the smoke grenades discharged we talked about the location of the machine-gun in relation to the red smoke. There were two intersecting canals with palm trees along them, and heavier vegetation and rice paddies everywhere else. The bad guys were near a group of huts next to the canal. Idaho Bravo estimated over a hundred, and later the intelligence guys raised that to almost 300. For the first time in the conflict the VC had taken over the area and held it for a couple of days. Frank and I talked about the attack headings, ordnance delivery schedule, and I told him to keep a sharp eye for ground-fire and to hold onto his socks because here we go!

I set up for a low-level (about ten feet above the trees) run, dropping one can of napalm and coming around again to make the second drop for any corrections. (Note: for you jocks who came along later in the war, up until now we were short of napalm, one of our best weapons, and every can dropped had to be put to good use. Also the nature of the terrain dictated making the same pass three times. Obviously a real no-no. Just keep in mind that up until this particular confrontation it had been a different war with small groups of VC. This occasion raised the stakes and added a new dimension which required us to do some re-evaluating of tactics).

I set up my pass along the axis of the canal, firing a

few rounds out ahead of me to keep their heads down. As luck would have it, the napalm can did not release, so I stayed low, told Frank not to come in yet as I jinked out of the hot area. A quick check revealed a circuit breaker had popped, so I reset it and set up for another pass. This time the can came off the wing as advertised and from the sound of Idaho Bravo he was happy with the results. Frank came in behind me and made his drop in the same general area.

Idaho Bravo gave me a seven-meter correction to my first drop and I made another pass for the second can. On the way in I saw some folks shooting at me from the banks of the canal. It was surreal. Here I was on a nice sunny day just flying along and these guys lined up along the canal pumping shots at me. So damn close were some of them I could see their shoulders recoil from the firing of the guns. I thought to myself, 'Now I know how a Canada Goose feels making an approach to a North Dakota grain field when the Ducks Unlimited guys open up on him'. I made the release and the can of napalm lit off. It isn't necessary to look around to confirm when a can goes off; there is a concussion wave that hits the airplane and lets you know it exploded. At night it is even more exciting because it not only gives you a kick in the pants, but lights up everything for a mile or so all around you.

On my very low-level jinking away from the target I noticed a faint sweet acrid smell. It was then that Frank made his attention-getting call. 'Lead! You are on fire! Lead! You are burning!' A glance inside the cockpit confirmed the worst. Very hot engine oil was gushing out of the right air ventilation duct, obscuring the instrument panel. Red warning lights began to glow through the oil, advising me things were not going well. One at a time I wiped off a key instrument to get more bad news; oil pressure fluctuating wildly, cylinder-head temperature above red-line, oil temperature red-line, generator warning lights and so on. So many red lights that I stopped wiping off the gauges because of so much bad news.

My main concern was to depart the area where I had been dropping cans of napalm on folks. They don't take many prisoners, and would like nothing more than to have me belly-in next to them. My next concern was to get some altitude with the failing engine. There were no ejection seats in the T-28; it was over the side like in the WWII movies. I had always set a thousand feet for the minimum to try to jump out, but now I was less than 700ft, so that option did not exist. I tried to climb, but it was useless; because with the increased power the very hot oil really sprayed around the cockpit. To compound my problems, the temperature of the oil and the chemicals in it were burning my eyes; it was all I could do to keep them open.

As the engine lost more and more oil it began to surge violently, seemingly vibrating out of its mountings. I tried to nurse the wounded bird northwards to a dirt strip some 30 miles away, but it soon became obvious the old girl was about ready to give up the fight. By now all forward visibility was gone, so I opened the canopy, and while it improved the visibility, the turbulence made the oil spraying around the cockpit even worse.

All this was academic, because the engine gave up the ghost with a few gasps and we were on our way down. I used the emergency hydraulic pump to lower the flaps while looking back at a long rice paddy I had just flown over a few seconds ago. I'm always amazed when I talk to others that have been in the jaws of death, at how efficient a person is in an emergency and how much you can get done in a short time under tremendous pressure. At a time like this, all the training and experience pays off in great dividends. Your mind is racing to provide answers to myriad problems. Shutting off switches, closing fuel selectors, pumping down flaps, making flight corrections, rechecking everything again. I recall being busy as hell, with no time for fear.

My final approach to the paddy had a short final and I was probably carrying enough airspeed for my wife, kids and all my buddies in the squadron. So I remember zipping over a rather large canal, my last obstacle, and reminding myself to slow this mother down before we make the belly landing. Probably a hundred knots, plus or minus a few. That might not seem like very much, but the next time you are on a freeway, think about taking a sharp right and driving through the nearest cornfield at 120 m.p.h. . . . puts it in a little more perspective when you think about it this way. The airspeed was slowing, and as the airplane dropped into what I thought was a rice paddy, it turned out to be something like a cane field with stuff sticking up six or eight feet high in about three or four feet of water.

Initially I just sunk into this growth as a blur of green paste hit the windscreen and shot past the open canopy. The T-28 hit bottom with a solid jolt and we began to slide. I recalled the story of the WWII fighter pilot who made a similar landing and pointed out the fact that, while there was no more pitch or roll control, the rudders still worked. I thought this was a good idea and would give me something to do before I either died or the airplane stopped. The good Lord was with me on this day, and the airplane began to slow down. At the end of the field I hit a mound of earth three or four feet high separating the fields. I remember feeling this tremendous thud, crash, bang, and then seeing blue sky as the airplane was catapulted straight up. This did not last too long, because the next thing I saw was blue water as I was coming down. My last thoughts were, 'I have come this far only to drown'.

There was a horrendous jolt, a deluge of water came in the cockpit and momentarily I blacked out. It could have only been a few seconds or so, because when everything cleared my right hand was on a very bent and deformed throttle trigger for the two 0.50-calibre guns that were firing under water at the time. I mused at this, thinking how odd it was that the guns could fire under water. This did not last long before I was on my way out of the airplane, now filling with water. Lucky for me it was only three or four feet deep.

My first concern was to check the condition of the Vietnamese 'observer' riding in the back seat. These guys only rode along with us on missions, spoke only Vietnamese and it seemed as though you never flew with the same guy twice. So it was hard to get to know them. But he was my responsibility, and when I climbed out on the wing and looked in the rear cockpit, he was not there! He later told me, through an interpreter, that the ride was very, very exciting, the oil was very hot and when I opened the canopy it was his cue to jump out. This he did at 700ft, and the "chute opened just above a banana grove. He landed, shit-canned his U.S. air force issue flight suit, donned his black pajamas and became one of the local boys!

Things back at the crash site were not as straightforward. My wingman was strafing out a few hundred yards in front of me. Because of the vegetation I could not see his targets, but assumed Frank was not shooting just for the hell of it. At this time there were no fancy survival radios for us to switch on and talk to wingmen. To my knowledge there were no helicopters down this far south, and the few we had would take hours to get down this far and by then it would be night and every VC and peasant in the Delta would be out on a full press hunt for the downed pilot. Things were just not looking good right then, and I was making plans for a night escape and evasion exercise.

From the back of the seat I took out a M-2 30-calibre folding stock carbine that had two 30-round clips taped to the stock. I inserted one clip in the magazine and test-fired it once. Then I took out my 45-calibre automatic from my shoulder holster and put the first round in the chamber. I then moved back into the heavy vegetation to await my fate. Frank made some low passes to ensure I was OK. I knew my buddies were working the problem, but from my vantage point it looked like an even horse race to see if they or the VC would get to me first.

I was covered with oil, and as I waded through the water and growth an oil slick mirrored my every move. I knew as soon as everyone could get organised they would most likely parachute in a company of South Vietnamese Marines to even the odds. I also knew it would take some time to get all this organised and it would not happen before dawn. It would be a long night mucking around in the field evading the bad guys.

Fortunately my buddies were indeed working on the problem and one of them flew over Ca Mau and saw a new UH-1A Huey helicopter sitting on the dirt strip. This was one of the very first sent to Vietnam. It seems as though Brigadier-General Stillwell was there, getting a briefing from some of his units. The Army pilots were contacted and with no hesitation whatsoever, were on their way to get me. By this time I recall there were other T-28s and B-26s which gave me a lot of confidence to hang in there.

Soon I heard the unbelievable sound of the Huey's now familiar whump, whump, whump as it closed in on my location. I down loaded my weapons and climbed on the skids of the chopper looking like a guy full of oil that had just survived a freighter sinking. The crew chief asked if I was hurt. I said ''No, just thirsty'' so they gave me a canteen and made me sit on the floor of the chopper because I would soil the seats of the plushed up General's helicopter!''

Tom's Vietnamese backseater, A3C Tung Nguyen Dinh was awarded, at an official ceremony, Tom's treasured parachute wings from Fort Benning. He was seen for several years hence wearing the wings and willing to tell anyone about his harrowing escape from the jaws of the death dragon. Tom went on to complete his tour of duty and flew another 40 or so missions, never quite forgetting his very, very close call.

THE SKYRAIDER ARRIVES

Finally, in March 1964 the decision was made to replace the Farm Gate T-28s and B-26s with twenty-five two seater A-1E Skyraiders. However, this decision came too late for two Air Force pilots and their Vietnamese observers. On 24 March 1964 one T-28 crashed after its wing sheared off during a bombing run and on 9 April a second T-28 plowed into a rice paddy after both its wings fell off during a dive.

The American presence in South Vietnam was increasing, however, and soon the Farm Gate detachment was replaced by the newly formed 1st Air Commando Squadron, Composite, activated in July 1963 and assigned to the 34th Tactical Group at Bien Hoa. The new squadron initially inherited six C-47s, four U-10Bs, thirteen T-28s and thirteen B-26s.

By the summer of 1964 the first of the Skyraiders had begun to arrive at Bien Hoa. The 1st ACS was given priority over the training requirements of the Hurlburt commanders, who needed the two-seater aircraft to train future Skyraider pilots. It would be June before the 16th and 17th Skyraiders off the modification line would arrive at Hurlburt.

The new Skyraider pilots adopted the callsign "Hobo," and, as with the Farm Gate mission, the official role of the 1st ACS was to train Vietnamese pilots and fly into combat with them in the two-seater aircraft. Generally however, the Americans did the work while the Vietnamese went along for the ride. Some months would pass before the order to take along the requisite Vietnamese was rescinded.

The E model Skyraiders were side-by-side two-seater aircraft with a large compartment behind the pilots, formerly used by the Navy to house two electronic equipment operators. The aircraft had been overhauled before delivery, but were still old by definition. However, the Skyraider was ideal for the conditions at that time; it could stay in the air for hours and carry a prodigious bomb load.

The Navy had actually stolen a march on the Air Force by transferring some of its Skyraiders to the Vietnamese Air Force (VNAF) in September 1960. They were given to the VNAF 1st Fighter Squadron at Bien Hoa, and Navy aviators were tasked with the job of converting the Vietnamese pilots to the Skyraider. The aircraft was a great improvement over the Grumman F8F Bearcat then in service with the VNAF, and was ideal for the type of warfare then in progress. The aircraft was almost 40ft long and had a 50ft wingspan, its huge four-bladed propeller turned by an eighteen-cylinder 2,700 h.p. Wright R-3350–26W radial piston engine that was the biggest and most powerful engine ever installed in a single-propeller aircraft. The Skyraider could carry up to 12,000lb of bombs,

rockets or napalm and mounted four 20mm cannon with 150
rounds each. It had a range of 1,100 nautical miles and could
loiter over a target for hours.

By the beginning of 1962 the VNAF had 22 Skyraiders in
its inventory, and the type would soon form the backbone of
the fledgling Air Force. With Nguyen Cao Ky, a former Skyraider pilot, as chief of the VNAF and later Prime Minister of
South Vietnam, the number of Skyraider squadrons increased.
They were also used by the élite VNAF 83rd Special Operations Group on missions over North Vietnam and Laos. The
Vietnamese pilots did not rotate home after a year in combat,
like their American counterparts. They flew their aircraft con-
tinually, logging thousands of hours, until it became their turn
to die. With such experience in the Skyraider the older VNAF
pilots became very good indeed.

As far as the 1st Air Commando Squadron, Composite, was
concerned, it soon became a Skyraider-only unit and remained
with the 34th Tactical Group until July 1965, when it was
assigned to the 6251st Tactical Fighter Wing, and then the 3rd
Tactical Fighter Wing from November 1965. In January 1966
it moved bases to Pleiku, and two months later was reassigned
to the 14th Air Commando Wing. The last move for the Hobos
was to Nakhon Phanom Royal Thai Air Force Base in December 1967, joining the 56th Air Commando Wing. Whilst at
NKP they flew air cover, close support, direct air strike, armed
reconnaissance and the famous SAR (Search and Rescue) missions.

CHAPTER 5

THE CALL TO ARMS, 1964

BACK IN THE STATES

ON 22 MAY 1964 the SAWC Director of Operations announced that the Australian-type bush hat worn with the Air Commando uniform was designated the "Air Commando Hat." At first, HQ TAC had refused to approve the wearing of the hat, but SAWC Commander General Pritchard appealed to the TAC Commander, pointing out the operational value of the hat and its morale benefit. The Air Commando uniform then consisted of jump boots, bloused green fatigues, the air commando hat and a blue scarf.

In July 1963 the Joint Chiefs of Staff approved the establishment of a special air warfare squadron in Europe and on 1 January 1964 Detachment 4, 1st ACW was activated at Sembach, West Germany under the code name Gold Fortune. On 1 July 1964 the detachment became the 7th Air Commando Squadron, assigned to USAF Europe. The unit was assigned six C-47s, four C-123s and two U-10s.

By the summer of 1964 the 1st Air Commando Wing had fifty A-1Es, six C-47s, four U-10s and forty-four C-123s in South Vietnam. From now on "pipeline" training for personnel going to Southeast Asia became the focus of life at Hurlburt Field during the Vietnam years. On 1 October the 4410th Combat Crew Training Squadron was reactivated to become the wing's largest squadron with responsibility for training of students heading overseas. Dual control A-1Es began arriving in great numbers for use in training student pilots en route to Bien Hoa. The eleven types of aircraft being operated by the Wing were now joined by two YAT-28s and one YAT-37 for testing and evaluation. The YAT-37 was a ground attack version of the T-37 jet trainer and would be put into mothballs for a couple of years until the idea resurfaced in the Combat Dragon project in 1967. One of the YAT-28 aircraft was eventually destroyed and the modified T-28 did not go into production.

Other arrivals during the year included Colonel Harry C. Aderholt, the new Wing Commander and the 317th Air Commando Squadron, Troop Carrier, together with the first C-123s for the Wing.

WAR AGAIN

On 16 March all semblance of peace in Laos vanished as the Pathet Lao, with North Vietnamese backing, attacked across the Plaines des Jarres. As the neutralists and Royal Lao government forces began to fall back, Washington approved the resumption of ''Yankee Team'' reconnaissance flights by Air Force and Navy aircraft. Over the next couple of months two Navy aircraft were shot down and only one pilot rescued by Air America, the only SAR organisation in place at that time. Laos was a bad place to get shot down; at the time of writing almost 600 American personnel are still listed as missing in action there.

In South Vietnam the Viet Cong turned July 1964 into the bloodiest month to date. The Special Forces camp at Nam Dong was attacked and 55 ARVN troops and two Green Berets killed. A fortnight later the Viet Cong ambushed 400 ARVN troops in Chuong Thien Province in the Mekong Delta; only 82 men walked away from the ambush. It became obvious that despite the assistance of 16,000 US military personnel, the South Vietnamese Army was unable to halt, let alone defeat, the Viet Cong insurgency.

An incident which took place during the following month allowed the United States to step in and assume overall control of the war. On 2 August a US Navy destroyer on intelligence gathering duty off the coast of North Vietnam in the Gulf of Tonkin was attacked by three North Vietnamese patrol boats. With assistance from aircraft from the USS *Ticonderoga*, they were sunk or driven off. However, two days later, the destroyer USS *Maddox*, was sent back into the area with a sister destroyer, the *C Turner Joy*. During the night of 4 August, amidst a thunderstorm, the destroyers reported that they were under attack again. Navy aircraft arrived overhead, but could find no sign of any attackers. Despite this the message that they were under attack was passed on up the line to the President himself. Within hours of the ''Tonkin Gulf incident'' President Johnson had authorised a retaliatory air raid on targets in North Vietnam. Before Johnson had finished his TV address to the nation to announce his decision, Lieutenant Everett Alvarez, a 26-year-old Navy pilot had been shot down and captured. He was to spend eight years as a prisoner of war.

On 7 August Congress passed the Southeast Asia Resolution, effectively giving the President and his advisers the power to direct an undeclared war against North Vietnam. As American fighter squadrons began to move into South Vietnam and Thailand, the North Vietnamese moved 30 MiG fighters to Phuc Yen airfield from China, and ordered the 325th Division of the North Vietnamese Army south down the Ho Chi Minh Trail.

PROVIDERS FOR THE AIR COMMANDOS

While Farm Gate was still in its infancy, Pacific Air Force (PACAF) looked around for more transport aircraft to send to Vietnam. TAC still had five squadrons of C-123Bs awaiting deactivation with the 464th Troop Carrier Wing at Pope AFB, so one of them was sent to Tan Son Nhut, arriving on 2 January 1962. Project Mule Train had begun. They were followed in May 1962 by a second squadron, which was joined at Da Nang by a third squadron in April 1963. The squadrons came under the control of the 315th Troop Carrier Group (Combat Cargo), activated on 8 December 1962. In 1963 permanent C-123 squadrons would be established in Vietnam to replace those on TDY.

As the remaining C-123 squadrons in the USA converted to the C-130 Hercules, the Air Force recommended in mid-1963 that all C-123s be transferred to the special air warfare force. The SAWC had been serving as the C-123 replacement depot for all Southeast Asia and special purpose C-123 requirements, including spraying and battlefield illumination variants. The remaining C-123s of the 464th Tactical Airlift Wing at Pope AFB were moved to Hurlburt Field with a nucleus of officers and airmen, and on 1 July 1964 they formed the 317th Air Commando Squadron, Troop Carrier. Pipeline C-123 training was also transferred to Hurlburt, and the C-123 units thereafter became part of the air commando tradition. In May 1968 a C-123 pilot, Joe Jackson, would become the only airlift pilot to win the Medal of Honor at a special forces base named Kham Duc.

Because of the heavy workload for the three C-123 airlift squadrons already in-country, Secretary of Defense Robert S. McNamara authorised a fourth squadron. Sixteen aircraft were sent to Vietnam from Hurlburt Field in September, and on 1 October 1964 the 19th Air Commando Squadron was activated at Tan Son Nhut. They arrived just in time, for widespread flooding had disrupted surface travel over much of Vietnam and additional airlift was required, not only for regular supply duties but for humanitarian relief missions as well.

In March 1965 the 315th Troop Carrier Group was renamed the 315th Air Commando Group, Troop Carrier, and its 19th, 309th, 310th and 311th squadrons became Air Commando squadrons. In May 1966 the first AGIL-equipped C-123 deployed to PACAF. AGIL, the Airborne General Illumination System, consisted of a bank of high-intensity Xenon lamps which provided longer and more constant lighting than flares, and could be directed to avoid blinding friendly forces. Power supply, cooling and drag problems were solved during the early 1966 test program run by the 1st Combat Applications Group. Although AGIL did not work over water, owing to light penetration, it was far superior for all land operations. One problem that the aircraft could not avoid was the fact that, with its lights on, the enemy on the ground could easily locate its position and fire back at it.

Major James R. McCarthy flew the C-123 with the 309th Air Commando Squadron from September 1965 to September 1966, and recalls his experiences:

"Prior to graduation from the Air Command and Staff College at Maxwell Air Force Base in Alabama in June

1965, about three dozen of us were told that we would become part of the facility after graduation. We could not refuse to accept the assignment, although people going to Vietnam would be taken off the list. After the meeting a dozen of us volunteered to go to Vietnam, and after graduation received orders to join the Air Commandos. We went to Hurlburt Field for ground school and aircraft transition training. Although we were all senior pilots with several thousand hours of flying time, we were checking out in aircraft we had not flown before. Six of us were assigned to C-123s, a couple went to A-1s and a couple to O-1s.

At the time I joined the 309th ACS, they were co-located at Tan Son Nhut Air Base, Saigon, with the 19th ACS. The 311th was stationed at Da Nang and the 310th at Nha Trang. Each squadron was composed of four flights with seven crew each. Our squadron also had a fifth flight; Ranch Hand. The Ranch Hand flight later became the 12th Air Commando Squadron. Also assigned to our squadron in 1966 was a group of Royal Thai Air Force pilots who also flew C-123s.

For the first two weeks in South Vietnam we usually were assigned to the 'milk run' missions; the cargo and passenger missions to Nha Trang or Da Nang. These were relatively safe areas and the airfields were large and well defended. It also gave the new guy a chance to adjust to the climate and the diet. You really could not appreciate the term 'Ho Chi Minh's revenge' unless you had experienced it. It can best be described as not knowing which end to put on the toilet, because it was coming out both ends at once. This could be a real problem at 5,000ft on a six hour mission. There was a saying by the troops that true happiness was a dry fart. There was a lot of truth in that statement.

When I arrived in Vietnam in September 1965 there were only four airfields that could accommodate C-130 aircraft. All of the other airstrips could only accommodate C-123s or C-7s. We basically had four missions; routine cargo/passenger missions to base camps, airlift support for Special Forces and South Vietnamese camps,

Cargo and Paratrooper drops to isolated villages and night-time flare support as required.

The night-time flare support flew under the code name Smokey Red. Each night, each squadron had to provide one Smokey Red aircraft and crew. The "plane would launch at dusk and fly all night if required. In the back end of the aircraft was a load of high intensity magnesium flares. When an outpost or camp was under attack they would call for flares from Smokey Red. On many occasions we worked with 'Puff the Magic Dragon' AC-47 gunships; when a flare caught the VC out in the open, Puff could make short work of them.

After a one-week flight checkout programme, I was assigned as a flight commander, then I was promoted to assistant operations officer and then operations officer. Our mission was to supply airlift support and night flare support as required. Our Frag Orders came from the ALCC (Air Lift Control Center); they determined the priority of the missions request.

In late 1965 the Viet Cong were trying to cut the country in half. There was never enough airlift available to fill all the requirements. Many of our missions in those days were resupplying the Special Forces camps along the Laotian and Cambodian borders. On many of these missions what we had on board the aircraft made the difference between some of these compounds surviving the night. Many compounds would be down to their last gallon of fuel oil to run their generators, or their last dozen artillery shells. A lot of these missions were night assault landings on 1,500ft dirt strips with no landing lights or runway lights. It was interesting flying.

One day my crew and I set a record for the most airlift tonnage carried in a single day by a C-123 in Vietnam. Because of heavy fighting around the Michelin rubber plantation near Dau Tieng, about 38 miles west-northwest of Saigon, a fresh ground unit had to be taken there from Phu Loi, about 30 miles away, and other troops and equipment moved out. They had estimated that it would take at least two days to airlift the entire unit with its equipment, but they were anxious to do it in one day if possible, because intelligence had indicated that the VC planned an all-out assault for the next day.

We started moving them at first light, and I told the Army ground commander that if he would have each load ready to go when an aircraft landed we would not shut down the engines. That saved quite a bit of time in turning the aircraft around. I also instructed him to have several fork-lifts on standby in case one broke down while we were loading the cargo pallets. The Colonel supervised the loadings himself, with one of our load-masters to help him judge the proper load per aircraft. I told the other C-123s in my squadron to stagger their refuelling times so we would not have more than one aircraft in the refuelling pit at any one time.

The airfields were two 1,500ft dirt strips located 20 minutes from each other. That allowed us to cram more flying time into each hour. The weather was perfect and we did not get too much groundfire from the VC. As dusk approached I had the ground commander station men on each side of the runway at 500ft intervals with flashlights that had paper coffee cups taped to their ends. The cups had been painted with black shoe polish, and the men were instructed to turn on their flashlights and point them up the glide slope when instructed to do so by a radio operator on the ground who was in contact with the aircraft. It was crude but effective, and the VC did not have fixed runway lights to shoot at. This was not an original idea of mine. It was part of our tactics manual for operating on dirt strips at night while under enemy fire. It was used by others many times during the war.

We flew 20 sorties that day and hauled 217,400lb of cargo, including 90,000lb of petrol, oil and lubricant; ammunition; vehicles and a 105mm howitzer, plus 635 troops. It was unusual because everything went right for us, and as far as I know that record was never broken by another C-123.''

Because of the heavy workload in 1965 and early 1966, aircraft maintenance suffered, as did the crews who were under strength until the newly formed 4410th Combat Crew Training

Wing came into being on 1 December 1965 at Hurlburt Field and increased the number of replacements flowing into Vietnam. Aircraft losses increased over this period because of the poor airstrips into which the C-123s were flying. Four aircraft were lost during landings at An Loc, Tuy Hoa and Qui Nhon. The hillside strip at An Loc was a particularly bad place to land, and half-a-dozen accidents were recorded in 1965/66, several resulting from collisions with helicopters sitting adjacent to the active airstrip. One C-123 landing at Dau Tieng struck a Chinook helicopter on one side of the runway and a UH-1D Huey on the other.

Less forgiving, though rarer, were take-off accidents owing to engine failure. Three C-123s were lost in this way, the first at an airstrip in the Delta, although all 75 men on board survived the crash landing in the rice paddies. The other two occurred in 1966, and 46 Americans died in the second of these accidents, which occurred at An Khe, the base of the 1st Cavalry Division (Airmobile). Flying in poor visibility near mountains was another cause of aircraft losses. The C-123s lacked navigational radar and were frequently used for deliveries into the highlands. In mid-1965 a C-123 from the 310th ACS flew into a mountain while attempting airdrops in marginal weather south of Pleiku, with the loss of all nine on board. In December 1965 a C-123 flying in limited visibility from Pleiku to Tuy Hoa without a navigator on board struck a cliff side and disintegrated. Eighty-one Vietnamese paratroops and the four-man crew were killed. Another C-123 flareship was involved in a mid-air collision with an A-1E north of An Khe in January 1966, with the loss of six crewmen.

· Yet another C-123 was struck by a Vietnamese aircraft while parked at Da Nang and destroyed, bringing the total losses to eleven for this period. This compared with eleven lost to all causes in Southeast Asia during the previous three years. Six C-130s were also lost in addition to the C-123s, and steps were immediately taken to try to reduce such attrition. Colonel Robert T Simpson, who assumed command of the 315th ACW in mid-1966, informed the crews, ''Our mission is not so urgent or pressing that we cannot afford time to accomplish it safely.'' Whilst the Colonel had a valid point, there was a war going on. James McCarthy and his fellow pilots found that the very nature of their job—carrying supplies to 150 different airstrips, some short, some narrow, some in valleys or on hilltops—was hazardous in the extreme, and if they flew in the approved Air Force manner the job would not get done. In addition to accidents, enemy groundfire and sabotage continued to reduce the transport fleet. During 1966 enemy sympathisers at air bases or amongst the South Vietnamese troops left live grenades or explosives aboard C-7 and C-130 aircraft, and at least two C-130s were lost as a result. During research for the author's previous book, *Vietnam—The Helicopter War*, (Airlife 1991) it was discovered that Marine CH-53 helicopter crews also found live hand grenades behind seats after South Vietnamese troops had been airlifted. It soon became standard practice to search aircraft carefully before take-off after hauling Vietnamese passengers.

WATERPUMP

Meanwhile, the civil war in Laos was coming to the boil again, and on 5 March 1964 Headquarters USAF approved the deployment of Detachment 6, 1st Air Commando Wing, to Udorn Royal Thai Air Force Base. The detachment, known by the nickname "Waterpump," consisted of four T-28s and 41 men, and its mission was to train Laotian and Thai pilots and maintenance personnel. Not coincidentally, this unit also provided a source of US controlled aircraft to augment the T-28s of the small Royal Laotian Air Force, and came directly under the control of US Ambassador Leonard Unger in Vientiane.

In July Lieutenant-Colonel William C. "Roadrunner" Thomas arrived to command the unit. A former Second World War and Korean War pilot, the super-fit commander ran everywhere, hence his nickname. During his tour of duty Waterpump achieved with 66 men what a regular air force unit would have required 350 men to accomplish. Sixteen C-47 pilots, twenty-six Thai T-28 pilots, nine Lao T-28 pilots and a dozen Air American T-28 pilots were trained, plus various maintenance personnel. The Air America pilots would fly cover for SAR missions. Sadly, four Waterpump pilots, flying two T-28s, were lost on one mission to causes unknown. They were Major Otis Gordon and Captains Ray Eason, Gus Albrecht and Lenny Hudson.

Don Schoknecht was serving with the Farm Gate detachment at Bien Hoa around this time.

> "When we started receiving the A-1Es, the AT-28s were being sent to Laos and Thailand, so I volunteered to go there. We got all the T-28s to the Air America complex at Udorn and proceeded to strip them of their Vietnamese markings and install Laotian markings. The first pilots I recall seeing were in civilian clothes and carried an old M-1 carbine and a Colt 45. I don't know who these people were, but I think they were our guys filling in until they got the Laotians trained."

Joe Holden was sent to Waterpump as an instructor.

> "We had three types of people to train; "C" pilots, who were Laotian kids 18 or 19 years old who could not speak English or fly at all, although we had a few older pilots who had been trained by both the Russians and the French; 'B' pilots, who were Thai nationals flying as mercenaries for the CIA, who would go from Udorn up to Vientiane and fly air support for General Vang Pao's 'secret' Hmong army in Laos. Finally we had 'A' pilots, civilian American pilots working for Air America and flying armed T-28s as escort for Air America H-34 helicopters on search and rescue missions."

Because of the increase in Pathet Lao combat operations in Laos, the Air Force extended and expanded the Waterpump detachment, and consequently more replacement pilot training had to be carried out at Hurlburt Field. Due to the extension of the operation, replacements left Hurlburt Field with 2,800lb of medical supplies to be used in a civic action program amongst the Thai people as well as for the assigned Air Commandos.

By 13 June 1965 Waterpump personnel had conducted over 60,555 medical treatments and immunisations for people in Udorn Province. Including Nakhon Phanom Province, over 96,000 Thais received medical attention between January and

June 1965. As time went by, Waterpump medical teams were busy in both Thailand and Laos, traveling to remote areas and dispensing thousands of pounds of medical supplies to treat malaria, typhoid fever, dysentery, tuberculosis and vitamin deficiency. In Laos they treated friendly wounded at a 100-bed hospital at Sam Thong, run by an Air Commando doctor, Captain Robert E. Jackson. The hospital had been constructed by US Aid, the Agency for International Development, and a blood bank was established to improve patient care for battlefield casualties. However, because neither Lao or Hmong tribesmen would give blood, bimonthly flights to Udorn were set up to collect blood donated by Air Commandos. Between July and December 1966 7,600 patients were treated at Sam Thong hospital, and medical staff performed four surgeries per day.

Detachment One of the 56th Air Commando Wing succeeded Waterpump and was in turn redesignated USMAC-THAI/TLD, although it was often still referred to as Waterpump as late as September 1974 when Norman Crocker, the chief of maintenance went home.

BRIGADIER-GENERAL "HEINIE" ADERHOLT: COMMANDO 1

A legend in the Air Commando community, Brigadier-General Harry C. Aderholt, "Heinie" to his friends, is a true combat leader, unlike many in the Air Force today. His flying career began during the Second World War and continued through Korea, when he was given command of Det 2, 21st Troop Carrier Squadron. The unit carried out hundreds of missions behind North Korean lines, including the recovery of parts from the new Soviet MiG-15 fighter for Air Force Technical Intelligence. A posting to the CIA followed, as head of their air training branch at "The Farm," and a second tour with them as Unconventional Warfare Planning Officer.

In January 1960 Heinie went to Okinawa as commander of the 1045th Operations Evaluation Training Group, a cover organisation providing specialised aid or supervision to certain overt and covert assets in Southeast Asia. This included supporting the CIA's Tibetan Airlift out of Takhli in Thailand, plus other activities in Laos and South Vietnam. One of his first tasks was to arrange the shipment of 1,000 weapons to Vang Pao, from their storage warehouse in Takhli in Thailand to Padong in Laos. He was next tasked with establishing a series of landing strips, called lima sites, throughout Laos. The nature of the countryside meant that most were only good for short-take-off-and-landing aircraft, and he was asked to find suitable aircraft to operate in and out of these strips. The Helio Courier was ideal, although Heinie did manage to spend a night at a strip in enemy territory when one failed on landing, and brought another down in a tree when it decided that it did not want to fly.

In 1962 Heinie went to the SAWC as Assistant Operations Officer, and then took command of the 1st Air Commando Wing as a full Colonel: After a spell at Clark Air Base in the Philippines, he went to Thailand to work with General John Singlaub of SOG fame, and was responsible for establishing the downed pilots' recovery service, now known as the Joint Personnel Recovery Center. Command of a flying unit followed, the 606th Air Commando Squadron at Nakhon Phanom Royal Thai Air Base, with a unit established along the lines of the Second World War Air Commandos; including transport (C 123s), fighters (T-28s), helicopters (UH-1Fs, not Sikorsky YR-4s), light aircraft (U-10s) and bombers (A-26 Nimrods). When the 56th Air Commando Wing was established at NKP, Heinie became the first commander.

After another posting to the SAWC as Director of Operations, he returned to Thailand and spent most of the rest of his career there in one capacity or another, ending up as Commander Military Assistance Command Thailand (MACTHAI). A lot of the work was covert or clandestine, including the Cambodian Airlift and Cambodian Air Force improvement plan, to bolster the defences of that country before disaster befell the population as Pol Pot's fanatics took over.

Two stories illustrate why Heinie's troops thought so highly of him. Not long after he took over as commander at NKP he was driving along the ramp when he saw a Sergeant running desperately towards him. He stopped and said, "What's the hurry Sergeant?" "No hurry now sir," came the reply, "I have just shit in my pants!" The sergeant explained that there were no latrines down at the flight line, and they had to go back up to the barracks when necessary. Heinie called the base commander on the radio, said there was an emergency at hangar two and told him to get down there straight away. When he arrived he told him to take the sergeant to the barracks, wait while he showered and changed and come back down. Heinie then told him, "Frank, you have failed in your support function. You have been so busy building churches, etc, that you have neglected the men's welfare. With the poor food and sickness on the base, there should be a latrine on the flight line where the troops spend most of their working day. You have got until sundown to build a two-holer latrine on the flight line, and if you don't get it done I will fire you." Needless to say, the latrine was built in time and Heinie ceremoniously declared it open that night.

Always protective of his troops, Heinie had another problem at Hurlburt when the jet jockeys they were training in O-1s started ground-looping them. Although the damage was minimal, higher authority decreed that, in future, any such accidents would result in the pilots going before a flying evaluation board and being transferred, effectively ending their career. Heinie called General Del Orden, the chief of Army aviation at Fort Rucker, and said, "Del, have you got any broken O-1s in your junkyard that I can have?" He replied, "Hell yes, we've got lots of them. How many do you need?" "Oh," said Heinie "five or ten will be fine." He sent his director of maintenance to collect the best of the O-1s and rebuild them, and henceforth, when one was damaged, they could sneak a spare in to keep up the numbers. Then they pranged a U-10, but as they did not have any spare ones, they rang the CIA and borrowed one, complete with USAF markings, and hid the pranged aircraft in the CIA's hangar until it could be repaired. While this was going on, the Tactical Air Command Inspector General (IG) arrived one night with a letter complaining that "These Air Commandos are trying to hide another major accident, etc." Heinie said, "Colonel, you don't believe that shit do you?" The Colonel replied, "Heinie, I don't have any choice. I've got to count your airplanes." "Go ahead," Heinie responded "then come over to the bar later and tell me how you did." The Colonel appeared later and informed Heinie that he had a major problem, as he was two aircraft short. Heinie told him not to worry, to have a few drinks and they would count them again in the morning. He then sneaked out to a telephone and told his director of maintenance, "Joe, you SOB, we've got the inspector general here and he thinks we are hiding another accident and we are two 'planes short. You get out there and correct it!" So they pulled out the extra aircraft and put them on the flight line. At eleven o'clock the next morning the IG returned to Heinie's office and said, "I can't figure this out, Heinie. I've counted the aircraft again and you've got three too many!"

SPOOKY ARRIVES

By the time the first Douglas AC-47 Gunship entered service in 1965, the aging cargo aircraft had already been around for 20 years. The mating of the old, dependable aircraft with the latest technology in machine-guns and the far-from-new concept of sideways-firing weapons was one of the better ideas to come out of the Vietnam war. It had long been known that an aircraft flying a pylon turn around a fixed point on the ground could keep that point in sight all the time. However, not until 1964 was it proved that an aircraft with sideways-firing guns could continuously engage a target on the ground and keep it under fire as it circled the target in a left bank.

Tests with the new 6,000-rounds-per-minute 7.62mm General Electric SUU-11A/A Gatling gunpod, fitted to a C-131, produced 25 hits on a 10ft rubber raft with just a one-second burst. Later tests showed that a burst could cover an area the size of a football pitch and put a round into every square foot. Such a weapon could prove a life-saver to the defenders of the hamlets and forts in the countryside of Vietnam, and field testing began in Vietnam at the end of 1964.

In October 1964 a test team arrived at Bien Hoa air base to convert a C-47 from the 1st Air Commando Squadron into a gunship. The aircraft was modified to carry three of the six-barrelled minigun pods on the port side; one would fire out of the open cargo door and the other two were mounted to fire out of the last two windows on the port side of the fuselage.

The gunship could carry 24,000 rounds of ammunition and 45 parachute flares with a burning time of three minutes each. The crew consisted of a pilot/aircraft commander, copilot, navigator, three gunners to maintain the guns and drop the flares, and a Vietnamese interpreter. The new gunship was originally designated an FC-47 (Fighter Cargo), but this was changed to AC-47 (Attack Cargo) after an outcry of protest by fighter jocks. Such was the success of the early gunship tests in Vietnam that an initial order for 26 aircraft was placed.

The first AC-47 squadron, the 4th Air Commando Squadron, deployed its 20 gunships to Vietnam in November 1965 under the code name Operation Sixteen Buck. The gunships were sorely needed, as the Viet Cong controlled most of the countryside and South Vietnamese morale was declining rapidly. The Seventh Air Force defined the squadron's mission as ''to respond with flares and firepower in support of hamlets under night attack, supplement strike aircraft in the defense of friendly forces and provide long endurance support for convoys'. The gunships were allocated the call sign ''Spooky,'' and also earned the nickname ''Puff the magic dragon,'' from those who had witnessed its nocturnal display of firepower. The roar of the guns and the sight of twenty tracer bullets per second reaching out towards the ground struck fear into the Viet Cong. Being a superstitious people, the Vietnamese took the name literally. Captured Viet Cong documents told of orders not to attack the Dragon, as weapons were useless and it would only infuriate the monster. In order to cover the whole of the country, detachments were established at Da Nang, Pleiku, Nha Trang and Binh Thuy. The squadron headquarters was at Tan Son Nhut near Saigon.

The first AC-47 gunships to reach Vietnam suffered from a shortage of guns, and 300 obsolete 0.30-calibre machine-guns were obtained to keep the squadron in service until the supply system caught up with them. Meanwhile, plans were under way to convert 53 old C-47s to gunships and equip each of them eventually with three General Electric GAU-2B/A gunpods.

The first year was a period of learning for the Spooky crews. They discovered that short bursts of three seconds were best. Very short bursts seemed to cause the guns to jam, whilst long bursts emptied the 1,500-round magazines too quickly and burned out barrels. With practice, the pilot who aimed the guns could compensate for what was known as ''Kentucky windage''; the variables involved in this included the slant range—the distance between the gun muzzle and the target; the airspeed—each knot of wind would displace the around 1.69ft per second of bullet travel; Gun Recoil—the aft fuselage swung to the right as the guns were fired, causing the rounds to fall short and to the rear of the target; and the saturation factor—how many bullets would land in a prescribed target area. For example, a four-second burst from one minigun at a slant range of 4,500ft would put 400 bullets in a circle 31.5ft in diameter.

By the end of 1965 two AC-47s had been lost. One was shot down by enemy ground fire on 17 December as it flew cross-country from Tan Son Nhut to Phan Rang. The second was on an experimental daytime recce/interdiction mission over Laos a week later when it transmitted a Mayday call and disappeared. The aircraft and crew were never found. Yet another gunship would be shot down in March 1966, whilst supporting the besieged Special Forces camp in the A Shau valley in South Vietnam.

In response to a request from the US Ambassador to Laos, it was decided to deploy gunships to Thailand to fly missions over Laos, and in February 1966 four were sent to Udorn Royal Thai Air Force Base (RTAFB), moving shortly thereafter to Ubon RTAFB. Two wars were under way in the country. Loyalist forces supported by the United States, or more accurately by the CIA, were fighting the North Vietnamese and Pathet Lao on the Plaines des Jarres, while on the border between Laos and South Vietnam attempts were being made daily to interdict the flow of men and materials heading south down the Ho Chi Minh Trail.

The operations over Laos will be covered in detail later in the book, but briefly the gunships were out of their depth over the heavily-defended Ho Chi Minh Trail, and following the trials over Laos the decision was made to confine the gunship to outpost and troops-in-contact support inside Vietnam.

Back in South Vietnam Spooky was proving its worth in the countryside, flying most of its missions at night when the enemy came out of hiding. On 15 July 1966 a company of

Viet Cong assaulted a 32-man Popular Front outpost in Phong Dinh Province. The attackers proclaimed by loudspeaker, "We are not afraid of your firepower." Thereupon, four AC-47s dropped 75 flares and expended 48,800 rounds of ammunition. Two F-100s dropped napalm on the enemy positions and the Viet Cong stopped the attack.

During the night of 11 October a record was established for the most 7.62mm rounds fired in a single night by an AC-47, when a gunship fired 43,500 rounds and 96 flares to aid a besieged outpost in Kien Phong Province. After using up its entire flare and ammunition load, the aircraft landed, reloaded and returned to the attack. The gunship was credited by the outpost commander with saving the fort.

In October 1966 eight AC-47s were sent to Nakhon Phanom RTAFB to join the C-123s, T-28s, U-10Bs and CH-3s of the 606th Air Commando Squadron, flying missions over Laos. Frequent enemy attacks on US air bases led to requests for more gunships to guard them during the hours of darkness. A second AC-47 unit, the 14th Air Commando Squadron, arrived at Nha Trang in October 1967, and eventually all areas of South Vietnam were covered by Spooky detachments. Usually there was one gunship on airborne alert from dusk to midnight and from midnight to dawn. A second AC-47 would stand by on runway alert. The 14th ACS became the 3rd ACS in May 1968.

Spooky often worked with the psywar C-47s of the 5th Air Commando Squadron. The psychological warfare aircraft flew under the call sign "Gabby," although they were known unofficially as "bullshit bombers." They were standard C-47s with a giant speaker mounted in the cargo doorway and carrying an ARVN official who would enunciate the benefits of the Saigon Government through a microphone. These aircraft would orbit at around 3,500ft while the speaker tried to persuade the Viet Cong to come over to the side of the Government. At the same time Gabby would warn them not to fire at the speaker aircraft lest great trouble would befall them. Unknown to Charlie, a Spooky gunship would be orbiting below and behind Gabby, and when the enemy began to fire at Gabby the roar of the Spooky miniguns would answer them. As silence descended again, Gabby would retort "See, I told you so!."

All was quiet in the Special Forces camp at Duc Lap on 23

August 1968, as the Green Beret advisors made their rounds of the camp defences. In their perimeter bunkers, the Civilian Irregular Defence Group Rhade and Hmong tribesmen, struggling to keep awake, rubbed their eyes and stared again into the darkness. Were some of the shadows outside the compound moving?

At 0105 hours the first mortar rounds exploded in the camp as yelling North Vietnamese sappers ran towards key positions. The whoosh of rockets reached the ears of the sleeping Green Berets as they tumbled out of their beds, grabbed their weapons and dashed outside. As the 95C NVA Regiment launched its first ground assault, the radio operator put out a frantic call for assistance.

The II Corps Direct Air Support Centre passed the request to the AC-47 gunship on airborne alert, and within seconds Major Daniel J Rehm, the pilot of Spooky 41, pushed the throttle to the firewall as the navigator scanned his maps. Forty-five minutes after the attack began, Rehm checked in with the compound's radio operator. "Spooky 41 overhead with flares and miniguns." They were just in time, the enemy had breached the wire and several fire fights had broken out within the compound.

Three thousand feet above the defenders the pilot settled his left shoulder into the Mark 20 Mod 4 gunsight, as used by the A-1 Skyraider, flipped the safety catch off the firing button on his control column, and directed the navigator to pass the order "Flare away" to the back of the aircraft. The kicker jerked the lanyard as he tossed the flare out of the open doorway and watched as it swung under its parachute, casting its 200,000-candlepower illumination over the countryside below. The attackers looked up as the night was turned to day, and began to search frantically for cover; they knew what was coming. The pilot rolled the aircraft into a left bank, squinted through the gunsight, compensated for the Kentucky Windage factor and pressed the firing button. The interior of the rear cabin lit up with an orange glow as two of the three miniguns belched out flame and smoke. With each gun spitting up to 6,000 rounds per minute and every fifth around a tracer, the sight and sound was impressive.

The pilot of Spooky 41 recalls:

"When we arrived, the buildings in the compound were all afire and the men were grouped in a blockhouse below the burning operations center. I set up a quick orbit of the area and began firing on targets about 200 to 300 meters from the camp. Almost immediately we began receiving intense anti-aircraft fire from four different points. I began with a long burst at a target from my miniguns, but when the tracers started to fly close to us, I moved to another altitude and began to 'peck' with short bursts at the enemy locations.''

As Major Rehm continued his attack, the crew in the back clamped their ear defenders firmly to their heads and attended to their duties; the navigator relayed orders from the pilot, the load master stood by the doorway with another flare and the two gunners prepared to reload the two guns when the unused third gun began to fire. Although the timely appearance of Spooky prevented the camp from being overrun, it took several days of attacks by gunships, tactical fighters, B-52s and armed helicopters, before the 4,000 strong enemy force broke off and withdrew. At times up to four AC-47s were on station and in 228 flying hours they expended 761,044 rounds. As the men at Duc Lap put it, Spooky truly became their guardian angel.

Both Spooky squadrons became Special Operations squadrons in 1968. The 3rd SOS was deactivated on 1 September 1969 and transferred its aircraft to the Vietnamese Air Force. The last Spooky mission was flown on 1st December 1969, when Spooky 41 of the 4th SOS recovered at Phan Rang air base in South Vietnam. Two weeks later the unit was deactivated. During the first six months of 1969 the two squadrons were credited with 1,473 enemy killed, a creditable achievement which their replacements would find hard to equal. The new AC-119G Shadow gunship was taking over Spooky's role and would be followed in time by the AC-119K Stinger and the AC-130 Spectre.

By the time of their replacement by the new generation of gunships in 1969, the AC-47 gunships had successfully defended over 6,000 hamlets and forts. In keeping with President Nixon's policy of Vietnamization the majority of the AC-47s were passed onto the South Vietnamese Air Force, while others went to the Lao, Thai and Cambodian Air Forces.

COMBAT CONTROLLER

The Combat Control Teams of the United States Air Force are descended from the Army pathfinders of the Second World War. The troopers trained to be dropped into enemy territory ahead of troop carrying formations to guide them into paradrop or landing zones. Although originally an Army mission, the Air Force decided to form its own teams at Donaldson AFB, South Carolina in 1953. Their basic role was to set up radio homing beacons and to mark out landing or drop zones with colored panels that could be seen from the air. They could also communicate by radio prevailing wind speeds and direction and assess any potential opposition on the ground. They were also skilled in morse code for long range radio communication.

Initially the combat control team members were trained in the Air Force speciality skills of radio operator/mechanic and later as air traffic controllers, although nowadays these élite men have their own speciality code. Charlie Jones joined the combat controllers in 1954 and after paratroop training he and his combat control team joined the 11th Airborne in Germany. In those days the combat control teams had to literally line a forward LZ with brightly colored panels to outline the runway or DZ for incoming aircraft. It often required a truck load of panels to do this. These days, the CCT members jump in a style which the old hands refer to as "Hollywood," where they carry the necessary equipment in their tunic or trouser pockets!

When the Air Force created Jungle Jim, they asked for combat controllers to join them and these first Air Commando combat controllers were commanded by Captain Lemuel Egleston, the "Gray Eagle." Working with the air commando air crews the teams soon developed the ability to guide aircraft into jungle airstrips at night using only flashlights with the beam directed skywards by coffee cups with the bottom cut out, placed over the lens.

Contrary to official air force policy that only officers or rated pilots could call in air strikes, the air commandos began to train their enlisted combat controllers in the skill. Instructors from the Air Ground Operations School at Keesler AFB were brought to Eglin to secretly teach the men how to guide in air commando T-28s to strike targets on the ground.

The first air commando combat controllers went to Vietnam in 1961, where the team leader, Sergeant Joe Orr won the first decoration in combat for a combat controller for his part in the attempted rescue of the crew of a downed C-123. With the rescue helicopter unable to land in the area, Joe was lowered by rope to the ground where he cut his way through the jungle to the crash site. Sadly, the crew did not survive the crash. Since ''combat'' decorations were not yet authorised for Vietnam, Joe was awarded the Soldiers Medal.

Master Sergeant Charlie Jones, Technical Sergeant Dick Foxx and A1C Charles Luckhurst replaced the first combat control team. They were assigned to a Special Forces A-team based at Boun Enaou, a Rhade village near Ban Me Thout in the Central Highlands. They had battery radios and jeep mounted UHF, VHF and HF radios to communicate with the Farm Gate U-10s, T-28s, and B-26s and could direct air strikes at night by using a rotating beacon in the village as a point of reference for the fighters and then giving them distance and heading to the trouble spot. Sadly, Dick Foxx was killed in a U-10 shootdown, together with Air Commando pilot Captain Willoughby Booth and Green Beret Captain Terry Cordell, during an operation to surround a Viet Cong company in October 1962.

In 1966, Charlie Jones went to Laos, to Site 20 Alternate, to direct air strikes for General Vang Pao out of the right seat of Continental Air Services Pilatus Porters. He flew some 400 missions in this manner. During several of these flights, the aircraft were peppered with ground fire. One day they were actually shot down, with Jones and the seriously wounded pilot barely making it to a landing at a friendly site.

One of the drawbacks of the job was that the Air Attaché would not allow them to mark targets with smoke rockets, so they had to guide in aircraft using features on the ground or by using the first bomb impact as a reference point. Wearing civilian clothes and known as Butterfly FACs, this handful of non-rated combat controllers performed sterling service directing air strikes until General Momyer heard about it and ordered them replaced by rated Air Force FACs.*

PROJECT DUCK HOOK

Project Duck Hook involved special C-123 training at Hurlburt for 38 Nationalist Chinese and 22 South Vietnamese. Ten of the 60 were interpreters. The training emphasised night low-level and bad-weather missions in mountainous terrain, utilising three specially configured aircraft. The nationality of these crewmen suggested that their future role might involve flying over territory where it would be extremely embarrassing to the United States if an aircraft was shot down and captured Americans were put on display. It did not take much imagination to figure out that they would be going to South Vietnam and flying "north."

Duck Hook was the first "Big Safari" project undertaken by Lockheed Aircraft Services, starting in February 1964. Six C-123Bs were reconfigured with Applied Technology Inc Reverse Repeater (ATIR) and Buster Transmitter Receiver (BSTR) electronic countermeasures equipment, an electronic warfare (EW) console and the AN/APN-153/ASN-25 Doppler navigation system. Later modifications included a model 190-C flight recorder to provide a record of flight data including Doppler ground speed and drift angle. In January 1968 the aircraft were fitted with the APR-25/26 radar homing and warning (RHAW) system and the AN/ALE-1 chaff dispenser, and in April 1968 conversion work began to modify the B models to jet-equipped K models. The aircraft were also painted in a seven-color camouflage scheme.

Duck Hook was initiated to improve support of Military Assistance Command Vietnam—Studies and Observation Group (MACV-SOG) special forces teams operating behind enemy lines. Colonel John Singlaub's SOG was authorised to

---

*The Steve Canyon program was the result, with young Air Force O-1 pilots being asked to volunteer from South Vietnam. Known as Ravens, the exploits of these men are legendary and readers may like to read Christopher Robbins' book of the same name for more details.

operate in North and South Vietnam, Laos, Cambodia, Burma, the southern provinces of China and Hainan Island in the Gulf of Tonkin. Seven countries, and there are, coincidentally, seven stars in the unit patch of the First Flight Detachment.

Helicopters were usually used to infiltrate, resupply and exfiltrate teams, but they did not have the range of the transport aircraft. In July 1964 Detachment 1 of the 775th Troop Carrier Squadron, with six specially equipped C-123s, left Hurlburt Field for Nha Trang. Although the C-123s improved the SOG's infiltration and resupply capabilities, the aircraft faced enormous problems. The enemy lacked the radar necessary for night intercepts, but their anti-aircraft network limited possible low-level routes into the North. The mountainous terrain was also a problem, restricting missions to moonlit or reasonably clear nights. By November only one resupply mission had been completed, and early work was restricted to high-altitude leaflet drops and routine air lift work.

The first reinforcement-resupply mission to North Vietnam took place on 25 December 1966. Seven more resupply missions to the north were completed in the first three months of 1967, and three teams of six were inserted in September and October 1967. However, only seven more missions took place up to the end of 1968.

The unit was known as the First Flight Detachment, and became part of the 14th Air Commando Wing at Nha Trang. One former member told the author:

"At First Flight we had a company of Nung guards that protected our compounds and our people. They were Chinese that stayed in Southeast Asia after the Second World War and intermarried with the Cambodians. They were mercenaries who were very reliable and excellent fighters as long as you paid them on time. A part of their contract was they could eat the heart and liver out of anyone they killed in combat. The NVA feared them and gave them a wide berth. There was a whole division of Nungs in the South Vietnamese Army, and President Diem was afraid they would take over the government in a coup, because they were so much better than any of his other divisions. When the Special Forces first showed up in Vietnam they needed guides that knew the language and who could be depended upon at times as bodyguards. Diem broke up the division and started assigning them to the Special Forces teams in company- and squad-size detachments. This solved his problems and gave the special forces a dependable help. Although the air base at Nha Trang got mortared several times and some of the people were shot at off base, our personnel or facilities were never attacked. I credit that to the fear the NVA and the Viet Cong had of our Nung guards.

Our missions behind enemy lines did tie up considerable forces, up to four Army divisions at one point, I was told later, that could have been sent to South Vietnam. They were searching for recon teams. The NVA were paranoid about having recon teams running around their countryside. Another mission would be to insert teams who had defective NVA ammo. They would find ammo caches along the Ho Chi Minh Trail and put the defective ammo in with the normal supplies. The ammo was designed so that when they fired the rifle it would blow up in their face. It didn't take long for the word to get around. Some intelligence debriefs on NVA grunts said they would only fire when some senior NCO could actually observe them. Again, a few defective rounds could have an impact on a lot of NVA personnel."

Major Owen Hitchings was flying with the 309th ACS when he volunteered for six months TDY with the First Flight Detachment. In August 1966 he became the second American SOG pilot to fly a psyops mission over North Vietnam. Before that, the missions were flown by Chinese or Vietnamese crews. An American escort officer would usually fly with the crew to Udorn, then the crew would continue on their own while he waited at the nearest radar site and followed the mission from there. However, as the war progressed, the Americans began to fly the missions themselves:

"Captain Fred Heitzhausen flew the first American-crew mission up North. My aircraft, nicknamed the 'Gray Ghost' because of its paint scheme, would be the sec-

ond. We were to fly in air force uniforms and the aircraft
would wear USAF markings, in case we were shot down
they could not accuse us of being spies. However, our
aircraft were usually sanitised before a mission. All US
markings would be removed and the only identifier was
a black letter inside the front door. Civilian flight
publications were put on board, and the crew carried
false civilian identity cards and wore civilian clothes.
The aircraft were painted grey and did not carry any
markings, although they were later painted black and
dark green. We had six C-123s then, four specially modified and using the call signs Whisky Bravo, Charlie,
Delta and Echo, and two normal trash-hauler models using the call signs Whisky X-Ray and Zulu.

We flew to Udorn in Thailand, and the following
night took off and headed for Vinh, just across the border in North Vietnam, where we were to drop leaflets
and small, parachute rigged radios set for the 'Voice of
America' frequency. We flew through the valleys of
Laos at 100-200ft with my copilot and navigator, maps
in hand, guiding me. After climbing to 14,000ft and releasing the leaflets and radios, the electronics warfare
officer informed me that a surface-to-air missile had
locked onto us.

I went into a split-S, descending at 5,000ft per minute
to break the radar lock, and then levelled off and headed
for Udorn. We were never sure whether the SAM had
been launched or not."*

*Owen was lucky that night. Rumour has it that the First Flight
Detachment lost two C-123s; one which crashed whilst on final ap-
proach to Tan Son Nhut, and one that disappeared on the way to
Taipei, where the aircraft were maintained by China Airlines.

CHAPTER 6

FIGHTING THE AIR COMMANDO WAY, 1965–'66

AMERICA WELL AND TRULY joined the war in March 1965, when the first Marines waded ashore at Da Nang and the Rolling Thunder bombing campaign against North Vietnam began. United States Navy aircraft carriers took up positions on Yankee and Dixie stations, off the coast of North and South Vietnam, while squadrons of attack aircraft moved into bases in South Vietnam and Thailand. Operation Barrel Roll had begun at the end of 1964, directed against enemy choke points where the Ho Chi Minh Trail crossed from North Vietnam into Laos. In April 1965 Operation Steel Tiger began, attacking targets in the southern panhandle of Laos.

The Joint Chiefs of Staff recommended a short, sharp bombing campaign against North Vietnam, to destroy the war-making capability of the country. Unfortunately President Johnson decided to ignore his military leaders and fought the war from the White House, with his civilian advisers. Such interference, together with the restrictions imposed by the White House, prevented the Air Force and Army commanders from bringing the war to an early end. It was going to be a long war.

American ground troops began to arrive in force during the year. The 173rd Airborne Brigade, a brigade from the 101st Airborne Division and the Big Red One, the 1st Infantry Division, would arrive during the year. The new helicopter-equipped 1st Cavalry Division (Airmobile) would arrive as the Viet Cong and NVA tried to cut South Vietnam in two. Following the siege of the Plei Me special forces camp, the Air

Cav troopers would meet North Vietnamese regular troops in the battle of the Ia Drang Valley.

As far as the Air Commandos were concerned, their Skyraider and Spooky gunship squadrons were outnumbered by the other USAF squadrons arriving in country. However, the organisation would grow until two Air Commando Wings were established in South Vietnam and one in Thailand. Many unusual and dangerous tasks would be thrown their way, including the support of special forces cross border operations.

PONY EXPRESS AND THE GREEN HORNETS

With the arrival of the 1st Cavalry Division (Airmobile) at An Khe in October and the news that three NVA Regiments were loose this side of the Cambodian border, the arrival on 8 October of yet another helicopter squadron probably went unnoticed. Unlike most helicopter units arriving in Vietnam, the 20th Helicopter Squadron and its fourteen Sikorsky CH-3C belonged to the air force and would later be assigned to the 14th Air Commando Wing at Nha Trang.

Up until this time, the only air force helicopter units in Vietnam were search and rescue detachments flying the HH-43 Huskie and later the CH and HH-3 "Jolly Green Giants." The 20th was given the nickname "Pony Express" and was basically a cargo carrying squadron. The Seventh Air Force described its mission as "to support various Air Force combat activities, such as the communication sites, Tactical Air Control System, air liaison officers, airfield construction, aeromedical evacuations, counterinsurgency operations, and to support/augment search and rescue forces in SEA if required. The unit will also be responsive to priority requirements of MACV."

The shortage of heavy lift helicopters at this time led to eight of the CH-3Cs being stationed at Da Nang from 10 December 1965 to 10 March 1966, to support the Marines until their CH-53s arrived. The CH-3s still at Tan Son Nhut were involved in the support of Army ground operations until the whole squadron moved to Nha Trang on 10 March to support the US 101st Airborne. Their work at Nha Trang mostly involved carrying 105mm howitzers out to mountain tops in the morning and back in the evening, because the Viet Cong owned the mountains at night. In June 1966, A, B and C Flights with eleven CH-3s moved to Udorn in Thailand, for employment in the unconventional warfare role. D Flight with three CH-3s remained at Tan Son Nhut.

The unconventional warfare role involved cross border operations into Laos, Cambodia, North Vietnam and Southern China. These operations were under the command of MACV-SOG, a joint-service high command unconventional warfare task force engaged in highly classified clandestine operations throughout Southeast Asia. The title SOG—Studies and Observation Group, was merely a cover to deceive people into thinking that it was performing an analysis of the lessons learnt to that point in the war.

MACV-SOG was activated in 1964 to assume the CIA's job of assisting, advising and supporting the South Vietnamese government's Special Exploitation Service, which conducted highly classified sabotage, psychological warfare and special operations against its neighbouring countries. MACV-SOG was assigned about 2,000 Americans, mostly Special Forces, and over 8,000 highly trained indigenous troops. It had its own air force, based at Nha Trang and eventually comprising the VNAF 219th Helicopter Squadron, the "King Bees," flying the H-34; a covert C-123 squadron known as the First Flight Detachment; a USAF C-130 squadron, and the 20th Helicopter Squadron.

In 1967 MACV-SOG reorganised its ground strike elements into three field commands; Command and Control North, South and Central (CNN, CCS and CCC). The detailed operations of these commands are beyond the scope of this book, but suffice it to say that their primary responsibilities included: **1** cross-border operations to disrupt the Viet Cong, NVA, Pathet Lao and Khmer Rouge in their own territories; **2** keeping track of all imprisoned and missing Americans and conducting raids to assist and free them; **3** training and despatching agents into North Vietnam to run resistance operations; and **4** "black" psychological warfare operations, such as establishing false NVA broadcasting stations inside North Vietnam. Other activities included kidnapping, assassination, the insertion of booby-trapped ammunition into the enemy supply system and the retrieval of sensitive documents or equipment, such as the black box from a U-2 spyplane which crashed on the wrong side of the Cambodian border in December 1966.

Ten of the eleven Pony Express CH-3Cs were conducting covert missions into Laos and North Vietnam when Major Doug Armstrong arrived in October 1966 to command the squadron's "B" Flight, known as the "Woodchoppers." He told the author:

"The call sign of all the 20th Helicopter Squadron CH-3s was Pony Express. Our symbol was a Pony Express rider, with the words "Pony Express" above it and "You Can Guess" below it. Our choppers were black to a very dark camouflage color and had no markings. We flew regularly into North and South Vietnam, Laos and Cambodia.

Our assigned primary mission was counterinsurgency. A typical mission took all day. After an intelligence briefing we would go to a forward base in Thailand or Laos and go for a ride in a Laotian registered airplane with a Laotian pilot and look over our planned landing site and the approaches to it, then return to base. Later that day we would take the choppers, usually two, and fly to one of several dozen sites in Laos where there was one American training team of what we called 'gomers.' Those Americans, who lived in the jungle, are a story in themselves. The gomers came from different tribes in the mountains, some from North Vietnam, China, Thailand and other places. Just before dark we would load them up and take them into the planned landing site at very last light. That gave them a chance to fade into the jungle without being chased until morning. Of course, it was a little hairy going down into the trees when we could barely see the branches. Often there were pungee stakes and sometimes nasty people with guns waiting for us. But we always successfully unloaded the team and got out of there. We used two helicopters, so one would carry the team and go in to land while the other circled high a short distance away in case the low guy

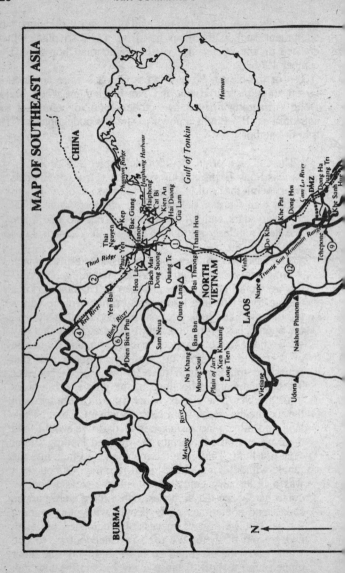

MAP OF SOUTHEAST ASIA

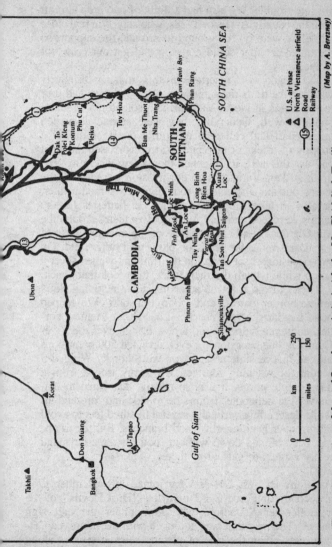

Map of Southeast Asia (with the Ho Chi Minh Trail).

(Map by A. Berzsnay)

got into trouble. We also had a flight of two prop aircraft with us, usually A-1Es or T-28s, who stayed in real close while we were on the ground to provide fire support so the other chopper could come in and get our crew out if necessary.

The teams we inserted in this manner primarily watched the trails through Laos, but we always had four to six teams in North Vietnam and sometimes in Cambodia as well. Generally, they were spaced about ten miles apart and called in all traffic on HF radio. If a convoy of trucks or elephants or troops passed one spot and not the next, intelligence then knew where to send in air strikes. Variations on our mission were to pull the teams out anywhere from four hours to a month later, or also to take supplies to them, i.e. batteries for the radios, kerosene and rice. We kept two teams around the Mu Gia Pass at all times. Some of the missions were to go in and mine the trails or blow up bridges, etc. On two occasions I sat down on the trail and waited several hours while a team did their work, then took them back.

The 20th did a lot of other missions including flood relief, border patrol, and cargo transport. We helped build a radar site very near the Laos/North Vietnam border, and even helped build a new bridge over the River Quai. On one occasion we even dropped 500 paratroops into an inaccessible area. I won the Sikorsky Winged S Medal for rescuing fourteen US Army troops from a deep jungle gorge. It was so narrow that I had to maneuver the helicopter from side to side and fore and aft while descending vertically several hundred feet to avoid hitting over hanging cliffs and branches. But the troops had been pinned down without food for three days and really wanted to get out of there.''

The Pony Express CH-3s were joined in September 1967 by a second Air Force CH-3 unit, the ''Dust Devils'' of the 21st Helicopter Squadron, who flew under the call sign ''Dusty.'' The new unit was equipped with the improved CH-3E and was given the role of placing seismic sensors along the Ho Chi Minh Trail, inserting roadwatch teams and, later, infiltrating MACV-SOG teams. The two helicopter squadrons were redesignated Special Operations Squadrons in August 1968. In the summer of 1969 the 21st SOS absorbed the "Pony Express" CH-3Cs of the 20th SOS and took over their mission.

For the greater part of its career, the primary mission of the 20th SOS was the infiltration and exfiltration of Special Forces teams in an operational area in Laos known as "Prairie Fire," which covered the vast Ho Chi Minh Trail network. In 1967 authorization was given for similar missions into Cambodia under the code name "Daniel Boone." Cross-border operations peaked in 1969 and early 1970, but heavy losses caused a reduction and eventually a halt to such work on 1 July 1970, when the politicians decided to cease US forays into Cambodia.

The 20th Helicopter Squadron received some Bell UH-1F Hueys in June 1967 from the 606th Air Commando Squadron at Nakhon Phanom Air Base (NKP) in Thailand. They had performed a variety of missions at NKP and in Laos, including support of the Thai Border Patrol Police. After joining the 20th, the UH-1Fs flew under the call sign "Green Hornet" and most were based at Nha Trang with the 14th Air Commando Wing, although a couple remained at NKP. Detachments were also located at various times at Kontum and Ban Me Thuot. By May 1968 their strength stood at fifteen Hueys and a detachment was established at Udorn Air Base in Thailand.

The Green Hornets initially used the UH-1F model Huey. The aircraft did not use the Lycoming engines fitted to the Army Hueys, but were built to accept the General Electric T58-GE-3 engine already in use in USAF CH-3 helicopters. This was a very powerful engine, and several design changes were made to accommodate it. The primary recognition feature of this model is the position of the exhaust stack, which emerges on the right side of the fuselage.

Not long after the Green Hornets began operations in Vietnam, some UH-1Fs were modified as gunships and redesignated UH-1Ps. The standard weapon load of the P model was a pair of XM-157A seven-shot rocket pods and two hand-operated GAU-2B/A pintle-mounted miniguns, which were located in each cargo doorway and could be fixed forward for firing by the pilot.

Usually, when a reconnaissance team was to be inserted "across the fence," four gunships would accompany the team's aircraft, together with a command Huey and a spare emergency recovery aircraft. A number of simulated landings would be made to confuse enemy watchers, and at one of these stops the team would get off, move away from the LZ and go to ground until they were sure that the coast was clear. Sometimes the team would be discovered and require immediate extraction. In difficult terrain, where no landing zones were available, McGuire rigs could be used to extract the team. These consisted of three ropes, each with trapeze wrist locks and a sling arrangement. The team member could clip his harness to the sling and be lifted out, trailing below the helicopter until a safe area could be reached to land and pick him up. The accepted rule was that the helicopter which inserted the team would also get them out. Occasionally, all hell would break loose.

On one mission, in February 1968, the nine-man Spike Team Maine was inserted in triple-canopy jungle and 10ft elephant grass near Attopeu, Laos. Unbeknown to them, they had landed on top of a 2,000-man NVA division headquarters and fierce fighting broke out as soon as the helicopters took off. The team comprised three Americans, led by Staff Sergeant Fred Zabitosky, and six Nung tribesmen. As the firefight raged the first helicopter took out several Nungs and Zabitosky and the other team members jumped aboard a second. Their helicopter was almost 100ft in the air when it was hit by a rocket propelled grenade (RPG), and fell to the ground, crushing Zabitosky's ribs. As A-1 Skyraiders strafed the LZ, Zabitosky staggered to the burning Huey and pulled out the two pilots before the fuel cells exploded. A rescue helicopter finally pulled all three men out at another LZ. The nine-man team reportedly killed 165 NVA regulars during the action, which led to Zabitosky receiving the Medal of Honor a year later. Because of the clandestine nature of the mission in supposedly neutral Laos, his citation states that the action took place in South Vietnam.

After the Green Hornets moved to Cam Ranh Bay in late

1970 they began to receive the twin-engined UH-1N. Initially developed by Bell for the Canadian Armed Forces, the UH-1N could carry a greater payload capacity and had the safety feature of two engines. The gunship versions had the XM-157A rocket pods and GAU-2B/A miniguns, or XM-94 rapid-fire hand-operated grenade launchers in lieu of the miniguns, capable of firing 400 rounds per minute. The Green Hornets were finally deactivated in March 1972.

SHOT DOWN AT PLEI ME

In October 1965 the communists tried to cut South Vietnam in half. Three North Vietnamese Army regiments crossed the Cambodian border with the intention of destroying three Special Forces camps, capturing Pleiku and pushing across the country to the sea. On 19 October the Special Forces camp at Plei Me, in northern II Corps, was attacked by 2,000 North Vietnamese Army troops. The camp was defended by 400 Montagnard tribesmen and a dozen Special Forces Green Berets. It soon became apparent that, rather than striking and running away as usual, the enemy were going to stay and fight. All available air support was scrambled to defend the camp, and it included Captain Melvin Elliott of the 1st Air Commando Squadron, whose flight of Skyraiders was diverted to the area. Following on from a flight of F-100s, the Air Commandos dropped napalm around the perimeter, so close to the camp that the pilots noticed that the igniters from the napalm cans were going over the wall into the trenches inside the compound. Mel told the author:

> "Two days later, on the evening of 21 October, I was in the officers' club having a drink with a friend from Hurlburt who was flying AC-47s. He asked me what medals I had been awarded during our tour there and I replied, 'The only ones left are the ones that hurt or scare you'. Then the phone in the club rang and it was the command post asking for A-1E pilots to go on alert. The pilots on alert had just departed on their third mission of the day and would have to be replaced. I rounded up

three other pilots and reported to the command post for briefing. Two of the pilots were scrambled almost immediately, and my wingman and I launched two hours later. We were to rendezvous with a flare ship and Army Caribou cargo 'plane over Plei Me.

We checked in with the flare ship, but the Caribou resupply attempt was cancelled. We had already dropped our napalm and CBUs outside the compound, and I informed the flare ship that we would have to leave the area shortly, but that we could strafe any likely areas with our 20mm cannon before leaving. The compound marked an area with a mortar around and I rolled in on a strafing pass. As I pulled off the target I noticed that things were quite bright. I looked at the left wing and it was ablaze. At this time I called my wingman and notified him that I was on fire. The wingman requested that I turn on my lights so he could see me. My thoughts at that point were that if he could not see me with the fire that was burning, he sure would not see the lights of the aircraft. At that point I planned to maneuver over the compound and bale out (we did not have the Yankee ejection system at this time). Before getting into position over the compound the flares went out, and it was impossible to see the ground. Before this happened the controls of the aircraft failed and I notified all concerned that I was baling out.

As I was attempting to bale out of the aircraft I became stuck against the rear part of the left canopy. My helmet was blown off immediately when I stuck my head out of the cockpit. A few days before I had cut the chin strap as the snap was corroded and would not unfasten. At this point the aircraft was out of control and was rolling due to the fire burning through the left wing. After freeing myself from the aircraft, I reached for the D-ring and discovered it was not in the retainer pocket on the parachute harness. However, I found the cable and followed it to the ring and pulled it. The 'chute opened and shortly afterwards flares lit up the area and I could see that I was going to land in the trees.

After landing in the trees, approximately 50ft above

the ground, I bounced up and down to ensure that the 'chute was not going to come loose and then swung over to the trunk of the tree and grasped a vine nearby. I had lost my hunting knife during the bale out, so I was forced to abandon the survival kit that was part of the parachute. After climbing down the vine to the ground, I sat down and thought about the situation for a short time and assessed what equipment I had. A 0.38-calibre revolver with five rounds of ammo, a pen-gun flare, a strobe light, a two-way radio, which at times was a luxury to A-1 pilots, my Mae West and a brand new chit book from the Bien Hoa Officers Club.

I got out my two-way radio and contacted my wingman, Robert Haines. I told him that I had him in sight and advised him when he was directly overhead and then instructed him to fly from my position to the compound and said that I intended to attempt to make it to the compound. Thirty minutes later he left the area to proceed to Pleiku to refuel.

I proceeded towards the compound, and when I felt I was getting close to the perimeter a severe firefight broke out. At this point I found a likely place to hide out and stayed there the rest of the night. Shortly after dawn I spotted an Army 0-1 orbiting the area and turned on my radio and called him several times before getting an answer. I had forgotten my call sign, and used my name when calling the Bird Dog. By identifying different landmarks the Bird Dog pinpointed my position. I stayed fast all day, and just after dusk the Bird Dog pilot told me that a Huey was coming to get me out.

I was told to get into the best position I could for the pickup and when the Huey arrived on the scene I moved from my hiding place onto a small trail through the brush. When the Huey came around with lights out I turned on my stobe. The Huey made two orbits, and on the third circle came in and turned on his floodlight. At that point a 0.50-calibre machine-gun opened fire about fifty yards from my position. The Huey turned off his light and left the area. Disappointed, I put my strobe in my pocket and got off the trail into the bush and laid as low as possible. About ten minutes later two North Vietnamese soldiers came down the trail with a flashlight. I was about twenty feet off the trail and flat on the ground. The two fellows were chatting as if they were out for a Sunday stroll, and shining their flashlight from one side of the trail to the other. On one of the sweeps of the light it came to within about two feet of me, and then the next sweep was beyond me. After the two fellows were satisfied that I was not in the area, I found a new hiding place and settled down for the rest of the night.

There was no sleep for me, as aircraft were in the area the entire time I was on the ground. Between them and the mortars it was quite noisy. One thing I learned during my tour at Plei Me was that a bomb must get quite close to an individual flat on the ground to cause him any great grief!

As dawn approached, my second on the ground, I heard the familiar sound of a C-47 orbiting the area. I got out of my hiding place and saw an AC-47 orbiting with the business side towards me. The aircraft made a couple of orbits as I was going around the trunk of a large tree similar to a squirrel who is being hunted. Shortly afterwards the AC-47 opened fire with his guns, fired a short burst and departed. I later learned that they had experienced an engine problem and returned to base.

Around 0800 hours I contacted a USAF Bird Dog in the area and through identifying landmarks, again approximately pin-pointed my position. The FAC said he was going to throw smoke grenades to get a better position on me. I didn't really think that was a good idea, but the FAC threw all the smoke he had, but never got close enough for me to see. He advised he was going for more smoke and left the area.

Another Bird Dog arrived and advised me that a chopper was coming to pick me up and to get into a suitable area. I moved into an opening clear of brush but full of grass five to six feet high and rather swampy underneath. Upon reaching the middle of this clearing I contacted the FAC and was advised that the chopper had been diverted on a 'Higher Priority' mission! This was really

the only time while I was on the ground that I was completely demoralised. I proceeded back to the place I had
hidden out all night and then decided that I was going
to move away from the compound to make it easier to
get picked up. During the move, about three-quarters of
a mile, I came across a small stream and washed my
face up somewhat and had a drink. This made me feel
somewhat better.

I came upon a rise in the terrain, and after the climb
I came upon a fair-sized clearing. I spotted a clump of
bamboo and started for it to hide out, when an object
darted out of it! After my heart started again I saw that
it was a wild pig. I crawled into the bamboo thicket and
contacted the Bird Dog orbiting overhead. I again pin-
pointed my position for the pilot, who said he was going
for some food and water as they did not know how long
it would be before I would be picked up. After he left I
realised that the only thing I had that I could open a can
with was my pistol and five rounds of ammo.

After thirty minutes I again contacted the Bird Dog,
and he said to come on the air again in fifteen minutes.
At the time I turned my radio on again I heard several
pilots talking on 'Guard' [the distress channel], several
of whom I recognised as A-1 pilots. The FAC said that
an Air Force HH-43 rescue chopper was about five
minutes out and that the A-1s would be dropping napalm
along a tree line about 100 yards from my position. He
advised me to move into the middle of the clearing as
soon as the A-1s passed over. Doing this, I spotted the
HH-43 coming in about twenty feet off the ground, directly towards me. The pilot got into position and was
forced to hover because of the brush in the grass. This
created a huge wave of grass that I was forced to crawl
through.

Upon getting to the chopper I was dragging many
vines that grew in the grass. The PJ [Para-Jumper rescue
crewman] on the chopper was hanging out the door and
I stepped on to, I thought, the skid, but instead got on
the wheel. As soon as I reached up the PJ told the pilot
he had me and away we went. However, the wheel ro-

tated and I was hanging by my arm and the PJ's arm. I looked up at him and said I was not going back down there alone as he pulled me into the chopper. This was about noon, and I had been on the ground for 36 hours.

After arriving at Bien Hoa an intelligence sergeant from Saigon was there to debrief me, and the most re-dundant question he asked was, 'Captain Elliott, were you scared at any time?' ''

On Monday 25 October a relief force of tanks, APCs and troops arrived at the camp, and the following morning the 2nd Battalion, 1st Brigade, 1st Cavalry Division (Airmobile) ar-rived by helicopter. The ground outside the camp was pitted with bomb craters and blackened by napalm and the number of enemy dead was estimated at between 800 and 900. Their plan to cut the country in half did not succeed, largely because of the arrival of the 1st Cavalry Division (Airmobile). Readers wishing to read further might like to refer to the author's pre-vious book *Vietnam—the Helicopter War* (Airlife 1991).

FORWARD AIR CONTROLLERS

It did not take long for the USAF to discover that their fast-moving jet aircraft found it difficult to locate and attack targets in the jungle. The problem was made worse if there were friendly troops in the area at the time, or indeed if there were troops-in-contact (TIC) with the enemy, urgently requiring air support. The area might also have contained friendly villages and their inhabitants, and fast-moving Phantoms or F-100 Su-per Sabres could not differentiate between friendlies or Viet Cong, unless they were shooting at the aircraft.

What was needed was someone in a low-flying, slow-moving aircraft to liaise with any troops on the ground and then mark the targets for the incoming fighters. Thus the For-ward Air Controller (FAC) was born. In the very early days of Farm Gate, English-speaking Vietnamese Air Force pilots in Cessna O-1 Bird Dogs were used, but they were soon re-placed by USAF FACs as American forces flooded into the country. In the early days in Laos, a handful of Air Commando combat controllers flew as unrated FACs in Air America aircraft to direct strikes against targets in that country. These very brave men, called Butterfly FACs, included Charlie Jones, known to all in the Air Commando Association. They were later followed by the "Ravens," young volunteer USAF pilots who directed air support for Lao irregular forces.

It became the job of the FAC, who usually knew the area like his own back yard, to talk to the troops on the ground, to find and mark the target with smoke rockets, and to direct the strike aircraft, giving them such information as what type of ordnance to use, from which direction to approach and leave the target and where to head if they were hit by groundfire.

The FACs started out flying the old Bird Dog, then in 1967 the twin-engined Cessna 0-2 arrived, followed eventually by the North American OV-10 Bronco. FAC squadrons, known as Tactical Air Support Squadrons, were formed, and they worked closely with all air force units, including the Air Commandos.

Someone, however, had to train the Forward Air Controllers, and the job was given to the Air Commandos in Florida. When the Department of Defense instructed the SAWC to increase its light aircraft training program for FACs heading for Vietnam, it became obvious that traffic in the Eglin complex had already reached saturation point. By the end of 1965, landings and take-offs at Hurlburt Field exceeded 11,000 per month. Consequently the Navy was asked to allow the air force to train FACs at Holley Field, in the southwest corner of the Eglin reservation, and permission was granted. Soon a portable control tower was in place, together with crash rescue equipment, and O-1E training continued at what eventually became a significant training establishment.

The Air Commando room at the Hurlburt Field Officers' Mess contains the pictures of their eight Medal of Honor winners. Two of the men were Forward Air Controllers. Although they served with Tactical Air Support Squadrons rather than with Air Commando or Special Operations Squadrons, they are considered by the Air Commandos to be brothers-in-arms, and therefore the rightful place for their stories is in this book.

Captain Hilliard A. Wilbanks was the first FAC to receive the Medal of Honor posthumously, for his actions on 24 February 1967 whilst flying visual reconnaissance ahead of the South Vietnamese Army 23rd Ranger Battalion. Captain Hilliard was familiar with the Central Highlands of South Vietnam and the rolling, forested countryside around Bao Lac and Di Linh. The chief inhabitants of the region were tribal Montagnards, or ''mountain people'' and, of course the Viet Cong. The South Vietnamese Rangers and their handful of American advisers were searching for signs of the enemy in the area around Di Linh, while Wilbanks circled overhead in his Bird Dog. A pair of US Army UH-1 gunships patrolled nearby.

The enemy had prepared their ambush well. The previous night the Viet Cong had forced local tea plantation workers to dig foxholes and bunkers on the hills west of Di Linh. The fortifications were camouflaged, and the enemy sat back to see who would fall into their trap. Early the following day the Viet Cong had decimated one South Vietnamese platoon and hit two other companies on the hillside. American advisers had been killed and their radios destroyed, so no warning of the danger could be communicated to the advancing Rangers. As dusk approached, Captain Wilbanks, flying his 488th combat mission, checked in by radio with Army Captain R. J. Wooten, the senior adviser, and flew lower to examine the terrain. Suddenly he spotted the camouflaged foxholes on the hillside and sent an urgent warning to Captain Wooten. Realising their ambush had been compromised, the Viet Cong opened fire on the FAC and the Rangers, who dived for cover as machineguns and automatic rifles opened up on them. The tea plantation offered the Rangers little cover, and the forward elements suffered heavy casualties.

Two other companies were pinned down, so Wilbanks fired a white phosphorous marking rocket towards the center of the enemy position and ordered the two nearby gunships to ''hit my smoke.'' Soon afterwards a third helicopter was hit by enemy groundfire, and Wilbanks advised the other gunships to escort it back to friendly territory. Another FAC in the area advised Wilbanks that fighters were on the way, but time was running out for the Rangers and their advisers.

Wilbanks saw movement on the ground. The Viet Cong were leaving their foxholes and advancing towards the badly outnumbered Rangers. The FAC banked his Bird Dog towards the enemy and fired another smoke rocket into their midst, diverting their attention but attracting their groundfire. Time and again Wilbanks dived low to fire his marking rockets at the enemy, flying into a hail of fire each time. When he ran out of rockets he opened the side window of the aircraft, poked out his automatic rifle and continued his attack. "Each pass he was so close we could hear his 'plane being hit," recalled Captain Wooten. On his third firing pass his luck ran out.

Another Ranger adviser, Captain Gary F. Vote, described the end of the gallant pilot's attack.

"He was no more than 100ft off the ground and almost over his objective firing his rifle. Then he began the erratic moves, first up, then down, then banking west right over my position. I thought he was wounded and looking for a friendly spot to land. I jumped up and waved my arms, but as he banked agâin I could see that he was unconscious. His aircraft crashed about 100 meters away, between us and the VC."

Captain Wilbanks was still alive when Captain Vote pulled him from the wreckage. The two helicopter gunships then returned and tried four times to land and pick up the wounded FAC. Finally, two Phantom fighters raked the enemy with their 20mm cannon fire and a helicopter swooped down to pick up Hilliard Wilbanks. Sadly, he died in the helicopter on the way to the treatment center at Bao Lac.

PROJECT QUICK SPEAK: PSYCHOLOGICAL WARFARE

Quick Speak was the project name for the psyops (psychological warfare operations) designated 5th Air Commando Squadron scheduled for deployment to Vietnam. The squadron consisted of sixteen U-10s and four C-47s, all equipped with loudspeaker systems and leaflet dispenser chutes, and they were to carry out operations as directed by the Joint United States Public Affairs Office (JUSPAO). To train the 5th ACS, together with the new AC-47 gunship unit, the 4th Air Commando Squadron, detachment 8 of the 1st ACW, was estab-

lished at Forbes AFB, Kansas, commanded by Colonel
William C. Thomas, back from his TDY with Waterpump.

While the 5th ACS were undergoing training, a TDY complement of six crews and four C-47s were sent to Vietnam in
August. Flying their first missions out of Nha Trang on 1
September, they soon discovered that new speakers were required. In order to use the old speakers the aircraft had to fly
below 1,500ft, where they were subject to groundfire. After
some delay, during which time one crew member was
wounded, new speakers arrived and were installed.

The TDY crews went home when the 5th ACS arrived at
Nha Trang in November 1965, starting operations in December. To supplement the speaker systems, leaflet drops were
made, and in the six months up to June 1966 the squadron
dropped more than 508 million leaflets. A major part of the
Chieu Hoi (Open Arms) programme, the leaflets urged the
Viet Cong to surrender to Government forces, promising them
good treatment and eventual repatriation to their families. In
general, the campaign was very successful and many enemy
soldiers came over to the Government's side. The biggest single operation conducted by the 5th ACS was its Tet program
in January. More than 130 million leaflets were dropped and
380 hours of speaker broadcasts were flown in an effort to
exploit the natural desire of Viet Cong and North Vietnamese
soldiers to be with their families during Tet, the nation's most
important holiday season.

Major Joe Buebe had been flying C-47s for seventeen years
when he joined the 5th ACS. He recalls:

"I flew tests for exhaust flame arresters and lost an engine and damn near never made it into Pham Thiet, because of a power loss on the good engine with the
arrester installed. I also tested out banner towing, but it
was not a good idea. I remember the day that Harvey
Toffet fired up his U-10 during a psywar demonstration
at Nha Trang. He started his take-off roll, turned on his
3,000 Watt speaker and played a tape recording of an
F-100 afterburner kicking in. It tore the roof down, and
some dumb Army General said, 'That's an awful loud
engine for such a small airplane!' "

Lieutenant-Colonel Ralph Evans was one of the psyops U-10 pilots:

"I flew Helio Couriers over enemy positions and over active battlefields, with a Vietnamese in the seat beside me broadcasting messages to the Viet Cong over a loudspeaker, mounted on the side of the aircraft. We also dropped leaflets over enemy positions and ran 'no-doze' night missions over the enemy, playing terrible noises and very loud music over our powerful loudspeakers.

The U-10 is a single-engined small aircraft, built originally for the civilian market. It had enormous wing flaps, fore and aft, which allowed for almost hovering flight, when needed. The castoring landing gear caused many pilots all kinds of trouble. In fact Air America, which also used the 'plane, welded the gear in a forward position because its pilots had so many ground loops with it.

We flew into every kind of unimproved strips out in the countryside and jungle. We dropped infiltrating agents off in some very weird places, guided at night by only two flashlights at midpoint on each side of an otherwise blacked-out, very short, dirt runway. We flew support missions for all of the forward Army positions, landing on the little, very much unimproved dirt runways they would hack out of the jungle.

The results of our 'Chieu Hoi' program were outstanding. While the Army was busy with a sometimes questionable body count, the psychological warfare program convinced 34,000 Viet Cong to give themselves up to our forces in 1967. These people were sent to indoctrination school and could be assigned to non-strategic duties with the Vietnamese Army."

The sister squadron to the 5th was the 9th ACS, and both joined the 14th Air Commando Wing at Nha Trang after it was activated in 1966. Colonel John S. Rogers flew with the 9th from June 1969, after it had been renamed a special operations squadron:

"The squadron was at Nha Trang in II Corps, with flights at Da Nang and Bien Hoa. I was sent to Da Nang as a Captain, the third-ranking officer under the commander and ops officer. The flight consisted of all lieutenants fresh out of pilot training. We had six Cessna O-2B Skymasters and two C-47s. The O-2s were equipped with speakers and leaflet chutes, the interiors were off-the-shelf factory, the exteriors in camouflage green paint.

I flew the O-2B, and the missions were simple; at night the Army would plot targets primarily over friendly territory where the locals would be good guys during the day and bad guys at night. All day we would orbit those targets, and, using a tape recording, send the government message to give up arms and receive money and other goods for the family. Sometimes we would have a Vietnamese on board to deliver a live message.

The O-2 was not armed, nor protected from enemy fire. We used to sit on our flak jackets for some protection. The C-47 was not equipped with speakers, but with a leaflet chute. Their mission was to drop leaflets over some of the same targets, but mostly over the higher country and out of the country like Laos.

Since we flew strictly VFR [visual flight rules] weather played a factor during the monsoon season. Some days we would stay home rather than fly a target at tree-top level. For speakers to be effective, we would fly between 1,000 to 2,000ft AGL.

Another mission we had was to fly an evening visual recon flight around the base, to help ensure the security of the base. Our 'planes would often come back with bullet holes from these flights. As far as I know, none of the 'planes were shot down while on any mission. The C-47 did manage to fly right through an Arc Light B-52 strike while over Laos one day. It seemed the morning intel brief plotted the B-52 mission incorrectly. We were at 10,000ft and the 'plane began to bounce around from the explosions directly below us. I was just riding around in the C-47 that day. That was the last

time I did that. From then on I just stuck to my own
'plane!''

THE ORGANISATION GROWS

The 1st Air Commando Wing possessed 117 aircraft at Hurlburt Field in October 1965. With so many aircraft and so little
space, the Wing headquarters was transferred to England AFB,
Louisiana in January 1966 and at the same time Detachment
2, 1st ACW was attached to the 4420th Combat Support
Group at Hurlburt. The 4410th Combat Crew Training Wing
remained at Hurlburt Field and the 1st ACW stayed at England
AFB until it returned to Hurlburt in July 1969.

With the expansion to two wings in SAWC, training requirements increased to an anticipated annual rate of 1285 aircrew
and 1800 maintenance personnel. Pacific Air Force (PACAF)
needed 66 more air liaison officers and forward air controllers
during the first ten months of 1966 and they needed 498 O-1
pilots by March 1967. The O-1 training program was now
gathering momentum, so the SAWC asked for a minimum of
25 O-1E/Fs for FAC training at Holley Field.

Another training requirement sprung upon the SAWC was
Project Phyllis Ann, involving two squadrons of airborne Radio Detection Finding C-47Ds to be used in Vietnam. Each
squadron would have eighteen aircraft, so Tactical Air Command and SAWC were asked to train 52 aircrews and ferry
the aircraft from the modification plant to Vietnam. Finding
qualified instructors was a problem as the Big Shoot and Quick
Speak C-47 programmes were also underway at the same time.

Between July and August the 6th ACS at Hurlburt should
have had fourteen A-1E, but never had more than four. These
were used in a test program conducted jointly by the services
to check out instrumentation pods used to determine accuracy
in finding specific targets and pilots ability to keep the aircraft
on course. At the end of August all four A-1Es departed for
Vietnam, leaving the 6th ACS with only four T-28s to perform
their mission of dive bombing, skip bombing, strafing and
rocket fire training.

More reorganisation was taking place in South Vietnam. On 8 March 1966 the C-123 equipped 315th Air Commando Group was raised to Wing status. At the same time, the 14th Air Commando Wing came into being at Nha Trang Air Base. The wing's operations included close and direct air support, interdiction, combat airlift, aerial resupply, visual and photographic reconnaissance, psychological warfare (including leaflet dropping and loudspeaker broadcasting), forward air control and FAC escort, escort for convoy and defoliation operations, flare drops and search and rescue. To carry out these operations the 14th ACW had five squadrons; The 1st ACS was transferred to them with 25 A-1Es, 4 U-10s and 6 C-47s; the 5th ACS was responsible for psywar activities, using 16 U-10 Helio Couriers and 6 C-47s; the 602nd FS(C) was there with its A-1s until transfer to Udorn RTAFB in April 1966; the 20th Helicopter Squadron arrived with its 14 Sikorsky CH-3C helicopters and later 15 UH-1Fs, and lastly the 4th ACS with its 16 Spooky AC-47 gunships.

Other squadrons joined the wing as time went by. A second psywar squadron, the 9th ACS, arrived in January 1967 with 16 U-10s and 6 C-47s. A second AC-47 squadron, the 14th ACS, was given to the Wing in October 1967, being renamed the 3rd ACS in May 1968. The 6th Air Commando Squadron and its Skyraiders was attached to the wing briefly from February to July 1968. They were joined by the 15th ACS in March. The 15th was equipped with Combat Talon C-130s and flew clandestine missions into North Vietnam and later Cambodia and Laos, in conjunction with the CH-3s of the two helicopter squadrons. The wing was also responsible for a new addition to the Air Commando inventory which arrived in July 1967, when 25 Cessna A-37 Dragonfly jets flew into Bien Hoa under the code name 'Combat Dragon'. The A-37s belonged to the 604th ACS and were ideal ground attack aircraft. Armed with a 7.62mm minigun and fitted with eight wing pylons capable of carrying 5,680lb of ordnance, they were faster than the Skyraider but inferior in range and payload. The last squadrons to join the 14th ACW were the AC-119 gunship-equipped 71st Special Operations Squadron (later renamed the 17th SOS) and the 18th SOS.

VALOUR IN THE A SHAU VALLEY

The first Medal of Honor for an Air Commando in Vietnam was won on a dark day for the US armed forces in March 1966. American soldiers were rarely defeated in open battle, but that changed on 10 March, when the North Vietnamese attacked the special forces camp in the A Shau Valley. The valley was a place to avoid like the plague; situated in I Corps Tactical Zone, two miles from the Laotian border, it was part of a major communist infiltration route from the Ho Chi Minh Trail in Laos, through the valley and into the populated areas of the northwest provinces and the ancient capital city of Hue. In an attempt to deny the Viet Cong and North Vietnamese Army the use of the valley, a Special Forces fortified camp had been established. Surrounded by steep jungle-covered mountains, the camp was manned by 17 Green Berets and 375 South Vietnamese Civilian Irregular Defense Group Soldiers.

At 0300 hours on 9 March the 95th NVA Regiment began a two-hour bombardment of the camp, followed by a probe of its southern defences. The enemy had planned their attack well; bad weather hampered fixed-wing support and the camp was outside artillery range. As the casualties mounted, two Marine H-34s flew in under the overcast and tried to pick up the wounded, but one was shot down and crashed in the compound.

Just before midday an AC-47 gunship was despatched to the valley and eventually the pilot, Captain Willard M. Collins, flying at almost treetop level, found his way under the clouds and made one firing pass at the attackers. During the second pass intense groundfire tore the aeroplane's starboard engine from its mount and silenced the other engine only seconds later. The gunship crash-landed on a mountain slope about seven miles from the camp, and one crew member had his legs broken. The other crewmembers prepared for an expected enemy attack and barely repulsed the first wave, fifteen minutes after the crash. A second attack, however, killed the pilot and the injured crewman. An Air Force rescue helicopter dropped through the clouds to pick up the remaining survivors just as another attack began. Using an M-16 rifle and a 0.38-calibre pistol, the copilot, Lieutenant Delbert R. Peterson, charged an enemy 0.50-calibre machine-gun position, but the brave lieutenant was never seen again.

The situation in the camp was desperate, and the defenders were sorely in need of more ammunition and medical supplies. Two C-123s from the 311th Air Commando Squadron, "Harry's Hog Haulers," were given the task. First Lieutenant Marc L. Bornn was one of the two aircraft commanders, and he recalls:

"I had just returned to Da Nang with First Lieutenant Herbert M. Busby after a resupply mission to Gia Vuc special forces camp in the Central Highlands. Mac Busby and I were both instructor pilots, designated the squadron's Lead Crew, which meant we performed most of the more demanding low-level paradrops and special missions.

At squadron Ops we received our briefing for our next mission, a low-level paradrop resupply of ammunition and medical supplies into the A Shau special forces camp, which was on the verge of being overrun by several thousand Regular North Vietnamese troops. This came as no surprise, as two days earlier I had flown in a 'plane load of Chinese Nung troops and their special forces advisers, to beef up the defences.

This particular camp was one of the 'sportier' locations to fly into. It sat at the south end of the ten-mile-long valley that was up to 3,000ft deep and extremely narrow, only half a mile wide in places. I knew that I could always expect to pick up enemy groundfire when in the A Shau.

Each aircraft was loaded with six pallets containing 1,800lb of ammunition and medical supplies and rigged for low-level paradrop. Since two aircraft were needed, I was paired up with Ronald Trickey, and Marc Busby was with William Devoe in the second bird. We all took off from Da Nang and flew northwest for about 30 minutes, climbing to about 8,000ft to top a solid cloud bank and upon reaching a point over the valley, checked in on UHF with an orbiting airborne command post C-130.

When I checked in on the Tactical FM frequency, which all aircraft and the A Shau camp were using, I could tell that the situation on the ground was grave and that our cargo was sorely needed. However, the weather was terrible, solid cloud cover from 8,000ft right down to within 50 to 300ft of the valley floor, completely obliterating any landmarks and the mountains that surrounded the valley.

As we orbited at 8,000ft above A Shau, we were in the company of many other tactical aircraft. There was a flight of A-1E Skyraiders, a flight of B-57 bombers, together with various other Air Force and Navy jet fighters . . . all waiting for a break in the weather to make our descent to A Shau. The only aircraft down in the valley at this time was an AC-47 'Magic Dragon' gunship, which had been shot down, and a flight of two Skyraiders performing strafing runs. One of these Skyraiders suddenly popped up through the clouds, flown by Major Bernard Fisher, from the 1st Air Commando Squadron, and he says that he knows of a hole down through the clouds to the valley floor and thinks that he could lead us in.

Both C-123s proceeded to follow Fisher as he dived through the hole in the clouds, with great hopes of breaking out in the valley and not the mountains. I had been trained as a fighter pilot and never thought I would see the day when I would have to put that training into practice, in order to attempt to maneuver this fully loaded assault transport through such a tight flight profile. The C-123s were on the tail of the Skyraider in a tight, almost vertical spiral with the vertical speed needle hitting over 4,000ft per minute! The turns had to be tight to stay VFR in the hole and not slam into the mountains. I put flaps, gear and full increase on the prop pitch in order to help slow the spiral dive. At these extremes, I knew that we were exceeding the aircraft's speed limits and g loadings, and the two loadmasters in the back were getting banged around pretty badly. We finally made it down to the valley, pulling out of the dive at about 50ft above the treetops, cleaned the aircraft up (retracting the gear and the flaps) and started to run down the valley to the camp.

The cloud ceiling at 100 to 250ft above the trees made it seem as though we were flying in some dingy twilight tunnel due to the narrowness of the valley. I flew down the side of the valley, as close to the treetops as possible, thus reducing our exposure to groundfire and hopefully ensuring that I would have enough room to execute a 180° turn if the clouds and fog became too severe. I estimated my position to be about seven miles North of the camp as I passed over Alui special forces camp, which we had abandoned months earlier. As we skimmed along towards our destination, we started picking up VC groundfire about five miles out. Looking out the open-sided cockpit window, I could actually see VC with their automatic rifles raised, firing at us as we passed over clearings. About this time we passed by the wreckage of the AC-47 gunship, and couldn't help thinking that it would have been nice to have had their firepower covering us. With each passing mile the enemy groundfire became more intense, with the addition now of 30-and 50-calibre machine-gun fire.

Through the misty gloom the camp now appeared, about a mile ahead, lying in a slightly wider portion of the valley. The only section of the camp still in friendly hands was the small triangular area and this would be our Drop Zone. Major Fisher and his wingman in their Skyraiders, together with two B-57 Canberras from the 8th Bomb Squadron at Da Nang, were now making low-level strafing passes while we prepared to make our drop passes. It was crowded, to say the least, with six different aircraft all manoeuvering in that very confined airspace in low light and visibility and with intense hostile fire. All of the aircraft and the camp were on a common FM radio frequency so the radio chatter was continuous and from all directions. During this last mile coming in over the camp we started to pick up 12.7 and 20mm anti-aircraft fire, in addition to the 30-and 50-cal machine-gun and small-arms fire, and not only from below, but from up on the valley walls as well, with some of the anti-aircraft guns almost firing down on us! It was like a classic anti-aircraft trap . . . they had us bracketed. Flying at treetop level kept a lot of the gunners from getting a good bead on us; by the time they started to walk the tracer into us, we were gone and they were firing into the treetops.

We lined up for our first drop pass, pulled up to gain altitude so the 'chutes would open on the pallets and to drop speed. We were now at our most vulnerable. The tracer fire was very heavy, criss-crossing in front of the nose and behind the aircraft. There was a sense of unreality about it, the red and green tracer rounds seemed to be floating at you like balls of cotton until they came abeam, and then they would accelerate at Mach 2 past you, all of this in a surreal miasma.

On our first pass we dropped two of the 1,800lb pallets on the DZ. I then dropped down to treetop level and cranked a hard left turn, mostly skidded with the rudder so that I would not put the wingtip in the trees, and headed back up the valley in order to give Mac Busby, in the other C-123 enough time to make his first drop and then to come hard around back over the DZ for his second drop. As he completed his second drop, and we were heading back for the camp again, we could see his aircraft completely bracketed by tracer. It was a wonder that he didn't take a hit. His last pallet missed the DZ and over the FM common frequency we heard that the VC were running to get it. One of the B-57 pilots punched his mike button and said, 'I'll take care of the bastards,' and he rolled in and pickled off a napalm canister on the VC. Now the surroundings looked even more otherworldly with the added orange glow from the napalm. The friendlies were able to recover the pallet with this diversion.

The camp radioed and advised us to abort our last drop pass, as the anti-aircraft fire on Busby's last pass had been so intense, but as we were within twenty seconds of the DZ we decided to press on, and we knew how badly-needed the ammo and medical supplies were. Strings of tracer were streaming all around us as we cleared the last pallet; we applied max power to get out and that is when we took a hit. It sounded as though someone had fired a 0.45-cal pistol right next to your ear. It was either a 12.7 or 20mm high explosive tipped shell, and it hit us in the belly, just aft of the cockpit. The explosion tore a 12in hole in the belly and turned the metal "skate wheel" cargo rollers into shrapnel.

Some of the shrapnel hit a large box of cargo tie-down chains that was positioned behind the cockpit, and the remainder went up through the upper fuselage, taking with it two wire bundles which provided electrical power for all the cockpit instrumentation! My immediate concern was the airworthiness of the aircraft and the safety of my crew. The flight controls were not damaged and the 'plane handled normally. I could set the power by the sound of the engines, and keep the aircraft upright as long as I had reference to the ground. We had the most basic instruments left, needle, ball, airspeed indicator and whiskey (magnetic) compass for the climb out of the A Shau valley in the clouds.

We were glad to leave the hostile arena below and climb up into the cloud cover, but we were not home free yet. We had to endeavour to keep the aircraft upright using the most basic of instruments and thread the eye of a narrow and precipitous mountain valley with a heading from a precessing magnetic compass. First Lieutenant David Hosley, our squadron paradrop navigator, gave me a heading to hold while we climbed out of the valley. We will never know how close or far we were from slamming into the valley wall when we topped the clouds at 8,000ft, it was the brightest and most glorious sun that I had ever seen.

Only twenty minutes had elapsed since we had plunged into the valley on Bernie Fisher's tail, but it seemed like an eternity. We got a radar steer back to Da Nang and landed uneventfully, to discover that we had also taken hits in the right prop and the tail.''

The heavily outnumbered defenders managed to keep the enemy at bay for the rest of the day and night, with C-123s dropping almost 400 flares during the night to illuminate the area. At 0400 hours on 10 March the NVA began their final assault, breaching the southern and eastern defences. With the enemy pouring into the compound, the defenders retreated across the runway to the communications bunker or into hastily-built fighting positions along the northern wall. Some CIDG irregulars fought bravely, while others surrendered to the enemy *en masse*. At 1000 hours the detachment commander asked that the camp be strafed and bombed with the exception of the communications bunker and the north wall.

By now another flight of Skyraiders had arrived above the clouds and was looking for a way down. Fortunately, Major Bernie Fisher and his wingman, Captain Francisco "Paco" Vazques were back on the scene, and they led the flight down through another hole in the clouds, followed by Wayne Dafford "Jump" Myers, the detachment commander of the 602nd Air Commando Squadron and the rest of his flight; Captains Hubert King, Jon Lucas and Dennis Hague.

Once under the clouds the Skyraiders found themselves in "The tube," as the narrow valley was nicknamed: there was little room to maneuver for the bombing and strafing runs against the attackers. The pilots were forced to fly straight down the valley, deliver their ordnance and then turn 180° and fly back the way they had come.

As the first four Skyraiders made their first pass down the tube, a score of anti-aircraft weapons and hundreds of automatic weapons opened fire on them. Captain Hubert King's canopy was shattered, so he pulled up and headed for the nearest airfield.

As Fisher led the two remaining Skyraiders back down the tube again, Major Myers felt his machine lurch. He recalled:

"I've been hit by 50 calibres before, but this was something bigger, maybe the Chinese 37mm cannon. Almost immediately the engine started sputtering and cutting out and then it conked out for good. The cockpit filled with smoke. I got on the radio and gave my call sign, Surf 41, and said, 'I've been hit and hit hard'. Hobo 51, that

was Bernie, came right back and said, 'Rog, you're on
fire and burning clear back past your tail!' I was way
too low to bale out, so I told him I would have to put
it down on the camp airstrip.''

As the blazing aircraft cleared the threshold, Myers realised
that he was going too fast to stop and raised his landing gear
for a crash landing. The belly fuel tank blew as he touched
down, and a sheet of flame followed the aircraft as it skidded
several hundred feet before coming to rest beside the runway.
Myers climbed out of the cockpit, ran along the wing and
sought shelter in the brush alongside the strip as the remaining
Skyraiders made repeated strafing attacks to protect the fort
and the downed airman. The Viet Cong were all around Myers, and there was no time to wait for a rescue helicopter.
Fisher decided to land and pick Myers up himself:

"I turned and touched down just about the end of the
runway. I used all the brakes I could, but the strip was
only 2,000ft long. This was the only time I was scared,
because it didn't look like I was going to be able to stop.
I hit the brakes as hard as I could and pulled the flaps
up, which gave me a little more weight on the brakes. I
think I must have been skidding on that steel planking.
It was a little bit slick from the dampness. I actually
went off the end of the runway a little way. There were
a lot of 55gal drums sitting out in the reeds, and in my
mind I was sure I would hit them. My tail did when I
turned, but the wing went right over the top of them.''

Fisher taxied back down the obstacle course, looking for
Myers, and hit the brakes as he saw him waving vigorously.
Myers ran as fast as his 46-year-old legs would carry him and
began to crawl up the trailing edge of Fisher's wing. Fisher
grabbed Myers and pulled him head-first onto the floor of the
cockpit. "It was hard on his head, but he didn't complain,''
said Fisher later. Major Fisher accelerated down the strip,
dodging the shell craters and debris, and lifted off, heading
for Pleiku Air Base in his Skyraider, which had been hit nine-

teen times. The remaining Skyraiders had continued to bomb and strafe the enemy until they ran out of ammunition, and after the battle 300 enemy bodies were counted along the wall of the A Shau outpost.

As the day wore on, the American high command realised that they had little choice left and their time was running out. Bad weather was restricting the air support operation and the camp had to be evacuated, which, under the circumstances, was easier said than done. Finally the decision was made to abandon the camp and at about 1730 hours sixteen Marine UH-34s, together with six UH-1E gunships, approached the camp. The plan was for the able-bodied men to fight a rearguard action while the wounded were taken to the LZ about 300 yards north of the camp. However, as soon as the helicopters approached, the South Vietnamese panicked and abandoned the wounded, pouring over the north wall towards the LZ. The helicopters found themselves swamped with men clambering over each other to get into the helicopters, and finally the Americans fired into the hysterical men to try to create some sort of order. Suddenly a recoilless rifle round hit one of the helicopters and it crashed nearby, the crew joining the Special Forces on the ground. A second UH-34 went down and three others were damaged. Only 69 defenders went out with the helicopters, including four Special Forces. The rest of the able-bodied survivors escaped into the jungle to escape and evade back to friendly lines.

The UH-34s of HMM-163 picked up about 100 more survivors from the jungle over the next couple of days. The losses were high; a total of 248 members of the garrison were dead or missing, including five Green Berets. The camp would not be re-opened, and its demise led to increased enemy infiltration of men and material through the valley into central I Corps.

As for "Jump" Myers and Bernie Fisher, and the other Air Commando pilots flying close air support that day, on 19 January 1967 President Johnson awarded Bernie Fisher the Medal of Honor for his actions. He was the first Air Force member to receive the medal for action in Vietnam. Sadly Colonel Wayne Dafford "Jump" Myers passed away on 23 May 1992.

BACK FROM THE DEAD:
THE RESCUE OF DIETER DENGLER

With US Navy aircraft carriers now on station in the Gulf of Tonkin, the colorful "Spads" of Navy Attack Squadron VA-52, the "Knight Riders" and VA-145, the "Swordsmen," appeared in the skies over North Vietnam. They made their debut on 5 August 1964, whilst taking part in naval air strikes against torpedo boat installations and petroleum, oil and lubricants (POL) sites in North Vietnam, in retaliation for real and imaginary attacks on Navy destroyers in the Gulf of Tonkin. One VA-52 Skyraider was shot down, the first American combat loss over North Vietnam.

For the duration of the war, US Navy aircraft carriers were present on Yankee Station, a geographical point in the Gulf of Tonkin, from which missions were launched daily against North Vietnam. Dixie Station was established off the coast of South Vietnam and a single aircraft carrier operated from that location, supporting the ground war in the South until the Air Force moved enough squadrons in-country to manage on their own.

It was rare for Navy pilots to be shot down and captured over South Vietnam, and to go down over the North automatically earned the pilot a place in one of half-a-dozen prison camps, such as the Hanoi Hilton, as the Hoa Lo prison in the capital of North Vietnam was known. However, to be shot down over Laos, while supporting the Royal Lao Army or attacking the Ho Chi Minh supply trail, was bad news. Officially there were no US forces operating in Laos, and the American government was still denying the fact when over 200 pilots had been killed or captured in that war-torn country. One such unfortunate pilot was Navy Lieutenant Dieter Dengler, who launched with a flight of four A-1Js from the deck of the USS *Ranger* on 2 February 1966. The four "Swordsmen" from VA-145 crossed North Vietnam and entered Laos near the Mu Gia Pass, a heavily defended infiltration point where the Ho Chi Minh Trail enters Laos from North Vietnam. Accurate anti-aircraft fire soon brought Dengler's aircraft tumbling to the ground in a crash landing from which he miraculously walked away. Captured by the Pathet Lao and thrown into a prison camp* with a handful of other American and Thai prisoners, Dengler was treated barbarically and his weight dropped from 170 to 90lb. Six months after his shoot down Dengler and some of the other captives overpowered their guards and escaped into the jungle. Days later, alone, starving and weak, Dengler lay down on a flat rock in the middle of a stream and prepared to die. Luck was with him however, as a flight of Skyraiders appeared overhead and, by a thousand-to-one chance, Lieutenant-Colonel Eugene P. Deatrick, commander of the 1st ACS, glimpsed his frantic waving. Within minutes a Jolly Green Giant rescue helicopter arrived to winch him to safety. Nothing was ever heard of the other escapees and, indeed, at the war's end the American government declined for political reasons to attempt to negotiate the release of the many American pilots then held captive by the Pathet Lao. History has largely ignored this disgusting state of affairs, and the majority of the men must surely now be dead. The possibility still exists, however, that American pilots may still be held in Southeast Asia, 22 years after the ceasefire.

PROJECT STRAY GOOSE: COMBAT TALON ARRIVES

The use of the Lockheed C-130 Hercules in what is generally known today as the Combat Talon project began at Pope Air Force Base, North Carolina, in 1966. The program involved the modification of a small number of C-130s to enable them to penetrate enemy defences in support of unconventional warfare operations. Four specially modified UWC-130Es (later MC-130Es) were deployed in late 1966 to Ching Chuan Kang Air Base, Taiwan, and later to Nha Trang Air Base in South

*Some months after Dengler's escape, the camp location was pinpointed and air commando Major Dick Secord, working with the CIA, organised a raid on the camp by native CIA guerrillas. It was a complete success and 82 "friendlies" were freed. No Americans were found however, but it was the only successful POW rescue staged during the whole war.

Vietnam, assigned as Detachment 1 of the 314th Tactical Airlift Wing.

The project actually started in September 1964 as a study project known as "Thin Slice," to support a classified South East Asia program called "Heavy Chain." Four C-130Es, including two Skyhooks (see below) were modified with electronic surveillance capability and a terrain-following navigation system, together with various additional electronic modifications and improvements during 1965. These modifications, which were made under the Rivet Yard I and II designation, were followed by further modifications over the following six years. These included fuel tank baffling, high speed low level air delivery system (HSLLADS), forward looking infrared (FLIR) and System 56 Self-Protection. Testing was carried out by the 1198th Operation Evaluation and Test Squadron, "Combat Sam," between 1964 and 1972.

Between July 1966 and June 1967 twelve more brand new C-130E(I) Skyhook-equipped aircraft were also modified under the Rivet Clamp project. They were fitted with aerial refuelling equipment, terrain following and terrain avoidance radar, an inertial navigation system, a high-speed aerial delivery system and the Fulton surface-to-air recovery system. The aircraft could penetrate hostile airspace at low altitudes, in night or adverse weather conditions, and locate small drop zones and deliver people or equipment with greater accuracy and higher speeds than possible with a standard C-130. Two were lost in 1967, so two standard C-130 aircraft were modified to the electronic configuration of the other aircraft. However, unlike the other Rivet Clamp aircraft, they were not fitted with the Fulton "Skyhook" recovery system.

Fulton Recovery system aircraft could be identified by the "open-arms" yoke fitted to the nose and they could be used to recover personnel or equipment from land or water. A man on the ground would don a protective suit and harness and then attach it to a 500ft nylon lift line, connected to a large helium filled balloon. The balloon would be inflated and the line lifted aloft. The pilot would fly towards the balloon, aim for the line, and grab it with the scissor-like arms fixed to the aircraft's nose, snatching the man from the ground with less shock than that caused by a parachute opening. The man would trail below and behind the aircraft until snagged and pulled into the open rear cargo door. During the Vietnam war no actual combat pickups or rescues were made, however.

The deployment to Vietnam was known by the code name Stray Goose, and the aircraft flew in support of MACV-SOG cross-border operations. Their first mission took place on 20 October 1966 and became a milestone in SOG airlift support, with the new C-130s able to carry more than twice the load for greater distances than the First Flight Detachment C-123s, and at greater speed. They also participated in the Fact Sheet Programme, in which 77 million leaflets and 15,000 gift kits were dropped over North Vietnam.

One C-130 was lost to mortar fire at Nha Trang in November 1967, and a second failed to return after a mission on 29 December 1967. The second C-130E, tail number 64-0547 reportedly struck a mountain in Laos, although a second report suggested that it was hit over North Vietnam and crashed in Laos. Apparently the aircraft commander, Major Edwin Osborne, was awarded a posthumous Silver Star for completing "a combat air drop of vital importance to unconventional warfare operations, after penetrating his aircraft through heavy hostile defences, marginal weather conditions and in an incompletely charted mountainous area to deliver the drop load." What happened thereafter is unknown. Chuck Timms, a former member of the unit, sent the author the names of the crewmembers, and they are included here to honor their memory;

> Major Charles P. Claxton, pilot.
> Major Edwin N. Osborne, Jr., pilot.
> Captain Gerald G. Van Buren, pilot.
> Major Donald E. Fisher, navigator.
> Captain Frank C. Parker, III, navigator.
> Captain Gordon J. Wenaas, navigator.
> A1C Edward J. Darcy, loadmaster.
> A1C James R. Williams, loadmaster.
> SSgt. Wayne A. Eckley, flight engineer.
> TSgt. Jack McCrary, flight engineer.
> SSgt. Gean P. Clapper, radio operator.

Although they were listed on the manifest as above, some may have performed other functions, such as the navigators, who may have been electronic warfare officers.

During its six years at Nha Trang the unit changed titles three times; in March 1968 to the 15th Air Commando Squadron, under the command of the 14th ACW, and in November 1968 to 15th Special Operations Squadron. In November 1970 the 15th SOS became the 90th Special Operations Squadron. In April 1972 the unit moved to Kadena Air Base, Okinawa, and in December 1972 it was again redesignated to its current title, the 1st Special Operations Squadron.

Although the squadron's name changed over the years, the mission remained the same; to provide tactical support to US and Allied special forces operating in Southeast Asia. During this period the squadron flew its MC-130Es in various unconventional-warfare campaigns; including psychological warfare operations over North Vietnam and covert resupply of special forces operating throughout the area. Since January 1973, when operations in Vietnam were terminated, the unit has been involved in proficiency training, support of unconventional warfare exercises and operational missions as directed by US Commander in Chief Pacific (CINCPAC).

The squadron moved to Clark Air Base in the Philippines on 15 January 1981. On 1 March 1981, when MAC assumed responsibility for the management of Special Operations Forces, the 1st SOS was assigned to MAC's newly established 2nd Air Division, with headquarters at Hurlburt Field. On 1 February 1987 the 2nd Air Division was deactivated and the 1st SOS came directly under 23rd Air Force, headquartered at Hurlburt. In April 1989 the 353rd SOW was established at Clark Air Base and the 1st SOS was placed under its management.

The 1st SOS MC-130Es of the 1990s are highly modified aircraft and include a highly accurate inertial navigation system, a FLIR sensor, a high-speed low-level aerial delivery system, electronic counter-measures equipment, a multimode terrain-following and ground-mapping radar system and an in flight refuelling capability. The aircraft are designed to penetrate hostile airspace at low altitudes, and crews are specially trained in night and adverse weather operations.

Apart from the 1st SOS, whose Far East Combat Talon detachment is known as "Combat Spear," the 7th SOS based in England as part of USAFE, also fly the Talon, under the code name "Combat Arrow." The 318th SOS "Combat Knife" at Pope AFB trained replacements for the two squadrons between 1967 and 1974, and then became the 8th SOS with the 1st SOW at Hurlburt Field. A fourth Talon squadron, the 15th SOS, flying the MC-130H Talon II, has recently joined the 8th at Hurlburt Field.

CAN SPOOKY KILL TRUCKS?

In January 1966 the decision was made to try out the AC-47 over the Ho Chi Minh Trail in Laos, in the truck hunting role. In February four aircraft from the 4th ACS detachment at Binh Thuy were sent to Thailand to join two others sent in haste to try to stop the North Vietnamese overrunning Lima Site 36 in Laos. One of the pilots, Captain Theodore M. Faurer, later recalled:

"Apparently William Sullivan, the American Ambassador to Laos, and General Westmoreland wanted more interdiction on the Ho Chi Minh Trail. The decision was made to unleash the AC-47 on the infiltrators. We were to become truck killers in Laos.

Our crew loaded all our belongings 'Okie-style' in the AC-47, motorcycles and all, and flew north to Udorn, Thailand. Three other crews and aircraft from other places joined in the migration north. As we flew north we wondered what was up. We didn't know why we were going to Udorn.

A couple of days of briefings and a few orientation flights provided the answer. Two slightly different wars had been going on up there. Kong Le and his forces were fighting in the Plaine des Jarres [PDJ] area, and of course the North Vietnamese were engaging in large-scale infiltration of men and equipment southwards along a series of roads and trails in the eastern portion of the Laotian panhandle. We were there to help the friendlies and to inderdict the infiltration. To our surprise, we learned that the US had been doing these two missions for a long time and that our losses had been significant.

Before starting our actual missions over the PDJ we flew a couple of day high-altitude orientation flights. We looked over the road network and couldn't help but see the inhospitable terrain. We also saw the bare brown areas on some of the hilltops. These were landing strips used by Air America, also based at Udorn, to resupply the friendly hill tribes. The remoteness of the area confirmed our doubts that we would be out of contact with anyone but those other unfortunate 'locals' on the ground. If we lost an engine it was highly unlikely we could get back out of the Plaine area and over the mountains of Thailand. The local joke about the remoteness of this operation was that the only way you were known to have had trouble was when someone noticed you were not at breakfast the next morning.

The typical mission in this area differed slightly from the delta operations. Usually there was only one mission a night, beginning at dusk. Again we often had an interpreter, but now he was usually a young Laotian T-28 pilot who was not only familiar with flying but with the target area as well. Usually he spoke fairly good English. The most frequent mission was to go out and find and attack our own targets along the road network. We did not find very many targets. The other variation, which we flew a couple of times, was similar to the technique used in the delta. However, once in contact with the ground, the scenario was interestingly different. The voice on the ground would tell you that they would fire an artillery flare. When it illuminated we would see certain buildings or something the voice had described. Our target was referenced from this and we would supply some firepower, then move onto the next target.

Of course, there was the time one of the air attachés requested that our crew drop some smoke bombs on the Chinese Embassy in Luang Prabang. The fact that it would be done in the daytime and against a defended and unfriendly target disinclined our detachment commander.

There was also the time we were sent up to the Plaine in the daytime to drop off some very important cargo at the friendly airstrip near Muong Houn. We found and landed on the long dirt strip which had been cut out of the side of the hill. Fortunately the Pathet Lao had already mortared it that day. To our surprise we saw a scene out of 'Terry and the Pirates'; Thai artillery, US personnel and Laotians, all living in primitive conditions. I'll always remember our departure as I said to Bill Powers, my copilot, 'Max power, Bill', as we watched the ridge lines approach, and approach, during take-off—we held the throttles in the full bent forward position.

The other mission, and a much more frequent one, was over the trails in the Laotian panhandle. Before describing a typical mission along the trails I need to provide my partial knowledge of some background. While still in the delta we heard some rumours about some of our squadron flying some new kinds of mission outside Vietnam. Then we heard about the loss of one of our crews in late December 1965. Seems there was a Mayday signal tracked over Laos, northwest of Pleiku, at the same time one of our aircraft was flying an experimental day recce/interdiction mission. The rumour had it that there was some doubt that it was our crew's Mayday; some spoofing may have been involved. In any case the aircraft and crew never returned. This was our second loss. The first had been my old advance party leader, Major Abbott, whose aircraft hit a ridge line in the Phan Rang area in the weather while on an administrative flight, just a week before the loss in Laos. I believe the report mentioned that bullet holes were found in the rudder and it was reported as a combat loss.

After the rumour about the loss of the second aircraft and crew, we did hear some rumours of night missions in Laos, but we knew no details. Our initial briefings upon arrival at Udorn filled in the picture. AC-47s were being flown from Pleiku and Da Nang against the Steel

Tiger and Tiger Hound sectors of the Laotian panhandle
(the areas just north and south of the 17th parallel). We
would now commence operations in a more northerly
sector of the panhandle.

Again we initially flew day orientation missions over
the known road and trail areas in our sector. We also
landed at Nakhon Phanom and visited with the FAC
personnel there who would provide us with intelligence
data collected during their daytime reconnaissance and
FAC missions. One other source of intelligence was the
reports sent back to NKP on HF radio by friendly Laotian road watch teams. As much as we admired their
courage, their information was always too old by the
time it got to us. There was no real time reporting.

Primarily our intelligence came from ourselves. We
watched for the trucks. Sometimes we could see their
lights. The area was full of fires, of about campfire size,
but quickly we were able to recognise their greater intensity. We also had a starlight scope and of course our
flares. We found plenty of trucks. My concern throughout my stay was whether we were destroying them.

The guns fired tracers, but they burned out prior to
hitting the ground if we fired from prescribed altitudes,
approximately 2,500ft above the ground. One of our
crews became notorious for firing the tracers at the
trucks and successfully setting them on fire. They also
took a lot of hits, but survived. We certainly could kill
people, drivers, included, but could 7.62mm bullets kill
trucks? We could fire on a truck for quite a while, return
to its exact location an hour later and find it gone. However, the truck drivers obviously did not like being shot
at, for they would pour on the coal and head for whatever cover they could find, whenever caught in our flare
illumination.

As in the delta, we worked the area all night, flying
missions from sunset until midnight and again from midnight until dawn. Also we frequently FAC'd fighters.
However, in the delta the fighters were passed to us in
response to a call from help from the ground. In Laos,
the fighters, from all services, were arriving in orbit ar-

eas on a preplanned basis. If no urgent target had arisen they would call us and ask for a target. All too often we had to put them against fords or other questionable targets. Except for the A-1s and B-57s, their success against individual trucks at night was not good.

At this point I want to mention a problem we encountered in designating targets for the fighters. Although all of our officers had been designated FACs late in 1965, my crew had not gotten deeply involved in this part of the mission until we went up north. Apparently the crews that had been FACing up north had discovered the need for a visual target designator. It was not enough to describe the target to a jet rolling in from 10,000ft or more above the ground at night, and often releasing its ordnance 5,000ft or so above the target. Some kind of marker was necessary.

Shortly after arriving at Udorn we were exposed to the Navy sea marker—our target designator. It was a rectangular block of wood with a red burning flare in the middle. The flare ignited a few minutes after release or a minute or so after reaching the ground. It continued to burn for about five minutes. This was an enormous help in providing a clearly identifiable point of reference for the fighters. However, it had the ballistics of a block of wood.

Usually we just threw out the marker, waited for the red glow and then advised the fighters that the target was on a specified azimuth and distance from the red light. A problem arose, however, when we wanted to pinpoint the target. A good case would be the time we discovered a bridge. It was not a normal bridge nor an even more common ford. It was a bridge that was kept below water level for use at night. The fighters couldn't see exactly where it was. As hard as we tried we couldn't place our rectangular bombs on target. In many ways this story of the sea markers was illustrative of the AC-47 program in Laos; the crews were trying their very best to make do with what was available, but their best just wasn't good enough.

Another operational difference we found in Laos was

being tasked to strike suspected truck parks and storage areas. Day reconnaissance and road watching would suggest such targets. If we were unable to find any trucks we could strike these suspected targets. This procedure turned out to be unique to this sector.

One other unusual mission arose before we left Udorn. We were told that a large force of enemy troops were taking an R and R [rest and recuperation] in southern Laos in the Attopeu area. They were causing considerable trouble, to the point of threatening to overrun a local large town. Our help was requested. My old aircraft commander, Major Jensen, and I were rounded up on the afternoon of 4 March and hurried on our way with a makeshift crew. We made radio contact with an American in Attopeu and fired on targets he suggested. The next night I returned at midnight with my crew, relieving Major Jensen and his crew, who had gone down there at sunset. However, this time we were to land at Savannakhet and receive a briefing.

We were met by Major-General Ma, a 34-year-old Laotian fighter pilot and chief of their Tactical Air Command. Later his name appeared in a *Time* magazine article. He was accused of participating in an attempted coup. We went up to a large thatched-roof building which had a sign over the entrance, 'Tactical Air Command Headquarters'. The largest room was full of people sleeping on cots. They were aroused and two large oriental doors were swung open to reveal a tactical display of southern Laos. After the briefing and over a cup of typically sweet oriental tea, General Ma chatted about the war. He said he flew missions every day in his T-28. He also commented that his Air Force used C-47s, but as bombers. The bombs were rolled out of the cargo door. Unfortunately this enlightenment had to end. Augmented with an Americanised Laotian fighter pilot, a recent returnee from training in the US, we headed out for another night against the unwelcomed Vietnamese forces. According to reports we killed a great many enemy troops.

By now the war was becoming more personal. We

began to hear of more of our own losses. Day operations continued to be risky. Our Da Nang detachment lost an AC-47 in the A Shau Valley when the special forces camp was overrun, and we also heard of a narrow escape by a crew sent to help in a day attack south of Da Nang. The miniguns were very effective against the troops in the open, but so were the enemy guns against the low and slow flying AC-47, especially in daylight.

We also heard the story about Major Jensen and the 0.50-calibre machine-gun. Apparently he convinced someone that he should do some airborne experimenting with a 0.50-calibre machine-gun mounted in place of the rearmost minigun, together with an Army starlight scope which enabled troops to see in the dark by intensifying reflected moonlight or starlight. He and his crew, my old crew from the Tan Son Nhut days, did not return one day. Nothing was ever heard from them.

We also knew from personal experience that our aircraft were coming up against increasingly effective anti-aircraft fire. The fighters, equipped with a radar warning device, had been picking up signals over the trails. We knew radar-guided guns and regular AAA were an increasing threat. In our most northern sector, for some reason, we had not come under too much fire. However, one night our gun-firing system malfunctioned and fired continuously for fifteen seconds, marking our position for the enemy on the ground. We coincidentally came under fire from what we judged to be a fairly heavy anti-aircraft gun. Reddish-orange bursts moved across the sky towards us as I, by reflex, tried to pull the firing button out, thinking it might be stuck. Our long dragon's tongue of tracer fire finally burned out after the longest fifteen seconds we had yet experienced.

All the other losses occurred without anyone knowing what had happened. Our experience might have ended with our loss. There was no one within radio range to advise if we got into trouble. The others lost just never returned, nor were they heard from prior to going down. However, all the losses were in the sectors to the south of ours in the panhandle, and therefore the crews were out of other detachments. The hardest hit was the sector just to our south, which was covered by the Da Nang detachment.

We were selected to trade with a crew at Da Nang that had asked to be reassigned due to the losses suffered. Being sent to die in wartime is one thing, but to leave a Thai base for Da Nang, after only a month, was another thing. Our new mission was interdiction in the sector just to the south of our old one. Fortunately our new sector became quiet, while the action increased in the area we had just left. The increased US effort seemed to bring increased enemy response, and the squadron's losses became concentrated in our old sector, which was now being covered by a detachment out of Ubon; the Udorn detachment having been forced to move due to ramp overcrowding.

By 30 June 1966 three AC-47s had been lost over Laos. Ironically, the last crew lost before these out-country missions ended was the crew which had asked to trade with our crew. Also, it was the first time anyone knew what had happened to one of our aircraft lost at night. Apparently a a C-130 flare ship heard a call from the AC-47. The transmission included something about a fire. The C-130 saw fire in the night sky. Another transmission included something about parachutes. For the first time the remains of the burned aircraft were spotted the next day, but no survivors were found.

I left Vietnam to return to the States on 20 July 1966, the same week that out-country AC-47 missions were terminated.''

LUCKY TIGER

The Lucky Tiger deployment involved the movement of the 606th Air Commando Squadron from Hurlburt to Nakhon Phanom Royal Thai Air Force Base during May-August 1966. They took with them twelve T-28Ds, six UC-123Bs, twelve U-10Bs and four UH-1Fs, and were joined in December by eight AC-47s. Colonel Harry C. Aderholt commanded the squadron. The role of the C-123s included the Candlestick flare-drop mission that had been previously performed by C-47s in South Vietnam and C-130 Blind Bat aircraft out of country. One of the Candlestick crew members was MSgt. Stephen A. Thornburg, who recalled his days with the 606th:

"Our call sign was Candlestick, and our mission was unarmed night recon along the complex of trails known as the Ho Chi Minh Trail. Our primary Ops areas were Steel Tiger; southern Laos and northern Cambodia, and Barrel Roll; northern Laos and the Plaine des Jarres. We went out night after night looking for traffic and supply points, and when we found either we would contact Moonbeam, Alleycat, or one of the other ABCCC [Airborne Command, Control and Communications] C-130s such as Cricket, for some fast movers to take out the target. We had to keep an eye out for AAA and try to keep from collecting hits. Most of the time the gomers used tracers, so we could see the flak coming up and call breaks to the pilot to get out of the way. Some nights you could tell it was going to be rough, as you could see exploding flak from horizon to horizon as you entered the playing fields.

The old '123 was a pretty rugged bird and took a lot of punishment. It had its faults, though. When it was raining outside it was also raining inside. The bird leaked like a colander, and even in Southeast Asia it could get cold in the back. The heater was a poor job and the heat never seemed to make it past the wheel well.

For the recon role we pulled the belly baleout hatch and the navigator lay there on the mattress looking out with a starlight scope, searching for targets. When he would spot something we would call up ABCCC and request fast movers with ordnance and try to light up the target with flares without taking hits in the meantime. As soon as a target was sure it was seen, they started throwing up whatever was available.

Often the flak was less of a threat than the fast mov-

ers. The F-4s were the worst to work with. They would
do a steep dive on the target area, pickle off their ordnance and then climb like hell before the AAA could
get a fix on them. It's a wonder we never had a midair,
as they almost run us down many a time. Its quite impressive when a Fox 4 goes screaming up between that
narrow space between your wingtip and horizontal stabiliser in full after burner. The flames leave you blind
for a few seconds and your sphincter sucks up so far
you can taste shit in the back of your throat!

When the flak gets real nasty you can hear it going
off and smell it exploding, and sometimes if it's real
close you can hear it pinging off the fuselage. One night
we took a solid hit down in Steel Tiger. We had been
working a truck park and were having to keep breaking
away from a persistent 37mm AAA gun, when another
gun nailed us good. The hit sounded like someone hitting an empty trash can with a baseball bat. Punched a
hole in the tail you could just about walk through. A
couple of nearby airbursts peppered the horizontal stab
pretty good as well. We decided we weren't wanted
there and decided to boogie on home. We had a good
pilot and despite the damage and the rudder being
jammed over a bit, we made it back to NKP.

We didn't have any armour on the '123s and we were
slow. We used to joke that evasive action consisted of
taking turns running around the cargo compartment. You
only got upset when both pilots were in the back evading
at the same time. Despite the violence of some of the
breaks to avoid AAA, we managed to do OK. Many a
time I would be carrying a flare to the ramp for launching when a break was called. The idea was to protect
the flare, as it burned at two million candlepower when
lit and would generate a hell of a lot of heat. You would
cradle the flare and walk up the side of the fuselage as
the break was called and back down again as the plane
levelled out. It could get hairy when a flare failed to
break away after launch. You would have to cut the
cable as the flare hanging behind the 'plane would light
you up for all the gunners on the ground.''

Norman Crocker joined the 606th in 1967.

'We had ten T-28s when I got there. Three crashed with
the loss of the one pilot, Captain Terry Koonce. Our
primary mission was night interdiction on the Ho Chi
Minh Trail. We were pulled off the Trail due to exces-
sive engine losses and flew close air support for the Laotian Army and escorted helicopters. I was later checked
out in the A-1 together with John Haken, Dale Ward,
Rich Hilland and Billy Mobley. We were to form the
cadre for the new 22nd SOS, but it was delayed for
political reasons and we went home. Billy and I went to
the 605th SOS with the 24th SOW in Panama and flew
T-28s until they were replaced by A-37Bs. The 605th
also had C-47s, but they were replaced with C-123s and
transferred to the 24th SOS along with U-10s and UH-
1Ps.'

OPERATION BIG EAGLE

On 8 June 1966 eight A-26A Invaders left England AFB for
Nakhon Phanom with Detachment 9, 1st ACW. The deployment, known as Big Eagle, marked the return of the B-26 to
Southeast Asia. The redesignation of the aircraft from B-26K
to A-26A had been authorised by Air Force Logistics Command on 30 April. They joined the 606th Air Commando
Squadron and its T-28s, UH-1Fs and C-123s.

Project Big Eagle involved the evaluation of the A-26A in
night interdiction of enemy lines of communication in Laos,
and the undersides of the aircraft were painted non-reflective
black before deployment. They faced a number of problems
operating out of their jungle air base. Bad weather caused a
number of sorties to be cancelled, and the pierced steel planking runway was very slick when wet and not long enough to
allow the aircraft to take off with full bomb loads. The propellers also suffered damage due to loose stones under the
PSP. There was also a high dud rate among the bombs and
flares initially available to the unit.

Despite these early problems the A-26As proved very effective in the night truck killer role. Using the call sign Nimrod, their night operations accounted for more than half of the total day and night truck kills during December 1966, even though they flew only four percent of the sorties in Laos. The aircraft could carry over 6,000lb of napalm, high explosive bombs or cluster bomb units, plus 1,600 rounds for each of the eight machine-guns. During the six-month test program Big Eagle flew 1,349 sorties, dropped 2,126 tons of bombs, expended 717,595 0.50-calibre rounds and released 8,349 flares.

The first combat mission, a daytime orientation flight over the trail, was flown in June 1966. A sharp-eyed or very lucky enemy gunner managed to shoot away the aircraft's rotating beacon, a hit that drew everyone's attention. These early missions were flown with the guidance of A-1 and T-28 pilots who knew the trail and the good and bad areas, and they were directed to targets by Airborne Command and Control C-130s. Blind Bat and Lamplighter C-130s provided flare illumination over target areas, and were later joined by Candlestick C-123s.

Because the squadron was comparatively small, the Nimrods usually operated one aircraft at a time, with a dusk-to-dawn coverage over the trail. Sadly the first combat loss occurred on 28 June 1966, when Captain Chuck Dudley, pilot, and First Lieutenant Tony Cavelle, navigator, were shot down. This was followed on 24 July by the fatal crash at NKP of Captain Glen Duke, pilot, and Miles Tanimoto, navigator. The last loss during the TDY period was in December, when Lt-Colonel Al Howarth, pilot, Captain Jack Bell, navigator, and Captain Harold Cooper, navigator were shot down whilst bombing a road in the Tchepone area. Thankfully they were picked up by helicopter after spending a night on the ground in Laos. Captain Cooper was on his dollar ride; his first combat mission.

Crews trained at Eglin AFB began arriving at NKP in mid-December on a permanent change of station (PCS) to replace the survivors of the dozen crews from the 603rd ACS who had deployed TDY for Big Eagle. Between July and December 1966 the 603rd had the unusual task of performing an overseas combat mission and a combat crew training mission at home. Project Big Eagle ended on 13 January 1967, and the aircraft remained at NKP with the new crews. The 609th ACS was activated to continue the A-26A mission on 15 September 1967, and became part of the 56th Air Commando Wing, which had been activated at NKP on 16 March. The new squadron carried the tail markings "TA," whereas the 603rd had used "IF" whilst training in the States. The new wing was commanded by Colonel Harry C. Aderholt.

NIMROD

With the end of the Big Eagle evaluation of the A-26A and the activation of a dedicated Invader squadron, the real Nimrod story began. They would hunt for trucks, while the enemy anti-aircraft artillery would hunt for them. By 1967 there were around 10,000 AAA weapons in Laos, ranging from the 21.5mm ZPU to the huge 57mm guns. It was a dangerous job.

On 22 February 1967 an A-26A was returning to NKP with battle damage. Whilst approaching the base an engine fire forced the crew, Captain James McCleskey, pilot, and Captain Mike Scruggs, navigator, to bale out. Tragically the aircraft blew up almost immediately after they left the aircraft, and the resulting explosion destroyed a second A-26A that had been escorting them home, killing Captain Dwight Campbell, pilot, and Captain Bob Scholl, navigator. The pick-up of the first crew was to be the last successful rescue of an A-26A crew member for the remainder of the Nimrod's time in Southeast Asia. The aircraft was not fitted with ejection seats, which might have been the salvation of some of the men lost during the following two years.

Truck hunting was a sport carried out relative to the weather prevailing in the area at that time of year. Between May and October the monsoon rains washed away the tracks and paths that made up the Ho Chi Minh Trail, and few trucks tried to make the journey from North Vietnam to the South. In September, however, the North Vietnamese Army road repair crews began to work on the trail in preparation for the dry season, November to May, when the trucks would carry supplies, fuel and ammunition to the communist forces in South Vietnam.

The area that the Nimrods worked during the dry season was known as Steel Tiger, a 50 by 150 square-mile section of the southern part of the Laos panhandle, bordering South Vietnam, and in the summer night missions would be flown in the Barrel Roll area of Northern Laos, including the Plaines des Jarres, working with the road watch teams. Two crews reached the magic 100 missions count, which meant that they could go home before their one year's tour was finished. Apparently this rule was only good if you flew jets and the crews were actually on their way home before the 7th Air Force sent them back to complete their full year. Sadly, none of them made it. Captain John Kerr, pilot, and First Lieutenant Burke Morgan, navigator, disappeared in the Barrel on 22 August 1967, and the squadron commander, Lt-Colonel Bruce Jensen, and his navigator, Captain Frank Smiley, suffered a similar fate in Northern Laos five nights later. Flights to the Barrel were put on hold for several weeks while the powers-that-be speculated on the fate of the crews. Was it AAA, North Vietnamese, or even Chinese MiG fighters, or did they fly into the mountains? No one ever discovered.

One innovation that appeared in the summer of 1967 was pioneered by Tom Wickstrom, and involved the use of an observer strapped in a seat and looking out of the A-26A bomb bay with a starlight scope. Another was the discovery of some Mark 34 and 35 funny bombs and their diversion to NKP. The funny bomb was an awesome weapon, and lethal against trucks or guns. Containing jellied fuel, cluster bomb units (CBUs) and white phosphorous, the bomb split its casing and ignited its contents while still falling, giving the appearance of a burning waterfall. When it hit the ground the CBU bomblets blew it around, so it covered approximately the area of a football field, destroying anything or anyone within that area. The new scope and bombs were used with enthusiasm by the Nimrod crews, including Captain Carlos Cruz, pilot, and Captain Bill Potter, navigator. Sadly they were shot down on 29 December 1967, together with their scope operator, A/1C Paul Foster, a combat control team member. Captain Cruz is listed as killed in action and his crew as missing in action.

Towards the end of 1967 and early in 1968 new crews arrived to replace the Nimrods who had survived a year over the trail. They were soon in action flying close-air-support missions for the Marine defenders of Khe Sanh, a fact often neglected in histories of the siege. As the 1967-68 truck hunting season drew to a close with the start of the rains, more Nimrods were lost to the enemy gunners. Captain Bo Hertlein, navigator to Lieutenant-Colonel Skip Shippey, was wounded while they were attacking gun positions on 24 April and died before the aircraft recovered at NKP. On 30 April Captain Bob Pietsch, pilot, and First Lieutenant Lou Guillermin, navigator, were lost, and both are still listed as missing in action.

The truck hunting season due to begin in November 1968 was to be a whole new ball game. President Johnson had ordered a halt to all bombing of North Vietnam, north of the 19th parallel, on 31 March. It was a naive attempt to persuade the North Vietnamese to begin peace negotiations, which effectively gave them breathing space to repair their roads, railways and bridges, increase the amount of supplies flowing South and begin to infiltrate 75,000 more troops down the Trail. In addition, the bombing halt allowed the enemy trucks a clear run from the docks in Haiphong to the border with Laos, and allowed them to move thousands of their anti-aircraft weapons from North Vietnam into Laos.

The Trail now became one huge shooting gallery, with trucks running the gauntlet of the Nimrods and the hundreds of other Air Force and Navy aircraft which became surplus to requirements following the bombing halt. The opposition was becoming stronger, however, with radar-controlled guns and, eventually, surface-to-air missiles being ranged against the aircraft hunting the trucks and supporting the forces of General Vang Pao.

One of the new pilots to arrive for the 1968–'69 truck hunting season was Paul Marshalk. He told the author:

"I was the first of my class to arrive. They were glad to see me as they had been flying twelve missions a night with fourteen pilots. Nine days later I was checked out and flying with an experienced navigator, wondering what I had gotten myself into. Our tactics consisted of two Nimrods and a FAC, a 'Nail' 0-2 from NKP or a Candlestick C-123 or Blind Bat C-130. Our favourites were the Candles, mostly because they flew above us at 7,000ft and could kick out flares and marks all night long. Also, being from NKP, we could talk with them about tactics and how things were going. We flew at 6,000ft and the Nails below us at 5,000ft, so they had to hold away from the target area when we were working. The FAC's job was to locate targets, usually using a starlight scope, but sometimes under flares and then direct us to the target.

The Low Nimrod would go after the trucks, while the High Nimrod would position himself to follow in, if he could pinpoint a gun position. If we got a good fix on a gun, both Nims would go after him, and as a result gunners sometimes became a bit reluctant to shoot at us, as the Nimrods killed a good many guns. Given a clean shot, though, they would hose us unmercifully.

The '26 was particularly well suited for night interdiction missions. We could carry a wide variety of armament and loiter for hours, waiting for the FAC to acquire a target for us. With a typical bomb load of eight napalms, a mix of 500lb or 750lb bombs on the wings, two funny bombs and up to five fragmentation bombs in the bomb bay, plus up to 2,600 rounds of 0.50-calibre for the eight machine-guns, we could make as many as 22 to 24 bomb and gun passes. Our average mission was three hours, but could go onto four, still landing at NKP with 200gal of gas after starting with 1,100.

Our intelligence told us that the NVA had as many as 2,500 people listening in on our strike frequencies, trying to figure out which airplanes were striking which targets, so they could coordinate the firing of the guns. The guns most fired at us were 23 and 37mm. If we saw the 37 tracers coming, always in clips of seven from each barrel, we could usually turn away from them. The 23s came up like a shotgun pattern of buckshot at a faster speed than the 37s, and if they had you there was little escape. When the 75s and 100s lobbed a shell at us from across the border, when we were working close to North Vietnam, whoever saw the muzzle flash would call it out and we all did a 90° turn until it exploded in the air, then we went back to our business.

We were no longer able to go into North Vietnam, because of the bombing halt, but we did a lot of work around the Mu Gia and Ban Karai passes, the two main entry points into Laos. In June 1969 we started flying up in the Barrel Roll area, where it was now the dry season, which I thought was convenient timing. To get there we had to fly over some pretty rugged mountains which reached as high as 10,000ft, all without oxygen. Since terrain varied greatly over small distances around the PDJ, we had to be exceedingly careful about where we were flying to avoid running into karst or mountains. The situation in the PDJ changed daily as the NVA and Pathet Lao fell back as the good guys advanced, but then the front lines rolled back rapidly the other direction."

The 1968-69 truck hunting season would be the last for the Nimrods. On 11 March 1969 Captain Neal Monette, pilot, and Major John Callahan, navigator, crashed near NKP after losing an engine due to fuel starvation. On 23 March Captain James Widdis, pilot, and Captain Bob Davis, navigator, were shot down in Commando Hunt near the Peanut Karst and killed. The last loss occurred on 8 July 1969, when Major Jim Sizemore, pilot, and navigator Major Howard Andre were shot down in Barrel Roll. The Nimrods were down to fifteen aircraft, plus nine more back at Hurlburt, and the decision was made to retire them. Apparently General John Ryan, Commander PACAF, did not want to keep open a long logistical pipeline for the few aircraft still in the inventory. Moremodern aircraft were now available, with an AC-130 gunship squadron operating out of Ubon. It was time for the Nimrods to return to the States, where most met their end in the boneyard at Davis-Monthan AFB in Arizona. Paul Marshalk has the last word:

"On 8 November 1969 the new truck hunting season began. It was like they had waved the green flag and the trucks were running and the guns were up. On my last mission, on the 9th, I discovered that they had changed the rules slightly by moving many radar-directed 23s and

37s into Steel Tiger, and nothing is more death to slow movers at low altitude than these. The AC-130s were supposed to replace us, but the ferocity of the AAA fire on the main part of the Trail was hard on the old transport, circling at 5,000ft with its flaps out at 140 knots. F-4s and other fast movers were really out of their element at night, flying around like bats out of hell in the dark, trying to find out where they were. When two of us sang the song 'F-4, F-4,' (see Appendix) composed by myself and my navigator Leon 'Crazy' Poteet, the night of our standdown party on November 10th, five F-4 drivers stood up and started for us on the stage. In an instant, the entire room stood, turned and defied them to do us harm. I heard, but cannot confirm it, that as we were partying that night we lost ten F-4s over the Trail trying to do our job. My God, what a cost.

Seventh Air Force didn't like much about the Air Commandos, because they wore funny hats, called each other by first names and hated the regular Air Force bullshit. The ultimate sin was that the '26s killed more trucks with old prop-driven 'planes than all their jets, at less than one twentieth of the cost per truck killed.''

"SANDY" SQUADRON

As the infamous Gulf of Tonkin incident of August 1964 opened the floodgate of US support for the war, a second US Air Force Skyraider unit arrived in Vietnam. The 602nd Fighter Squadron, Commando, joined the 1st Air Commando Squadron at Bien Hoa as a part of the 34th Tactical Group, becoming operational on 15 October 1964. The 602nd would be followed by the 6th and 22nd Air Commando Squadrons as the war progressed.

On 27 July 1965 John L. Larrison led the first ever flight of Skyraiders to Udorn on a "special mission" to cover search and rescue operations for the first attacks on the surface-to-air missile sites around Hanoi. Shortly afterwards the squadron began sending detachments to Udorn on TDY to escort Jolly

Colonels John R. Alison (left) and Philip G. Cochran, commanders of the 1st Air Commando Group. (A.R. Van De Weghe)

Lt. Carter Harman (extreme right) together with his crew chiefs (left to right) S/Sgts Warren McArtney, John Mauter and James Phelan and the Sikorsky YR-4 helicopter *Pink Elephant* in which he carried out the first ever combat rescue. (Carter Harman)

Lieutenant Robert A. Beck in the P-51 he was shot down in on 25 February 1945, whilst flying with the 2nd Fighter Squadron over Central Burma. (Bob Beck)

A flight of four of the forty P-51s that took part in the longest fighter sweep of the Second World War, from Cox's Bazaar, India to Don Muang Field, Bangkok, Thailand. Captain Eason leads the flight in P-51 number 51 *The Hungry One*. Note long range fuel tanks. (Walter R. Eason)

A Farm Gate B-26 dropping napalm on a target in the Plain of Reeds. (George Crowe/Tom Wickstrom)

After surviving his successful crash landing in his T-28 on 9 September 1963, Tom Schornak went on to teach student pilots to fly the A-1E Skyraider. (Tom Schornak)

VNAF Skyraiders and Farm Gate C-47s and T-28 on the Bien Hoa ramp in December 1961. (USAF 98641)

A flight of Ranch Hand C-123s spraying defoliants. The original Aerial Spray Flight became the 12th Air Commando Squadron. (Jack Spey)

A 1st Air Commando Squadron A-1E rather the worse for wear following a landing at Bien Hoa. (Don Schoknecht)

This C-123B Provider crash landed at a special forces camp in September 1966. (USAF 98541)

Colonel William C. 'Roadrunner' Thomas, commander of the Waterpump detachment, standing third from right, together with instructors and students. (William C. Thomas)

Bernie Fisher (left) and 'Jump' Myers (right) after their brush with death in the A Shau Valley. (AFSOC/PAO)

Lieutenant Marc L. Bornn and his C-123 at the A Shau special forces camp before it was overrun by the North Vietnamese. (Marc L. Bornn)

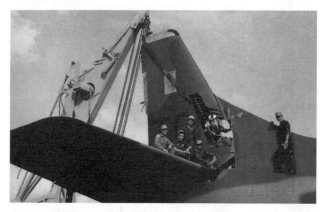

Stephen Thornburgh's C-123 took a hit from a 37mm AAA gun whilst flying a Candlestick mission in the Steel Tiger area of Laos on 14 May 1971. The pilot is in the hole and Stephen is on the right. (Stephen Thornburgh)

The prototype Air Rescue Service HC-130H testing the Fulton Recovery System off the coast of California. The 'downed aviator' has been snatched by the recovery system and will now be winched in over the rear cargo ramp. (Guy Aceto/Air Force Magazine)

Green Giant rescue helicopters over Northern Laos and North Vietnam. A flight of four Skyraiders would normally be launched to cover a rescue mission, using the "Sandy" call sign. One pair would be the Low element and the other pair the High element. On a typical mission Sandy 1 and 2 would be the low pair with the flight leader, Sandy 1, designated the On-Scene Commander (OSC). They would scramble and race to the rescue area to try locate the downed pilot and to keep the enemy away from him. In the meantime the high pair would be escorting the rescue helicopter (and often a back-up) to the scene. Following instructions from the OSC the Sandy flight, and other aircraft when necessary, would try to suppress the enemy groundfire and lead the low-bird helicopter in to pick up the downed crewman, while the high-bird helicopter stayed out of range nearby in case it was needed.

The Skyraiders could loiter over a target for hours, absorb a lot of punishment and carry a large amount of ordnance. A standard SAR load would comprise six pods of 2.75 in white phosphorus rockets, each pod containing seven rockets; six 100lb white phosphorus bombs; one 7.62mm gunpod with 1,500 rounds of ammunition, and the 20mm wing-mounted guns. In addition, each aircraft carried one 150gal external fuel tank on the right stub pylon and one 300gal tank on the centerline pylon.

One problem that the Sandy crews had to contend with was the possibility of coming across North Vietnamese MiG fighters once across the DMZ. In September the 1st ACW sent two A-1Es to Nellis AFB, Nevada, to take part in Feather Duster II, testing offensive and defensive manoeuvres against Russian MiG aircraft. Later in the war two Navy pilots would each shoot down a MiG in air-to-air combat.

In April 1966 the 602nd moved the whole squadron to Udorn RTAFB, and in April 1967 were assigned to the 56th Air Commando Wing at NKP. They flew strike, reconnaissance, escort and many search and rescue missions using the call sign "Sandy." Although several TDY groups of pilots had flown SAR missions out of Udorn in late 1965, they did not use the call sign "Sandy." That originated when Captain W. J. "Doc" George led four replacement A-1Es to Udorn and his Bien Hoa departure call sign was "Sandy." On arrival at Udorn Doc was asked what call sign he would like to use while there, and he replied "Sandy." The name stuck.

A word on other Skyraider call signs from Lew Smith, a 602nd pilot:

"Circa 1965-66 the 1st Air Commando Squadron operated with the call sign 'Hobo' and the 602nd out of Nha Trang with 'Spad'. Call signs related to the area of operations and not the mission; fragged missions to Steel Tiger and Barrel Roll carried the call sign 'Firefly', and those to Rolling Thunder 'Dragonfly'. This scheme lasted until there was a move to NKP and other squadrons were created. The 602nd would change to 'Sandy', the 6th SOS would take over 'Spad' and the 22nd SOS would inherit 'Zorro' from the T-28s of the 606th ACS at NKP."

Lew kept a diary of his time with the 602nd, and a small portion, reproduced here, shows the life and times of the Skyraider pilots, dicing with death over Laos and North Vietnam.

"Jim Crane, Dick Rosecrans and I arrived at Nha Trang on 16 March 1966. The rest of my 'express' class, Ben Skelton, Dick Needham, Tom Wolfe, Tom McDaniel, Jim Loven, Mick Spillane and Sid Boston, were to follow shortly. The 602nd had already lost two pilots KIA in March and three in October 1965. Fred McPherson was to be the first KIA in 1966. These were in South Vietnam. Oscar Mauterer was to become the first casualty in third-country operations. Detached to Udorn, he was declared MIA after baling out over the Mu Gia Pass, between North Vietnam and Laos.

Dick Willsie was in command and the big talk at the time was 'Jump' and Bernie's big day at A Shau, "Operation X' as the Udorn detachment's operations were labelled, and the rumour that some from the 602nd would be PCS'd to Udorn. I sat alert at NKP for the first time on 11 April, but didn't get a scramble until the 16th. By the 18th I had been on four pickups. On the 19th Dick Robins was scrambled into Mu Gia Pass after an O-1 that was reported to have 'spun-in'. Robbie got in, saw the FAC still strapped in the inverted wreckage, and was killed as he manoeüvred in the valley. On the 26th the whole squadron moved into Udorn, PCS.

On 1 May Jim Ingells was shot down just north of Ban Ban. The Udorn SAR had no luck, so we scrambled out of NKP. The Jolly Green got shot up in a stiff firefight, so Jim got his aerobics and a night out in the hills of northern Laos. The next morning, with no opposition, he got the honor of being the first of us to get picked up in this 'out-of-country' operation. We had finally had this very important 'first'.

By 10 May everyone was becoming well worked into the new operations and its intensity. SAR tactics were evolving rapidly, then six pilots were to be levied to O-1s. On the 16th I was flying as 'Dragonfly 23', with Lew Daugherty as '24'. We were on armed recce in Route Package One, just north of the DMZ. Just west of Dong Hoi Lew spotted a truck through the scud below. I cleared him in and followed. He fired as I broke through in trail and I spotted the last of the fire behind him and from his nine o'clock. He hadn't seen the gun, but they had ranged in on him and were dead on me and I took two rounds in the engine.

Since it was burning a bit better than it was running, I called '24' and left the machine, sans Yankee. (We did not have the Yankee extraction system, then, we had the original low altitude egress system; aluminium and fingernails). As my 'chute blossomed, looking between my feet I saw my 'plane impact. On the first oscillation down I was in bamboo and, bouncing once or twice, came to a stop six feet from the ground.

I made good contact with Lew while on the run, buried my helmet (still brilliant white, before camo was issued), smeared my face with the two sheets of carbon paper always in my pocket for that purpose, and secured myself inside a large, rotted-out stump. Ed Griffin and Dick Needham, who were airborne when we went into RP1, were still around and arrived shortly with a full SAR load. Leo Martin and Dick Rosecrans were escort-

ing the Jollies in from NKP. ETA one hour. Daugherty
and I made contact every five minutes.

That team did a classic job of fire suppression and
preparing the area for the JGs. It was from this perspective that my development as a Sandy really took giant
steps. Using the full range of ordnance, the Sandies
wasted 'that gun' and a lot of unfriendlies all around.

The Jolly Green was cleared in and I popped my
smoke on command. It drifted down the ravine and up
over the facing ridge. The helo came right to it and I
told him I was transmitting for him to take a steer. When
I let up on the button he was telling me that his direction
finder was out. So I vectored him to me and he got the
tree penetrator to me on the second try in thick under-
brush. As soon as I was straddled and strapped on the
penetrator it was the ride of a lifetime as the helo started
the exit route with the hoist just starting up. I could still
hear small-arms fire all around. He hugged the terrain
down his predetermined route, now being laced with the
Sandies' CBUs and napalm. Then I was hoisted up and
taken back to NKP. After this, I was off to Bangkok for
R and R and met Bob Weekly, a Jolly Green pilot. He
told me that he had lost a total of seven windscreens in
his exploits as an HH-3 pilot.

On the 26th Bob Bush, on a SAR for a downed F-
105 pilot near Mu Gia pass, was downed by hostile fire.
His experience, as most were in some regard or other,
was unique. He was the first, and I think the only, to
make contact with friendlies on the ground. After a Mex-
ican stand-off, of sorts, they made friends and contact
with the helicopter and he returned.

9 June was Black Thursday. Ted Schorack (Sandy 31)
and Bob Bush (Sandy 41) were killed in a mid-air collision after extracting an F-105 jock out of North Vietnam. Just hours later Jerry Caskey was hit and baled out
near Lima Site 50 and was picked up by an Air America
Huey. Tom Wolfe was killed on the 29th in an A-26
shoot-down while it was on a strafing run on Route 911
and 912. He was giving a local area check out to the A-
26 crew on their first mission from the jump seat. He

had been reassigned to O-1s, but he was still one of us at the NKP bar.

On 31 July Dave Lester, 'The Birdman', had his shoot-down. As appropriate to his name, he never touched the ground. Landing in a tree and tying himself off securely, 'The Birdman' stayed perched there until we arrived and Jolly plucked him right off his limb.''

Lieutenant-Colonel Jerry Ransom commanded the 602nd from November 1966 to December 1967, by which time he had become the first A-1E pilot to fly 100 missions over North Vietnam. He later returned to NKP as deputy commander of operations with the 56th SOW. He passed away in October 1990. The 602nd was deactivated in December 1970.

CHAPTER 7

THE SECRET WAR IN LAOS, 1967–'68

HURLBURT SITREP

THE 4410TH COMBAT CREW Training Wing at Hurlburt Field was activated on 1 December 1965 and would move to England AFB in July 1969. In early 1967 the Wing comprised four squadrons; two were at Hurlburt, the 4408th CCTS training C-123 crews and the 4409th training A-1E and T-28 pilots, including Vietnamese students. The 4410th CCTS at Holley Field primarily trained O-1 Forward Air Controllers and students flying the U-10 and O-2. In December the 4407th CCTS would be activated to assume the mission of the 4410th while that unit began training crews in the new OV-10 Bronco FAC aircraft. The fourth squadron, the 4412th CCTS was at England AFB, training C-47D and AC-47D pilots. On 1 April the 4532nd CCTS was activated to fly A-37Bs and assigned to the Wing. Later in the year both the 4412th and 4532nd were reassigned to the 1st ACW at England AFB.

The first jet-equipped C-123K arrived at Hurlburt Field on 5 January and the first of 76 of the type to be ferried by the 319th ACS to Vietnam departed on 10 April.

At the start of 1967 there were 385,000 US troops in South Vietnam and almost 7,000 had been killed to date. They were facing almost 300,000 communists, including over 100,000 NVA regular troops. Some 165,000 tons of bombs had been dropped on North Vietnam, but their impact had not altered the determination of the enemy to continue the war. Almost 400 US aircraft had been lost so far.

General Westmoreland now had seven US divisions, plus various minor units under his command. Two and a half Korean divisions and an Australian-New Zealand force were in-country, in addition to the resident eleven South Vietnamese divisions. 1967 would be the year of the big battles, as Westmoreland tried to push the enemy away from the centers of population and to dig the enemy out of their traditional strongholds. When it suited the Viet Cong and NVA, they stood and fought. When it did not, they moved back to their sanctuaries in Laos and Cambodia to rest and re-equip to fight another day.

ZORRO AT NKP

The increase in fighting in Laos and the establishment of the Ho Chi Minh Trail as the primary supply route for the enemy forces in South Vietnam, led to the organisation on 8 April 1967 of the 56th Air Commando Wing at Nakhon Phanom Royal Thai Air Force Base. One of the units assigned to the Wing was the 606th Air Commando Squadron and in September, the 609th ACS joined them, with their A-26A Counter Invaders. In 1967, the Skyraider-equipped 1st and 602nd Air Commando Squadrons also moved to NKP from South Vietnam and were joined by the 21st Helicopter Squadron and its CH-3s. By now the T-28 had been taken out of service in South Vietnam and was about to write a new page of history in the skies over Laos. Captain Jack Drummond flew the T-28 not only over Laos as a USAF pilot based in Thailand, but in Laos and Cambodia as a civilian.

"In 1966, I was flying out of Ubon Royal Thai Air Force Base in C-130 'Blind Bat' flare ships. The Ho Chi Minh Trail was being used extensively to transport men and supplies to the battlefields in the South and it was the job of the Air Force to interdict this traffic. In the daytime it was no problem, but most of the traffic moved at night and the Air Force was ill equipped to attack trucks moving on the ground at night. Our C-130 was equipped with flares and a starlight scope, which we would use out of the back door of the plane to try to see truck lights moving on the ground. If we found any trucks we would drop flares and then B-57s would try to bomb them. We were not very successful, because our equipment was not very good and no one had much experience of night interdiction.

I had been flying for about six months when another call sign turned up one night—''Zorro''. When I asked him what he was, he said he was a T-28 out of Nakhon Phanom Royal Thai Air Force Base.* After the mission I called Nakhon Phanom and discovered that there was a small detachment of T-28s based there to try to interdict the traffic on the Trail at night. They could fly lower and slower than the B-57 jets and the accuracy of their ordance was much better.

I had been a pilot for six years and had always wanted to be a fighter pilot, so three or four months later I managed to get an assignment to T-28s and returned to Hurlburt Field in Florida, where I saw my first T-28. I did my transition flying in a T-28D-5 with five or six older pilots and finished the course in early 1967.

One month later I was back at Nakhon Phanom, or Naked Fanny as it was nicknamed. The base was different from the other air bases in Thailand; for one thing there were no jets there, they were all old airplanes, T-28s, C-47s, C-123s and B-26s. The Wing Commander at NKP was Heinie Aderholt, and he had been instrumental in replacing the C-130 flare ships with the C-123. This was basically because it had a door in the floor that could be removed, so the starlight scope could be used to look straight down from the bottom of the 'plane.

We would usually only fly one mission each night, or occasionally two. We were about 90 miles west of the Ho Chi Minh Trail, and the early flight would take-off just about sundown for a thirty-minute flight out to the working area. We also had O-1 Forward Air Control aircraft working with the C-123s; when the flare ship found some trucks and dropped its parachute flares, the

*The 22nd SOS was activated at NKP in October 1968 and their Skyraiders also used the call sign ''Zorro''.

O-1 would fly down and mark the targets for the fighters with its smoke rockets. The O-1s would also work the Trail on their own, with a starlight scope operator in the back and carrying around four flares in addition to smoke marking rockets. The O-1s had their rotating beacons masked so that you could only see them from the air.

The ordnance we carried on these missions varied quite a bit. We carried napalm, cluster bomb units— CBU14 and CBU25, Mark 47 white phosphorous bombs, which were quite small but very effective, as the white phosphorous would hit a truck and stick to it while it burnt. Heinie found some fire bombs once that the B-29s had used to burn Tokyo down, and we carried those. They weighed about 500lb and had a 2ft-diameter flat nose and they really stressed the T-28 carrying them. We had three ordnance stations under each wing and might carry two napalm bombs, two CBUs and two of something else. Each CBU had six tubes, which could be fired individually, giving us a total of twelve passes.

On a typical napalm pass we would use a 15° to 20° dive, rather than the low, flat delivery usually recommended in daytime, and instead of releasing the bomb at 100ft above the ground we would release it at 500ft. The more passes you made, the more accurate you became. With the new generation of fighters coming into service, equipped with bombing and attack computers, we called the T-28 computer the 'TLAR computer': That Looks About Right. We would try to hit the first truck in a convoy, to stop them so that we could attack the rest at our leisure. Then the O-1 or C-123 would come over and drop more flares, so you could attack the rest of the convoy. This had to be done as quickly as possible to allow us to leave the area before the local anti-aircraft fire (AAA) became too hot and started to affect our accuracy. It was hard to see us at night, so the AAA fire was usually of the barrage type. Later, radar directed AAA was moved in to guard the Trail, and that was another matter.

I got on a hot streak with trucks for about a month or

so, and I was able to destroy at least one truck each
night. It was the height of the dry season and more
trucks were running than had ever run before. The anti-
aircraft fire was more intense than ever, and we usually
encountered 37mm AAA guns which fired a seven-or
nine-round clip and was effective up to around 4,500ft.
Its best range was about 1,500ft and the rounds were
bright orange and slow moving, so if you saw them you
could avoid them. The 57mm rounds were more red than
orange, and their range was higher, around 7,500-
8,000ft, with an effective range of around 4,500ft.
Around January or February of 1968 they came up with
four-barrel 23mm guns with a rapid rate of fire, and they
could traverse the hell out of it. The rounds were white
and it looked like a water hose being sprayed at you.
We were more afraid of those than of any other.

We did not actually lose any airplanes to groundfire
though. We lost three or four 'planes, but we don't actually know why we lost them, whether they ran into
the mountains or got shot down, we never knew. We
did not have any return to base with battle damage.''

About January 1968 Heinie Aderholt went home and was
replaced by a new wing commander. The Air Force was
plagued with restrictions and rules of engagement for most of
the war. Many came direct from the civilian war managers in
Washington, and they often affected the success of missions
and caused a needless loss of lives. The new wing commander
told the T-28 pilots that, instead of flying alone at night, they
had to fly with someone in the back seat. Furthermore, he
insisted that they did not fly below 4,500ft, which meant it
was extremely difficult to hit the targets. He, or higher headquarters, also insisted that the T-28s should not fly into areas
circled in red on their maps, because of the high density of
AAA guns there. However, it was obvious to the T-28 pilots
that the reason that all the guns were sited there was because
that was where you could find all the trucks.

Life became boring for the pilots. They could not find the
trucks, no one shot at them, and the FACs did not want to

work with them; they wanted to work with the B-26s or F-4s and find the trucks. So, in order to carry out their mission effectively, some pilots decided to report the wrong co-ordinates and worked with the NKP FACs, finding trucks and getting shot at. In late January Jack Drummond was out one night with a Blind Bat flare ship and they told him on the radio, "Hey, Zorro, we got trucks you can't believe, there's fifteen or twenty of them down here. They're stopped and we can't get any fighters, can you help us out?" However, they were right in the middle of one of those big red circles, where pilots were not supposed to go. The trucks would have been carrying ammunition and supplies for the Viet Cong and NVA troops fighting the American and South Vietnamese forces in South Vietnam. To Jack Drummond, his duty was clear. He was the only man on the spot, restrictions or no restrictions.

Jack rolled in on the trucks, and by the time he had finished at least a dozen were in flames. The groundfire was the worst he had ever seen. So as not to excite the bureaucrats back home, he reported his co-ordinates as being just on the edge of the red circle and went home elated. On his arrival the T-28 pilots threw a party at the officers' club. However, about midnight a telex came in from the C-130 crew, complimenting him on his low flying, etc, etc, all the things that he was not supposed to do. In the morning the vice-wing commander went down to Jack's trailer and woke him up. He said, "Jack, I just can't believe what you did last night. It was superlative and you are in a world of deep shit. The wing commander is going to have your ass, and you have got to go see him about six o'clock. You are off the flying schedule." Jack wondered frantically what to do. Was he going to be court martialled? Then he remembered a name that Heinie had left him, some-one to call if he got into trouble. Jack called the number, and found himself talking to the assistant US air attaché at Vien-tiane in Laos. Heinie had previously told him that Jack was an excellent T-28 pilot, and in a matter of minutes Jack found himself assigned to Laos. Before he put down the telephone, the attaché said, "By the way, don't bring any uniforms." A C-47 arrived at NKP about four o'clock, picked up Jack and departed; destination Laos.

TROPIC MOON

With the flood of North Vietnamese troops and supplies down the Ho Chi Minh Trail increasing every year, greater emphasis was put on obtaining night interdiction aircraft to try to slow down the enemy's nocturnal movements. During the first half of the year the 1st Combat Applications Group at Hurlburt had been working with a contractor to develop a low-light-level TV (LLLTV) system for use in Vietnam. Eventually three of the B-57s at Phan Rang were fitted with pod-mounted LLLTV systems in a program lasting from December 1967 to July 1968 and known as Tropic Moon II. Although the equipment required at least one-quarter moon illumination, the encouraging results had led to the withdrawal from service of the last B-57Bs, which were returned to the Martin factory in Baltimore for conversion to B-57G Night Intruders.

These B-57G Tropic Moon III aircraft contained three sensors; forward-looking radar, infrared and LLLTV, plus a lasering device. The last was used in conjunction with the new generation of 'smart bombs', whereby the 500lb laser-guided bombs followed a beam aimed at the target by the aircraft and, as long as the crew kept the beam on the target, the bomb would usually hit it. The 13th Tactical Bomb Squadron was reactivated and equipped with the B-57Gs, and in September 1970 they deployed to Ubon Air Base in Thailand and became part of the 8th TFW. On 12 December 1970 one of the B-57Gs was lost whilst flying a night mission deep in southern Laos. The aircraft apparently collided with a Cessna O-2 FAC in the dark, although the crew ejected safely and were picked up the next morning.

With the rundown of Allied participation in Vietnam, the B-57Gs in Thailand departed for the US in April 1972. They were transferred to the Kansas Air National Guard, who used them until 1974, when they were retired and later scrapped.

TESTING THE NIGHTINGALE

Vietnam was the testing ground for many new additions to the
Army and Air Force inventory. The Air Commando and Special Operations squadrons were tasked with testing most of the
innovations, and one of these crossed paths with Tom Garcia,
a pilot with the 20th Helicopter Squadron in the latter months
of 1967. Tom and the Green Hornets in their UH-1F Huey
helicopters were flying insertions and extractions for SOG out
of Kontum in South Vietnam. He recalls:

"A single example of a device called the Nightingale
came my way in Kontum in the latter months of 1967.
Like the E-63 Urine Sniffer, tested by my unit that same
year, I saw the item only once, tried it out and never
heard anything about it again.

Our mission of the day was a Special Forces insertion
along the Cambodian border west of Duc Co. The team
included two SF troopers plus four Montagnards. The
primary helicopter's crew consisted of two pilots and
two M-60 gunners. That meant the insertion chopper
carried ten people and enough gear for the SF team to
live in the jungle for a week without any outside support.
No problem for an Air Force UH-1F Huey with its powerful GE engine.

There was a backup slick, ready to swoop down and
rescue everyone should the primary 'copter be shot
down, have engine failure or suffer some other unfore-
seen major difficulty. Two Air Force gunships were part
of the group. They were equipped with GE 7.62mm
miniguns and dual rocket pods. Finally, I brought up the
rear in a third slick. Sort of a backup for the backup. I
was supposed to hang back, way back, and stay high,
out of the range of small-arms ground fire. My altitude
allowed me to serve as a communications link with
home plate.

The day before, someone, probably an SF operations
type, had given me the Nightingale. It was, as I recall,

a plywood board about 30in by 30in, maybe a little larger. There was an initiator arming device which, with a time delay, set the thing off. I was told the Nightingale produced a loud racket, sounding 'just like a firefight'.

The idea was to drop it near a team insertion. The fake firefight would certainly confuse the issue as to what was happening and who was doing what to whom, should any enemy troops be in the area.

I thought it was a neat idea and was determined to drop down and plant it 300 meters from where the team landed. Maybe there were no NVA in the area and all the noise would make no difference one way or the other. But, if there were bad guys a little more noise (five helicopters were already making plenty of 'here come the Americans' commotion) would just add to the fun and might serve the intended purpose.

The terrain was ideal. Light tree cover in gently rolling hills with plenty of open grassy areas. It would be easy to find a spot. I got the impression that the rest of my crew, copilot and gunners, didn't share my enthusiasm for the operation. The insert slick had a backup slick plus two gunships for cover. We didn't have anyone particularly interested in keeping an eye on us, and the landing site was one picked out on the spur of the moment, not one specifically selected during the previous weeks reconnaissance mission.

Everything went like clockwork. As I saw the insert ship start its final approach I dove down to a quick landing, actually a low hover, in a dry creek bed between two small hills. One of the gunners armed the Nightingale and tossed it out.

I suppose it activated on schedule, but we were long gone by then. When the SF team returned to base at Kontums FOB II a week later, I was off on another mission in a different part of Vietnam and didn't get to ask if they had anything to report about our small part of the operation.

As far as the United States Air Force is concerned the Nightingale project is a very minor historical footnote, perhaps completely forgotten by now, almost 25 years after the fact. This story will, at the least, preserve the knowledge of the 20th Helicopter Squadron's operational use of it once, during the year 1967.''

The next use of fire-fight simulators, as far as the author is aware, took place in November 1970 as a diversion for a heliborne raid on Son Tay prison camp, deep inside North Vietnam. Perhaps Tom Garcia's tests with the Nightingale were successful after all.

COMBAT DRAGON

During 1967 there was much discussion concerning the need to replace the aging A-1 Skyraider in the close-air-support role. Money was short, and the cost of another aeroplane was a primary consideration. Because of the T-37's reliable service history and low cost, someone came up with the idea of using a version of the "Tweety Bird" trainer. A YAT-37 model was produced as a prototype of the A-37 attack aircraft. It was basically a T-37A re-engined with two General Electric J-85 jet engines boosting the thrust from 1,800lb to 5,600lb. Eight hardpoints for ordnance were added, together with two permanently fixed wing-tip fuel tanks. Several guns were looked at including a German 20mm and the 7.62mm GE gatling gun. The Gatling gun became the standard arm, with modifications as the test program was in progress.

With the standard Cessna high-lift wing, excellent performance was expected, although somewhat speed-limited when compared with F-100s or other high performance aircraft. Later versions were equipped with in-flight refuelling probes as well, giving the aircraft unlimited range. The cockpit never was pressurised, restricting normal operating altitudes to 25,000ft by regulation. However, for some reason the YAT-37 had been put on the shelf for two years, when it suddenly reappeared with an urgent requirement to be tested in a combat environment. The 604th Air Commando Squadron was to fly the A-37A under the project name Combat Dragon.

Colonel Louis W. Weber was at Nellis AFB in 1967, working in the Combat Analysis Division, when a theatre war exercise (TWX) came in, saying that they wanted an operational plan written that would test the A-37 in combat:

"It took a little over three weeks to write and coordinate the plan and subsequently get 'Combat Dragon' on the road. Since I had a free hand, some unique things could be written into the plan; one was painting half the fleet in a sky blue color scheme to compare the number of hits received by a blue aircraft as compared to the olive drab and thus to determine the effectiveness of a different camouflage scheme. We also wanted to demonstrate an extended maximum response rate to a simulated attack through use of a surge operation, in which we would fly the airplanes day and night to see whether pilots, maintenance or other factors might be limiting.

All A-37A aircraft were original T-37A aircraft retrieved from the boneyard at Davis-Monthan AFB in Arizona. We received our first modified production aircraft in May 1967 at England AFB, Louisiana, and the base became the site of future combat crew training. We flew the A-37 six times a day, and as each new production model was received it joined the flying schedule. By the time we deployed to Bien Hoa in July 1967 we had flown over 1,000 sorties and had received nine of our twenty-four aircraft. The aircraft were crated and flown out in C-141s and reassembled on arrival. Thirty-nine aircraft were to be modified, with fifteen remaining at England AFB for training and/or replacements.

Our first combat missions were flown on 15 August 1967, and by 30 September we had flown 1,673 combat sorties. Generally each aircraft was flown four times each day, and in the first seven months of operation we flew 10,000 combat sorties. We lost some airplanes on the ground and in the air, but generally our losses were light. The airplane proved to be very satisfactory for the work we were doing, and as a result new production was started on the A-37B.

Our call sign 'Rap' was unique. We used 'Dragon' at first, then for political reasons we were asked not to use that call sign. We quickly came up with the shortened form of the first name of a friend of mine, Rapely Y. McBurney—Rap. It stuck and became a matter of pride; if you got a Rap on your target you had the best.

When we tested the 'surge' in South Vietnam we covered all the fragged missions that Seventh Air Force could generate for us, and found that they ran out of targets before we ran out of capability. In fact, we had more airplanes in commission at the end of the test than at the beginning.

Single-engine operation became an accepted procedure on longer-range missions, or when loiter time was needed. We would go quickly to altitude and shut down one engine at a time. The airplane would hold its altitude or descend slowly, saving fuel.

We could carry 250, 500 and 750lb bombs, fire rockets, CBUs and other ordnance. The 7.62mm minigun had a weak point which gave us trouble; firing at 6,000 rounds per minute developed a tremendous volume of exhaust gas, and venting that gas could cause engine roll-back or gun-bay explosive damage. Even adding a half-speed switch did not seem to help."*

THE DUST DEVILS IN LAOS

In September 1967 the second Air Force Sikorsky CH-3 unit arrived at Nakhon Phanom Royal Thai Air Force Base. Known

*The A-37A proved so successful that a B model was produced and flown by the 604th SOS and the 8th and 90th Attack Squadrons (later designated Special Operations Squadrons) attached to the 3rd Tactical Fighter Wing at Bien Hoa. The 8th and 90th absorbed the aircraft of the short-lived 310th and 311th Attack Squadrons in late 1969. The B model was also flown by the 603rd SOS, 4406th CCTS and the 4532nd CCTS back in the US. The 8th SOS flew their last combat sorties on 30 September 1972. The following day they transferred to Clark Air Base in the Philippines and were attached to the 405th Fighter Wing. Eventually they would rejoin Special Ops as an MC-130 squadron.

as the "Dust Devils," the 21st Helicopter Squadron was equipped with the improved CH-3E. This model had uprated T58-GE-5 1,500 s.h.p. engines and was armed with two Emerson Electric TAT-102 pod-mounted turrets. The turrets were mounted on each sponson and fired using gunsights at the port and starboard personnel doors. Each turret contained a General Electric six-barrel T 62mm minigun and an 8,000-round ammunition storage feed system. More than 180° traverse was achieved on each side of the aircraft to give complete 360° coverage with overlapping fire forward.

The squadron was initially tasked with placing seismic sensors along the Ho Chi Minh Trail, inserting Road Watch teams and, from late 1968, infiltrating MACV-SOG "Prairie Fire" teams. The Road Watch teams operated along the length of the Laotian panhandle, gathering intelligence and harassing the enemy. The "Prairie Fire" insertions into Laos, and later into Cambodia from Thailand, were hard work. Apart from the long distances involved, each mission meant two crossings of the enemy's main panhandle infiltration corridors, and the high-altitude flying necessary to ensure safety from groundfire was hard on engines.

The "Pony Express" CH-3Cs of the 20th Helicopter Squadron, which had been in Thailand since June 1966, were still flying lift and supply missions into Laos and North Vietnam. Some missions were flown to infiltrate, supply and recover Allied teams inserted north of the DMZ. One such team was recovered by a CH-3, escorted by one of the new Lockheed AC-130 gunships, from the area of the Ban Karai Pass on 21 August 1968. These clandestine missions officially ceased after the bombing halt of 1 November 1968. Three months earlier, on 1 August 1968, the 21st Helicopter Squadron had been redesignated the 21st Special Operations Squadron (SOS) and the 20th Helicopter Squadron had become the 20th SOS.

In the summer of 1969 the 21st SOS absorbed the "Pony Express" CH-3s of the 20th SOS and, with a complement of fifteen CH-3s, took over their mission as well. One high-priority task was hauling POL, food, water and equipment to several isolated radar and communication sites. One of these was the ill-fated Lima Site 85, and a CH-3 went down on approach to the site in December 1967, three months before the site was taken by the communists.

As the fighting escalated in Laos, the need for heavy-lift helicopters became evident, and from 1967 onward US Army Chinooks and Flying Cranes, together with Marine CH-53s, were detached to north Thailand from Vietnam. In August 1970 the 21st began to re-equip with the larger Sikorsky CH-53C. This aircraft had twice the power and three times the load-carrying capacity of the CH-3.

During 1969 communist fire brought down and destroyed six CH-3s in Laos, and one other was destroyed by the enemy after a crash landing. By the time of the ceasefire in Laos on 22 February 1973, the Air Force had lost a total of eleven CH-3s in Laos and six others elsewhere in Southeast Asia. The introduction of the CH-53 reversed the trend. As with the CH-3s, they were still used in pairs in case one aircraft was brought down, but the use of high-speed, steep approaches to landing zones and effective air support by A-1E Skyraiders kept losses down to two ships, both in 1971; one near Long Tieng and the other near South Vietnam during Operation Lam Son 719.

Along with its many other duties, the 21st SOS was used increasingly for tactical troop lifts, hauling Hmong and Royal Lao battalions in airmobile assault and reinforcement operations. The squadron made its last major combat assault on 20 January 1973, when seven of its CH-53s and two Air America Chinooks transported over 1,000 troops to reopen the Vientiane-Luang Prabang highway.

Following the ceasefire, the squadron remained at NKP, ready to evacuate Americans from Laos or Cambodia. Air America operations continued inside Laos and the Royal Lao Air Force expanded its helicopter strength to 26 H-34s. Two-and-a-half years would pass before the Pathet Lao finally won the war in Laos. During that period the 21st SOS remained in Thailand, through the fall of Cambodia and South Vietnam to a bitter postcript to the war in May 1975, when the squadron would be decimated at Koh Tang Island off Cambodia, following the seizure of the US vessel *Mayaguez*.

A NEW ERA

The year 1968 saw the dawn of a new era for the Air Commandos. On 1 August all Air Commando units were renamed Special Operations Squadrons and Wings. The Special Air Warfare Center was renamed the Special Operations School. Although this was a break with tradition, at least the new designations reflected the roles of the various units more accurately.

Back in the USA General Corbin, SAWC commander and an instructor pilot from the 4409th CCTS, flew the first production model OV-10A Bronco from the North American Rockwell plant to Hurlburt Field on 26 February to initiate Project Combat Bronco. Student training on the new FAC aircraft began in May, and by July 24 aircraft had arrived.

In February the Secretary of the Air Force approved a program to develop AC-119G, AC-119K and AC-130 gunships, following on from the success of the AC-47. On 1 March the 4413th CCTS was organised at Lockbourne AFB, Ohio, and assigned to the 1st ACW at England AFB. Their mission was to train combat aircrews in the new gunships. In May the 71st Air Commando Squadron, Reserve, was called to active duty at Lockbourne AFB to train in the AC-119G Shadow and take the aircraft to Vietnam to join the 14th Air Commando Wing. The first AC-119K would arrive at Lockbourne AFB in November and another squadron would be activated in 1969 to take the AC-119K Stingers to Vietnam.

The success of the A-37A Combat Dragon deployment was such that an A-37B model was built, and on 1 October the 4406th Combat Crew Training Squadron was activated to fly the type. The first A-37B would arrive on 10 February 1969.

Back in Vietnam, 1968 also heralded the beginning of the end for United States involvement in Southeast Asia. On 30 January the Viet Cong and North Vietnamese launched their infamous Tet Offensive, in which nearly every major city, provincial capital and military installation in South Vietnam was attacked with varying degrees of success. In Saigon itself the American Embassy was attacked by a sapper team, and although they were contained and killed, the pictures sent shock waves around the world. Tan Son Nhut airbase was attacked by 700 Viet Cong, and personnel at the 7th Air Force Command Center and USMACV headquarters grabbed weapons and ran out to help defend the base. The ancient capital city of Hue was seized and had to be recaptured house by house. Were the communists really on the run after four years of fighting by US ground troops?

Although the communists were soon driven back to their sanctuaries, leaving over half of their number killed or captured, the Tet Offensive and the seige of the Marine base at Khe Sanh sent the Washington administration into a state of shock. Now was the time to take advantage of the huge losses suffered by the Viet Cong and take the war to the enemy. Soviet and Chinese support could have been cut by mining the North Vietnamese harbours and ports and abolishing the prohibited zones around Hanoi, Haiphong and along the border with China, thus opening the way for a massive air campaign to destroy the war-making capability of North Vietnam. However, President Johnson was despondent and announced a bombing halt north of the 19th parallel on 31 March, in an attempt to persuade the North Vietnamese to begin peace negotiations. He also announced that he would neither seek nor accept nomination for a second term as President of the United States. America was now committed to a negotiated, as opposed to military settlement of the war, and the process began with major concessions to the enemy.

The North Vietnamese responded to the bombing halt by increasing the amount of supplies flowing south and starting to infiltrate 75,000 more troops down the Trail. They now had plenty of AAA weapons to spare, and started to strengthen their anti-aircraft defences over the trail as well. On 1 November, following the advice of his negotiating team in Paris, Johnson ordered a halt to all bombing of North Vietnam. Four long years would pass before the bombers would fly north again.

By 5 November, when the elections were finished, America had a new president, Richard M. Nixon. Before his tenancy at the White House was ended by the Watergate scandal, Nixon would at least take some of the strong measures demanded by

the military during Johnson's reign, but at the end of the day
the public wanted their boys home, and the public elected the
president.

THE SPADS OF THE 6TH SOS

In March 1968 the Skyraider-equipped 6th Air Commando
Squadron deployed from England AFB to Pleiku Air Base,
South Vietnam, where its primary role was working with
Army Special Forces and covering SOG teams inserted in
Laos. They also maintained a forward alert unit at Da Nang
to handle SAR missions in South Vietnam, a task performed
in North Vietnam by the 602nd ACS. The 1st ACS "Hobos"
had just moved from Pleiku to NKP, but left one flight behind
to provide experienced cadre for the new squadron. Lieutenant-Colonel Normal F. Repp took command of the squadron
as the ranking officer, with eight months' in-country experience. The 6th used the call sign "Spads," and their twenty
aircraft, mostly single-seat J models with a few H and Gs,
carried the tail code "ET."

Lieutenant-Colonel Wallace A. "Jack" Ford commanded
the squadron while at England AFB, but he was lost on 24
May 1968 whilst on a mission over South Vietnam. The Special Forces men were determined to recover Jack's remains for
his family. They were driven off twice, but were successful
on their third attempt.

Lieutenant-Colonel Sidney L. McNeil was recommended
for a Silver Star for covering the withdrawal of a special forces
team that stumbled into an NVA base camp in Laos on 11
January 1969. Sid's flight destroyed twenty military structures
and observed two secondary explosions and fires as ammunition caches blew up. The patrol leader estimated that twenty
NVA had been killed in his vicinity alone, before a helicopter
lifted his team out without loss. Given the choice of Huey
gunships, Phantom jets or Skyraiders, a trapped Green Beret
would always ask for a Spad.

The squadron had a lot of problems with old ammunition,
and Air Force Logistics Command would not give them bore-

safe rounds until they had used up the 20-year-old stuff. O'Dean E. ''Stretch'' Ballmes discovered the same problem:

''The 20mm ammo belts were loaded with a ball round, a high explosive round, an armour-piercing round, an incendiary then tracer, and this was repeated over the length of the belt. No matter what you were shooting at, every fifth around was the correct round. However, the sear mechanism frequently did not extract the brass, and if the next around was H. E. it would explode on contact with the non-extracted brass. That happened to me whilst on a strafing run south of Da Nang. There was the loudest explosion I had ever heard from my starboard outboard gun, and my wingman said, 'Stretch, you're on fire, better punch out!' The bird still wanted to fly, though, so I headed for Da Nang. I was flying a G. model and could not see the right wing, nor the 50 meters of flames trailing from it.

Fortunately, on approach to Da Nang the fire went out and I landed, turned off the nearest taxiway with a fire engine, exited the cockpit and ran like hell. The inboard two-thirds of the wing was a skeleton, only the outboard third had skin. That's what that sweet lady was flying on. Thirty days later she had a new wing and was back in combat.''

Harold G. Pierce was squadron operations officer in March 1969 when the NVA launched a large-scale attack across the border from their sanctuaries in southern Laos. Their targets were the Special Forces camps at Ben Het and Dak Seang. Pierce says:

''We worked with 'Elliot' FACs to protect the C-7 Caribou cargo aircraft, trying to drop supplies to the cut-off camps. About an hour before the scheduled drop we would mark the enemy gun positions with WP rockets, and VNAF A-37s, flown by superb pilots, would drop 500lb bombs on them. When the C-7s were only a couple of minutes out, we would lay a wall of smoke between the approach corridor and the major remaining threat, then continue to attack any positions that opened fire as the C-7s made their drops. After about ten days the NVA withdrew."*

FLYING WITH THE LAO

As we read earlier, Captain Jack Drummond took a job with the air attaché in Laos after incurring the wrath of the 56th ACW commander for ignoring the restrictions and regulations and destroying an enemy truck park with his T-28. Across the border he found himself in another world;

"I flew in a C-47 to Vientiane and was met by a jeep sent by Colonel Gus Sonnenburg, the Air Force Attaché in Laos. I had no idea what I would be doing, just that it involved T-28s and that I would be wearing civilian clothes, not military uniform. I was taken to the "Ice House," where the air force personnel assigned to Gus stayed when they were in Vientiane. A message was waiting for me there, telling me to come in and see Gus the next morning.

Gus took me to the early morning briefing which covered the air activity in Laos the previous day. It was broken down into three elements; what the US Air Force had done in Laos the day before; what the "Ravens," the USAF Forward Air Controllers in Laos, had found and done the day before; how many strikes they had put

---

*The 633rd Special Operations Wing was activated on 9 July 1968 at Pleiku air base, South Vietnam. Commanded by Colonel George P Birdsong, its motto was ATTACK. It only had one squadron, the 6th SOS. The squadron had a comparatively short life span from mid-1968 until it was deactivated on 15 November 1969, the pilots joining the 1st, 22nd and 602nd SOS at NKP. Some pilots did remain at Da Nang, named Operating Location Alpha Alpha (OLAA), as a detachment of the 56th SOW. The 633rd SOW was deactivated 15 March 1970.

in and finally what the Royal Laotian Air Force had done.

After the briefing Gus told me that he felt fortunate to have me there and that Heinie Aderholt had told him that I might show up at some time or other and that he had a place where he could use me. He emphasised that we could not be seen as being military personnel because of the 1962 Geneva Convention on Laos, the signatories having agreed to withdraw all military personnel from Laos. He gave me a cover story, which was that I was a US Government Forest Ranger and I thought that rather funny because I had just spent the last few months trying to burn down the largest quantity of forest that I could, in my hunt for North Vietnamese trucks.

Gus explained about the other non-US personnel working in Laos, namely pilots from the Thai Air Force, who were seconded to the Laotian Air Force to gain combat experience by flying T-28s. They called them the ''B'' Team. They flew out of Vientiane and were basically mercenaries, flying missions given to them by the Central Intelligence Agency (CIA) element in Laos.''

The Royal Lao Air Force operated out of Vientiane, Savannakhet, Pakse and a northern base at Luang Prabang. In addition, T-28s flew from the CIA base at Moung Soui. Some pilots were Hmong tribesmen who had been trained by the Americans, and they flew specifically for General Vang Pao, in support of his forces. A cousin of Vang Pao, Lee Lue, became one of the best pilots ever to climb into the cockpit of a T-28. When he was finally killed he had logged over 5,000 combat missions in the aircraft.

In 1964 Detachment 6 of the 1st Air Commando Wing had been established at Udorn Royal Thai Air Force Base, to train Lao and Thai pilots and ground crew under the project name ''Waterpump.'' They came under the direct control of the US Ambassador to Laos in Vientiane. The Lao pilots were given English language training, and then went through ground school and onto basic flying training in the T-28. Advanced flying training followed; formations, instrument flying, etc, and then gunnery training before graduation. Their instructors were originally Air Commandos, but the regular US Air Force officers took over. However, they had little T-28 experience. After graduation, the Lao pilots were assigned to a squadron at one of the previously mentioned locations.

The US Air Force had a parallel organisation at each air base, as part of Project 404; an air operations center consisting of a commander, a chief of maintenance, a radio guy, two or three aircraft technicians and a couple of others to maintain communications equipment and a medic cum flight surgeon for the Lao pilots. The AOC commanders had never been T-28 pilots before, and Jack's new job was to be the new AOC commander for both Pakse and Savannakhet. He recalls:

"I was told to look like a civilian; to grow my hair and not call the men assigned to me by their rank. I was not to tell anyone that I was in the military, and I was not to let my men salute me or call me captain. My job was to see if I could help the T-28 squadrons at the two bases to become more effective in their air-to-ground role and support of Royal Lao Army units around Savannakhet in Military Region III and Pakse in Military Region IV. My biggest disappointment, though, was an order direct from the US Ambassador that I was not allowed to fly combat missions in the T-28 with the Lao pilots. The defense attachés office had an assistant attaché at Savannakhet who monitored our radio channels to ensure that this rule was not broken. How I was supposed to teach the Lao pilots anything, when I could not fly in combat with them, was not explained to me.

I then went over to the Lao Air Force Headquarters and discovered that they had no idea what was happening at Pakse or Savannakhet, nor how many aircraft were there or how many pilots or ground crew were with each squadron.

The next morning I flew out to Udorn, to the Waterpump facility, to discover how their maintenance system worked. Only minor maintenance was carried out by the squadrons, the bulk of the work was carried out at Udorn. Each base had around 24 T-28s, and if you had a badly damaged 'plane, it had to be flown to Udorn and exchanged for a new one. When the T-28s came out of the Air America repair facility they looked, flew and smelled new and were repaired to Air Force standards.

I looked at the pilot training organisation at Water-pump and discovered that despite 150–200 hours of flying training the Lao pilots were sent out to the squadrons with only ten hours solo time in the T-28.

The next morning I signed for a T-28 and flew down to Savannakhet. The base had a single concrete runway and a short squat control tower. However, the bomb dump and flight line were just dirt, and when the rainy season began it all turned to mud. In addition, only 250lb bombs were being used as the bomb loader was broken and 250lb was all the Lao munitions people could lift at one time.

I was quartered with a handful of intelligence guys who worked for the assistant attaché at Savannakhet. I discovered that when I was flying missions out of NKP and wanted to attack a target that was not fragged (previously assigned) or given to me by a Raven, a US Air Force Forward Air Controller, it was these guys who would have to give me permission, and they were young, first lieutenant kids, working from maps on the wall in their operations center!

I also met the local CIA operative, who was referred to as the CAS guy, which stands for Controlled American Source. CAS was what the CIA called themselves in Laos. They were there to act as the command and control element for the mercenary forces in Laos; the Hmong tribesmen in the North and the Thai Army Units assisting the Royal Lao Army in the South. They also controlled the ground recon teams that were inserted into the Ho Chi Minh Trail to gather intelligence and the Thai Air Force 'B' Team of T-28 pilots.''

It soon became obvious to Jack that there were two types of pilot in the Lao T-28 squadron at Savannakhet. The flight leaders probably had flown 1,000 combat sorties in the T-28 and the squadron leader 3–4,000 combat sorties in T-28s and in T-6s and Bearcats that he had flown for the French. The young guys from Waterpump had only ten hours' solo, and one mission with live ordnance before they got there. There was no-one in the middle. In addition, they had only dropped hard bombs, no napalm, no snakeyes (with drag-inducing fins that deployed after release to slow the bomb down to ensure that the aircraft was clear of the blast before it exploded) or CBU's, cluster bomb units which opened to release a number of smaller bombs to cover a wider area.

The squadron commander calmly informed Jack Drummond that, "The younger guys learned through doing, and if they did not learn they died." In the USAF the height of aspiration for a pilot was to fly fighters, but in the Lao Air Force the height of aspiration was to fly C-47s. If you flew T-28s you just flew and flew and flew until you died and then you did not fly them any more. "Fly until you die" was a common saying, and to get out of T-28s you had to bribe your way out. Jack soon decided to try to improve matters:

"I wanted to do three things. Firstly to find out the younger pilots' capabilities and then design a training program to teach them to become good combat pilots without killing themselves. Secondly, I wanted to improve the airfield, and thirdly to try to improve the tactics of the squadrons at both Savannakhet and Pakse.

I visited Pakse and found that the squadron there was in just the same condition regarding organisation and experience, although their airfield was in better shape. One good point was that there was no assistant air attaché at Pakse. In order to assess the guys, I had to fly with them, but I had to ensure that I did not speak on the radio or allow myself to be seen by the assistant air attaché. I realised that the training at Waterpump was totally inadequate, and there was a long history of accidents, from taxying accidents to pilots coming off the target and turning the wrong way and never being seen again.

I began a ground school at Savannakhet for the younger guys, and eventually obtained enough pierced steel planking from NKP to cover the taxiways and bomb dump. I tried obtaining the stuff through normal channels, but got nowhere, so I went to the CAS guys and told them that if they wanted effective air support they were going to have to do something about the airfield. A couple of days later they told me that there was up to $40,000 available to buy what I needed. In addition, I found some 120lb white phosphorous bombs in the bomb dump, which were desperately needed by the T-28s flying night missions from NKP. I shipped the bombs by barge to NKP and swapped them for the pierced steel planking. I then paid local labour to lay the planking at Savannakhet and even had enough money left over to build new squadron buildings at Savannakhet and Pakse and to start a fund for relatives of pilots killed in action.

I recall two combat missions that I flew in Laos. One day, while I was flying an O-1 which belonged to the Raven Forward Air Controllers, I found an enemy truck park in the trees. I returned to Pakse and told one of the Ravens what I had found, and decided that I was not going to share my truck park with anybody. I went back out in a T-28, accompanied by the FAC, and spent the afternoon bombing the trucks. The bomb damage assessment was between 25 and 30 trucks destroyed.

On another occasion a Raven came in and told me that he had found a bridge over a river in a remote area near the Thai border, and that he could see truck tracks and other evidence that it was being used by the enemy. I went out in the afternoon and found a truck convoy crossing the bridge. I called 'Alleycat', the airborne command and control ship, and requested flights and spent the next 45 minutes working four flights of Phantoms, trying to drop this little bridge into the river. Well, they dropped bombs all over that part of Laos, but did not hit the bridge, so I flew back to Savannakhet and got a T-28 loaded with four 500lb bombs and two pods of CBUs and went back after my bridge. I rolled in on my first pass and dropped my first bomb right in the middle of the bridge and it fell into the river. I then flew along the road and attacked the trucks which had crossed the bridge. The Raven who had told me about the bridge went back later and took a photograph of the remains of the bridge. He gave it to me inscribed with the words, 'To the best bomber in Southeast Asia'. I still have that picture on my wall today.

One day I went to Udorn to borrow one of the two RT-28 photo-reconnaissance birds, to help the CAS guys get some pictures of the China Road that was being built by the enemy across northwest Laos to Thailand. The colonel commanding Waterpump refused to let me take one of the aircraft, because he said it was the only way his guys could get combat sorties. Apparently they had been flying photo sorties out of Udorn and logging them as combat missions in order to qualify for their air medals. I asked him how many guys he had, and he replied, 'About seventeen'. I said, 'Well, I have got about forty air medals and you can have seventeen of them'. I then went out and got in the airplane and flew off with it.''

MEDAL OF HONOR AT KHAM DUC

Following the loss of Lang Vei in February 1968, the only remaining Special Forces border camp in I Corps was that at Kham Duc. Located ten miles from the Laotian border on the extreme western fringe of Quang Tin Province, the camp served as a base for Allied reconnaissance teams and a training site for Vietnamese Civilian Irregular Defense Group troops. The first Special Forces A-detachment had moved into Kham Duc in September 1963, and found the outpost to be an ideal border surveillance site. It was, however, a difficult place to supply.

This border region southwest of Da Nang was one of the most rugged in Vietnam, and was nearly uninhabited except for the Vietnamese military dependants, camp followers and merchants living across the airstrip in Kham Duc village. The camp, village and airstrip were all situated in a mile-wide bowl, surrounded by jungle and hills which rose abruptly to heights of over 2,000ft. Although C-130 crews had been using the 6,000ft asphalt runway for years, they detested the difficult landings, made dangerous by the weather and the terrain, with the Ngok Peng Bum ridge to the west and the high Ngok Pe Xar mountain looming over Kham Duc to the east.

In the early hours of 10 May the forward operating base of Ngok Tavak, built around an old French fort five miles from Kham Duc, was attacked by a battalion of NVA troops. At the same time that the attack on Ngok Tavak began, the camp at Kham Duc was blasted by heavy mortar and recoilless-rifle fire. This continued throughout the day as the 1st VC Regiment of the 2nd NVA Division moved into positions encircling the camp. At first light C-130s began to arrive with reinforcements from the American Division, and despite the communist shells falling on the runway, 900 Americans and 600 Vietnamese troops had arrived by nightfall.

As the enemy ground attack began during the early morning darkness of 12 May, General Westmoreland reviewed the situation and determined that the camp lacked the importance and defensibility of Khe Sanh. He directed that the camp be abandoned and that the defenders be evacuated by air, despite the strong enemy presence.

By 1000 hours, three of the camp outposts were in enemy hands and company-size NVA assaults were taking place on three sides of the main perimeter. Army and Marine helicopters managed to extract some of the troops, but a Chinook was shot down, blocking the runway until engineers managed to drag it clear. At about 1100 hours Major Ray D. Shelton brought his C-123 Provider in and took 70 people on board, including 44 American engineers. Despite heavy automatic weapons fire and a dozen mortar detonations near his aircraft, Shelton took off safely.

Heavy ground-fire led to the orbiting C-130 command and control ship postponing any further evacuation attempts for the time being. At noon a massive NVA attack was launched against the main compound, but was stopped by ground-support aircraft hurling napalm, CBUs and 750lb bombs into the final wire barriers. By the middle of the afternoon only 145 persons had been evacuated by the one C-123 and fifteen helicopter sorties. A dozen more transports were orbiting nearby, waiting their turn to go in, and with time running out another attempt was made at 1525 hours.

Major Bernard L. Bucher made a steep approach from the south in his C-130 and landed despite numerous hits. More than 100 panicking civilian dependants crowded aboard, and Bucher began his take-off run. He chose to take-off towards the north, either unaware of, or disregarding, the concentration of enemy forces in that direction. As the aircraft cleared the northern boundary it was struck by enemy tracer fire, crashed, and burned with no survivors.

Landing behind Bucher was a C-130E flown by Lieutenant-Colonel William Boyd, Jr., who made an initial go-around just before touch-down. He loaded another 100 people aboard and took off to the south, banking after lift-off so that the aeroplane would be masked by the rolling terrain. Boyd landed his Hercules safely at Chu Lai despite numerous bullet holes and a smoke filled interior. For this flight he was awarded the Air Force Cross.

Lieutenant-Colonel John R. Delmore flew in next, spiralling down from directly overhead. As he neared the ground, bullets tore through the aircraft and, with all hydraulics gone, and almost out of control, the Hercules smashed into the runway. The wrecked aircraft came to rest at the side of the strip and the fortunate crew scrambled out unhurt. They found some shelter and were soon picked up by a Marine helicopter.

The loss of two aircraft in a matter of minutes did nothing to inspire confidence in the remaining transport crews orbiting above. However, three more C-130s flew in and withdrew the last defenders. This final evacuation was made possible by close-in air strikes, with fighters laying down a barrage along both sides of the runway during the run-in and while the transports loaded. Lieutenant-Colonel Wallace crossed the field at right angles in his C-130E and made a 270° turn at maximum rate of descent with power off and gear down. Touching down, he made a maximum-effort stop and was immediately swamped by 100 panicking Vietnamese. The loadmaster had to rescue a women and a baby trampled in the rush as the civilians and the last few Americans dashed aboard. Wallace took off to the south and safety just as a helicopter swooped down to take the Special Forces command group out of the camp.

As the advancing NVA infantry took over the camp, a near-tragedy occurred. A C-130 flown by Lieutenant-Colonel Jay Van Cleef was inexplicably instructed by the airborne control center to land the three-man combat control team which had already been evacuated earlier in the day. Van Cleef protested that the camp was almost completely evacuated, but the control center insisted that the team be returned and left.

Obediently Van Cleef landed his aircraft, and the three controllers ran towards the burning camp. He waited patiently for another two minutes for passengers waiting to be evacuated, and when none appeared he slammed the throttles open and took off. He duly notified the control aircraft that they had taken off empty, and was shocked to hear the control aircraft then report to General McLaughlin that the evacuation of Kham Duc was complete. His crew immediately and vehemently disabused the commander and pointed out that the camp was not evacuated, because they had, as ordered, just deposited a combat control team in the camp. There was a moment of stunned radio silence as the reality sank in. Kham Duc was now in enemy hands—except for three American combat controllers.

Meanwhile, Major John W. Gallagher, Jr, and the other two controllers took shelter in a culvert next to the runway and started firing at the enemy in the camp with their M-16 rifles. The command post asked a C-123 to try to pick the men up, but as the aircraft touched down it came under fire from all directions. The pilot, Lieutenant-Colonel Alfred J. Jeannotte, Jr., could not see the team anywhere, and jammed the throttles forward for take-off. Just before lift-off the crew spotted the three men, but it was now too late to stop. The C-123 took to the air and, low on fuel, turned for home. Jeannotte later received the Air Force Cross for his actions.

The C-123 behind Jeannotte was being flown by Lieutenant-Colonel Joe M. Jackson and Major Jesse W. Campbell. They arrived just as the command ship requested that someone make another pick-up attempt. Jesse Campbell radioed "Roger. Going in."

Joe Jackson had been a fighter pilot for twenty years before being assigned to transport duty. He had flown 107 missions in Korea and had won the Distinguished Flying Cross. He knew that the enemy gunners would expect him to follow the same flightpath as the other cargo aeroplanes, and decided to call upon his fighter-pilot experience and try a new tactic. At 9,000ft and rapidly approaching the landing area he pointed the nose down in a steep dive. Sideslipping for maximum descent, with power back and landing gear and flaps full down, the Provider dropped like a rock. Jackson recalls:

> "The book said you didn't fly transports this way, but the guy who wrote the book had never been shot at. I had two problems, the second stemming from the first. One was to avoid reaching 'blow up' speed, where the flaps, which were in full down position for the dive, are blown back up to neutral. If this happened, we would pick up even more speed, leading to problem two, the danger of overshooting the runway."

Jackson pulled back on the control column and broke the Provider's descent just above the treetops, a quarter of a mile from the end of the runway. He barely had time to set up a landing attitude as the aircraft settled towards the threshold. The debris-strewn runway looked like an obstacle course, with a burning helicopter blocking the way a mere 2,000ft from the touchdown point. Jackson knew that he would have to stop in a hurry, but decided against using reverse thrust. Reversing the propellers would automatically shut off the two jets that would be needed for a minimum-run take-off. He stood on the brakes and skidded to a halt just before reaching the gutted helicopter.

The three controllers scrambled from the ditch and dived into the aircraft as the surprised enemy gunners opened fire. In the front of the aircraft Major Campbell spotted a 122mm rocket shell coming towards them, and both pilots watched in horror as it hit the ground just 25ft in front of the nose. Luck was still on their side, however, and the deadly projectile did not explode. Jackson taxied around the shell and rammed the throttles to the firewall. "We hadn't been out of that spot ten seconds when mortars started dropping directly on it," he remembers. "That was a real thriller. I figured they just got zeroed in on us, and that the time of flight of the mortar shells was about ten seconds longer than the time we sat there taking the men aboard." Within seconds they were in the air again, and one of the combat team recalled, "We were dead, and all of a sudden we were alive!"

General McLaughlin, who had witnessed the event from overhead, approved nominations for the Medal of Honor for both pilots, who landed safely back at Da Nang to discover that their C-123 had not taken one hit! In January 1969 Colonel Jackson received the Medal of Honor in a ceremony at the White House. Major Campbell received the Air Force Cross and the rest of the crew were awarded Silver Stars. The battle had resulted in a total North Vietnamese victory, for the last Special Forces border surveillance camp on the northwestern frontier of South Vietnam had been destroyed.

COLONEL JONES, MEDAL OF HONOR

On 1 September 1968 Lieutenant-Colonel William A. Jones III, the commander of the 602nd SOS, proved beyond doubt that a Sandy pilot would go to any length to effect the rescue of a downed pilot, and was awarded a Medal of Honor as a result of his actions. Only twelve were awarded to Air Force pilots during the war, and two of these went to Skyraider pilots. The citation for the medal tells the story:

"For conspicuous gallantry and intrepidity in action at the risk of his life above and beyond the call of duty. On 1 September 1968, Colonel Jones distinguished himself as the pilot of an A-1H Skyraider aircraft near Dong Hoi, North Vietnam. On that day, as the on-scene commander in the attempted rescue of a downed United States pilot, Colonel Jones' aircraft was repeatedly hit by heavy and accurate anti-aircraft fire. On one of his low passes, Colonel Jones felt an explosion beneath his aircraft and his cockpit rapidly filled with smoke. With complete disregard of the possibility that his aircraft might still be burning, he unhesitatingly continued his search for the downed pilot. On this pass he sighted the survivor and a multiple-barrel gun position firing at him from near the top of a karst formation. He could not attack the gun position on that pass for fear he would endanger the downed pilot. Leaving himself exposed to the gun position, Colonel Jones attacked the position with cannon and rocket fire on two successive passes. On his second pass, the aircraft was hit with multiple rounds of automatic weapons fire. One around impacted the Yankee Extraction System rocket mounted directly behind the headrest, igniting the rocket. His aircraft was observed to burst into flames in the center fuselage section, with flames engulfing the cockpit area. He pulled the extraction handle, jettisoning the canopy. The influx of fresh air made the fire burn with greater intensity for a few moments, but since the rocket motor had already burned, the extraction system did not pull Colonel Jones from the aircraft. Despite searing pains from severe burns sustained on his arms, hands, neck, shoulders and face, Colonel Jones pulled his aircraft into a climb and attempted to transmit the location of the downed pilot and the enemy gun position to the other aircraft in the area. His calls were blocked by other aircraft transmissions repeatedly directing him to bale out, and within seconds his transmitters were disabled and he could receive only on one channel. Completely disregarding his injuries, he elected to fly his crippled aircraft back to his base and pass on essential information for the rescue rather than bale out. Colonel Jones successfully landed his heavily damaged aircraft and passed the information to a debriefing officer while on the operating table. As a result of his heroic actions and complete disregard for his personal safety, the downed pilot was rescued later in the day. Colonel Jones' conspicuous gallantry, his profound concern for his fellow man, and his intrepidity at the risk of his own life, above and beyond the call of duty, are in keeping with his highest traditions of the United States Air Force and reflect great credit upon himself and the Armed Forces of his country.''

ENTER THE SHADOW

The loss of six AC-47 gunships over the Ho Chi Minh Trail made it clear that a new gunship was needed. The Air Force wanted a bigger gunship with a vast increase in payload and performance, to enable them to fit more guns and ammunition, together with new systems including night observation devices, to locate the enemy during the hours of darkness. The C-130 was chosen as the next gunship, and was designated the AC-130 Spectre Gunship II. It would eventually evolve into the most powerful gunship ever built, but the Hercules was much in demand in the transport role and a shortage of airframes caused a slow start to the project. In the meantime, the Seventh Air Force in Vietnam wanted more gunships as soon as possible, preferably with the ability to operate over the Ho Chi Minh Trail as well. The AC-47 was now out of the question, so the Air Force turned to the venerable Fairchild C-119 Flying Boxcar.

The C-119 had a better performance than the C-47, together with a large interior, and it was readily available "off the shelf" as it already equipped some squadrons of the Air Force Reserve. On 17 February 1968 a letter of contract was awarded to Fairchild-Hiller Corporation to modify 26 C-119G airframes into AC-119G gunships, and a further 26 into a more advanced AC-119K for the truck-hunting role. The modifications were to be carried out at Fairchild-Hiller's facility in St Augustine, Florida. The C-119s were withdrawn from Air Force Reserve units, in particular the 434th Troop Carrier Wing in Indiana, who would also supply many of the AC-119 crews. The new gunship would be equipped with four 7.62mm SUU-11A/1A minigun pods and, with the increased ammunition load carried within the larger interior, the AC-119G would be about 25 percent more effective than the AC-47. Other new equipment included an AVQ-8 20kW Xenon searchlight, a night observation sight, an LAU-74A flare launcher, a General Precision fire control computer and a TRW fire control safety display to ensure that the aircraft did not open fire on friendly troops.

The AC-119G crews underwent gunship training at Lockbourne AFB in Ohio, and then moved down to Eglin AFB for jungle training. The first of the new gunships was delivered in May 1968, exactly 100 days after the contract was let. The AC-119G would be used by the newly activated 71st Special Operations Squadron, and they deployed to South Vietnam in November 1968, joining the 14th Special Operations Wing at Nha Trang air base. The new gunship squadron needed a call sign, and to their dismay the call sign "Creep" was allocated. After a howl of indignation from the squadron crews this was changed to "Shadow" as of 1 December 1968. The 71st began flying operational sorties and combat evaluation on 5 January 1969. The AC-119Gs performed satisfactorily, except in the FAC role, where they were too slow, hard to maneuver and vulnerable to enemy groundfire. They were also very heavy, and were limited to six hours flying time.

Most Shadow targets would be located as a result of armed reconnaissance sorties, when an aircraft would be assigned to patrol a "box," an area bounded by precise co-ordinates. They would fly at around 500ft and search for a target with the night observation device, or by using the flares or searchlight. When a target was identified, the gunship plotted the co-ordinates and called the controlling agency for clearance to fire. When clearance was received, the Shadow would climb to 3,500ft and usually select a semi-automatic firing mode, bank into a left orbit and open fire. Many of the AC-119G boxes were located west of the cities of Kontum and Pleiku, where the borders of Cambodia, Laos and South Vietnam converged. One Shadow attack on an enemy troop concentration and storage area north of Pleiku air base touched off 80 secondary explosions. By March 1969 the 71st had received its full complement of eighteen AC-119Gs. Back in the US work was continuing on the AC-119K, and this model, and more of the service history of the Shadow, are described in the next chapter.

PROJECT BLACK SPOT

Project Black Spot began in December 1965 and was designed to give the air force a self-contained night attack capability to seek out and destroy enemy trucks on the Ho Chi Minh Trail at night. Two C-123Ks (54–691 and 54–698) were modified by E-Systems of Greenville, Texas and given the designation NC-123K. The aircraft were tested by the 1st Combat Applications Group to determine the feasibility of integrating either automatic or manual release of weapons. The project cost over $14 million and the 1st CAG provided crew training as well as testing.

Major Charles A. Boerschig was with the project from the start and flew combat missions over Laos. He told the author:

"The aircraft were fitted with a long nose fairing that housed a Forward Looking Radar with a Moving Target Indicator function. A revolving ball turret was installed under the nose and housed a Forward-Looking Infra-red sensor (FLIR), a Low Light-Level TV (LLLTV) and a laser range finder. The turret could rotate in both azimuth and elevation, thus giving the sensor operator the ability to track targets off the aircraft's line of flight. The aircraft was also fitted with an advanced navigational system and passive Infrared (IR) detectors.

The moving target radar was very ineffective in detecting targets, so target acquisition was made by the TV and FLIR. The two sensors, mounted side by side, worked very well together. For example, when the truck drivers would hear the airplane, they would turn into the jungle if possible, to hide. The TV would very often be blocked out by the foliage, but the heat from the engine would still be visible on the FLIR, enabling us to drop bombs on him.

The system was envisioned to carry two dispensers, but due to all the equipment and modifications, the aircraft could only carry one dispenser. Even with one dispenser we were still taking-off over the gross weight limitations. We developed a schedule that called for one aircraft and crew to fly two sorties each night. We would fly the first mission, then land at a base such as Pleiku, to rearm and refuel for the second mission. We had a special bomb loading carrier, which would be loaded

with a dispenser. A C-130 would pick up the loader and
its crew and ferry it to the base to be used.''

Two rectangular aluminium weapon dispensers for Cluster
Bomb Units (CBUs) were stacked within the fuselage, each
container holding thirty-six CBUs. Depending on the type of
CBU carried, the containers could hold between 2,664 and
6,372 one pound bomblets. They were released through twelve
openings in the cargo floor that aligned with the twelve cells
(each containing three CBUs) in the weapons dispenser. The
lower fuselage contained twelve inward opening doors that
aligned with the openings in the cargo floor, forming a chute.
Bomblet release was controlled by a weapons panel in the
forward fuselage and in the event of emergency, the entire load
could be jettisoned manually.

To supply the electrical power required to operate the armament system and sensors, the engine generators were replaced by alternators and these were cooled by air scoops fitted
to the top of each engine nacelle.

Before deploying to Vietnam, the two aircraft were sent to
Osan Air Base, South Korea to be evaluated against the high
speed infiltration boats used by North Korea to land agents in
South Korea. They remained in South Korea from 19 August
until 23 October and then deployed to South Vietnam for a
combat evaluation of the weapons system by the 1st Combat
Applications Group.

Using the Black Spot callsign the two aircraft began operations on 15 November, flying out of Phan Rang Air Base,
with mission staging areas at Binh Thuy and Pleiku. During
the combat evaluation period sixty-nine sorties were flown
over the Mekong Delta and the Ho Chi Minh Trail. One mission in particular went very well. Charles Boerschig continues:

''Due to the limitations of the canister type munitions,
we had to operate at 4800ft exactly. This would cause
problems due to weather, but we had no choice. The
navigator would direct the aircraft to our area using the
moving-map display, which was one of our most effective pieces of equipment. Once in the area we would

pick out the Trail on the TV and FLIR sensors and direct
the aircraft using them. Due to the limitations of the
sensors we would have to point the turret at a very steep
angle, so when we did pick up a target we would have
very little time to get the aircraft over the point where
we could get an effective bomb release. More often than
not we would not have time, so we would have to turn
around for a second try. The computer would hopefully
track the target, although it was not all that reliable. I
developed a system of holding hands with the FLIR operator, in that we would both have a hand on the master
joy-stick and have the pilot make a shallower turn than
normal. With both of us working the joy-stick we got
much more accurate results.

On one particular night we were in and out of the
clouds and there was not much traffic moving. We did
find a couple of trucks, and we used the same both hands
on the joy-stick technique, so we dispatched both of
them. We continued over the Trail, but there wasn't any
more traffic moving. I had done some studying on the
way the NVA operated their trucks. Each driver had his
own truck and section of the Trail and he would drive
his truck to his stopping point where the truck would be
unloaded and the cargo transferred onto another truck
for the next section of the route. These areas were called
truck-stops or truck-parks. I deduced that the ideal location for one would have a fairly large open area for
positioning the trucks; jungle areas close by to hide in
and a stream nearby would be a plus. I had picked out
one such location in our search area, so I decided to go
take a look. Sure enough, when we got close we got
some good indications, but there were no real definite
targets showing. It was getting late and we didn't want
to take any bombs back home, so we made a drop. All
hell broke loose! We got several secondary explosions
and started what the co-pilot described as a fire as big
as a couple of football fields. We made a couple of more
runs to get rid of all the bombs, then returned to Ubon.
We had quite a night. We received credit for over half

of the truck kills that had been made by all the aircraft flying that night!''

The two aircraft were credited with a total of 151 boats and vehicles destroyed and 108 damaged, with secondary explosions noted on 261 targets. They completed 77 percent of all missions and had an inservice rate of 84 per cent.

The combat evaluation ended in January 1969 and the aircraft were returned to the States for demodification and storage in the "boneyard" at Davis-Monthan AFB in Arizona. No further C-123s received the modification, because better systems were about to be tested over Laos. Spectre was on its way.

GREEN HORNET MEDAL OF HONOR

By 1967 nearly 300 Prairie Fire patrols had been sent into Laos, and the enemy were increasing their efforts to track and destroy these teams. The Green Hornets of the 20th Special Operations Squadron were still carrying out their prime mission of supporting the teams, and would lose five UH-1 helicopters in this role in 1967–68. At the end of 1968 a routine infiltration mission ended with the award of the Medal of Honor to one of their pilots.

The six-man Special Forces reconnaissance team had been inserted without problems in a heavily forested area not far from the Special Forces camp at Duc Co. It was 26 November, and as the five Hueys made their way home, they had little inkling that the day would end with the award of two Air Medals, eleven Distinguished Flying Crosses, one Silver Star, one Air Force Cross and the highest of them all, a Medal of Honor for First Lieutenant (later Captain) James P. Fleming. Three of the Hueys were UH-1F Slicks, including "Slick 1," Fleming's aircraft. The two others were gunships, and all were low on fuel and anxious to return home.

As sometimes happens, the team encountered a large enemy force and the team leader, Lieutenant Randolph C. Harrison, requested evacuation, or in Special Forces terms, exfiltration. The Huey flight immediately turned around and returned to the area to find their FAC, Major Charles E. Anonsen, circling the team, who were trapped with their backs to a 30-yard-wide river.

The team marked their position with smoke and the two gunships dived down to pour a hail of minigun fire into the enemy surrounding the team. Both gunships came under fire from machine-gun positions 200 yards from the river, and they switched their attack to them, destroying two before Captain David W. Miller's Huey took some hits and had to withdraw. He cleared the area, but his engine soon failed and he had to autorotate to a landing in a small clearing. Major Dale L. Eppinger, the pilot of "Slick Lead," followed Miller's ship down and picked up the crew minutes before enemy troops arrived to destroy their gunship.

With one gunship down and the lead Slick away picking up the crew, the second Slick departed owing to lack of fuel, leaving only Fleming's Slick and the other gunship, together with the circling FAC. The situation was critical, as the two remaining aircraft were running low on fuel and ammunition. The FAC told the Green Berets to move 20 yards to a small clearing on the river bank, and sent Fleming in for the pickup. As Major Leonard Gonzales positioned his gunship between the Slick and the enemy, Fleming tried to get into the clearing. However, it was too small, and he fought to hold the front of his helicopter's landing skids on the river bank, with the tail boom extended out over the river.

Suddenly the enemy launched another attack, the gunfire rising in an ear-shattering crescendo as the team's radio man told Fleming that they were pinned down and could not move to the clearing. Fleming backed away from the bank as his door gunners put down a barrage of covering fire. Gonzales watched Fleming break clear and recalled, "It was a sheer miracle that he wasn't shot down on the take-off."

On the ground, the Special Forces team ringed their position with Claymore mines and hoped that Fleming could get in again. Fleming was wondering the same thing: "The first time we went in I wasn't really conscious of the danger. You know, it was what we had been trained to do, and so we did it. But then I guess it all got to me. Dave Miller getting shot down, the heaviest hostile fire I'd ever seen . . . frankly I was scared to death!''

Once more Fleming took his helicopter down, dropping almost to the surface of the river, where the banks could help shield him from the enemy. The enemy knew where he was going now, and concentrated their fire there. A series of explosions occurred as the enemy hit the Claymore mines and the six team members dashed for their lives, killing three more of the enemy on their way to the clearing. Fleming again hovered with his skids just above the river bank as the breathless team dashed into the clearing. One of the door-gunners, Staff Sergeant Fred J. Cook, fired his M-60 with one hand as he reached down to help the Green Berets aboard. Fleming later recalled, ''Sergeant Cook is about five feet seven and weighs not much more than 120lb. But those Special Forces boys, some of whom were 200lb or more, said that Cook literally lifted them into the helicopter with one hand!'' Despite a hail of lead as thick as a swarm of locusts, nobody was hit. As the last Green Beret dived on board, Fleming backed away and turned east down the river. Only then did he notice the bullet holes that had appeared in the windshield.

SPECTRE, THE ULTIMATE GUNSHIP

The Lockheed AC-130 ''Spectre'' was the ultimate gunship. It was a far cry from the early AC-47 ''Spooky'' and the AC-119G ''Shadow'' and AC-119K ''Stinger'' gunships. The first AC-119G squadron arrived in Vietnam in November 1968, and the first AC-119K squadron a year later in November 1969. Between those dates, only four, and later six, AC-130 gunships were operating over the Trail pending delivery of more advanced ''Spectres.''

The first AC-130 had arrived in Vietnam for field trials in September 1967, and its success led to the decision to modify more of the type. However, the Air Force could not spare any of its C-130 fleet; they were all needed for airlift duties. Seven early-model JC-130s were available, though, and the first of these was converted to gunship configuration by June 1968 and combat operations began with four aircraft in October.

The AC-130A was armed with four 7.62mm minigun modules and four 20mm M-61 Vulcan cannon. Two of each were mounted forward of the main landing gear on the port side of the aircraft, and two of each aft of the gear. In addition, a night observation device (NOD) was fitted, a sophisticated instrument which enabled the user to see targets on the ground by utilising the available star or moon light. The NOD, and a primitive infrared sensor to detect the heat from truck engines, were fitted to the port side of the aircraft, and a fire control computer was installed, linking gunsight, sensors and guns and to coordinate all the variables involved in a sideways-firing weapons system. A steerable illuminator was also mounted on the port side, comprising two 20kW Xenon arc lamps giving off visible, infrared or ultraviolet light. These early AC-130s were operated by the newly formed 16th Special Operations Squadron, attached to the 8th TFW at Ubon Royal Thai Air Force Base. The Commander of Spectre Crew Number One was Lieutenant-Colonel William Schwehm, whose one-year tour of duty began in September 1968. He recalls:

"The primary mission of the AC-130 gunship was the destruction of enemy trucks, although on a few occasions we did fly fire support missions for friendly ground troops. During one year, my crew was credited with the destruction of 228 trucks, three anti-aircraft guns and the probable destruction of another 67 trucks and one helicopter. In all we were hit five times by anti-aircraft fire, with two crewmembers killed and three wounded. I was blessed with a good crew and what I consider to be the finest airplane ever built. Although the AC-130s we flew were the first C-130s built, they were sturdy and, modified as AC-130s, were state-of-the-art in weapons systems.

Most of my 126 combat missions were flown at around 4,500ft above the ground and at 145 knots. I was with the first group of four crews which formed the 16th SOS, and the most aircraft we had assigned during my tour was five. We did a lot of local modification during my tour, because we were in the learning process. Together with Carl Cathy, the commander of the 497th

Tactical Fighter Squadron, I drew up the procedure for the F-4 escort business. We flew with no external lights, so I had our maintenance people come up with a shielded rotating beacon for the top of our aircraft, so that the escort pilot could see us from above.

All of our missions were over Laos, since President Johnson's prohibition of North Vietnamese airspace was on at that time. This allowed the North Vietnamese to bring a good part of their anti-aircraft artillery into Laos, which they did. It was not unusual to receive 300 to 500 rounds of AAA on one four-hour mission. We did encounter AAA rockets, however, I do not believe we got any radar-controlled SAMs. We did get radar controlled gunfire, and halfway through my tour we had the jamming equipment installed in our aircraft.''

The night flights over the Ho Chi Minh Trail were always hazardous, even with F-4 escorts to take on the anti-aircraft guns. Bill Schwehm's luck finally ran out on 24 May 1969, when his crippled Spectre (64–1629) was destroyed in a crash-landing at Ubon RTAFB. The Spectres were beginning to hurt the North Vietnamese, and one of the things that Bill Schwehm's crew were told at the briefing on that fateful night was that Russian advisers were known to be assisting the North Vietnamese gunners in an effort to get one of the gunships.

Spectre became one of the main players in the Commando Hunt interdiction campaign in the southern Laos, Steel Tiger area of operations. This 50 × 150-mile area encompassed the two major mountain passes, Mu Gia and Ban Karai, on the border with North Vietnam and Laos, plus the part of the Trail running south on the Lao side of the border. During the first truck-hunting season of 1968–69 the NOD was the primary sensor used by Spectre, because it was simple and reliable. The other equipment could be affected by haze, smoke and light fog.

Later Spectres received the ''Surprise Package'' modification, which replaced the earlier eight guns with two 20mm Gatling guns, and two 40mm Bofors cannon. Low-light-level TV, tested under Project Tropic Moon, plus improved infrared equipment, enhanced the night vision and detection capability. The two 20kW illuminators were replaced by a 2kW model, to lessen the chances of a surface-to-air missile locking onto its heat signature. Black Crow (BC) equipment, used to detect NVA trucks by picking up electromagnetic radiation emissions from their ignition systems, was installed from mid-1969 onwards.

When the Spectres were equipped with all of the various sensors the crew would carry five navigators, one of whom was an electronic warfare officer to operate the Black Crow and defensive systems. A table navigator would sit on the flightdeck with the pilots and flight engineer and direct the course of the gunship until a target was found. The other three navigators and the electronic warfare officer made up the sensor team and occupied a small room inside the cargo compartment called the booth. From the crew of thirteen or fourteen they were the only ones who could not see outside with the naked eye. One would be the fire control officer, and the other three operated the LLLTV, IR or BC sensors, sitting in front of TV monitors and control panels with joysticks to aim the sensors. The LLLTV console received a standard black and white TV picture from wide-and narrow-angle TV cameras hung from a giro-stabilised platform looking out of an opening slightly forward of the two 20mm cannon. They amplified existing light 60,000 times and produced a picture on the screen as if it was daytime. A Pave Way I laser designator mounted on the bottom of the platform could provide a pulsed beam of energy for guiding sensor-headed bombs, later carried by F-4s. The IR console received its picture from a globular detecting unit protruding from the port side wheel well. The unit would sense infrared energy radiated from the ground; cool objects would appear gray or black on the monitor, warm objects appeared light colored, and the wheels and engine of a moving truck would show up white. The IR had both search and track modes of viewing, and both the IR and LLLTV pictures centered around electronic cross-hairs.

Black Crow was the ears of the gunship. It picked up electromagnetic radiations from internal combustion engines and displayed them as green dot clusters on a grid-faced cathode ray tube, indicating the range and azimuth to the source of the signals. The sensing unit was mounted under a glassfiber radome near the left side of the gunship nose. The BC console also contained radar homing and warning equipment for detecting radar scanning and tracking by enemy AAA and SAM sites.

The pilot would follow the table navigator's directions until the sensors located a target, then he would "take guidance." This would mean following a steering bar, driven by the computer, that would lead the pilot to the correct point in the sky to begin the 30 degree left bank to circle the target. When the pitch steering bar moved to the point where both bars were centerd, the pilot would look over his left shoulder into the gunsight and continue flying to bring the moving reticle and fixed reticle together when he could commence firing. It was a real juggling act since the co-pilot was operating the throttles to maintain airspeed and flying the elevator on autopilot to maintain altitude while the pilot flew ailerons and rudder to align the guns (fixed reticle) with the target being tracked (moving reticle). Exacting crew co-ordination and pilot-copilot finesse were absolutely essential to effective shooting. The pilot fired the guns blind and depended on the sensor operators to inform him of the results. In the back of the plane, gunners would load and service the guns, while a "scanner" hung over the rear cargo door to warn the pilot of any AAA fire heading their way and to call "breaks" as necessary. Often one of the gunners would hang out of the right-hand cargo compartment window to add another pair of eyes to spot AAA threats.

Countering the enemy AAA fire was a continuing problem. During the 1968–'69 and 1969–'70 truck-hunting seasons the AC-130As were armed with four 7.62mm machine-guns and four 20mm cannon. They flew over the Steel Tiger area about 5,000ft and stayed out of the range of small-arms fire, although their 7.62mm rounds were spent by the time they reached the ground. Flying higher than 7,500ft to avoid enemy 23mm AAA fire caused the 20mm rounds to tumble in flight, and fewer than half detonated upon impact. With the 40mm Bofors fitted, Spectre could stay at about 8,500ft, out of range of NVA's 37mm guns, but still within range of the 57mm guns. If the Spectres climbed higher than 10,000ft, oxygen became a problem, and it was not unknown for a gunner to pass out

THE SECRET WAR IN LAOS, 1967–'68   225

until the aircraft descended to a lower altitude.

By the time of the 1970–'71 truck-hunting season, some of the earlier AC-130s had received partial Surprise Package modifications, including the 40mm guns, but concern was mounting regarding the accuracy of bomb damage assessments (BDAs). Twenty thousand trucks were claimed damaged or destroyed during 1969–'70, equal to the complete North Vietnamese rolling stock, but the trucks continued to run. In May 1971 the Seventh Air Force required a truck to suffer a secondary explosion or sustained fire to count as destroyed. Direct hits counted as damage only. Crews would normally use high-explosive rounds for the first few shots and then switch to incendiary (misch metal) rounds to light-off fuel leaks or explosive cargoes. The resulting explosions and fires made it much easier to determine when a truck had been ''killed''.

A second Spectre was downed in April 1970 and surface-to-air missiles became a threat in 1971. From then onwards, the BC and illuminator operators and the rear scanner would try to detect a SAM launch and if one was seen, the IO would observe the flight of the missile until impact was imminent, then call for the pilot to dive, to try to break the lock of the missile on the aircraft. It was a risky business. To try to stay ahead of the game, an AC-130E model was in the pipeline, with better ECM equipment and chaff dispensers to counter the SAM threat. In addition, an Army 105mm howitzer would be installed in place of the aft 40mm gun, with the advantage of greater range and 5.6lb of explosive per shell, compared to the 40mm guns 0.6lb.*

*At the time of writing, the AC-130E, now fitted with new engines and redesignated AC-130H, is still in service with the 16th SOS and the AC-130A with the reserve. However, the AC-130U is soon to appear on the scene and will be discussed in a later chapter.

CHAPTER 8

FIGHTING A LOSING BATTLE, 1969–'71

VIETNAMISATION AND REORGANISATION

DURING 1968, 16,511 US military personnel were killed, the highest number for any year of the war. Public opinion was turning against the war, and Richard M. Nixon had just been elected as the new president. Gradual disengagement became his new policy, and from 1969 onward the US began to run down its war effort and a program of "Vietnamisation" was begun with the intention of bolstering the Vietnamese armed forces. While the war continued, the training of Vietnamese aircrew increased as plans were made to expand the VNAF into the third largest air force in the world.

By the end of August the first US troop withdrawals had begun. The North Vietnamese were dragging their feet at the peace talks, and refused to make any concessions, despite the US bombing halt and troop withdrawals. In October, a quarter of a million anti-war protesters invaded Washington, DC and marched on the Pentagon; the war was being decided not in Vietnam, but on the streets of the United States.

With the end of the Rolling Thunder bombing campaign, the fighters and bombers were redirected against the enemy infiltration routes through Laos and Cambodia. It must have been very frustrating to the pilots risking their lives hunting for individual trucks, usually in the dark, when it would have been a much more effective use of air power to have destroyed the stockpiles near the ports in North Vietnam, from where the trucks began their journey.

Richard Nixon was made of sterner stuff than Lyndon Johnson, and when the North Vietnamese launched a mini-Tet offensive in February, he authorised B-52 bombing raids against enemy sanctuaries in Cambodia. Operation Breakfast was to be kept secret, and over the next fourteen months B-52s, flying and bombing according to Combat Skyspot instructions, dropped over 100,000 tons of bombs in what collectively became known as Operation Menu.

At Hurlburt Field, the first six months of the year saw 1,044 aircrew graduate, including 45 Vietnamese A-37 pilots. The Dragonfly was proving popular with both American and Vietnamese pilots, and it was to become South Vietnam's principal strike aircraft. Gunship training was proceeding apace, and the 18th SOS was activated at Lockbourne AFB and assigned to the 1st SOW. The unit would fly the jet-equipped AC-119K Stinger, and they received their first aircraft in March.

In July the Headquarters 1st SOW at England AFB and 4410th CCTW at Hurlburt Field exchanged locations and commanders. The A-26 equipped 603rd SOS transferred from England AFB to Hurlburt and prepared to retire their last aircraft to the desert boneyard at Davis-Monthan AFB in Arizona. They were followed by the 319th SOS, who had by now flown 133 C-123Ks to Vietnam and brought 100 B models home. The 4408th CCTS was given 25 C-123s from Hurlburt and England AFB and was reassigned to the 317th Tactical Airlift Wing in September.

As a part of the exchange of bases, the 1st SOW took over the Hurlburt based 4407th, 4408th, 4409th and 4410th CCTS at the same time. The 18th SOS and 4413th CCTS at Lockbourne AFB were reassigned to the 4410th Combat Crew Training Wing (CCTW). In August the 4473rd CCTS was activated at Eglin AFB Auxiliary Field No 3 and assigned to the 1st SOW. They were to operate the Beech YQU-22A Bonanza radio-controlled aircraft on intelligence gathering missions over the Ho Chi Minh Trail as a part of the Igloo White programme. The movement of enemy troops or trucks would be detected by sensors sown along the Trail by aircraft, and the data transmitted to the QU-22 and thence to the "Dutch Mill" surveillance center at NKP. Airstrikes could then be directed to the appropriate areas. Five YQU-22As had been deployed to NKP in March 1969 as part of the Pave Eagle 1 programme. Camouflaged Lockheed EC-121Rs from the

553rd Reconnaissance Wing were also used in this role.

In October the OV-10 equipped 4409th CCTS became the 549th Tactical Air Support Training Squadron and the 0-2 equipped 4410th CCTS became the 547th Special Operations Training Squadron. Both units remained assigned to the 1st SOW. As 1969 came to an end, the 603rd SOS began to re-equip with the A-37B, replacing their venerable A-26s.

THE FLOATING RUNWAY AT NKP

Not all Air Commandos spent their working day in the air. Some had jobs on the ground, with problems far removed from those who flew the missions. Colonel Thomas R. Owens was the base commander at NKP from June 1968 to July 1969, and then at Hurlburt Field from July 1969 to September 1972. It was his third war. He described some of his days at NKP to the author, including the tale of the floating runway:

"The Wing Commander at NKP commanded all activities of the wing and had three subordinate Colonels under him. The Director of Operations, the Director of Material and the Combat Support Group Commander, also known as Base Commander. At NKP I had an interpreter who went everywhere off base with me. He was especially valuable when we attended a civic function in town or a meeting with provincial officials.

The Provincial Governor was a military police officer, as were most of his staff. I was invited to attend the annual Red Cross ball that was the social event of the year. At about midnight three shots rang out and a man lay dead in the entrance to the hall. As it turned out, one contractor had shot another one, but someone said it was OK because they didn't like each other anyway! As soon as the firing started, the Governor and his staff all had guns in their hands. They did not shoot, but all disappeared within minutes. It seemed to break up the party.

We had two flag poles out in front of base headquarters, one for the Thai flag and one for the United States flag. One day my interpreter came in and told me that we had to raise the Thai flag pole because it was not higher than the US one. Apparently anything representing the King had to be higher than anything else. Pictures of the King and Queen hanging on office walls had to be the highest in the room. We complied by raising the Thai flag pole six inches higher than ours.

One night we had an airplane accidentally drop its ordnance a short distance after take-off into the thick forest. By the time we got to the site a group of Thai farmers had gathered up the bombs and started to dismantle them, so they could sell the component parts. One blew up and then they all blew. Three people were killed instantly and four more seriously hurt. Within hours my interpreter had located the families and paid them for their loss. We always kept plenty of Bhat on hand and a finance officer to disburse it in such a situation.

The Thai base commander was an Air Force Colonel who had trained in the States at Vance AFB, Oklahoma. He was friendly and spoke perfect English, but he never wanted me to come to his office, since that was where personnel, truck drivers etc, came to purchase their base entry permits. This money went to pay the salaries and expenses of his personnel. He had to generate enough money to support his personnel and airplanes that were maintained at NKP. I'm not sure that he got rich off the operation, but that was the system.

We had a very active civic action unit on base that operated in the local area. We had two-and three-man teams that lived in the local communities and gave medical services and advice to the local people. The teams were all enlisted USAF personnel, and we supplied them by air on a periodic basis. We also had a festival to raise money to buy books for the local schools. We bought the books in Bangkok and transported them up country, and then used helicopters to carry them out to the local schools, usually in a 40–50-mile radius. It was always a big day when the helicopter would arrive. All the local officials would be out to greet us and then have us come to the school for the presentation.

The heavy rainfall in northeast Thailand was a problem for air operations, disrupting flying as well as any work being accomplished on the ground. Maintenance requirements increased due to the high humidity and corrosion, regardless of the type of equipment being maintained. These problems were magnified at Nakhon Phanom due to the older and many different types of aircraft. The base had been hacked out of the rainforest, which grew at such a rapid rate it was difficult for the Civil Engineers to build and repair facilities to keep up with the mission. The engineers who maintained the airfield had to be alert to all sorts of emergencies, some of which were not covered in any engineers' classroom or manual.

To keep up with the base expansion, a large Rapid Engineer Deployable Heavy Operational Repair Squadron Engineer (Red Horse) detachment was permanently located at NKP. During the 1967-'68 dry season they built an asphalt parallel taxiway that doubled as a runway while the main runway was being built and later repaired. During the same dry season they prepared a base and laid an aluminium runway which held up well when it was dry. This was the first time this type of aluminium runway had been used under combat conditions. As it turned out, NKP was an ideal testing ground for the new expensive planking. During the rainy season in late 1968, more than 20in of rain fell during one 24-hour period. The volume was just too much for the airfield drainage system, and the water poured over the runway to a depth of 3-4ft. This caused several hundred feet of runway to float about 50ft downstream. By the early morning of the second day of continuous rain it began to let up. The resources of the Base Civil Engineers and Red Horse were marshalled to move the runway back into place. Bulldozers, front end loaders and road graders were put in place on each side of the displaced portion of the runway. They gently pushed the aluminium section back into place while the day's missions were being launched and recovered on the parallel taxiway. By mid-afternoon the runway was back in place, none the worse for the floating episode.

During the following dry season the aluminium runway was removed, cleaned, and made ready to ship out. Red Horse again came to the rescue to rebuild the runway. They installed double the number of 36in culverts, and added five feet to the low portion of the runway. Then almost 10,000ft of runway and 1,000ft over-runs were paved with asphalt. This action seemed to give a permanent fix to the problem of the 'Floating Runway.' "

"SPOOKY" MEDAL OF HONOR

It is to the credit of the Spooky crews that one of their number became the only enlisted man, and indeed the youngest man in the Air Force, to win the Medal of Honor in Vietnam. The evening began for Spooky 71 when it took off at 2000 hours on 24 February 1969 from Bien Hoa Air Base near Saigon on a routine patrol around the capital. One of the eight-man crew that night was 23-year-old Airman First Class John L. Levitow, who was filling in for a sick friend. As the gunship's loadmaster it was his job to set the timing and ignition controls on each flare before passing the three-foot, 27lb cylinder to the gunner, who would pull the lanyard to trigger the flares time-delay firing mechanism and then throw the flare out of the open cargo door at the command of the pilot, to descend by parachute to the ground below.

Just after midnight Spooky 71 had finished a fire support mission against enemy positions outside of Bien Hoa when it received a request for illumination near Long Binh, the large military complex just north of Saigon. The pilot, Major Ken Carpenter turned towards Long Binh where flashes on the ground marked the Viet Cong mortar positions. As the gunner Sergeant Ellis Owen began to drop illumination rounds the gunship was rocked by a tremendous blast. An enemy 82mm mortar shell had struck the right wing and exploded, rocking the entire plane. A three foot hole was blown in the side of the fuselage, sending shrapnel flying across the cabin.

Four crewmen, including Levitow were knocked off their

feet and as Owen fell he inadvertently pulled the lanyard from a flare. The cylinder rolled across the cabin, fully charged. In ten seconds the parachute canister would explode and in another ten the magnesium flare would ignite, with a blast of heat up to 4,000° Fahrenheit.

Levitow had over 40 shrapnel wounds in his right leg and hip, but he helped one of the more severely wounded men to the front of the aeroplane and then turned and noticed the flare between the number one gun and some ammunition cans. "From that point I don't remember anything. My mind went blank," he said later. He moved to the back of the aeroplane and began to drag the flare to the door, his wounds leaving a trail of blood on the floor. Almost losing consciousness, he finally reached the door and pushed the flare out. Moments later it exploded with a brilliant white flash. For his courage Levitow received his nation's highest award on 14 May 1970.

STINGERS OVER THE TRAIL

Back in the States, a further 26 C-119s had been modified as jet-equipped AC-119Ks specifically for the truck-hunting role. Two M61A1 20mm Gatling guns were installed, in addition to the four GE MXU-470 minigun modules now fitted to the AC-119Gs. A AN/APN-147 Doppler terrain following radar was fitted, together with a Texas Instruments AN/AAD-4 Forward-Looking Infra-red set, Motorola AN/APQ-133 side-looking beacon tracking radar and a Texas Instruments AN/APQ-136 search radar with a moving target indicator mode.

The first AC-119K was delivered to the 18th Special Operations Squadron at Nha Trang on 3 November 1969. They were given the call sign "Stinger" and combat operations commenced at the same time as the combat evaluation, known as Combat King. Used almost exclusively in the truck-hunting role, the Stinger's twin 20mm guns could destroy most makes of Soviet trucks, but were ineffective against light tanks. Later in the war some Stingers would relinquish all the 7.62mm armament in favor of carrying more 20mm ammunition. At first the K model gunships were based in flights at Phu Cat, Da Nang and Phan Rang. However, they were so far from the

Ho Chi Minh Trail that two flights were eventually moved to Udorn and NKP, from where they could roam the Trail at will.

The 18th SOS joined the 17th SOS* under the command of the 14th SOW, which was in the process of moving from Nha Trang to Phan Rang and deactivating the 4th SOS, who gave their AC-47s to the VNAF.

Prior to its redesignation, the 71st SOS was involved in an unusual mission when one of its aircraft arrived over a friendly compound which had lost its electric power during a Viet Cong attack. A doctor was performing a delicate operation on a wounded South Vietnamese soldier when the power failed. When informed of the situation the Shadow pilot, Lieutenant-Colonel Burl C Campbell, banked his aircraft into a tight orbit over the compound and switched on its one million candle-power illuminator. The light enabled the doctor to complete the operation successfully and the Shadow headed for home.

Sadly, the first casualty for the 17th SOS occurred on 11 October 1969 when "Shadow 76" crashed on take-off from Tan Son Nhut Air Base with the loss of six crew members. A second Shadow was severely damaged a month later when its right undercarriage collapsed on landing at the Marines air base at Chu Lai. The first Stinger was lost on 19 February 1970 whilst on short finals to Da Nang Air Base. The approach went normally until the flaps and undercarriage were lowered about two miles out and at 500 feet altitude. A sudden power loss in the port engine and jet pod prevented the pilot from maintaining directional control or altitude. The aircraft was destroyed in the resulting crash landing, but the crew luckily escaped with only minor injuries.

1970 was a quiet year for Shadow operations over South Vietnam. Most of the enemy main-force units had withdrawn to their sanctuaries in Laos and Cambodia, so many gunship missions were now flown over the border areas and in defense of special forces outposts. On 28 April, the 17th SOS lost another Shadow when an engine failed on take-off from Tan Son Nhut Air Base and crashed, killing six of the eight crew

*The 71st SOS, which had been operating the Shadow for a year before the Stingers arrived, had been redesignated the 17th SOS in June.

members. The G models were so heavy that with one engine out they could only climb at 100ft per minute, compared to the K model with its two underwing J85 jet engines and 960ft per minute climb rate, following the loss of one engine. Soon afterwards the Air Force reduced the G models maximum gross take off weight to allow a 150ft per minute rate of climb on a single engine.

Less than a fortnight after the crash at Tan Son Nhut, a Stinger operating out of Udorn in Thailand was almost lost, but for an outstanding display of airmanship by its crew. It was one o'clock in the morning and the Stinger was orbiting a heavily defended road section near Ban Ban in Laos. They had already destroyed three trucks and were now receiving heavy anti-aircraft fire. Suddenly, the whole cargo compartment lit up as anti-aircraft shells tore into the right wing and sent the aircraft into a sickening dive. Captain Alan Milacek called "Mayday, Mayday, we're going in," and ordered the illuminator operator to jettison the 1,100lb flare launcher. Within the seconds the aircraft had descended 1,000ft with the two pilots struggling to pull the aircraft out of its dive, as the crew prepared to bale out.

By using full left rudder, full left aileron and maximum power on the two starboard engines, they regained stabilised flight. The crew then proceeded to throw out every possible item to allow the crippled aircraft to clear the mountains between them and safety, and Milacek made a successful no-flaps landing at Udorn at 150 knots (normally 117 knots). When the shaken crew climbed out of the aircraft they discovered that about a third of the right wing, a 14 foot section and aileron, had been torn off. Fifteen months later Captain Milacek and his crew were awarded the Mackay Trophy for the "most meritorious flight of the year."

The 18th SOS lost its second Stinger on the night of 6 June 1970, when its port propeller went out of control shortly after take-off from Da Nang. The pilot tried to return to base, but the situation deteriorated and the crew baled out over the South China Sea east of Da Nang. The empty aircraft continued seaward, creating a certain amount of excitement as it headed towards China's Hainan Island. It eventually went to a watery grave, but all crew members except one were recovered safely.

Following President Nixon's new policy of Vietnamisation, United States combat units began to return home. The 14th Special Operations Wing was deactivated in September 1971 and most of its AC-47 and AC-119G gunships were given to the South Vietnamese Air Force. The 17th SOS gave its aircraft and equipment to the Vietnamese 819th Combat Support Squadron at Tan Son Nhut and were tasked with training two dozen crews by 1 May 1972. They were well on their way to achieving that figure when the North Vietnamese launched their Easter invasion of South Vietnam on 30 March.

Some of the heaviest fighting took place around the city of An Loc, which was surrounded by North Vietnamese Army units. An AC-119K being flown by Captain Terry Cortney on a daylight mission was hit by 37mm anti-aircraft fire and lost the starboard engine and jet, along with some parts of the wing. As the aircraft began to lose height the pilot held the aircraft steady so the crew could bale out. As the copilot swung in his parachute he saw the aircraft enter a right bank and crash into the ground. Captain Cortney stayed with his aircraft and saved his crew, and was nominated for a posthumous Medal of Honor. Sadly it was not approved.

MSgt. Stephen Thornburg, who we met earlier whilst flying C-123 Candlestick missions out of NKP, returned in 1972 for a tour on the Stinger. He recalls:

"Most of my time was spent at Bien Hoa and Da Nang. The Stinger was an awesome weapon against troops, and we saved several isolated outposts in danger of being overrun. Although our gross weight was supposed to be limited to 84,000lb we regularly exceeded that in order to carry additional ammo. We even took off with minimum oil to carry more ammo. When all six guns were on line at the same time, the recoil would push us out of orbit.

One special forces camp we were working in August 1972 was cut off for over a week, and only airpower kept them from being overrun. We worked for them from dusk to dawn, when TACAIR took over. At times the defenders would fall back to their bunkers and have us spray the compound with minigun fire. They would come back up after the sweep and we would go back to working the perimeter. We would radio them for status and they would call back, "Sixty in the wire plus spare parts. KEEP SHOOTING. Every time you shoot it looks like hamburger flying around here." After about a week or two of this they were finally extracted. Weeks later, mass graves were found in the nearby swamps. We had taken quite a toll of the attackers.

The most impressive sights were when we would catch a convoy of ammo and fuel trucks on the Ho Chi Minh Trail. They would cook off for hours and were spectacular to watch. Their fuel was often transported in drums, and they would shoot up into the night sky as they were hit. It was like giant roman candles as they rocketed up on jets of burning fuel. When the fuel/air mixture reached the right combination, the drum would burst; it could be seen for miles. The ammo trucks were impressive as well; if they were carrying explosive rounds we could get a real good secondary explosion, and if the load was small-arms ammo it could cook off for quite a while and rounds would shoot across the ground in all directions.

The '119 could be a pain to fly at times; we were almost always over gross weight and the aircraft's center of gravity was way out. The 'planes were also prone to shed things like cowl flaps and panels, and the parts would often bounce off the fuselage and lodge in the boom.

The worst flight I can remember was in September 1972 at Bien Hoa. The 'plane had just come out of major maintenance, but it was a piece of shit. As usual we had to taxi at speed to keep the cylinder-head temperature within limits. Right after take-off the right engine ran away and the prop would not feather. The pilot attempted to recover at Bien Hoa and began to turn; he brought the jet on the right side up to 100 per cent and lowered the flaps. However, the left inboard flap jammed between the boom and fuselage, and now we had asymmetrical flaps to complicate the existing problems. Despite all this the pilot did a terrific job and put it down on the runway. As luck would have it, the brakes on the left side froze up and dense white choking smoke came pouring in through the gun ports. The pilot stopped the 'plane and ordered "Abandon ship." I killed the fuel flow to the GTPU as I left the 'plane and it took three minutes before the GTPU died from fuel starvation. At the same time the fire department reached the 'plane without managing to run any of us down. They tried to spray the hot brakes, but could not depress the water cannon far enough, so the water missed the brakes and instead went into the gun ports. So the aircraft sat on the runway, brakes smoking, water pouring out of all the rivet holes, right engine smoking and leaking copious quantities of oil on the ground and the crew running for shelter in case the pig decided to cook off.''

NO SAFE HAVENS

Although President Nixon wanted to withdraw American troops from Vietnam and leave the South Vietnamese to continue the war alone, he was not afraid of taking drastic decisions while US troops were still at war. Apart from the Ho Chi Minh Trail, another infiltration route existed, known as the Sihanouk Trail. The communists were being allowed to land supplies at the Cambodian port of Sihanoukville and truck them to their sanctuaries on the border with South Vietnam. Two main areas were known as the Fishhook and the Parrot's Beak, the former supposedly containing the Viet Cong's Central Office for South Vietnam (COSVN). It was estimated that enough supplies were getting through to support two-thirds of the enemy activities within South Vietnam, and 40,000 enemy troops were in residence, supplying arms and assistance to the local Khmer Rouge insurgents and running the sanctuaries and supply bases.

President Nixon authorised the unthinkable, an attack across the border, in early May 1970 to clear the enemy sanctuaries in Cambodia. The troops of the 1st Cavalry Division (Airmobile) were ecstatic; now they could hit back at last. More importantly, the invasion would buy time for the United States to continue its withdrawal, while the South Vietnamese learned to stand on their own two feet.

Although 4,800 communists were killed and thousands of tons of supplies and ammunition captured, the invasion provoked a backlash of public opinion in the States. Violent demonstrations rocked the college campuses, and a nervous senate passed the Cooper-Church Amendment which prohibited the use of American ground troops in Cambodia or Laos after 30 June. The decision by Congress to forbid American troops to cross the border (officially) played into the hands of the enemy. Now they knew they were safe. When a similar cross-border incursion into Laos took place the following year, using South Vietnamese troops on their own, it was a dismal failure.

Another important decision made by the new President was to authorise an airborne raid into North Vietnam, to try to free some of the 500-plus American prisoners of war scattered around various prisons. The camp chosen was Son Tay, 28 miles northwest of Hanoi, and the raid would prove to be one of the most important milestones in the history of Special Operations.

One other minor milestone that may have gone unnoticed was the first night air-to-air refuelling of an A-37B of the 603rd SOS at Hurlburt Field on 26 March. Two months later Dragonfly jets from the unit flew non-stop to Howard AFB, Panama, being refuelled by KC-97 tankers during their six-hour flight. September saw the 317th SOS at Hurlburt receive five new UH-1N helicopters, followed by four more as training began on the type.

Things were far from quiet in Thailand as the year began. On 12 January Ubon RTAFB was attacked by a small force of communist sappers who attempted to destroy aircraft with satchel charges. Five of the raiders were killed within a few feet of the Blind Bat C-130s. The Skyraider force was being reduced as well, with the 22nd and 602nd SOS deactivating in September and December respectively, leaving only the 1st SOS still flying Skyraiders.

COMBAT MEDIC

The humanitarian side of the Air Commandos is seldom mentioned, particularly the medical effort in Thailand and Laos. One of the "Docs" involved was Hap Lutz, who was on a tour of duty in Savannakhet, Laos (Lima Site L-39) in 1970 when he came up with the idea of constructing the first Royal Lao Air Force hospital. Hap pointed out the benefits to the Lao personnel and their dependants to Arch Gordon, the Air Operations Center commander, and to the Lao Wing Commander Thongdy, and was given the green light to go ahead.

Hap was given a long single-storey building by the flight line, and began to turn it into a 30-bed hospital. Contacts at World Medical Relief, Detroit, produced huge amounts of medical supplies, shipped to Hurlburt Field and thence to Udorn, Thailand, and onto Savannakhet, Laos. Help was also on hand in the shape of Explosive Ordnance Disposal (EOD) men on two-week detachments from NKP; Marshall "Doc" Dutton, Jim "Big Knife" Lawrence, Joe Allaire, Tony Sichmiller, Ardell Race, Jim Russell, Darrel "Mac" McCombie and C. O. Bost, together with Charlie Day, the line chief at the base. These men begged, stole or borrowed what was needed to equip the building. An old French tower was discovered and modified to supply water, floor tiles arrived in Lao T-28s, and the building was painted and fitted with curtains.

When the medical supplies arrived, beds, mattresses, IV stands, desks, etc, were put in place. The Royal Lao Army provided a field ambulance and sent their flight surgeon Somchith to the school of aviation medicine in Texas. The grand opening was attended by all the big wheels of the Royal Lao Air Force and Army, the CIA, USAID, USIS, the French and Filipino communities, Prince Boun Oum, the air attaché and air commandos.

In addition to hospital duties, Hap also ran an outpatients' clinic in his own quarters every evening and saw about 300 patients a week, plus emergencies. It was a fine example of the Air Commando "Can Do" attitude.

A book could be written about Hap's experiences alone. He related one of them to the author:

"Roy Dalton, Colonel, retired, and I were posted to Nongbulao, Laos, to assist the Royal Lao Army Commander, Colonel Thao Nheuphet, take Donghene, a village some eleven klicks away. He was to direct air operations and I was to care for the sick and wounded. "Captain Loy," as he was affectionately called, (call sign Dance Band) and I (call sign Ben Casey) were bunkered down in leaky tents and sleeping bags that exceeded even the tradition of our commando training.

We bathed in the nearby river, always conveyed to and from with our two Second World War tanks and several machine-gun-laden jeeps and many personal guards. We subsisted on local animal capture, sticky rice, local grasses, reptiles and insects. Wheeler's sheep camp was vacationland by comparison.

Just when the "Outta sight, outta mind" syndrome takes over, something marvellous happened. It was Christmas, windy, blustery and a chill was in the air. I was manning the radio, and Captain Loy was in a staff meeting with Colonel Nheuphet and his commanders. I distinctly heard a chopper in the distance. Radio silence was abruptly broken and the chopper pilot ID'd and asked for permission to land. Simultaneously, the staff meeting broke up and everyone took their procedural positions.

An Air America H-34 appeared and Captain Loy granted permission to land. After the roar of the engine subsided, the blades' whirling faded and the dust settled, out stepped Air Attaché "Pappy" Pettigrew, our big boss. Ann, his wonderful wife, had prepared us a turkey dinner and "Pappy" was delivering it, plus a bottle of Crown Royal and White Horse scotch! Into the hinterlands of hell he brought it. His generosity and thoughtfulness on what was otherwise a dismal Christmas will always be remembered."

THE SON TAY RAID: A PERSONAL PERSPECTIVE

By the spring of 1970 there were over 500 American prisoners of war in North Vietnam. They were held in a dozen scattered camps and were undergoing torture and maltreatment daily. Negotiations to free them had so far failed, so the decision was made to try to spring some prisoners from one of the camps. In June 1970 the Joint Chiefs of Staff asked Brigadier-General Donald D. Blackburn, Special Assistant for Counter-insurgency and Special Activity, to draw up plans for a raid on Son Tay prison, to free the 50 American prisoners held there. It would not be an easy operation, as Son Tay was 28 miles northwest of Hanoi, the capital of North Vietnam.

Rather than launch a hasty rescue operation, detailed plans were formulated to ensure that every eventuality was covered and that nothing was left to chance. This delayed the start of the operation for five months, until just before midnight on 20 November, when one HH-3E and five HH-53s carrying 59 Special Forces troops took off from Udorn in Thailand. Most of the helicopter crews and the helicopters themselves belonged to the Aerospace Rescue and Recovery Service, as did the HC-130P Hercules refuelling aircraft. Two C-130E Combat Talon pathfinder aircraft were to be used during the final stages of the assault, one from the 7th Special Operations Squadron and one from Detachment 2, 1st SOW.

The plan was not unduly complicated. Using in-flight refuelling, the six helicopters would fly from Thailand, across Laos and into North Vietnam. While various diversions were taking place locally and across North Vietnam, the task force would close on the camp under cover of darkness. The single HH-3E "Banana 1," with a small assault force, would be crash-landed inside the prison compound while two HH-53s, "Apple 1 and Apple 2" would disgorge the bulk of the assault force outside. The wall would be breached and the prison camp buildings stormed. Any North Vietnamese troops found inside would be killed and the POWs would be released, taken outside and flown home in the HH-53s.

Major (now Colonel retired) Jay M. Strayer was the copilot

of "Apple 2," and his personal recollections from that raid
prove the old adage that if anything can go wrong, it will. The
trick is to anticipate such eventualities and make alternative
plans if possible; a lesson almost forgotten by special forces
planners in later years. Jay told the author:

> "I spent 12 of my 28 years in the Air Force with the
> Aerospace Rescue and Recovery Service, and am proud
> of the fact that, in Southeast Asia, we successfully res-
> cued 2,780 combat crew members, including some
> Army, Navy and Marines who would have been cap-
> tured or otherwise lost. One pilot who we could not save
> from captivity was Tom Curtis, a Captain then, with
> whom I'd served in Germany in the very early 'sixties.
>   Tom replaced me as the HH-43 rescue detachment
> intelligence officer at Nakhon Phanom in May 1965.
> Three months later Tom was shot down near the Mu Gia
> Pass, between Laos and North Vietnam, while attempt-
> ing to rescue an F-105 pilot named Willis Forby. Tom,
> his flight mechanic and pararescueman were the first air
> rescue members to be captured and made POWs. His
> copilot was separated and later allegedly killed by some
> natives as he was attempting to walk out. Little did they
> know it, but some seven-and-a-half years later Tom and
> Will Forby would fly home from Hanoi on the same C-
> 141 freedom bird—probably the record for taking so
> long to effect a successful rescue!
>   Five years and three months after Tom was captured,
> at deserted Takhli air base, Thailand, on the eve of 20
> November 1970, after three months of intensive training,
> I sat staring for the first time at the list of POWs who
> were known to be in the Son Tay prison camp. I was
> shaken when I saw my good friend Tom Curtis's name
> on the list. I literally trembled and broke out in a cold
> sweat as I wondered if it might be possible that I would
> be the one to rescue my friend.
>   I had been on my third trip to Southeast Asia, twice
> in HH-43s, and had arrived again at Udorn air base,
> Thailand, in June 1970 to fly the HH-53. In late July or
> early August a headquarters request came down for a

couple of experienced rescue helicopter pilots to return to Eglin for participation in a special project. Although I had just arrived from the States and had no special interest in returning so quickly, I said yes, together with Captain Bill McGeorge, and we returned to Florida.

I was impressed with our introductory meeting with (then) Brigadier-General Leroy Manor, telling us that we were about to embark upon a very key mission and that it was important we do not discuss what we were doing, how we were preparing, or try to guess what the mission objective was. He never placed any classification on it like "Top Secret." He simply stated that if the wrong people got an indication of what we were up to, it would likely get us all killed. I was duly impressed and it must have been an effective caution, because we all returned from the mission intact.

I was impressed with the special need for teamwork as we flew never-before-tried formations at night, and without lights. Flying at night only added to the mystery of the mission, as did the emphasis on radio silence, a factor that would get us into trouble later. We did learn the importance of teamwork, for that was certainly the key to success and survival. It became readily apparent that something special was in our future. At that time, hijacking commercial airliners and kidnapping company executives in foreign countries were in vogue, and we guessed that we were going to rescue a high government or company official from some terrorist group. I remember that the Air Force officers were let in on the mission quite some time before we left Eglin.

The original mission date was in October, but a typhoon in the area delayed us a month. We left Eglin in two C-141s at 0200 hours in the morning of November 12, and arrived at Takhli at 0300 hours the same day . . . my family would learn of our purpose with the rest of the nation ten days later.

One might think the selected raiders were young daredevils, but this was not the case. The average age of the Green Berets was 35, and the average age for the Air Force helicopter pilots was 38. A major at the time, I was 36. The group averaged about 18 years of service and about half the force was eligible for retirement.

I particularly remember the Army leader, Colonel Arthur D. Simons. Nicknamed ''Bull,'' he clearly looked like one tough sonofabitch. Somewhat short and stocky in stature, with a shaven head, he looked much like the TV character ''Kojak.'' Although it is twenty-three years ago, I distinctly remember him telling me a few hours before mission launch, during some small talk premission banter, ''If you flyboys don't pull us out, not to worry, we'll walk out without you!'' The thing I remember most about the exchange is that he came across believable; he made me believe that if there was anyone who could pull off such a feat, he could.

As I recall the intelligence study, we might be facing 50-60 guards and could expect some surface-to-air missiles along with some AAA and aggravation from MiG fighters. Also there was a ground force training camp about half-a-mile to the south that could give us trouble in two ways; the troops quartered there and the fact that, in dim light, the compound looked very much like the Son Tay prison camp.

Although the POW list included fewer than 70 names, we were prepared to take out as many as 100 POWs. It was planned from the start that it would be the HH-3s final mission, for there was no room for it to land inside the compound without the rotor blades hitting a tree or some other obstacle. A planted explosive charge would ensure the enemy could make no use of it after our departure. The two HH-53s, call signs Apple One and Apple Two, each with half the assault force, would land outside the south wall. With this almost simultaneous attack on both the inside and outside, we believed we could achieve the surprise necessary for success.

We had a last-minute-huddle-type briefing to check weather and to go over the radio-out procedures for the 'umpteenth' time, and one of the mission leaders pulled the cover off a large sign that said 'FUCK COMMUNISM.' We all cheered and the tension seemed to subside for most of us. We were not too fond of communists at the time, and after being frustrated so many times by our government's 'rules of engagement,' it seemed that at long last we were going to get in a solid blow without mid-mission interference for a change!

We boarded the C-130s for the short trip to Udorn air base. I remember I was in sort of a slow-motion dream-state as I disembarked with my personal gear and walked by my squadron friends, all standing out on the porches and wherever there was a place to watch. They all spoke a quiet word of greeting and wished us good luck, but none asked what we were up to. They had been ordered to stand down a couple of days or so before, to ensure their aircraft were in top mechanical condition for us to use. Even the tower operator was ordered to ignore our taxi-out without radio transmissions.

I climbed aboard into the left seat of Apple Two and worked through the starting checklist with Lieutenant-Colonel Jack Allison, the aircraft commander, our flight mechanic and the two pararescuemen. Just as we had practised, the formation lead HC-130P refueller aircraft, Lime 01, got off on time, as did the rest of us, the HH-3 Banana and five Apple HH-53s. We routinely fell into the seven-ship formation, three helicopters stacking high on each side of the leading HC-130 at about 1500 feet AGL. There was a partial moon and some clouds that we climbed through, when suddenly the call came to 'break, break, break!,' indicating that someone had lost sight of the formation lead and we were to execute the formation break-up procedure.

Each helicopter turned to a predetermined heading and climbed to a predetermined altitude for one minute and then returned to the original heading. The effect was a very widely separated formation, each helicopter 500ft above the other and at varying distances away from the lead HC-130. I could see other members of the formation flying in and out of the clouds, and I thought we had blown the mission we had hardly started. Apparently, a strange airplane had almost flown through the formation and someone had called the lost contact procedure to avoid a mid-air collision. As it turned out, our planning for such possible events, and the training for such, resulted in a rather routine formation break and with a subsequent rejoin being completed successfully.

I don't recall exactly how many checkpoints there were on the way across the Plaine des Jarres of Laos; I believe there were about ten. At check point seven, I think, Apple Three was to exchange places with Apple One. Slipping from its outermost position in the formation, Apple Three was the designated gunship and lead ship from the initial point (IP) five miles out from the objective and where the lead C-130 would split away from the helicopter assault group. The first indications of things to come was the difficulty Apple Three had getting Apple One's attention to move back out of the way for Apple Three's new position. I believe a flashlight beamed into Apple One's cockpit finally shook the crew out of their lethargy.

In the meantime, we had all topped off our fuel tanks from the lead HC-130 and had quite deftly exchanged formation leads from him to the just-arrived, blacked-out C-130 with all the fancy electronic gear.''

As the raiders crossed the border into North Vietnam, diversionary attacks were being launched all over the country. The Navy launched a raid from the east on the port city of Haiphong. Ten air Force F-4 Phantoms were flying MiG combat air patrol to screen the force from enemy fighters, while an F-105 Wild Weasel decoy force launched a diversionary raid on enemy surface-to-air missile sites. Five A-1 Skyraiders with the call sign Peach One to Five, arrived on station to suppress ground fire around the prison camp. They were flown by men from the 1st and 56th SOW, and were probably the first Skyraiders ever to have flown so far North.

Now flying below 500ft, the helicopters prepared to assault the prison compound, while the two Combat Talon aircraft dropped napalm markers and firefight simulators nearby. Jay Strayer continues:

''Tension was building up by this time, as we neared the IP for the final approach to the camp. I had done most of the flying up to this point, and Jack Allison took over the controls for the final phase. I in turn picked up the navigation duties during this critical phase of the mission.

As we had rehearsed so many times, the lead C-130 led us over the last mountain range and down to 500ft above the ground. At the IP, they, along with Apple Four and Five, popped up to 1,500ft to fly directly for the camp. A single radio transmission with the last vector heading to the camp was made by the C-130's navigator and we continued on, maintaining a disciplined radio silence.

Now we were only four—Apple Three in the lead with the HH-3, Apples One and Two following in trail, with 45-second separations between. I was particularly interested in this phase, for I had done the procedural planning for getting us separated in a manner that would allow room for each to "do his thing," while at the same time not delaying the following bird's initial assault details.

As we neared our objective I sensed we were not going the right way to the Son Tay camp, and mentioned it more than once to Jack. Quite suddenly I was sure of it; we were about to land at the military camp to the south of Son Tay! The amazing thing to me at the time, and remains so, is that no-one had the forethought to break radio silence and say so! Indeed, Apple Three had almost taken the camp under fire, discovered his error in time, turned north to the correct place, but apparently never thought to mention it to those of us following."

The pilot of Apple Three had been distracted by a "transmission failure" warning light that had started flashing, and by the flares dropped by the Combat Talon C-130E over the compound. He decided to ignore the warning light, but had drifted 200 yards to the south and saw another installation similar to the camp a further 200 yards away. Finally realising he was off course, he turned towards the camp and his gunners opened fire, destroying the two guard towers and a barracks beyond the camp. He gained altitude and flew a further mile and a half to a rice paddy, where he would set down until the assault force and POWs called for extraction.

Banana 1, the HH-3E, also followed Apple Three off course, and was almost in the hover when they, too, realised their error and turned away. As planned, the pilots of Banana 1 crash-landed their HH-3E inside the prison compound, where high trees tore off its rotor blades and tipped the aircraft over. The troops inside scrambled out and began systematically clearing the cell blocks, killing every North Vietnamese that got in their way.

No matter how well-planned an operation, something always goes wrong, and in this case the HH-53 carrying the main assault group deposited its troops outside the wrong compound. Jay Strayer watched it happen:

"Apple One, carrying Bull Simons and half the assault force, actually landed and cleared Bull and his troops out and was just taking-off when I broke radio silence and yelled, "You're in the wrong place!" several times. I recall being enraged, frustrated, dumbfounded and with some other feelings I've since forgotten about, but quickly advised Jack to turn North to the right place and alerted Lieutenant-Colonel Sydnor in our helicopter that the "Bull" was out of the play and "Plan Green" was in effect and he and his group were in charge.

And charge he did. We landed him and his force just outside the south wall and, as they were disembarking, our pararescueman proceeded to empty his 3,000-rounds-per-minute, six-barrelled minigun, with every second or third around incendiary (every seventh was normal), into the nearby barracks. I was awestruck as I sat watching. The scene reminded me of a picture I had once seen of a burning building wherein the frame, windows and doors were outlined in red and was very bright against the surrounding darkness. I had never seen this kind of destruction so close, and it was very, very impressive.

We departed and listened to Apple One having difficulty relocating Bull Simons' group. We offered to pick them up, for I was sure I could guide Jack directly to them, but Apple One declined our offer and we found an out-of-the-way rice paddy where we could sweat out the final moments of the search for our POWs. It was frustrating to listen to Apple One's frantic calls for Bull Simons to signal or make some visible sign that would help relocate him for pickup.''

On the ground, Bull Simons and his troops soon realised they were in the wrong place; the compound was ringed with barbed wire, and when they blew a hole in the surrounding wall they saw a two-storey building inside. Son Tay prison camp did not have any two-storey buildings. The place was soon alive with hostile troops, and an intense firefight ensued. Unbeknown to the intelligence services, the compound was full of Chinese or Soviet advisers, and the assault force killed a number of them before they retraced their steps and re-boarded Apple One. The raid was now only eight minutes old.

The only good thing to say about the mistake is that it did deal a severe blow to the nearest enemy reaction force to the prison camp. For good measure Simons called in the Skyraider close-air-support team to destroy the footbridge between the now blazing compound and the prison camp.

Soon, both assault teams were in action, clearing the prison camp and its surroundings and killing or wounding all the North Vietnamese guards in the process. However, reports started to come in from the men searching the cell blocks, "Negative items." Within minutes it was confirmed that the prison was empty; the POWs had been moved.

The assault force hastily withdrew and were picked up by the HH-53s. Twenty-seven minutes into the raid, the last of the troops were airborne, and six minutes later the HH-3E was destroyed by explosives left on board. There had only been two lightly wounded casualties amongst the assault force, although a couple of the aircraft carrying out diversionary raids elsewhere had been shot down.

Forty-five minutes out of Son Tay, Simons pulled out his code book and sent a radio message to General Manor at his command post at Monkey Mountain near Da Nang; "Negative prisoners, previously moved." Apparently, the well in the compound had dried up and the nearby river had flooded, coming to within a few feet of the walls, so the prisoners had been moved on 14 July, four months previously. It was claimed that "Intelligence" had not detected the move, although the author has heard conflicting accounts of this intelligence failure. Jay Strayer's opinion is that, "I cannot see why such a high-calibre force would have been exposed so dangerously unless some of our men were expected to be there," so we will leave the story there.

Despite the intelligence failure, the raid was a tactical success. The assault force got to the camp, took their objective, and all of them got out again safely. As it happened, the POWs had been moved to a new prison camp in an Army barracks at Dong Hoi, 15 miles east of Son Tay. Awoken in their cells at their new prison, nicknamed "Camp Faith," by the sound of surface-to-air missiles being launched, the prisoners realised that Son Tay was being raided and that they had missed their ride home. However, they knew for sure that America cared and that attempts were being made to free them. Morale soared. Within days, all of the POWs in the outlying camps had been moved to Hanoi. Men who had spent years with just one or two others for company found themselves sharing a cell with dozens of others. From their point of view, the raid was the best thing that could have happened to them. They now had comrades to share their existence with, they could organise themselves, and the guards were too busy digging trenches to hassle them.

In October 1992 the author met General Leroy Manor at the Air Commando Association office in Fort Walton Beach, Florida. I asked the General about the raid, and whether or not it would have been successful. He replied, "If the prisoners had been there, we would have brought them home." He was probably right.

CHAPTER 9

WINDING DOWN THE WAR, 1972–'75

THE LAST DAYS

ALTHOUGH OPERATION LAM SON 719, the February 1971 invasion of the enemy sanctuaries in Laos by the South Vietnamese Army, was generally a failure, with the ARVN troops beating a hasty retreat, it did buy more time for Vietnamisation as the Americans returned home. In December President Nixon authorised Operation Proud Deep, the largest series of air strikes against North Vietnam since 1968. They were long overdue.

By March 1972 most of the US combat troops had gone and nearly all of the USAF squadrons had pulled out of the South Vietnamese air bases. On 30 March the first of ten North Vietnamese Army divisions crossed the DMZ into South Vietnam. The Easter Invasion had begun. Quang Tri, Loc Ninh, An Loc, Dak To, Kontum and Pleiku were the targets.

Over the next three months, the US responded by deploying fighters and bombers to bases in Thailand and South Vietnam and beginning B-52 bomber strikes against targets in southern North Vietnam. In May Nixon authorised Operation Linebacker I, and full-scale bombing of North Vietnam resumed. The ports were mined and the railroad bridges between China and North Vietnam were destroyed. By the end of June 106 bridges had been destroyed in North Vietnam, together with all major POL storage sites and the pipeline running south to the DMZ. The invasion slowly ground to a halt, and most of the captured towns were retaken, but it proved impossible to throw the enemy back over the border.

By December 1972 Nixon had been re-elected as President

and, with the Paris Peace Talks going nowhere, he authorised
Linebacker II, the full-scale bombing of targets in and around
Hanoi and Haiphong. Eleven days of B-52 bombing raids persuaded the North Vietnamese to continue talking, and a ceasefire was finally signed on 27 January 1973. South Vietnam's
President Thieu signed under pressure from Nixon, despite the
fact that half the North Vietnamese Army was still camped in
the jungles of South Vietnam. America wanted its POWs
home, regardless of the eventual fate of South Vietnam. However, the American POWs held by the communists in Laos
and Cambodia were simply ignored by Nixon and his chief
negotiator, Henry Kissinger. They never came home.

THE SECOND FAC MEDAL OF HONOR

The 20th Tactical Air Support Squadron was activated in
South Vietnam in May 1965, and operated from Da Nang Air
Base from that date until the unit returned to the States in
January 1973. Flying under the ''Covey'' call sign, one of its
members, Captain Steven L. Bennett, was to become the second Forward Air Controller to win the Medal of Honor posthumously during the Vietnam war. He was flying an OV-10
Bronco aircraft, a significant improvement over the traditional
mount of the FACs, the O-1 Bird Dog.

Captain Bennett was 26 years old, and had been in country
for only three months before that fateful day of 29 June 1972.
His back-seater was Captain Mike Brown, a Marine company
commander who had volunteered for temporary duty in Vietnam to assist Air Force FACs in directing naval gunfire. They
took off from Da Nang air base around 1500 hours and headed
northwest along the coast to Quang Tri, where they spent two
hours adjusting naval gunfire against enemy troop concentrations near the city. As a replacement FAC had not arrived,
they remained on station for an extra hour, directing two
flights of Navy A-6 Intruders against ground targets and then
flying low to survey the results of the strike. Meanwhile, a
mile away, a platoon of ARVN troops was pinned down at a
fork in a creek by a heavy force of North Vietnamese Army
troops. The platoon's situation was desperate when a US Ma-

rine ground artillery spotter radioed an emergency call for help.

Bennett heard the call and responded immediately, flying towards the fork in the creek. Because the enemy troops were so near the ARVN patrol, the FAC could not call in naval gunfire, and there were no fighters in the area to help. However, Bennett had his own guns, and dived towards the creek bank, firing at the attackers amidst a hail of gunfire from the ground. After his fourth strafing run the enemy began to withdraw, leaving many dead and wounded behind. However, on his fifth pass Bennett's luck ran out and his aircraft was hit by a shoulder-fired SA-7 Strella missile which hit the port engine and exploded, spraying the cockpit with the shrapnel and debris and slightly wounding the back-seater.

The situation was grim. The port engine was gone and the left landing gear was now hanging limply in the air stream. They were also on fire. Bennett turned the crippled aeroplane and headed for the water. In the back, Captain Brown transmitted "Mayday! Mayday! This is Wolfman four-five with Covey eight-seven. We are in the vicinity of Triple Nickel (Highway 555) and 602, heading out feet wet."

Steven Bennett struggled to keep the Bronco flying straight and level as the remaining engine tried to turn the aircraft. Unable to gain height, they passed just 600ft above the beach and the American ships offshore. As they reached open water they jettisoned the fuel tank and rockets and prepared to eject. The Marine back-seater looked over his shoulder and discovered that his parachute was gone. "What I saw was a hole about a foot square from the rocket blast and bits of my parachute shredded up and down the cargo bay."

After Captain Brown informed his pilot that he could not bale out, the flames subsided and hope returned. Quickly the FAC turned southeast down the coast, trying to reach Da Nang, which had the equipment to foam the runway and soften the inevitable crash landing. However, they would never make it. The fire flared again and a chase 'plane confirmed that they were close to exploding.

The only option open now was to ditch the OV-10 in the sea. It was extremely dangerous, because that type of aircraft did not ditch well, and every Bronco flyer knew that no pilot had survived a water landing before. Steve Bennett eased the aircraft down in a slow descent towards the water as the two men completed their pre-ditching checklist. They touched down about a mile from the shore, and Captain Brown remembers, ''We dug in harder than hell.'' The landing gear caught in the sea before the Bronco cartwheeled and flipped over on its back.

In the submerged rear cockpit, the Marine struggled frantically to free himself. He unstrapped and tried to get out through the top of the canopy. Finding his exit blocked, he pulled himself clear through an opening in the side and yanked the toggles to inflate his life preserver. On the surface he found only the aircraft's tail section still afloat. He swam around the tail, but could not find Bennett. He pulled himself down the tail section and back underwater, fighting to reach the front cockpit. He only got as far as the wing, and when he surfaced for the second time the OV-10 had gone under. A few minutes later, around 1900 hours, Mike Brown was picked up by a Navy rescue helicopter. The next day Steve Bennett's body was recovered from the smashed cockpit of the submerged aircraft. He had had no chance to escape.

The citation which accompanied the Medal of Honor included the words, ''Captain Bennett's unparalleled concern for his companion, extraordinary heroism and intrepidity above and beyond the call of duty, at the cost of his life, were in keeping with the highest traditions of the military service and reflect great credit upon himself and the United States Air Force.''

GOING BACK TO THE WORLD

As a part of the Vietnamisation programme, the remaining USAF Skyraiders were to be transferred to the South Vietnamese Air Force. The last Skyraider unit, the 1st SOS at NKP, began to lose theirs in October 1972, and they flew their last mission on 7 November. The unit was moved without personnel or equipment to Kadena Air Base on 15 December, later becoming a Combat Talon squadron.

Steve Thornburgh and the 18th SOS were also preparing to go home:

"We finally moved all of our AC-119K Stingers into Da Nang around November 1972, because of the impending ceasefire. All of the aircraft due to be given to the Vietnamese had to be in-country by that date. In December we painted NVAF markings on the aircraft, and although we were still flying them, they now belonged to the VNAF.

After the ceasefire the 18th SOS deactivated and we came under the 6498th Air Base Defense Wing. Our small detachment under Colonel Deering was to train the Vietnamese until 1 March 1973. By now most of the US forces had left, together with most of the sophisticated equipment. One morning we landed around 0400 hours just as the fog was rolling in. Another Stinger left at the same time, piloted by Lieutenant-Colonel Simon. When they came back the fog had closed in solid and they could not see the airfield. The GCI radar at Da Nang had been removed and Chu Lai had been closed. They did not have enough fuel to go down to Tan Son Nhut and the coastal airbases were socked in.

Finally, they had to point the aircraft out over the South China Sea, put it on autopilot and bale out. They all got out OK, but lost one of the Vietnamese crew when they were picked up by boat the next morning. He had failed to jettison his parachute when he hit the water, and it snared the boat's propeller and dragged him through it before anyone knew what was happening. Further flying was cancelled after that and we left the base the next day. We were the last Americans out of Da Nang."

Another unit finally going home was Project 404. Major Jack Spey was one of many Air Commandos assigned to the project, and he told the author:

"Established in the mid-sixties, Project 404 was a military assistance and advisory group trying to assist the

Royal Lao Government in its war against the communists, without disturbing the neutrality of the country. Whereas Waterpump trained the Lao pilots, 404 would provide assistance to the Royal Lao Air Force squadrons flying in the five Military Regions.

The organisation was a part of the US Ambassador's "Country Team." We reported to the official US Air Force attaché in Vientiane, who in turn was responsible to the ambassador. The official attaché's office comprised a full Colonel with three or four assistant attachés and a couple of typists and NCOs. We had our command post upstairs in the attaché's building, and ran an operations and intelligence branch there. I was a major and Chief of Combat Operations, running the command post, and I reported to the Director of Operations. There were around eight of us, including a Chief Forward Air Controller and a Chief AC-47 Gunship adviser, the latter to advise the gunships that had been given to four of the military regions. We also had five radio operators/technicians manning the communications center. These were combat control team members from Hurlburt Field.

We were the headquarters or the command post for the five Air Operation Centers out in the military regions. Each AOC would advise the local Lao wing commander and assist with the smooth running of the Lao Air Force squadrons. There were usually seven to ten US personnel from 404 attached to each AOC, including an officer with operations experience, a maintenance first sergeant, aircraft electrician, an ordnance man (gun-plumber), supply specialist, communication specialist to maintain the radios and navigation equipment and a medic. [see Combat Medic story]. Each military region also had USAF FACs, responsible to the AOCs, flying O-1s maintained by Air America at Udorn.

Project 404 was a small, low-profile organisation of around 140 people. We wore civilian clothes and referred to each other as Mister; no ranks were used. The rule was keep it simple and limit the bureaucracy. As a result our small organisation killed more enemy for less dollars than any other war the United States has fought, and that included the cost of supporting and maintaining the Royal Lao Army and Air Force and the CIA-backed Irregular Forces.

The Operations section of 404 had a number of functions. They had to monitor and provide guidance to FACs through the AOCs in the field and schedule RLAF T-28s into 100-hour inspections at Udorn with Air America. They had to monitor the expenditure of ordnance and schedule sorties within the military regions. The communications center was in contact with the airborne command post orbiting Laos twenty-four hours a day and co-ordinated any air requirements. They were also in contact with the five AOCs and had direct lines to Air Force headquarters in Saigon and NKP, and even an emergency line to the State Department Duty Officer in Washington. Any requests for additional air support came into the command post, and they could direct any US air, including gunships at night, if required to support Royal Lao and Irregular Forces.''

In mid-1973 as the ceasefire began to take effect, the 404 personnel began to return home, leaving a few supply specialists behind to help the RLAF establish a logistics supply through its government, without the direct assistance of the USAF.

SPECTRE OVER CAMBODIA

As United States participation in the war in South Vietnam came to an end, there was still plenty of work to be done in Laos and Cambodia. Captain Bobby Clark, a Spectre aircraft commander with the 16th SOS at Ubon, describes some of the missions from those days:

"Immediately following the January 1973 ceasefire in Vietnam, most of my missions focused on armed reconnaissance along truck routes in Steel Tiger in Laos. I also flew a few close air support missions for troops in contact [TIC], but recorded no significant BDA [battle damage assessment] on any of these missions. I believe the official cutoff date for Laotian missions was 15 March 1973.

From 1 March 1973 onward all of my missions were flown over Cambodia. These 69 missions were about evenly split between close air support of TIC and armed recce. Three of the missions were convoy cover missions to escort supply ships coming up the Mekong River to Phnom Penh. One mission was a truck convoy escort mission.

Due to the SA-7 missile threat we were directed to operate no lower than 9,500ft AGL while over Cambodia. Above 7,500ft AGL, which became the normal working altitude due to small-arms fire, our 20mm Gatling guns were very ineffective due to around tumbling. We would still use them if well clear of friendly troops because even non-exploding rounds would deter the enemy.

Close to midnight on the evening of 24 March 1973 my aircraft arrived overhead a small friendly post northeast of Phnom Penh. The post was under attack, and we quickly received permission from the airborne command post ''Moonbeam'' to fire. The FAG [forward air guide] on the ground gave us co-ordinates and we fired for effect. From our vantage point we could easily see the tracers from all the incoming fire. I fired the 40mm from LLLTV guidance, while the IR tried to track the FAG. The FAG kept calling us in closer and closer to his position as friendly lines were being overrun. Frequently the groundfire was turned on us, and we could see the tracers arc up ineffectively towards us. Most of the fire was 12.5mm or 14.7mm, and could not reach our altitude. When my 40mm rounds (very similar in effect to a 40mm grenade) were hitting within 15 meters of the FAG, he frantically called us to start working away from his position. Once well away from the FAG we used our 20mm guns to cover a wider area and force the enemy to retreat. I completely 'Winchestered' [used all ammo], and we returned to Ubon. During post-flight inspection of the aircraft (55–0029) we found a single three-inch shrapnel hole in the right-hand horizontal stabilizer. The hole was made from above, so sometime during the fire-fight a 23mm gun must have slipped unnoticed into the fray and exploded a round above the aircraft. We were surprised!

During the evening of 3 June 1973 we were tasked to fly armed reconnaissance along the Tonle Sap River north of Phnom Penh, in an area where Khmer Rouge guerrillas were thought to be organising a supply point. We located a number of smaller boats gathered around a larger craft near where a road approached the river. 'Moonbeam' confirmed the boats as enemy and cleared us to fire. The smaller boats began to scatter as we began firing 40mm rounds into the larger craft which TV was targeting for me. I started several small fires on the large boat and then fired at the smaller craft, which IR could follow more easily than TV. Suddenly, both TV and IR were overwhelmed with a bright 'blossom.' I was look-ing through the gunsight next to my left shoulder and saw the same brilliant explosion. Whatever was on the larger craft had let go with a vengeance! When the sen-sors recovered from the blinding we could find no evi-dence of boats, only scattered fires along the river banks. Review of the BDA video tapes after landing revealed that nineteen boats had disappeared.''

During the early hours of 24 July 1973 Bobby Clark launched with a ragtag crew, a mixture of several different crews rather than his usual ''hard'' crew. As they neared the objective the table navigator made contact with the FAG, who begged them to open fire as the friendlies were being overrun by the enemy. However, ''Moonbeam'' was having trouble communicating with the FAG, and it was a court-martial of-fense to fire without permission. The IR was detecting hun-dreds of hot spots, which were enemy soldiers pouring fire into the FAG's position.

The situation was critical, so Clark told the crew to prepare to drop flares so there would be enough light for the TV to track targets, and instructed the table navigator to radio the FAG that they were opening fire with their ''big guns,'' the

105mm carried by the AC-130E/H. The other officers were nervous; the fire control officer was talking against the orders on his private telecom with the TV and IR operators and the EWO, so Bobby interrupted him and told him to get on with the job.

What the guys in the back did not consider was the reaction on the ground when the bad buys heard on their radios that the "big guns" were about to open fire, and saw the flares turning night into day. Spectre had drawn its guns first, and the bad guys turned and ran.

It took 30 minutes before permission was received to fire, by which time the enemy troops were crossing a small bridge a mile away that served as an excellent choke point. As the sun rose Bobby put the guns on semi-automatic and put every round they had into the mass. The crew was euphoric, and the fire control officer and Bobby became good friends over the drinks that HE bought that morning!

As the 15 August 1973 approached, the day on which US air support would cease, the Spectre crews started to pull daytime alert duty, just as if they were flying F-4s. Bobby Clark recalled:

"On 13 August we were sitting under the gunship wing for shade while the copilot, Lieutenant Hegler, remained in the terribly hot aircraft, monitoring the radios. Suddenly he began shouting for us, and we all bolted for the aircraft, as we understood that we were to launch. The INS [inertial navigation system] was already running, so I quickly strapped in and called for the starting engines checklist. As soon as number three was running I called for the before-taxi checklist and began to taxi out to the runway on one engine. The copilot and flight engineer started the other engines and ran through all the clean-up items to make sure we had all systems set. When I reached the runway we were cleared into take-off position and accomplished the engine run-up checklist during the take-off roll. We were airborne at 1434 hours, six minutes after alert. The crew was magnificent!"

WATERPUMP AND THE CAMBODIANS

Jack Drummond finished his time with Project 404 in Laos and returned to the United States. For the next couple of years he flew the A-7 Corsair and A-37 Dragonfly, and 1974 found him attending the Armed Forces Staff College at Norfolk, Virginia. One day he received a telephone call from Heinie Aderholt, who told him, "Jack, I need you again. We've got this really neat deal over in Thailand. . . . " Heinie had been recalled to active service as a General and was commander US-MACTHAI. By then the US Congress had pulled the plug on Southeast Asia. The Americans were out of South Vietnam following the so-called Peace Agreement, and all direct aid to Laos and Cambodia had been halted in August 1973.

Jack said "Yes" to Heinie, moved his family to Florida and flew to Udorn to join the Waterpump organisation. He recalled:

> "Heinie wanted to do for the Cambodians what we had done in Laos, but on a smaller scale; training and equipping the Cambodian Air Force. The situation was different now though, because in Laos we were restricted by the terms of the 1962 Geneva Convention, but in 1974 in Cambodia we were restricted by United States laws. I was never able to fly combat sorties there, and spent my time living in Bangkok, supervising the training program at Waterpump in Udorn, visiting the Cambodian fighter squadrons and trying to do on the ground as I had done in Laos. Additionally, I flew aircraft from the various bases back to Bangkok, where the Cambodian Air Force aircraft were maintained by a company named Thai-Am. It was the same sort of deal that we had in Laos, flying the aircraft back to Udorn for repair.
>
> The Cambodian pilots were much more aggressive than the Lao had been, and did a yeoman job of providing close air support in their T-28s for the Cambodian Army. Unfortunately we had the same problems there as we did in Laos, with low pay and pilots trying to haul

contraband to make up their money. One day I was told
that there was a T-28 at an outlying field that had suffered an accident on take-off. I went over and found the
aircraft sitting on its tail at the end of the runway. It was
obvious that the center of gravity was much further aft
than I had ever seen on a T-28, and when I opened the
baggage compartment I could see why. The compartment, which could normally carry roughly 35-50lb
weight, was filled with 150-200lb of salt in bags. Salt
was in very short supply in Phnom Penh, and when the
Cambodian pilots had flown their combat sorties they
would land at an outlying field and buy salt to sell when
they got back. However, when the pilot had tried to take
off, the plane tipped backwards on its tail and could not
lift off. I was concerned about the structural damage that
the salt was doing to the T-28s, and found corrosion
everywhere. In the end we had to get the pilots a C-47
to haul salt in!

Working at Waterpump, I was able to improve the
training program and produce better pilots than the Lao's
who had been trained there years before. However, from
middle to late 1974 the war in Cambodia started to go
to hell in a hand basket. The Khmer Rouge had ringed
Phnom Penh, the capital, and the flight line was under
rocket fire, then, as the enemy got closer, it came under
105mm howitzer fire and it became difficult to get the
aircraft refuelled.

By March 1975 the war was coming to an end in
South Vietnam and the country was being overrun by
the North Vietnamese. As the South Vietnamese retreated they left fully-functioning aircraft and airfields
for the enemy to capture, and we wanted to make sure
that this was not repeated in Cambodia. Heinie asked me
to devise a plan to evacuate the whole of the Cambodian
Air Force to Thailand when the need arose.

We planned to move as many of the families to Thailand as possible, and stored fuel and ordnance at a base
north of Phnom Penh so that when the day came we
were going to withdraw to the base, load the fighters
with ordnance and the transports with people, and fly to

Thailand, bombing Phnom Penh airport on the way out. That's exactly what happened in the middle of April 1975, after the US Embassy staff were evacuated from Phnom Penh and Cambodian President Lon Nol left the country.

We took every member of the Khmer Air Force and their dependants who wanted to go, and headed for Thailand. There were too many dependants for them all to go on the transports, so the T-28 pilots put fathers, wives and mothers in the back seats of the airplanes and made their last combat sortie with their loved one in the back seat with them. Then we all headed to U Tapao, a Strategic Air Command base in Thailand.

We only gave the base fifteen minutes warning that we were coming, and 175 Khmer aircraft and about 1,400 refugees showed up. Strategic Air Command nearly had a fit as T-28s landed with the bomb arming wires still hanging from the ordnance stations, and with loaded guns. The base came to a halt as Americans stared in amazement as some of the T-28 backseaters took off their helmets to reveal long black flowing hair! One young Huey pilot landed his helicopter amidst the B-52s on the alert pad, having run out of fuel. He had between 15 and 25 people on board.''

Jack Drummond remained in Thailand for two more weeks, until he was asked to help arrange a similar evacuation plan for the South Vietnamese Air Force when the country finally fell on 30 April. When that evacuation took place, some hundreds more aircraft arrived safely in Thailand, but that is another story.

THE COMMUNISTS WIN

The years 1974 and 1975 saw the end of the United States' involvement in Southeast Asia, and communist victory in Laos, Cambodia and South Vietnam. American aircraft and combat troops were no longer in South Vietnam and they would not return. Despite US attempts to bolster the Cambodian Air Force, such as the C-123s supplied under Operation Flyswatter in July 1974, the Khmer Rouge tightened their grip on the countryside and continued to isolate the towns.

Back in the US, the Air Force announced in May 1974 that the C-130-equipped 919th Tactical Airlift Group was to be converted to AC-130A gunships, and on 1 July 1975 the unit was redesignated the 919th Special Operations Group, the only special ops group in the Air Force Reserve. The gunships were to be flown by the 711th Special Operations Squadron, based at Duke Field (Eglin Auxiliary Field 3), and they were operational by July 1976.

In 1975 Cambodia was about to take a giant step back into the dark ages as Pol Pot's supporters closed in on Phnom Penh. On 1 April 1975 President Lon Nol left the country and the US Embassy was evacuated on the 12th. A third of the population would eventually disappear in a genocide, the like of which had not been seen since the days of the Nazis. Finally the inevitable happened in South Vietnam on 30 April 1975, when the North Vietnamese took Saigon and the long war came to an end.

Laos would hold out a little longer, following a ceasefire agreed in February 1973 and the cessation of US air support that April, but in December 1975 the King abdicated, ending a 600-year-old monarchy, and the Pathet Lao and North Vietnamese took over. They then instigated a program of genocide against the Hmong people, using concentration camps to contain and starve to death Hmong and others, including most of the Lao royal family. Hmong still living in their villages were subjected to air attack and bombardment by chemical weapons, banned by the international community but supplied by the Soviet Union. Men, women and children died the most horrible deaths, while others fled across the Mekong River to live in dismal refugee camps in Thailand. The tragedy of the Hmong continues. Abandoned by their American friends, they now suffer forced repatriation by the United Nations and the Thai government, back into the hands of their sworn enemies in Laos. The whole sad story can be read in the book *Tragic Mountains* by Jane Hamilton-Merritt (Indiana University Press, 1993).

*   *   *

Amongst such momentous events, brief mention should also be made of the 656th Special Operations Wing, established on 14 May 1975 and activated 30 June at NKP, Thailand. Comprising the 21st SOS with its CH-53s and the 23rd TASS with OV-10s, and commanded by Colonel Robert D Janca, it was formed to absorb resources left at NKP following movement of the 56th SOW. The wing was charged with closing the US portion of NKP and, with the attached squadrons, certain contingency operations. Before the wing was deactivated on 22 September 1975, the 21st SOS would be decimated at an island off Cambodia named Koh Tang.

THE *MAYAGUEZ* AND THE GLORY TOUR

The 21st SOS was one of the last US units to leave Southeast Asia. Lieutenant-Colonel John Denham was the squadron commander for this "Glory Tour," which saw their CH-53s participate in Operation Frequent Wind, the evacuation of American citizens from Saigon, before the city fell to the North Vietnamese, and the evacuation of Embassy staff and others from Cambodia as a part of Operation Eagle Pull.

On 12 May 1975 Khmer communist gunboats seized the American spy ship SS *Mayaguez* in international waters in the Gulf of Thailand. At the time of its capture the ship was 60 miles southwest of Cambodia, near the Poulo Wai Islands. The next morning Navy reconnaissance aircraft located the ship steaming to Koh Tang Island, midway between the Poulo Wai Islands and the Cambodian mainland. That night the first AC-130 gunship arrived and discovered Cambodian gunboats shuttling between the *Mayaguez* and a large cove at the northern end of the island.

On the morning of the 14th a fishing boat made a dash for the mainland, carrying the crew of the *Mayaguez*. Despite warning shots fired by the Spectre and riot control gas dropped by USAF tactical aircraft from Thailand, the ship reached the shore and the captives were taken to another island, just off the mainland. However, the United States did not know that the crew had already left the island, and, after sinking a number of gunboats throughout the day and night, the decision was made to seize the *Mayaguez* and recover any crewmembers being held on Koh Tang Island.

During the early hours of the 15th, six HH-53 Jolly Green rescue helicopters and five CH-53s using the ''Knife'' callsign of the 21st SOS on-loaded 230 Marines and prepared to land them on the island. Unfortunately, no one had any idea how many defenders were on the island. The answer was soon forthcoming. The helicopters were heading for two beaches on the island, not knowing that the communists were well dug in at the edge of the jungle and armed with automatic weapons, rocket launchers and mortars.

As dawn broke, Knife 21 and 22 made their approach to a small beach on the western side of the island. Knife 21 was being flown by the squadron commander, and the minute the helicopter touched down and the Marines began running down the rear ramp the Cambodians opened fire. As soon as the Marines were offloaded Denham tried to take-off, but one of his two engines had been disabled and the aircraft severely damaged. As he headed out to sea the crew jettisoned everything they could, but a mile out from the beach the helicopter sank into the ocean. S/Sgt. Elwood Rumbaugh, the flight mechanic, pulled the copilot out of the sinking helicopter and Denham helped him inflate his life jacket. However, when he looked around S/Sgt. Rumbaugh had disappeared and was never found.

Knife 22 received similar treatment, and Captain Ohlemeier was unable to land his Marines. With fuel streaming from the damaged helicopter, he raced back towards Thailand to make an emergency landing before his fuel ran out.

Knife 32, flown by First Lieutenant Michael Lackey, picked up the three survivors from Knife 21 and headed for the west beach. As the Marines began to offload, a rocket tore a gaping hole in its side and exploded inside the passenger compartment. Incredibly, only one Marine was wounded, although one of the flight mechanics was hit by groundfire and seriously wounded. With 75 holes in his helicopter, Lackey lifted off and sped back to base, arriving just in time to save the flight mechanic's life.

The situation was grim on the other side of the island as well. As Major Howard Corson, flying Knife 31, and First

Lieutenant John Shramm in Knife 23 hovered to land their Marines on east beach, they ran into a barrage of fire. A hail of bullets struck Knife 23, damaging the rotor system and one of the engines. As the helicopter began vibrating severely Shramm ordered the rear ramp opened and crash-landed on the beach as the entire tail section was torn off. The four crew and all 20 Marines survived the landing and dashed to the cover of the tree line.

Knife 31 was not so lucky, and exploded in flames after being struck by rockets or RPGs. The copilot was killed and Major Corson severely injured as the helicopter crashed at the water's edge. Thirteen of the 26 Americans were killed and the survivors struggled out to sea, where they were picked up by US naval vessels. An hour after the assault began, five out of the eight helicopters in the first wave had been put out of action and only 54 Americans were ashore.

Supported by AC-130 fire, the second wave of Jolly Greens had more success landing their Marines. However, three hours after the assault began, a Thai fishing boat flying a white flag set out from the mainland. On board was the entire crew of the *Mayaguez*, who were transferred back to their own ship, which then steamed away under its own power.

The problem now was how to recover the 131 Marines and five crewmen from the island. The decision was made to re-inforce, then withdraw the Marines, assisted by Navy aircraft from the USS *Coral Sea* and Spectre gunships. This took the whole day, and was achieved solely because of the bravery of the helicopter crews. It was a sad end to almost fifteen years of special operations involvement in Southeast Asia.

As the American public and the new President Ford turned their backs on Laos, Cambodia and South Vietnam, the special operations force dwindled to a shadow of its former self. At the height of the war there were 550 aircraft in the force, but by July 1976 the 1st SOW at Hurlburt Field was down to five MC-130E Combat Talons (8th SOS), nine AC-130H Spectres (16th SOS) and six helicopters; four UH-1Ns and two CH-3Es for the 20th SOS that had been reactivated that January.

CHAPTER 10

OPERATION EAGLE CLAW: LEARNING THE LESSONS AGAIN, 1980

INTERNATIONAL TERRORISM, THE NEW ENEMY

AS THE VIETNAM WAR came to an end and the dominoes; South Vietnam, Laos and Cambodia, fell to the communists and their allies, America's armed forces underwent great soul searching and a reduction in their capabilities. The longest and most expensive war in America's history had been lost by the politicians, but the military took the blame.

The effect of the end of the war was felt at the Air Force "boneyard" at Davis-Monthan Air Force Base in Arizona. By June 1973 there were 6,000 aircraft and helicopters in storage, the largest number since it opened in 1945. The Air Force Special Operations units were hit hard in the post-Vietnam years. The Skyraiders, Shadows and Stingers had been left behind in Southeast Asia; the Providers had gone to the reserves and the Nimrods were in the boneyard. Even the AC-130 gunships were scheduled for deactivation or transfer to the reserve. They were not funded beyond 1979 in the Air Force budget. The MC-130 Combat Talons were old and in need of significant new modifications. The only Air Force deep penetration helicopters were being operated by search and rescue squadrons and there was a general feeling amongst pilots and aircrews in the Air Force that the Special Operations Force was not a career-enhancing assignment.

Special Operations, never enthusiastically supported by the major commands, was being pushed into the side lines. The Navy was about to decommission its only special operations-capable submarine and the seven active duty Army Green Beret Groups from the Vietnam war days, was reduced to three.

Outside of the United States, the world was changing. International Terrorism was a new virus spreading with complete disregard of national borders. On 27 June 1976, an Air France Airbus with 254 passengers on board, was hijacked whilst enroute to Paris from Israel. The four terrorists, two members of the Baader-Meinhof Gang and two Palestinians, directed the pilot to fly to Entebbe Airport in Uganda. At first the outside world accepted the word of Idi Amin, the Ugandan ruler, when he stated that he was attempting to bring the hijacking to a peaceful conclusion. The hijackers demanded the release of 53 terrorists in various jails, including a member of the Japanese Red Army, responsible for the murder of 26 people at Israel's Lod Airport in 1972.

It soon became apparent that Idi Amin was actively supporting the hijackers and when they threatened to start executing the passengers on 1 July, Israel's Prime Minister and cabinet decided to give them what they wanted. As a result the execution deadline was extended and a hundred non-Jewish passengers were released.

Finally, 106 hostages remained under guard in the Old Terminal at Entebbe Airport. With the exception of the Air France crew, all were Jews. In the face of such anti-Zionist action Prime Minister Rabin had no choice. To negotiate with the terrorists would have been a sign of weakness and would probably have perpetuated the terrorist problem. A rescue mission would be launched.

At 2300 hours on 3 July 1976, the first of four Israeli Air Force C-130 transport aircraft touched down at Entebbe Airport, after a 2,200 mile, seven and a half hour flight from Israel. Within minutes, Israeli Commandos had assaulted the terminal, killing every terrorist and Ugandan soldier that they could find. Four armored personnel carriers accompanied the commandos, to keep Ugandan reinforcements at bay and to destroy a squadron of MiG fighters parked nearby. Ninety minutes after the assault began, the hostages and soldiers were on their way home, after a refuelling stop in nearby Kenya.

Yet another success was achieved by the West German Counter-terrorist Unit GSG-9, when they conducted an assault on a hijacked Lufthansa Boeing 737 in Mogadishu, Somalia in October 1977. The assault resulted in the death of three of the four hijackers and the rescue of 82 hostages. The German troopers had been trained by the British Special Air Service, who would successfully and in spectacular fashion recapture the Iranian Embassy in London, a decade later.

Could the United States carry out such operations? This question was asked by President Jimmy Carter and resulted in the formation of Delta Force, an élite commando unit, under Colonel Charlie Beckwith at Fort Bragg, North Carolina. However, having the men to do the fighting was only one half of the problem. Did the United States Air Force have the means to carry them into battle? The answer was No.

OUR EMBASSY IN IRAN HAS BEEN TAKEN!

Special Operations took on a whole new meaning on 4 November 1979, when a mob of Iranian ''students'' occupied the United States Embassy in Tehran, seizing 98 staff and local employees. They demanded that the United States return the exiled Shah for trial, in accordance with the wishes of their leader, Ayatollah Ruhollah Khomeini.

Within days US President Jimmy Carter had ordered a ban on US oil purchases from Iran and froze $5 billion in Iranian assets in the United States. However, as he reviewed his alternatives he realised that he was well and truly up the proverbial creek without a paddle. Was America to declare war to rescue the hostages incarcerated in the Embassy buildings? If he did, would they be killed before anyone could get to them? What were the chances of freeing them by a sudden raid under the cover of darkness?

It was easier said than done. Whilst the US Army had the men capable of taking down the Embassy and freeing the hostages, in the shape of the newly formed Delta Force, the logistics involved in transporting the force to the heart of the capital city of a hostile nation without discovery, and then recovering them and the hostages, was to tax the ingenuity of the US armed forces to the limit.

The Pentagon became a hive of activity as the various services were scoured for leaders and planners. Ideas were formed then discounted as the various alternatives were explored. In the meantime the Iranians were content to hold the Embassy employees hostage, to the continuing embarrassment of the United States.

Colonel James H. Kyle was summoned to the Pentagon one week into the crisis to act as deputy commander of the Joint Task Force. A former Spectre pilot with combat experience over the Ho Chi Minh Trail, Kyle had spent ten years in special operations. The biggest question he had was, "Why didn't we already have a counterterrorism force ready to go?" He later recalled, "The irony of the situation struck me. Special Operations is the outfit needed to counter this and other types of terrorism, and yet is fighting for its existence each budget cycle as the bucks go up for grabs. The emphasis and most of the funds, is lavished on new-generation fighters, bombers, missiles or transports."

At that time the special ops fleet, battle-scarred and weary from Vietnam, was run down and neglected. There were only fourteen MC-130 Combat Talons, four in Europe, four in the Pacific and six in Florida, with three or four undergoing maintenance at any one time. Their one plus point was that seven of them could be refuelled in the air, thus extending their range. By comparison, a standard TAC airlift squadron would have sixteen C-130s, with almost 50 to a wing. Spectre gunships were available, but there were no special operations helicopters capable of carrying a large assault force over long distances.

Major-General James Vaught was appointed Joint Task Force commander, with Jim Kyle in charge of the air force part of the mission and eventually designated the on-scene commander at the staging base for the rescue force in the Iranian desert. The assault troops would be Delta Force, commanded by Colonel Charlie Beckwith, who would lead his men in the assault on the 27-acre Embassy compound. The problem was, how to get them there?

DOES ANYONE HAVE A PLAN?

One of the biggest problems facing the dozens of planners in the Pentagon was the lack of helicopters. Although the Air

Force had HH-53 Super Jolly Green Giant rescue helicopters and the men to fly them, the decision was made to use the Navy RH-53D Mine Countermeasures version of the Sea Stallion, which could carry 6,000lb more cargo than the HH-53. The aircraft could fly 750 miles unrefuelled with 20 men on board, and with folding tail boom and rotor blades could be stored below decks on an aircraft carrier. In addition, because of the possible mine-clearing requirement in the Straits of Hormuz, they would attract little attention from Soviet spy satellites. They were to be flown by crews from the Marine Corps.

The Navy originally supplied pilots to fly the mission, but they were replaced by Marines. At the time the 20th SOS had six crews qualified to use the new night vision goggles, who had been training in night low-level tactics under combat conditions in the desert. Nine of their people were former HH-53 pilots, and could have been requalified in short order. Jim Kyle's request to use them was turned down by higher authority.

Eventually, a rescue plan was pieced together. The operation, named Eagle Claw, would take place over two nights. On Night One three MC-130s would depart Masirah in Oman carrying 139 men; Delta Force, combat controllers, Farsi-speaking translators and truck drivers. They would head for a spot in the Iranian Dasht-e-Kavir desert between the coast and Tehran, code-named Desert One. One MC-130 would arrive an hour before the other two, check that the area was clear with his FLIR, then land roadblock teams and combat controllers to set up the landing zone and start the tactical air navigation (TACAN) beacon operating. When the rest of Delta Force arrived, two of the three MC-130s would unload and depart for home. Three EC-130s would follow the MC-130s. These were borrowed from a Tactical Airborne Command and Control squadron, and flown by special operations crews. Each would carry two 3,000gal fuel bladders to refuel the helicopters. Eight RH-53s would lift off from the USS *Nimitz*, sailing in the Gulf of Oman, 50 miles from the Iranian coast, and head for the rendezvous with the '130s at Desert One.

Fifteen minutes after the last EC-130 was to arrive, the helicopters should appear, refuel and on-load Delta Force within 40 minutes, then fly for a further two hours to the drop-off point 50 miles from Tehran. Agents already in-country would lead the troopers to a hide site to wait until the following night. The helicopters would fly to a larger site 50 miles further on, camouflage their helicopters and wait for Delta to summon them on Night Two. The MC-130 and the EC-130s would return to Masirah. With Delta Force and the helicopters hidden by dawn, the Joint Task Force headquarters would monitor the Iranian communications circuits to see if the insertion had been detected and to obtain a final situation report on the hostages.

On Night Two, 100 Army Rangers on board four MC-130s would leave Wadi Kena in Egypt, accompanied by three AC-130 gunships. The Rangers, supported by one gunship, would attack and secure Manzariyeh airfield, upon which would land two C-141 jet transports flying from Daharan, Saudi Arabia, ready to evacuate Delta Force and the rescued hostages. One AC-130 would support the assault on the Embassy and one would suppress any fighter activity at nearby Mehrabad Airport.

Using locally-procured trucks, Delta Force would head for the Embassy while a separate team was tasked with rescuing three of the hostages held at the Ministry of Foreign Affairs. The assault would begin just before midnight on Beckwith's command, and take between 30 and 45 minutes to complete. At least six of the eight helicopters would be required, four to land at a soccer stadium near the Embassy to collect Delta Force and the majority of the hostages, and two to pick up the team from the Ministry of Foreign Affairs. The helicopters would extract the rescue team and hostages and take them to Manzariyeh airfield, where they would be loaded onto the C-141s and flown to safety. The Rangers, MC-130s and AC-130s would return to Egypt. The helicopters would be destroyed in place. It was a complex plan, prepared over five months and would require skill, teamwork and luck to carry it off.

FAILURE

At 1705 hours local time, 24 April 1980, the troops at Masirah received the message ''Execute mission as planned. God speed." At 1805 hours the first MC-130 "Dragon One," piloted by Lieutenant-Colonel Bob Brenci, was airborne. One hour later the eight helicopters on the *Nimitz* launched and headed for the coast, flying 100ft above the water in near total darkness. The helicopters and C-130s all crossed the coast at low level and continued towards Desert One. The problems began 140 miles inland.

Despite a clear-weather forecast before the launch, the first MC-130 ran into a Haboob, a milky layer of suspended dust often caused by the effects of earlier thunderstorms. For the crews flying at night with night vision goggles, it was the last thing they needed. The MC-130s could navigate with their terrain-following radar and inertial navigation systems, but for the helicopter pilots the problem was much worse.

Suddenly, whilst flying at 200ft above the ground, the pilot of Bluebeard Six, one of the RH-53s, saw his Blade Inspection Method (BIM) warning light flash on. The BIM warns of a loss of nitrogen pressure inside the aluminium rotor blades, so the pilot landed, checked the blades and confirmed that the helicopter was no longer airworthy. Bluebeard Eight landed and picked up the crew, then continued inland.

To the helicopter pilots the haboob looked like a wall of talcum powder ahead of them. Initially visibility was reduced to less than half a mile, but soon they could not see the ground, nor each other. The flight leader in Bluebeard One decided to land, and Bluebeard Two followed him. The other helicopters did not notice and continued on their journey.

At 1045 hours Iranian time the first MC-130 landed at Desert One. Hearing the news over the SATCOM link, Bluebeard One and Two launched again and headed north. During the 20 minutes they had sat on the desert floor Bluebeard Eight caught up with the rest of the flight, now led by Bluebeard Three. However, Bluebeard Five, carrying Colonel Chuck Pitman, the senior Marine, was experiencing problems with instruments. In near-zero visibility the pilot saw that one of his primary flight instruments, the pitch and roll indicator, had failed, as had the TACAN and the radio-magnetic heading indicator. To make things even worse, they lost sight of the rest of the formation. The pilot doubted that he could navigate his way past two mountains in his path and find Desert One.

He decided to abort and return to the *Nimitz*, and the Marine leader agreed. It was an unfortunate decision. They had been fighting the dust for one hour and fifteen minutes and were only one hour and twenty minutes from the rendezvous site. In thirty minutes more they would have been clear of the dust.

The helicopter assault force was now down to six. The first three finally arrived at Desert One an hour late, and the rest arrived 15 minutes later. The pilots were badly shaken by their ordeal, but they had made it, including the gutsy Captain B. J. McGuire, whose Bluebeard Two had lost its second-stage hydraulic system, which powers the number one Automatic Flight Control System and the backup portion of the primary flight controls. In peacetime the pilot must land as soon as possible, because sustained flight with only the first-stage hydraulic system invites a complete control lockup. However, he decided to continue onto the rendezvous.

After landing at Desert One, McGuire discussed the problem with Ed Seiffert, the pilot of Bluebeard One and now senior Marine, who informed Jim Kyle and Charlie Beckwith that Bluebeard Two could not go on. Flying with a full load of 20 troopers and their equipment, there was a danger of overtaxing the remaining hydraulic system and causing an accident. With Beckwith insisting that he needed six helicopters and Seiffert insisting that he had only five serviceable, Kyle passed the recommendation to abort onto General Vaught, who concurred. It was a devastating blow.

Worse was still to come. As Bluebeard Three hovered in a cloud of sand to move past EC-130 "Republic Four," it drifted 90° to the right and struck the port side of the tanker aircraft. Night was turned to day as both aircraft exploded in flames. There were fourteen crewmen on the EC-130 together with part of Delta Force.

Sergeant James W. McClain, Jr, was an assistant loadmaster on the EC-130E. At the time of the collision he was assisting in closing up operations. Upon seeing the explosion he immediately moved to assist another loadmaster in opening the left paratroop door. Met by a sheet of flame, they slammed it shut in a hurry and began to assist in calming the panicking troopers and maintaining control. Once the right paratroop door was open and personnel were exiting, he heard a troop commander shouting and pointing at the door, and saw that panicking personnel had begun to pull the door closed as they exited. Pushing his way to the cargo ramp, and leaning out over the trapped group of personnel, he managed to push the door up and open. After pinning the door open he directed the remaining personnel to safety.

Ensuring that no-one remained in the cabin, he began to move forward to the cockpit. At that time the safety pilot escaped down the stairs from the flight deck, just before the galley bulkhead collapsed, blocking the stairway exit. Two Delta Force troopers rescued the badly burned radio operator just before another explosion occurred. The explosion blew Sergeant McClain out the right troop door onto the desert floor. Upon rising, he saw flames pouring out of and around the aircraft and began to move away to safety. While moving away, he saw a dazed fuels specialist who was unable to move. He picked the specialist up and carried him to an awaiting aircraft and safety. He also organised a small group of survivors and led them to an awaiting aircraft. He suffered minor burns and a back injury as a result of his actions. Sergeant McClain was later awarded the Airman's Medal for extraordinary heroism.

As soon as possible, the remaining C-130s on-loaded the rescue force, including the Marine helicopter crews whose aircraft were to be abandoned, and retraced their route back to Egypt. It had been a courageous attempt, but it had failed.*

THE REASONS FOR FAILURE

Years after the failure of Eagle Claw, Jim Kyle listed the four main reasons, in his opinion, why the operation failed. The Air Weather Service was unable to predict the severe dust conditions that caused so many problems for the Marines. The

---

* Five members of the 8th SOS lost their lives in the inferno; Captain Harold L. Lewis, Jr., the aircraft commander; Captain Lyn D. McIntosh, copilot, Captains Richard L. Bakke and Charles T. McMillan II, both navigators, and Tech Sergeant Joel C. Mayo, flight engineer, together with three of the Marine Corps enlisted helicopter crewmen.

aircrews could have received more low-level, bad-weather training, but at the end of the day, despite the sand and poor visibility, six of the helicopters did find their way to Desert One in the end.

Poor communications and flawed command and control was another problem. The various flight packages and individual aircraft were unable to communicate securely with each other, or with headquarters. The communication procedures were designed for radio silence under visual flight rules conditions. When the helicopters wanted to ask for navigation assistance or advice regarding abort decisions, they were unable to do so. Some of the communication systems were incompatible with others, and the Marines had also removed the inter-aircraft radio components from their helicopters. They could communicate with each other in flight only by hand and torchlight, a method useless in low-visibility conditions.

Command and Control began to fail when the helicopter pilot carrying the senior Marine turned around and flew back to the aircraft carrier. The leaders in the command post at Wadi Kena had no helicopter experts with them, and did not take any steps to restore central control when it became obvious that it was every man for himself in the dust.

The most controversial issue is that of the helicopter abort decisions. Using Marine pilots to fly Navy aircraft was not a good idea. A Navy pilot will view a BIM warning as a nitrogen-gas leak from the rotor blade, and will normally complete a combat mission. A Marine views the warning as a crack in the blade that may be expanding and may cause a catastrophe if the operation is continued. He will abort the mission. Indeed, three Marine CH-53s had crashed because of this condition, whereas the Navy had lost none of their RH-53Ds. If the pilot of Bluebeard Five had been able to communicate with someone familiar with the Navy models, he may have continued onto Desert One. It would also have been a good idea to carry a comprehensive stock of spare parts, including rotor blades and hydraulic parts, on one of the C-130s. The blade could have been changed in 30 minutes, and the failed hydraulics on Bluebeard Two in 45 minutes.

When Kyle talked to the pilot of Bluebeard Two years later, the pilot told him that he had wanted to continue flying with the degraded hydraulic system, but that Ed Seiffert overruled him, believing the risk to be too great. This was, however, their Super Bowl, and if the pilot felt it safe to fly, maybe he should have been allowed to do so. It would have made all the difference.

Bluebeard Five was carrying Colonel Chuck Pitman, the Marine commander, when it turned around and flew back to the carrier whilst only 145 miles from Desert One. If he had continued through the dust for another 30 minutes he would have been in the clear, but instead he flew back through the dust for an hour and a half to the coast. Because of disorientation problems (vertigo) he could not stay in formation with Bluebeard Seven, and had problems with malfunctioning instruments. The copilot wanted to continue, but the pilot wanted to go back, and he was not overruled by the senior Marine. He also broke radio silence to inform the carrier that he was returning. Could he not have broken radio silence to ask for a weather report or assistance?

Poor tactics by the helicopters were also a factor. A CIA Twin Otter had flown into Desert One a month before the raid to check the ground and conceal landing lights under the sand. On the way back they picked up radar signals at 3,000ft that may have been Iranian, but were probably from American ships. However, the Marines were under the incorrect impression that they had to fly at 200ft or lower to avoid radar detection, thus confining themselves to the areas of suspended dust. Last, but not least, someone on the JTF staff miscalculated that it would take four hours and twenty-five minutes for the Marines to fly the 600 nautical miles from the carrier to Desert One. They actually required five hours and twenty minutes, flying at 100 knots, regardless of the dust problems. This miscalculation put the C-130s on the ground one hour before they needed to be there, burning more fuel and exposing themselves to discovery for a longer period.

There are a number of reasons why the operation failed, many of which could have been avoided. At least seven of the helicopters could probably have reached Desert One, and at least six could have flown Delta Force forward to continue their mission. To add insult to injury, when the EC-130 and the RH-53 started to blow up at Desert One, sending debris towards three of the parked Marine helicopters, the crews abandoned their aircraft, leaving classified documents for the Iranians to discover next day. These included the routes to and from Tehran, various landing zones, call signs and the location of the truck warehouse in Tehran. Fortunately the agents waiting for Delta Force managed to escape capture, but it certainly had a detrimental effect on any second rescue mission.

There were many lessons to be learnt from the failure of the operation. The most important of these was that a well-trained, integrated organisation was needed to carry off such raids in the future. It should have its own helicopters and aircraft, planners and maintainers, and leaders schooled in the art of special operations. It would be long in coming, but it would happen in the end.

PAVE LOW AND HONEY BADGER

Despite the failure of the first hostage rescue attempt, planning for a second raid began right away. This operation was code named Honey Badger, and Dick Secord, a former Air Commando, was given the job of planning it. It was to be different to the first raid in that they only had eight helicopters, but this time there would be 95. The force would include the first six Pave Low HH-53Hs, just transferred to special operations from the Air Rescue and Recovery Service; the Army's first operational company of 20 UH-60 Blackhawk helicopters, plus supporting CH-47C Chinooks from the 101st Airborne Division and even specially modified Hughes OH-6 Loach scout helicopters, modified to carry several fully-armed Delta Force troopers on a special outside platform. Over 100 aircraft and almost 4,000 men would be taking part.

The basic plan was to use two Ranger battalions to seize Mehrabad Airport in Tehran and land C-5s, C-130s and C-141s carrying the assault helicopters. The helicopters were to have been on their way two minutes after their transport aeroplanes' loading ramps hit the tarmac. Spectre gunships would orbit overhead, while a flight of Navy F-14s would provide combat air patrol in case any enemy warplanes were launched. KC-135 tankers would refuel the aircraft. Delta Force and other special operations units, whose identities remain classified, would try to rescue the hostages from the various locations.

The Pave Low HH-53Hs would have been used as pathfinders for the force, utilising their FLIR and LLLTV sensors,
Doppler/inertial navigation systems and terrain following/
avoidance radar. However, the operation never took place because of the difficulty in pinpointing the locations of the hostages, who had been moved after the abortive first raid. The
situation was finally resolved when the Iranians released the
hostages as President Ronald Reagan took over from Jimmy
Carter.

The Pave Lows were here to stay, though, and on 17 June
nine of them joined the CH-3Es and UH-1Ns of the 20th SOS,
commanded by Colonel Wild Bill Takacs. The "Green Hornets" had to give away their CH-3Es as part of the deal, but
the new helicopter was worth it.

A DECADE OF EVOLUTION

The years following the failure of Eagle Claw were traumatic
for the Special Operations Forces. Major-General Hugh Cox
recalls the decade leading up to the establishment of Air Force
Special Operations Command (AFSOC) as a separate major
command:

> "When one ponders the successes of Special Operations
> in the 1980s, you sure can't attribute it to enlightened
> leadership, stable organisations or universal support of
> the special ops mission. As history has shown, Generals
> and Colonels can screw up in spades, but the troops will
> usually pull it off and succeed in spite of the difficulties.
> One only has to look at how Special Operations person
> nel of the Army, Air Force and Navy succeeded in Op
> eration Just Cause in Panama and Urgent Fury in
> Grenada, not to mention the as yet largely undisclosed
> triumphs in Desert Shield/Storm, to know that Special
> Operations Forces (SOF) personnel are the cream of the
> services crop. There were many other still classified op-

erations in the decade of the 1980s that are known only to those directly involved. The bottom line is SOF has demonstrated its value as one of the pre-eminent instruments of national power by its successes over the last few years.

The 1980s were marked by controversy, inter-service and intra-Air Force rivalries, jealousies and frequent disruptive reorganisation before the emergence of AFSOC with its own major command status. I was in the midst of it, as the vice-wing and later wing commander of the 1st SOW, the commander of the now disestablished 2nd Air Division, the first director of operations and later the deputy commander in chief of the new unified command for special operations, the US Special Operations Command, SOCOM.

After the failure at Desert One morale was low, the wing was over-tasked and SOF personnel were still suffering from lack of promotions and general higher headquarters indifference. The high-pressure preparations for the planned second hostage rescue attempt had also taken its toll. What turned the tide was the coming together of some key leaders in positions of responsibility in the 1st SOW and overseas SOF units, such as Bob Mayo, Hugh Hunter, John Roberts, Robbie Robertson, Jim Hobson, T. O. Williams, John Gallagher, Bill Takacs, Wayne Corder, Bob Brenci and others too numerous to mention. They were tough, experienced guys, motivated by the importance and sheer excitement of the SOF mission. They brought the 1st SOW and the Air Force Special Operations Force out of the doldrums of post Desert One and set them on the path of success.

Their task was not easy, because the institutional and organised Air Force was generally indifferent to the SOF mission. Officer promotions in the AFSOF were the lowest in the Air Force, and personnel who had participated in Eagle Claw were getting passed over. The turnaround started when Lieutenant-General Larry Welch took over command of 9th Air Force and the 1st SOW began reporting to him. Department of Defense and Congressional attention increased and money started to flow into the special operations missions area.

However, we were then hit by the decision by the Air Force Chief-of-Staff, General Charlie Gabriel, to transfer the AFSOF mission from the Tactical Air Command (TAC) to the Military Airlift Command (MAC). The news hit Hurlburt like a late summer hurricane, and the immediate response was largely negative. SOF troops viewed TAC as a command of warriors, and the move to MAC was viewed by most SOF personnel as a definite step down and an indication that the Air Force leadership considered them as 'trash haulers' and combat supporters, not leading-edge, point-of-the-spear warriors.

General Jim Allen, the CINCMAC, had campaigned for the AFSOF mission based on the premise that MAC would support AFSOF and make it better. However, it became immediately apparent during the TAC-MAC transition meetings that MAC intended to assimilate the AFSOF into its existing organisation and mission. They wanted to place AFSOF in its Aerospace Rescue and Recovery Service (ARRS). Their rationale was that special ops was no different than rescuing a downed aircrew member and ARRS would do both missions. I heard a MAC General say that any MAC C-130 aircrew member could do the special operations mission, and that flying at 250ft altitude, at night, in rough terrain and in bad weather was no big deal! It should be duly noted that he had never done it!

I set about to use what TAC influence I still had to preclude the AFSOF losing its identity and specialness that I believed would occur if the AFSOF was assimilated by the ARRS. The result was that TAC insisted on 'separate and distinct' and a new numbered MAC Air Force, 23rd Air Force, was established, with separate subordinate commands for Rescue and Special Ops. The ARRS would remain the same and a new MAC air division would be formed to have command over all AFSOF worldwide. On 3 March 1983 the 2nd Air Division was activated, and I moved from command of the 1st SOW to Commander, 2nd Air Division.

Although we had accomplished much, dealing with MAC headquarters was painful from the start. There was a not too well hidden intention, particularly at HQ MAC, to take the 'special' out of special operations. As if to illustrate the point, during the first year of AFSOF under MAC there were only a handful of SOF experienced personnel placed on the 23rd Air Force and HQ MAC staff! MAC also assigned non-volunteer pilots to fly the low-level Combat Talon mission in MC-130s. The MAC leadership refused to acknowledge that there actually were airlift pilots that didn't want to fly in close proximity to mother earth. As a result, we had our share of pilots that either didn't want to fly the Talons or were unsafe doing so.

The most significant operation in the young life of the 2nd Air Division was Operation Urgent Fury in Grenada, in the fall of 1983. Army and 2nd AD SOF units spearheaded the invasion of the island of Grenada, and SOF were in charge and largely planned and executed what has become a symbol of US commitment to just causes in the 1980s and '90s. It marked the emergence of US resolve to use its military might when it was in the national interest, whereas such resolve was certainly absent prior to the start of the decade, and SOF was at the point of the US spear!

After a year as the first commander of 2nd Air Division I was promoted to Brigadier-General and shipped out of SOF, despite the position of vice-commander 23rd Air Force being vacant at the time. That position was filled by someone from the C-141 airlift world, with no SOF experience, and I went to West Germany. Whilst there I was visited by Congressman Earl Hutto, an enthusiastic SOF supporter whose district encompasses Hurlburt Field. After many discussions I sent him a 'think paper' in late 1984, which suggested that as long as other services controlled the SOF purse strings, SOF would remain low priority and subjugated to other military capabilities. The 'conventional' military mind predominant in the services would never properly resource the SOF because the mission area was viewed as relatively unimportant to most. I recommended a unified command for SOF, with a CINC who had his own cheque book.

In 1985, in the Defense Authorisation Bill for 1986, there was language inserted that directed the creation of a unified command responsible for all SOF, and its four-star CINC would be responsible for organising, training and equipping his forces with defense dollars specific to that purpose. It gave the CINC responsibility for SOF personnel and the power to hire and fire. I'm proud of the little part I played, but little did I know this was just the beginning of a fight that's not over yet.

While events in Washington and elsewhere in the mid-1980s were leading up to the law establishing US SOCOM and its service components, the long knives at 23rd Air Force and HQ MAC were slicing away at the AFSOF. The 2nd Air Division was disestablished and all SOF units began reporting to 23rd Air Force head-quarters, whose staff was by far predominated by per-sonnel who didn't know how to spell SOF and seemed indifferent to learning.

In 1985 23rd Air Force was commanded by an airlift-er who was proceeding to combine Air Rescue and Spe-cial Ops in Special Warfare wings, along with hospitals, missile site support and a partridge in a pear tree. In effect, it used special ops priority and resources to sup-port the non-SOF service mission of rescue. SOFs re-sources are earned and exist to service the other warfighting CINC's special ops missions, not the Air Forces service responsibility of air rescue.

In the spring of 1987 US SOCOM was created by law, and activated at MacDill AFB, Florida. It was led by US Army General James J Lindsay and created to fulfil all the expectations for the SOF as embodied in the 1985 legislation that created it. I came on board as its first Director of Operations and Training, J-3. One of the first battles was with 23rd Air Force's Foward Look plan that combined Rescue and Special Ops into one mission area and organisation. After a visit to the newly relocated 23rd Air Force HQ at Hurlburt Field, the plan was quashed, and out of the debris came the doctrine that says that the Air Force's rescue mission is only done by SOF as a by-product of its SOF mission or as directed by a CINC with appropriate authority.

Despite this, MAC tried to combine Air Rescue and Special Ops training at Kirtland AFB, New Mexico, a MAC base with a MAC wing commander 1,300 miles away from Hurlburt Field. It became clear that to move all AFSOF training to Kirtland was unwise and unaffordable with such a small force, and only a small amount of training was transferred.

Even after SOCOM took over the AFSOF, MAC continued to task SOF units, and many brave and dedicated special operators threw their bodies in front of the MAC/23rd AF train to stop it, so that CINCSOC could assert its legislated authorities and responsibilities. After about a year as director of operations, I moved up to the position of Deputy, CINC. General Lindsay finally concluded that the shotgun marriage of CINCMAC and CINCSOC over the AFSOF was indeed a marriage of convenience and probably wouldn't work in the long run. Following an attempt by MAC to re-assign HC-130 refuelling aircraft that belonged by law to CINCSOC, General Lindsay called General Larry Welch, the Chief of Staff of the Air Force and said he wanted MAC out of the picture.

General Welch agreed, and we decided to try to go for major command status. I secretly did not think it was attainable, but it would at least draw the line in the sand on the issues; CINCSOC wanted total control of the AFSOF as envisaged in the law creating the command. To my total and pleasant surprise, after many months of fighting with MAC staffers at the Pentagon, the Air Staff got Chief of Staff's approval to create the Air Force Special Operations Command! I went home that evening and celebrated with many martinis.

The creation and activation of AFSOC occurred in mid 1989, and since that time has established itself as the Air Force component of the US Special Operations Command. After the formation of AFSOC I decided I could die happy, and chose to retire early from the Air Force. I had burned more than a few bridges with three- and four-star Air Force leaders over my advocacy of the joint AFSOF mission with my unfailing support of the unified SOF command, US SOCOM. So I happily stepped out and left the fights for the AFSOF to others.''*

*Hugh L. Cox, Ill, is now a Major-General with the Alaska Air National Guard. A fuller account of his trials and tribulations before the founding of AFSOC appeared in the December 1992 issue of the Air Commando Association newsletter.

CHAPTER 11

THE INVASION OF GRENADA, 1983

OPERATION URGENT FURY

GRENADA, AN ISLAND IN the Caribbean Ocean, was once a British possession, but won independence in 1974 when the corrupt and heavy handed Eric Gairy became Prime Minister. In 1979 he was overthrown in a bloodless coup by the Marxist New Jewel Movement, led by a leftist named Maurice Bishop. He proved little better than Gairy, becoming a communist dictator and forming a People's Revolutionary Army and Militia. Fidel Castro, the Cuban dictator, saw the possibilities of a Marxist government only 90 miles north of South America. It would make an ideal staging base for aircraft flying to Africa to further the Cuban cause in Angola, and a supply depot and training base for guerrilla and terrorist groups throughout the Caribbean basin and southwards. However, the one airstrip on the island was too short for long-range aircraft. Soon, hundreds of Cuban "construction workers" began building a new airport at the southern tip of the island, on a narrow spit of land called Point Salines. In addition, the Soviets agreed to supply the Marxists with $20 million worth of arms via Cuba.

The presence of Soviet and Cuban military personnel and equipment so close to the United States' sphere of interest caused concern, particularly as the new airport featured armored fuel storage dumps, ammunition storage bunkers and military style "hot-refuel" fuel transfer points built into the ramps. The 9,500ft runway was quite capable of accommodating the latest Soviet strike, reconnaissance and transport aircraft.

In October 1983 Deputy Prime Minister Bernard Coard, together with the head of the Army, led a coup to overthrow Bishop, and he was shot dead during the upheaval. Nine of his followers were executed at the same time, and martial law was declared. There were 600 American students, tourists and retired citizens on the island, and plans were being made to evacuate them when the Organisation of Eastern Caribbean States (OECS) formally asked Barbados, Jamaica and the United States to join with it in military action to restore order and political stability to the country. The member nations of the OECS, Dominica, St. Lucia, Grenada, St. Kitts-Nevis and St. Vincent and the Grenadines, had signed an agreement in 1981 to take whatever steps might be necessary to preserve the stability of the region. President Reagan and his advisers approved a plan for a full-scale assault on the island, to secure and evacuate American and certain foreign citizens, to neutralise the Grenadian army and any other armed forces on the island and to restore stability and democracy to Grenada.

The opposition was not to be underestimated. There were 5,000 men under arms, with Cuban advisers, and Commander-in-chief, Atlantic (CINCLANT) was only given four days to organise the invasion. Navy Task Force 120, organised around a carrier battle group and Task Force 124, the 22nd Marine Amphibious unit, would command the operation, named Urgent Fury. The Marines would land near Pearls Airport, at the northern end of the island, while securing the southern end would be a joint services task. Navy SEALs were to reconnoitre the Point Salines airport and guide a combat control team in to place radio and navigation beacons for the C-130 transports carrying two battalions of Army Rangers, who would land and secure the airport. Then they would race to the nearby medical campus to secure the American students.

SEALs were also to scout Pearls Airport for the Marines, seize the island's main radio station and rescue Britain's Governor General, Sir Paul Scoon, who was under house arrest. Delta Force was to release the political prisoners held at Richmond Hill Prison. The 82nd Airborne Division would then fly into Salines airfield to relieve the Rangers, SEALs and Delta Force and mop up any pockets of resistance.

The assault did not go according to plan. On 23 October sixteen SEALs and two boats were to be dropped by two MC-

130s off the southern end of the island, then climb into their Boston whalers and rendezvous with a destroyer. They were to take on more SEALs and three combat controllers and head for Salines airport. The parachute jump was to take place at dusk, so the men could still see the water, to release their lines before impact and locate their boats. However, the drop was made six hours later, in pitch black darkness from a height of 2,000ft. In addition, the men had been overloaded with equipment, and when they finally hit the water four of the team went under and never resurfaced. Seven of the men found their whaler and started the reconnaissance mission, but had to abort when a Grenadian patrol boat came near. They tried again the following night, but their outboard motor died and they drifted for eleven hours before being picked up by the destroyer. The Rangers bound for the airport would have no advance information on the airport or its defences.

SEALs did get ashore and checked the coastline near Pearls airport, finding it unsuitable for an amphibious landing. The Marines would have to assault the airport by helicopter and risk the fire from the 23mm anti-aircraft guns based there. Fortunately, there was a clear area 700 meters from the airport, and the CH-46s landed the Marines there instead.

By the time the Army's 160th Special Operations Aviation Battalion had been alerted for the operation, loaded their UH-60 Blackhawks aboard C-5 transports, flown to Barbados, assembled the helicopters and flown the 170 miles to Grenada, it was broad daylight. The Marines had almost secured Pearls airport and the Rangers were dropping at Salines. The nine aircraft carrying 100 SEALs and Delta Force troopers had lost the element of surprise and the enemy were waiting for them.

One UH-60 dropped an eight-man SEAL team at the radio station, where they quickly overpowered the guards. However, reinforcements arrived and after a firefight the SEALs withdrew. The station was later destroyed by air.

The two Blackhawks carrying the 23-man SEAL team tasked with rescuing the Governor-General had a bad start. The pilots could not find the residency at first, and when they came to a hover over the poorly chosen landing zone they came under fire from guards within the walls of Government House. The SEALs fast-roped the 90ft to the ground, but the helicopters were driven away by the fire, taking with them the SEAL's second in command, three diplomats and the team's SATCOM equipment, used to communicate with headquarters.

The SEALs disarmed the police on guard and moved the Governor and his staff to a room in the center of the mansion. They then took up positions around the house to repel the forces surrounding them. It took four hours for a Spectre gunship to arrive, but it stayed through the night and kept the enemy at bay. At sunrise the next day Marines arrived to relieve them. The rescue operation that should have lasted just a few minutes took more than 24 hours.

The other six Blackhawks carrying 60 Delta Force men were heading for Richmond Hill Prison. The plan to land at night, while the guards were asleep, had gone out of the window. They were awake, alert and waiting for the helicopters. As the helicopters flew along the valley floor, the defenders of the prison could fire down on them, aided by troops at Fort Frederick, the Army headquarters across the other side of the valley. One Blackhawk was shot down, the pilot killed and the crew and passengers badly injured. Because of uncoordinated communications between the services, the wounded would have to wait 3½ hours for a Navy medevac helicopter to arrive. Four other Blackhawks had wounded on board, and they broke off the mission and took them to ships waiting offshore.

The task of capturing the runway at Point Salines was given to the Army's 75th Rangers on board the Combat Talons of the 8th SOS. The commander of the squadron, Colonel (now Major-General) James L. Hobson, Jr. describes the mission:

"After notification of the operation, five of our MC-130Es and crews departed Hurlburt Field at noon local time on 24 October 1983 and flew to Hunter Army Airfield, Georgia. After weather, intelligence and course-of-action briefings, we loaded the Rangers and equipment on our aircraft and departed around 2000 hours local on the 24th. We received one in-flight refuelling, arrived in the area of Grenada around 0300 hours local, and entered a holding pattern about 75 nautical miles east of the island.

The original plan called for the numbers one and two Combat Talons to fly down the runway at 0500 hours local, 30 seconds apart, and drop an Army Ranger 'seizure package'. Their responsibility was to clear the runway of any obstacles and secure the perimeter of the field. Then, 30 minutes later, the number three Talon aircraft and two 'slick' non-Talon C-130s would airland and unload additional Rangers.

Unfortunately, an AC-130 gunship flying high over the island detected vehicles and obstructions on the runway (through its LLLTV). As a result, the airborne mission commander directed everyone to airdrop instead. [The chaotic scene inside the C-130s as the Rangers struggled to don parachutes, rehang equipment and hook up for the jump can only be imagined.]

The first two MC-130s departed the holding pattern, 75 miles west of Point Salines, in order to meet their original 0500 hours local drop time. The weather in the area was poor; thunderstorms in the vicinity and poor visibility. About 25 nautical miles west of Point Salines the number one Talon lost its inertial navigation system. Since it was in the weather, the aircraft commander called over the radio, 'NO DROP'. He was concerned that in the poor weather and with no accurate means of navigation, he might possibly drop some Rangers in the water.

The Air Mission Commander told both the number one and two Talons to 'hold south of the IP (initial point) and join up behind number three Talon when he comes by'. All three would then drop 30 seconds in trail.

I was flying the number three Talon, whose original mission was to be the first to airland at 0530 hours local and deplane the Battalion Commander and his command and control staff. We were now directed to be the first to airdrop, followed by the numbers one and two Talons. I left the holding pattern to make good my 0530 hours drop time. After slowing down and approximately two miles from the end of the runway (the runway was the drop zone), a searchlight came on from the control tower area and illuminated our aircraft. Obviously there was no element of surprise.

We proceeded to the end of the runway and dropped our load of 41 Rangers from an altitude of 500ft above the ground. Immediately, there was heavy AAA and small-arms fire (7.62mm and 23mm). After the Rangers left the aircraft, we banked hard right and descended to 100ft above the water and exited the area.

Meanwhile, the number one Talon was 30 seconds in trail behind me, and when I departed the drop area, the Cuban resistance zeroed in on him. Before he could make his drop, his aircraft was hit with small-arms fire and he elected to call 'NO DROP.' During the hot wash [after-action meetings], he explained his decision not to drop. The AC-130 gunships were circling overhead and he wanted them to suppress the enemy fire to prevent a potential heavy loss of life.

For the next 30 minutes the gunships suppressed the airfield defences, and about one hour later the remaining Talons and C-130s dropped their loads of Rangers. Later that afternoon we all recovered at Roosevelt Roads Naval Air Station, Puerto Rico. For the next week we conducted psyops operations in the form of leaflet drops on the island, urging the Cubans to surrender. We finally returned home to Hurlburt Field on 30 October.''

By 0730 hours the Rangers had reached the medical school and recovered the students. They then learned that there was a second campus, with 233 Americans, on the west coast of the island. At 1600 hours an assault force of CH-46s and CH-53s, covered by Marine Cobra gunships, A-7s and AC-130s, landed more Rangers at the campus and evacuated the occupants to safety.

The final objective for the Rangers was Camp Calivigny, the main Army training base atop a cliff five miles east of Salines. Navy A-7s and an AC-130 attacked the camp as Blackhawks carrying two companies of Rangers skimmed the surface of the sea towards the camp. As the first four UH-60s popped up over the rim of the 150ft cliff, they discovered that they had little room for landing. The second and third aircraft landed within the compound, whereupon the third UH-60 crashed into the first. The fourth UH-60 also lost control and crashed into the first two. Three Rangers were killed and four others injured. Only one Cuban was discovered in the camp.

Eventually two dozen Cubans were killed on the island and 661 others were rounded up for deportation. The Governor-General and all of the Americans on the island had been rescued without loss, and the brutal Grenadian regime had been removed. The Cubans and Soviets would have to look elsewhere for allies. However, there were many lessons to be learnt by the special operations community, including the important requirements of detailed planning and up to date intelligence. They would do better next time.

23RD AIR FORCE CREATED

During 1983 the Aerospace Rescue and Recovery Service was merged with the Special Operations Forces to form the 23rd Air Force. However, the creation of AFSOC in 1990 would see the air rescue service returned to Military Airlift Command control, although AFSOC kept their HC-130N/P tanker aircraft, with the exception of those operated by Air Force Reserve and Air National Guard units. They also took over most of the HH-53 fleet and modified them to MH-53 standard for special operations. This largely left the front-line air rescue service with only UH and HH-1s and HH-3Es, although the HH-60G has since replaced some of the HH-3Es. Because special operations then had the big helicopters, they inherited much of the combat search and rescue mission, something that is not part of their true role. However, as they were to find during the Gulf War of 1991, they were stuck with it.

CHAPTER 12

THE INVASION OF PANAMA, 1989

OPERATION JUST CAUSE

ALTHOUGH THE UNITED STATES is separated from the South American country of Panama by Mexico, Guatemala, El Salvador, Honduras, Nicaragua and Costa Rica, it has had a vested interest in the internal affairs of the country dating back to the 1850s, when the US concluded a treaty allowing transit rights across the isthmus, coastal positions for the defense of the future canal, water reservoir and support sites, and partial control of Panama City and Colon, the projected termini of the canal. Construction began in 1907, and the Panama Canal was opened in 1914, allowing travel between the Pacific Ocean and the Caribbean Sea.

Despite strong opposition at home, President Jimmy Carter signed a treaty in 1978 that will turn over control of the canal to Panama in 1999, although the US still retains complete right of access to the area and is permitted to intervene militarily to protect the canal and other US interests.

Colonel Manuel Antonio Noriega became commander-in-chief of the National Defense Forces in the mid-1980s, a position which actually controlled the reins of power in the country, despite an elected President. A dishonest leader, with fingers in many pies from gun-running to drug trafficking, Noriega soon fell out with the US and started down the dangerous path of brinkmanship. On 16 December 1989 the National Assembly of Panama, under Noriega's control, declared that Panama was at war with the United States. On that day Marine Lieutenant Robert Paz was murdered by Panamanian soldiers at a road block, and a US Navy officer and his wife who witnessed the incident were detained and abused. The following day President George Bush authorised the execution of Operation Just Cause, which had several objectives. They were to capture General Noriega and deliver him to the US to face drug charges; the protection of American personnel and US interests under the Panama Canal treaty; the restoration of democracy in Panama and the establishment of the elected government, which had been prevented by Noriega.

The headquarters of the US Southern Command is based in Panama City, and various Army posts and Navy and Air Force bases are dotted around the former Canal Zone. Howard AFB is situated at the Pacific end of the canal, and usually houses Special Ops aircraft on detachment. The assault would be carried out by forces already in place in Panama, together with troops flown in from the US. For obvious reasons, achieving surprise would be difficult.

The Special Operations contribution to the operation was supplied by the 1st SOW at Hurlburt Field, who committed three MC-130Es from the 8th SOS, two HC-130 tankers from the 9th SOS, seven AC-130H gunships from the 16th SOS, two AC-130A from the AFRES 919th SOG and five MH-53J helicopters from the 20th SOS. Some aircraft were deployed to Panama before the assault, and others flew direct to their assigned targets from the US. On 19 December a C-5 Galaxy airlifted four MH-60s from the 55th SOS to Howard AFB.

The US Army also committed special operations helicopters, in particular the 160th Aviation Group (Task Force 160) with twelve AH-6 Little Birds, ten MH-6, seven MH-47E and seventeen MH-60K Night Hawks. Their special forces troops included the 75th Ranger Regiment, the resident 7th Special Forces Group (Airborne) and the 1st Special Forces Operational Detachment D—Delta Force. Together with Navy SEALs they formed the Joint Special Operations Task Force (JSOTF) under the command of Special Operations Command, South (SOCSOUTH).

Operation Just Cause began in the early hours of Wednesday 20 December. Five task forces were deployed for the assault. Task Force Bayonet, with its light tanks and infantry was to destroy the Panamanian Defense Force Headquarters in La Comandancia, and was aided in this task by AC-130H gunships which eventually blew the building apart. This task force was also responsible for the capture of Paitilla airfield, where Noriega kept his private jet aircraft, but this was one mission that did not go so well. Normally an Army Ranger mission, the task was given to the Navy's SEAL teams, with air support from an AC-130 if required. The SEALs were ordered to disembark from their rubber raiding craft and advance down the runway, but they soon came under fire from PDF troops. A radio breakdown aboard the AC-130 prevented the SEALs from bringing the gunship's weapons to bear, and in a firefight that ensued in front of the hangars four SEALs were killed and seven others wounded. Ninety minutes would elapse before medevac helicopters arrived to evacuate the wounded.

Task Force Red was spearheaded by an Army Ranger battalion, supported by 82nd Airborne troops, who jumped into Torrijos airfield and the Puma Battalion barracks just outside the airport. A second Ranger battalion was led into Rio Hato airfield by two F-117A Nighthawk stealth fighters which dropped 2,000lb bombs to shock the defenders. The troops parachuted from MC-130Es and engaged some of Noriega's most loyal units in fierce fighting. Later an MC-130E provided refuelling and rearming support for Army helicopter gunships and another MC-130E, which had suffered propeller damage, executed the first three-engine C-130 short-field, night-vision-goggle take-off.

Task Force Pacific brought twenty C-141B-loads of reinforcements, who formed a second wave to parachute into Torrijos airfield and then blocked a bridge over the Pacora River to prevent PDF forces advancing into Panama City from the east.

Task Force Semper Fidelis, comprising a company of US Marines and a company of light armored infantry, seized the bridge of the Americas, the only access into Panama City from the west.

Task Force Atlantic, consisting of 82nd Airborne and 7th Light Infantry troopers, captured the electrical powerplant at Sierra Tigre, the Madden Dam and Gamboa Prison. The prison was taken by Delta Force troops, who freed an inmate jailed for running the CIA agent radio network in Panama. The raiders arrived in specially modified MH-6 Little Bird Army helicopters flown by the 160th Special Operations Aviation Regiment.

Spectre provided much needed surgical air support to ground troops at many locations on 22 December, and an AC-130H controlled the surrender of from 200 to 300 PDF troops at Penonome airfield. The aircrew illuminated the field and directed the PDF to form up shoulder-to-shoulder to await the formal surrender to ground forces. This illustrated the respect they had for the gunship.

Despite all attempts to locate him, General Noriega remained on the run until 24 December, when he sought refuge in the Vatican Embassy in Panama City. Soon Delta Force troops surrounded the embassy grounds and an AC-130H gunship orbited overhead. A waiting game ensued, with MH-53 helicopters hovering above the embassy and loud music being played by psyops units. One important prisoner, Lieutenant-Colonel Deal Cig, was removed from David, Panama, by an MC-130E flown by Colonel George Gray, the 1st SOW commander. The runway had a crater which reduced its usable length to only 3,900ft, but Colonel Gray landed successfully, picked up the prisoner and delivered him to Howard AFB.

Captain Thomas R. O'Boyle, a 20th SOS MH-53 pilot, was later singled out for praise for flying several critical sorties. These included leading a difficult four-aircraft night urban assault into downtown Panama City, a night assault on General Noriega's beach house and an eight-aircraft assault to secure the prison camp at Playa De Golfa.

On 3 January 1990 General Noriega surrendered at the Vatican Embassy and was flown by helicopter to Howard AFB. From there an 8th SOS MC-130E flew him to Florida to stand trial on drug charges.

SPECTRE OVER PANAMA

The contribution to the success of Just Cause by the Spectre gunships of both the 16th SOS and the 919th SOG deserves special mention. Five AC-130H from the 16th SOS flew for eight hours in an unprecedented five-ship formation direct from Hurlburt Field to Panama, despite harsh weather conditions and two heavyweight aerial refuellings en-route. The lead gunship, commanded by Captain Brian K. Dougherty, arrived over Torrijos airport at H-Hour, just prior to a 56-ship airdrop of men from the 82nd Airborne Division and 75th Ranger Regiment. Using their 105mm howitzer they destroyed the Panamanian 2nd Infantry barracks and HQ and the troops therein, together with three anti-aircraft artillery positions, allowing a safe and resistance-free airdrop. They also halted a convoy of reinforcements by destroying the lead vehicle, before proceeding to Rio Hato airfield to provide a further three hours of close air support.

Two AC-130Hs were tasked with destroying nine targets within La Comandancia, the Panamanian Defense Force Headquarters compound, including the barracks and AAA positions. New tactics were to be used, with the aircraft flying a concentric two-ship orbit, with one at a higher altitude than the other. These tactics had never been used in combat before and called for firing within 50 feet of the lower gunship. To preclude shooting down their wingman, the crew fired using night vision goggles, which had also never been accomplished before in combat.

The upper crew set off a huge secondary explosion with the first of their 105mm rounds, before answering a call for help from US ground forces to suppress enemy fire coming from the Comandancia building itself. The first 40mm round scored a direct hit on a PDF gun position that was firing rocket-propelled grenades at US troops less than 20 metres away.

The lower gunship fired thirty-five 105mm rounds at three targets in less than four minutes and then identified and destroyed three 0.50-calibre machine-guns that posed a threat to them and other aircraft in the area. After La Comandancia had been destroyed and overrun, the aircraft supported Marines engaged by PDF troops at Fort Amador.

The gunship assigned to support the ill-conceived SEAL attack at Paitilla airfield had a night of mishaps and malfunctions. They initially experienced "Many severe tactical system malfunctions" and had to return to Hurlburt Field. Some quick trouble-shooting and a hot-refuelling saw them on their way again. However, once over Paitilla airfield, as they initiated pre-strike procedures, another malfunction occurred, preventing them from firing. Such sophisticated systems cannot be expected to work all the time, but it may possibly have saved some of the SEALs if close air support had been available. No doubt lessons have been learnt from the incident.

Military Airlift Command gave the Tunner Award to the AC-130H crew commanded by Captain Mark Transue for their extraordinary achievement while providing close air support during Just Cause. They completed their eight-hour flight from Hurlburt Field and arrived over Rio Hato airfield ten minutes before H-Hour. They soon began receiving heavy AAA fire from every section of the air base, home to two PDF Rifle Infantry Battalions. They only had couple of minutes to suppress the fire before the arrival of fifteen C-130s carrying 500 Rangers.

The IR operator located their first target, a ZPU-4 quad-barrel AAA gun and destroyed it with their 105mm howitzer. Two armored personnel carriers received similar treatment as the Rangers jumped into the combat zone. Once on the ground they called upon the gunship for close air support and several targets were destroyed, including an enemy truck containing CS tear gas packets to incapacitate the Rangers. For five hours the gunship orbited the base, destroying another ZPU-4 and the barracks area with many of its occupants. Thereafter they provided support to friendly forces at Paitilla airfield, before landing after almost sixteen hours in the air.

The President's Award for the top AFRES crew was given to the crew of a 919th SOG AC-130A commanded by Major Clay McCutchan. They were the first combat aircrew airborne during Just Cause, sent aloft to provide air base defense for Howard AFB during the early phases of the operation. After returning briefly to the base, they were airborne again to disperse intruders at the main gate, before the 24th Composite Wing Air Operations Center (AOC) directed them to support a ground party under fire. As they again returned to Howard, the AOC directed them to destroy three armored personnel carriers heading towards a US installation. Fortunately the crew checked first and discovered friendly forces around the vehicles, which had been captured earlier. A serious incident was avoided by their professionalism.

The crew flew two more sorties and were instrumental in the safe recovery of twenty-nine Americans held hostage in the Marriott Hotel. They eventually logged fifteen hours of combat time and continued to provide support for the next three weeks of the operation.

CHAPTER 13

WAR IN THE PERSIAN GULF, 1990–'91

A MAJOR COMMAND AT LAST

In 1987 the US Special Operations Command (USSOCOM) was established, to fill a growing need for a capability to respond to crisis. The 23rd Air Force became the Air Force component for USSOCOM, and in 1989 all non-special operations force assets were removed from that organisation. A milestone was finally reached on 22 May 1990, when, amidst regular air force cutbacks, Special Ops was elevated to a major command. On that date the 23rd Air Force was redesignated Air Force Special Operations Command and established at Hurlburt Field, to exercise operational or administrative control of all US Air Force special operations forces. AFSOC is now an Air Force major command and the Air Force component of the unified US Special Operations Command. The AFSOC motto is "Air Commandos—Quiet Professionals."

Together with the Army Special Operations Command at Fort Bragg, North Carolina, the Naval Special Warfare Command at Coronado, California, and the Joint Special Operations Command training and standardisation unit at Fort Bragg, they report to the Commander-in-Chief, USSOCOM, at MacDill Air Force Base, Florida.

The AFSOC mission is to organise, train, equip and educate Air Force special operations forces for worldwide deployment and assignment to regional unified command for conducting:

- Unconventional warfare.
- Direct action.
- Special reconnaissance.

- Counter-terrorism.
- Foreign Internal Defence.
- Humanitarian assistance.
- Psychological operations.
- Personnel recovery.
- Counter-narcotics.

When established, Air Force Special Operations Command consisted of three Wings, the 1st SOW at Hurlburt Field, and two others overseas, comprising 111 fixed-and rotary-wing aircraft of five different types and twelve different models.

The 39th Special Operations Wing, soon to move to RAF Alconbury in the United Kingdom, and designated the Air Force component for Special Operations Command Europe, comprised the 7th SOS formerly based at Rhein-Main in Germany, flying the MC-130E Combat Talon, the "Dust Devils" of the 21st SOS, equipped with the MH-53J Pave Low, and the 67th SOS with the HC-130P/N Combat Shadow. The 353rd SOW was at Kadena Air Base in Japan, and is the Air Force component for Special Operations Command, Pacific. Its squadrons are the 1st SOS, flying the MC-130E, the 31st SOS with the MH-53J, and the 17th SOS with the HC-130P/N. The two wings would be renamed Groups and restructured in 1992, the 39th SOW becoming the 352nd SOG and the 353rd SOW becoming a SOG, their lineage going back to the 2nd and 3rd Air Commando Groups that were activated during the Second World War.

DESERT SHIELD: PREPARING FOR WAR

On 2 August 1990, in pursuit of long-standing claims to its neighbour's territory, 100,000 Iraqi troops invaded the tiny Persian Gulf state of Kuwait. The Emir of Kuwait fled to Saudi Arabia, together with thousands of his countrymen. The next day the United Nations Security Council demanded the immediate withdrawal of Iraq's forces. With hundreds of Iraqi tanks poised on its border, threatening to invade the most important oil-producing country in the world, Saudi Arabia requested assistance from the United States. President Bush agreed, and Operation Desert Shield was initiated; the largest military airlift the world had ever seen. The same day, Iraq's President Saddam Hussein ordered the rounding up of hundreds of Westerners in Kuwait and their incarceration at strategic targets within Iraq and Kuwait; a human shield against any bombing campaign.

Soon a multinational force was assembling in Saudi Arabia, including American, British, French, Egyptian, Canadian and Italian troops and aircraft. Within two months almost 200,000 American troops had arrived in the region. By 18 December the multinational force totalled 490,000, including 270,000 Americans. To support their troops the US Army also brought with them 1,000 helicopters, including the MH-6 and MH-60s of the 160th Special Operations Aviation Brigade. As the buildup continued, aircraft carriers and marine assault landing ships arrived in the Gulf; armored battle groups assembled and began acclimatising and training, and a hundred different types of aircraft from a dozen nations began to flood into Saudi Arabia to prepare for war.

Fortunately, Saddam Hussein freed the hostages in December. A multi-location rescue plan would have been a nightmare for the special operations forces, if indeed it would have been attempted at all. There were, however, plenty of special operations assets in the theatre, ready to go to war again.

In early August 1990 the 1st SOW deployed to King Fahd international airport in Saudi Arabia. They took with them AC-130H Spectre gunships from the 16th SOS, MC-130E Combat Talons from the 8th SOS, HC-130P/N tankers from the 9th SOS, MH-53J Pave Low helicopters from the 20th SOS and MH-60G Pave Hawk helicopters from the 55th SOS. Their maintenance was to be carried out by crew chiefs and specialists of the 834th Aircraft Generation Squadron, the 834th Equipment Maintenance Squadron, the 834th Component Repair Squadron and the 655th Special Operations Maintenance Squadron.

The 39th SOW in England moved to Incirlik Air Base in Turkey as a part of Operation Proven Force, and their activities are detailed later in this chapter. In addition, AFSOC also had EC-130E(RR) aircraft from the 193rd Special Operations Group, Air National Guard, from Harrisburg, Pennsylvania.

Their EC-130E(RR)'s would perform Commando Solo psyops broadcast missions, targeted against Iraqi troops inside Kuwait and Iraq with the aim of persuading them to surrender. Two EC-130E(RR) aircraft were initially deployed to Saudi Arabia, and the unit was mobilised to field a third when the ground war began. It is also believed that some of the unit's four EC-130E(CL) Comfy Levi aircraft deployed to perform the highly classified Senior Scout intelligence gathering mission, but this has not been officially confirmed.

The Air Force Reserve also had a part to play. The 919th Special Operations Group at Duke Field, Florida, received the call to arms. (The 919th became a Wing on 1 June 1992). Comprising the MH-3E-equipped 71st SOS in Arizona and the AC-130A-equipped 711th SOS in Florida, the unit reports to AFSOC during wartime. The 71st SOS was called to active duty on 21 December 1990, and deployed to Saudi Arabia in January 1991. The unit reported directly to the 1st SOW during Desert Shield and Desert Storm, and returned to Tucson, Arizona, in March 1991.

Elements of the 711th SOS at Duke Field were called up to active duty on 17 January 1991. Five of the unit's ten AC-130A gunships flew out on 30 January en route to the Gulf, and on 3 February more than 300 personnel deployed. During the short Desert Storm operation, reserve aircrews flew more than 125 combat hours. The MH-3E helicopters from the 71st SOS based at Davis-Monthan AFB in Arizona, flew combat search and rescue, and AC-130A Spectre gunships from the 711th SOS provided airbase defense for King Fahd airport.

After all diplomatic efforts to persuade Iraq to withdraw from Kuwait had failed, Operation Desert Storm began on 17 January 1991. After 5½ months of preparation the coalition forces were ready to carry the war to the Iraqi aggressors, and at the forefront of the order of battle would be special operations forces.

DESERT STORM: INTO THE BREACH

After months of negotiations and Iraq's steadfast refusal to withdraw from Kuwait, Operation Desert Storm was launched to liberate the country by force of arms. At 0220 hours on 17 January 1991 the offensive began. Two pairs of MH-53J Pave Low helicopters from the 20th SOS led the way, followed by eight AH-64A Apache attack helicopters. Their objectives were the two Iraqi early-warning radar sites to the west of Baghdad and 700km inside Iraqi territory that had to be destroyed before the armada of Tornadoes, Stealth Bombers, F-15 Eagles, F-111s and others could fill the skies over Iraq. Task Force Normandy crossed the border into Iraq ahead of the first US and Allied warplanes, using the Pave Low's state-of-the-art navigation and terrain-following systems to weave their way to their targets. Timing and the element of surprise were essential to the success of the mission, and the helicopters hugged the ground as they crept under the Iraqi radar net. The targets were electronically linked, and had to be destroyed at the same time. If the Iraqis detected either the helicopters or the attacking force, a warning would be sent to Baghdad and anti-aircraft artillery and surface-to-air missiles would be ready to take a heavy toll on the coalition bombers.

The Pave Low helicopters arrived undetected and illuminated the radar sites with laser target designators. The Apache's Hellfire missiles could not miss, and both targets were destroyed before they could raise the alarm. The electrical generators were the first to be hit, then the communication facilities and finally the radars themselves. In less than two minutes the Apaches fired 27 Hellfire laser-guided missiles, around 100 70mm rockets and some 4,000 rounds of 30mm ammunition. The code word "California" was flashed back to General Schwarzkopf at Central Command Headquarters in Riyadh, and within minutes Baghdad received its first air raid of the war. Saddam Hussein was being given a message that he clearly understood; the Allies were serious and he was now at war again.

The raid was planned and led by Major Corby L. Martin, an Air Force Academy graduate, who developed joint formation procedures and team cohesion during eight rehearsal missions. As the radar sites exploded in flames, the sky was filled with small-arms fire and infrared missiles, making egress difficult for the raiders. However, Martin led the Apaches to safety and then accomplished a blacked-out, low-altitude (below 500ft) join-up with an HC-130 Combat Shadow tanker to refuel. Martin eventually flew 45 combat hours in 33 sorties during Desert Storm, and led the first US/British helicopter operation in combat. The team flew more than five hours over featureless terrain in the search for a British Special Air Service patrol missing in action nearly 200 miles inside Iraq. The team had been discovered by Iraqi troops and had split up to escape and evade back to friendly lines. Unfortunately, only one courageous trooper made it back to the border. The others were killed or captured and returned at the end of the war. Major Martin's efforts during Desert Storm were rewarded with the 1992 James Jabara Airmanship Award.

The air war was to be split into four distinct phases, covering the first week or ten days of hostilities. In Phase 1, air superiority was to be gained over Iraq and Kuwait, and Iraq's strategic attack capability was to be destroyed. That meant the nuclear, chemical and biological production facilities and the "Scud" missile launching and storage sites. The command and control structure was to be disrupted. Phase 2 was aimed at suppressing the air defences of the Iraqis in and around Kuwait. Phase 3 required continuing attacks against phase 1 and 2 targets, while shifting the main weight of the attack against Iraqi army units in Kuwait. Phase 4 would be the air support of ground operations, when they finally began. Because of the large number of aircraft available, the first three phases ran concurrently.

On 18 January Iraq fired the first Scud missiles into Israel in an attempt to draw that country into the war and split the coalition forces. Within hours the "Great Scud Hunt" had begun. Reconnaissance aircraft searched the skies while special forces patrols searched the ground, trying to destroy as many missiles and launchers as possible. The MH-53Js from the 20th SOS were heavily involved in the hunt, moving to a forward operating location at Al Jouf and eventually flying more than 60 missions behind enemy lines.

By 24 February, after 100,000 sorties had been flown by the coalition air forces, the Iraqi defenders had been softened up enough to start the ground war, and at 0400 hours that morning American, British and French armored formations crossed the border into Kuwait and Iraq. The enemy defences crumbled, and 5,000 prisoners were taken during the first ten hours. As the surviving Republican Guard formations moved forward to oppose the thrusts, they were attacked from the air. Two A-10 pilots claimed 23 tanks destroyed on one day alone. Saddam Hussein responded by ordering the destruction of public buildings in Kuwait and the destruction of 500 oil wells, filling the skies with smoke and fire.

On 26 February, as Allied forces continued to outflank and cut off the Iraqi forces in Kuwait, the enemy began to withdraw. Once out in the open they were easy meat for the ground-attack aircraft, and a turkey shoot began. The 200 strong A-10 force alone accounted for over 1,000 tanks, 2,000 armored personnel carriers and artillery pieces and 1,400 other vehicles. A US spokesman listed the enemy options that day as, ''If they try to go back to Basra, the Air Force will kill them. If they go to the other side of the Tigris, the bridges are down. If they try to move south into Kuwait, they will run into coalition forces and the US Marines.'' The end was not far away.

As the fires from hundreds of oil wells filled the sky from horizon to horizon with thick black smoke, across the border flew five Pave Low helicopters, escorted by Pave Hawk gunships, their destination the US Embassy in Kuwait city. Hovering over the buildings, Army Special Forces rappelled down onto the roof of the Embassy to raise the Stars and Stripes and to check for booby traps. Resistance fighters and special forces teams driving heavily-armed fast attack vehicles raced around the city, searching for pockets of enemy troops.

Kuwait city was in Allied hands by 27 February, and the surviving Iraqi forces were in full retreat. Faced with the total destruction of his armed forces and even the occupation of his country by coalition forces, Saddam Hussein agreed to a ceasefire. At midnight Washington time on the 28th, 100 hours after the ground war began, President Bush called a halt to the fighting. Whether or not the Allied forces should have been allowed to carry onto Baghdad and overthrow the Iraqi dictator, only time will tell. In the author's opinion that is what should have been allowed to happen. History has a habit of repeating itself.

BEYOND THE CALL OF DUTY

The AC-130H Spectre gunships also had a role to play in the conflict. Stephen Thornburg, whose Southeast Asia exploits in the AC-119 and C-123 were recounted earlier, went out to the Gulf with the 16th SOS. He recalled:

"We had four aircraft in place by the first week of September. At the time our location was classified, as we were not operating out of an existing military field. In fact our site was still under construction throughout the deployment. We were lucky enough to be in hard quarters; many of the workers fled after the Kuwaiti invasion and some units were able to contract out the vacant trailers. Although we had central latrines, and were four men to a room 10ft square, at least we weren't in tents. Until additional security personnel arrived we were responsible for our own ground and security defences.

The weather was still very hot, up to 112° Fahrenheit and higher most days. The initial problem was the heat, as it could fry the electronics and damage the circuit boards in the sensors. The dust was also a real problem, as it hung in the air and caused problems for the IR and the LLLTV. It caused both a thermal blanket and a visual impairment for the LLLTV. The airborne grit also scratched the scanner's blisters and the lens on the sensors.

By December the temperature had gone to the cold side and, as hot as it had been before, it seemed damned cold at 50°F and below on the ground. In flight it was worse. Aside from the flightdeck and the sensor booth, the rest of the aircraft was as cold as the outside air, and also there was a wind chill factor to contend with. The AC-130 has many openings for various guns and sensors, etc, and channels the air through, so the gunners and loadmaster are constantly cold during the cooler months."

One night the gunships knocked out two Iraqi radar sites and a mobile Scud missile launcher. It was risky business, though, and one gunship pulled 5g to shake off an Iraqi surface-to-air missile launched at it. Sadly, the Spectre crews did not escape unscathed during Desert Storm. One of the casualties was "Spirit 03," an AC-130H from the 16th SOS. Before the start of the ground war, the Saudi Arabian border town of Khafji had been overrun by an Iraqi surprise attack, and as night fell an AC-130, call sign "Spirit 01," was sent to stop other Iraqi columns approaching the town. It destroyed eight Iraqi armored personnel carriers (APCs) and caused others to disperse or retreat. The aircraft was also taking AAA fire from enemy troops on the road below, including 23, 37, 57 and 100mm guns. They were being fired optically, but eventually the Iraqis started firing artillery flares to try to silhouette the aircraft. The flares looked like Strella shoulder-fired heat-seeking SAMs and occasionally lit up the sky around the gunships' orbit.

Around 0200 hours "Spirit 01" ran out of ammunition and left the area. It was replaced by "Spirit 02," but the AAA fire had grown so intense that it had to leave the area after twenty minutes. After a lengthy delay, "Spirit 03" flew into the target area. Initially the gunship did not encounter as much AAA fire as the other two ships, then, about 0600 hours an Iraqi SAM hit the port wing of "Spirit 03" and exploded just above a fuel tank, blowing off the wing. The crippled aircraft did a barrel roll into the shallow water just off the Saudi coast. The fourteen crew members rode the aircraft in and none survived.*

The gunship was probably vulnerable because it stayed in the area for about half an hour after dawn and became visible to the gunners below. Spectres are night animals and would

---

*The crew are respectfully listed here as Major Paul J. Weaver; Captains Dixon L. Walters, Arthur Galvan, and William D. Grimm; First Lieutenant Clifford Bland, Jr.; Senior Master Sergeant Paul G. Buege; Master Sergeant James B. May, II; Technical Sergeant Robert K. Hodges; Staff Sergeants Timothy R. Harrison, John P. Blessinger, John L. Oelschlager and Mark J. Schmauss; Sergeants Damon J. Kanuha and Barry M. Clark.

normally avoid daylight, but the friendly troops on the ground needed help and the gunship did not desert them.

Gunships also played a part attacking fleeing Iraqi troops on the "Highway of Death" during the Iraqi rout from Kuwait. They spent little time in the airbase defense mission as there was little threat of Iraqi assaults against Allied bases, other than from Scud missile launchers once Desert Storm had begun. By the end of May the 16th SOS only had two aircraft left in country to support rescue missions and on call to provide airborne artillery support if necessary to quell any outbreaks of fighting during the setting up of the peace monitoring teams. These two aircraft returned to the States at the end of May.

Another Hercules variant, the MC-130E Combat Talon, also saw action over the desert. In August 1990 the 8th SOS deployed four Combat Talons to the Saudi Arabian desert in support of Operation Desert Shield. At the onset of Operation Desert Storm three of them were airborne in support of helicopter refuelling and psychological operations.

On 7 February 1991, two MC-130Es took off, each carrying a 15,000 pound BLU-82 bomb. The BLU-82 is the largest conventional bomb in the world and was used in Vietnam to create instant landing zones in the jungle. In the closing days of the Vietnam war one was dropped on an enemy position four miles from Xuan Loc in South Vietnam. The entire city shook as if rocked by an earthquake, and all the lights went out. The explosion destroyed the entire headquarters of the 341st North Vietnamese Army Division. In Iraq and Kuwait they were used to clear Iraqi minefields and other border defences, and the 8th SOS dropped at least nine more before the end of hostilities.

Psychological warfare also played a part in the defeat of the Iraqi ground forces. The day before a BLU-82 was to be dropped, an MC-130E showered the enemy lines with leaflets in Arabic, warning the Iraqi troops to surrender, because "Tomorrow, if you don't surrender, we're going to drop on you the largest conventional weapon in the world." The next day, after the bomb was dropped and its effects felt, more leaflets were dropped, warning, "You have just been hit with the largest conventional bomb in the world. More are on the way."

In one instance the campaign led to the surrender of an Iraqi Battalion commander and his staff, who crossed into Saudi Arabia carrying some of the leaflets and maps of the mine-fields along the Kuwaiti border. This intelligence coup enabled the minefields to be breached within hours of the start of the ground war. Combat Talons also dropped over sixteen million leaflets inside Iraq and Kuwait. During Operation Desert Calm they continued to support search and rescue, air-land opera-tions and resupply missions until August 1991.

The credit for the destruction of Saddam Hussein's terror weapons, the Scud missiles, must also go to the Special Forces. Pave Lows dropped US Special Forces and British Special Air Service teams inside western Iraq to hunt down and destroy the missiles before enough could be fired against Israel to force that country into the conflict. When the mobile launchers or their command or supply centers were discovered, the teams either attacked themselves, or called up Allied air-craft to launch laser-guided bombs at the target, while it was "painted" by a laser illuminator held by one of the troopers.

THE RESCUE OF SLATE 46

As the Allies continued their bombing campaign to soften-up the Iraqi defences before the ground offensive began, other jobs were found for the Special Operations helicopters. Allied aircraft were being shot down, and search and rescue missions were tasked for the MH-53Js. They were now flying in the traditional role of their brother HH-53 Super Jolly Green Gi-ants, veterans of the Vietnam war, who plucked pilots from the ground in Laos and North Vietnam while Skyraider escorts suppressed enemy groundfire. Now their escorts were Fair-child A-10 Thunderbolt tank busters, still using the "Sandy" call sign.

On 21 January a Navy F-14A Tomcat was shot down by a SA-2 surface-to-air missile 180 miles inside Iraq at about 06: 30 hours. Both pilot and radar intercept officer (RIO) ejected and reached the ground in one piece, although the RIO was captured soon afterwards. The pilot, Lieutenant Devon Jones, walked across the desert for a couple of hours without finding anywhere to hide, so he then used his survival knife and helmet and dug a hole three feet deep. He climbed in and waited. In the meantime, the Pave Lows had been searching for three hours until they ran low on fuel and returned to the Saudi airfield at Arar to refuel. While they were there, two A-10s located the downed pilot and the MH-53Js, led by "Moccasin 05" lifted off again and headed deep into Iraq. Tracked by an Air Force E-3A Sentry Airborne Warning and Control (AWACS) aeroplane, the rescue helicopters raced across the desert at low level, crossing a four-lane highway en route to the pilot's position.

The Iraqis had been monitoring the pilot's radio calls and were closing in on him. The rescue helicopter now found itself in a race against time, to reach the pilot before the Iraqis. A covered truck, possibly a radio direction-finder vehicle, was fast approaching the pilot, then the A-10s saw it and opened up with their cannon. The truck burst into flames only 100 yards from the hidden pilot. The MH-53J was closing fast, flying five feet above the ground, and as it got within 50 yards of the pilot he popped out of his hole and ran towards them. The relieved pilot climbed aboard for the 150-mile journey back to the border. He had been on the ground for eight hours.

The MH-53J that picked up the pilot was flown by Captain Tom Trask, and the copilot was Major Mike Homan. Sandy Lead, A-10 pilot Captain Paul Johnson, later received the Air Force Cross and his wingman, Captain Randy Goff, the DFC. The RIO, Lieutenant Larry Slade, spent six weeks as a POW enduring mental and physical torture before his release.

BATMAN AIR BASE AND GOTHAM CITY

As part of the coalition build-up, the United States Air Forces in Europe deployed forces to Turkey under the code name Proven Force. Many were based at Incirlik Air Base, and flew almost 5,000 sorties against targets in northern Iraq, out of range of the aircraft based in Saudi Arabia. By the time the first missions were flown, on 18 January, 100 aircraft were in residence.

One of the units that arrived was the 39th SOW from England. The force included Wing headquarters, plus the 7th SOS (MC-130), 67th SOS (HC-130), 21st SOS (MH-53J), 667th Special Operations Maintenance Squadron (MH-53 and HC-130 maintainers) and the attached Detachment 1, 1723rd Special Tactics Squadron (parajumpers and Combat Controllers). They then moved four MH-53Js and four HC-130P/Ns, plus maintainers, special tactics and a supporting staff, forward to Batman Air Base, 150 miles from the Turkish/Iraq border. Built with NATO infrastructure funds, Batman is located approximately 60 miles east-southeast of Diyarbakir Air Base. The 20th had eight MH-53Js in the south and the 21st had five in the north, plus two from the 20th. The three helicopters left at Incirlik were training with special forces personnel recovery teams.

Colonel Bobby Clark volunteered to accompany the 21st to Turkey. As chief of the 39th SOW Combat Readiness Division he was best qualified to pull together the mission planning effort. Some of the crews had rescue backgrounds, and would need to learn how to sneak into enemy territory. He recalls:

"I was at Batman Air Base, where search and rescue was our main preoccupation, but not a doctrinal tasking. We flew only one operational mission, but trained steadily. The site was bare-base for us, as the Turkish Air Force had taken over all of the buildings for fighter-bomber operations.

We were quite proud that we moved the helicopters, aircrews, maintenance, special forces and support troops forward and became operational in 48 hours. By close of play we had about 500 men living in Gotham City, named from the Batman comics.

We lived and worked in tents. What a crazy place that was; the high desert with temperatures dropping to 14° Fahrenheit at night. It snowed and rained, and we lived in a sea of mud until it froze! We had no showers or proper washing facilities for the first two weeks.

Unfortunately, we did not conduct any special operations missions from Batman Air Base, probably due to Turkish veto power over everything we did.''

Colonel Mike Russell, the commander of the 21st SOS, described the role of the Pave Low helicopters:

"We only flew one rescue mission, three days after we arrived, but the pilot had been captured before we actually launched. The call sign of the pilot, a wing commander, was 'Corvette 03.' He had hit a target near Baghdad but could not make it back across the border and had baled out. He had evaded capture for a day or so and we had been put on alert, but were told to hold. Twenty-four hours passed before we were told to execute and we finally launched two MH-53Js. Captain Grant Hardan was the flight leader.

It was very deep into Iraq; five hours flying time to the pickup site. Unlike the Vietnam days, we usually fly at night if possible and without an escort. A-10s essentially have no night capability. However, some fighters were sent from the southern tier to hit some targets in the area as a diversion, and others were to authenticate the identity of the survivor prior to pickup.

When the fighters tried to contact the man on the ground they were met with a AAA barrage that watered their eyes. They tried again and were met with another barrage, so they were told to terminate the mission and return home; it was obvious he had already been captured. The mission was successful in that we penetrated the defences that we needed to penetrate and get five hours into the area. If the survivor had still been there, we would probably have made a successful pickup."

One of the other missions delegated to the squadron was the location and destruction of bombs jettisoned by F-111s returning home from unsuccessful missions. There was a 15-mile-deep wall of AAA that extended across the whole of the border between Turkey and Iraq, and it was effective up to 18,000 or 20,000ft. The F-111s would go over the top, but if the Iraqis sent up any fighters they would egress the area, because they did not have a good air-to-air capability. They jettisoned their bombs on the border, rather than land with them, but the Turkish authorities went ballistic when they found out. Even though the bombs were inert, they could have been recovered by the PKK terrorists and turned into weapons. The 21st had to fly in explosive-ordnance disposal teams who would fast-rope to the ground, set charges on the bombs and be hoisted up quickly before the explosives detonated.

After the war the squadron returned to England, but two weeks later they were ordered to pack up again and return to Turkey to participate in Operation Provide Comfort. Although a ceasefire existed between the coalition forces and the Iraqis, they were not prevented from driving the Kurdish tribes in northern Iraq towards Turkey. Soon the mountains were full of fleeing, starving refugees, who needed food, medical care and shelter. The squadron was tasked with cargo hauling and lifting special forces teams into the Kurd's camps to organise relief sorties. On more than one occasion they had to evacuate casualties caused by mines, including at least one American serviceman. At the time of writing, helicopters from the 21st are still on detachment to the area.

ELECTRONS, NOT BULLETS

"Our motto is 'Electrons not bullets,'" said Colonel Lawrence F. Santerini, commander of the 193rd SOG, when discussing the role of his EC-130E(RR) psyops aircraft during Desert Shield and Desert Storm. "We found that by putting out psyops to the enemy, talking them into surrendering, we saved lives on both sides of the fence."

On Thanksgiving Day 1990 the 193rd began broadcasting "Voice of America" into the Kuwait theatre of operations, helping to prepare the battlefield psychologically by offering the Iraqi soldiers food, bedding and medical care if they surrendered, and reminding them of the consequences if they did not. During Desert Storm their efforts were rewarded when thousands of Iraqis began surrendering to the Allied forces. Leaflet drops were apparently the most effective, together with radio broadcasts and loudspeaker messages. The text of one message broadcast on 11 February 1991 was along the lines of: "Your only safety is across the Saudi Arabian border. That is where the bombing and the starvation stop. The Joint Forces

offer you asylum. They offer you a warm bed, medical attention and three filling meals a day. Embrace your Arab brothers
and share in their peace.'' It is estimated that 100,000 Iraqi
troops surrendered or deserted by the war's end.

The 193rd is usually tasked by the State Department, who
will evaluate the "problem area." Messages are produced at
the Army's 4th Psychological Operations Group at Fort Bragg,
North Carolina, and approved by the State Department before
delivery to the 193rd. Sometimes a linguist from the Army or
someone in-country will fly with the crew, depending on the
mission. Once airborne, the mission control chief and five
electronic communications system operators occupy their
"search," medium-and high-frequency, very high frequency
and ultra-high frequency, or audio positions in the mission
compartment. The compartment has cassette and reel-to-reel
recorders, a video recorder, television monitors, receivers,
noise modulators, transmitters and a live microphone.

The mission control chief, together with the theatre commander's planning staff, plans where the orbit areas will be
set up to hit the target audience with the best possible signal.
Rather than trying to overpower a signal, they normally try to
broadcast on an open frequency. The search operator monitors
radio and television frequencies to find one that is clear of
other broadcasts and is within range of the target. The operators tune up transmitters inside the aircraft and corresponding
antennae on the outside of the aircraft, depending on the frequency being used. Signals can be transmitted from either side
of the aircraft, depending on the direction of the target. An
electronics operator plays the message tape through a video-
cassette recorder or tape deck to other operators, who transmit
over the airways. To ensure that the target audience is listening, other psyops units can drop leaflets to inform people of
the frequency being used. Very often the messages are in a
native language, and it can be months before the crews know
the result of their efforts. One last word regarding these efforts; during one mission, with multiple aerial refuellings, the
Rivet Rider stayed aloft for 21 hours, claiming a record for
the C-130.

PAVE PIGS

Although the 71st SOS was called to active duty on 21 December 1990, they had already been preparing for two months. Their MH-3E helicopters were fitted with satellite communications sets, FLIR turrets at the aft end of the aerial refuelling probes, Trimble Global Positioning receivers and Dalmo Victor APR-39A(V)1 radar warning receivers. On 10 January 1991 they loaded four privately-dubbed ''Pave Pigs'' and 105 personnel aboard a C-5 transport and set off for King Fahd airport in Saudi Arabia. Four days later they were flying night training missions over the desert.

The squadron did most of its training at night, using ITT AN/AVS-6 ANVIS night-vision goggles (NVG). The MH-3E cockpits were made NVG compatible using flip-down filters in 1990. One of the problems encountered was the inability at night to distinguish sand dunes when landing, so they set up water patterns for landing on land. Six chemlights would be thrown out each side of the aircraft to form a lane and provide the reference for a safe approach and landing.

Because the MH-3E is basically a modified HH-3E Jolly Green Giant rescue helicopter, capable of landing on water, the squadron was assigned over-water search and rescue responsibility in the Persian Gulf, and provided transportation for special forces units working off the coast of Kuwait. The SAR missions were escorted by MH-60G Pave Hawks, and the SOF insertions and extractions were covered by MH-53J Pave Lows. They also had the sad task of locating the wreck of the Spectre gunship ''Spirit 03,'' which they found in the water on 27 February.

The squadron was also forward-deployed to medevac casualties once the ground war had begun, and two MH-3Es were routed between Iraqi anti-aircraft sites to pick up five badly wounded Saudi soldiers on 24 February. Only one pilot ejected in the area covered by the Pave Pigs, and he was recovered by a US Navy ship. However, the pier used as a forward operating location came under fire from an Iraqi FROG missile battery, and the 71st proved that an MH-3E can be airborne from a dead start within 90 seconds.

Working with the new equipment was an experience for the crews. Usually the crew comprises two pilots, a flight engineer and one or more scanners, who watch for threats, talk the pilots into landing zones and manage any customers on board. They also man the M60D machine-guns or the new M240E rapid-fire guns, although the latter did not arrive in time. Nor did the Lockheed Sanders ALQ-144(V)3 IR jammers or the Tracor ALE-40 flare and chaff dispensers. The crews faced the IR missile threat with scanners pointing flare pistols out of the cabin windows and cargo ramp.

Dedicated FLIR and Global Positioning System (GPS) operators were also carried at first, but then the flight engineer was tasked with working the FLIR and the copilot to tie the GPS into navigation routines. The FLIR station in the cabin had a nine-inch monitor, a video recorder and a control pendant that could be carried to the cockpit. A six-inch monitor in the center console showed both pilots where the flight engineer was looking. Although not integrated into the navigational system as on the MH-60G or MH-53J, the FLIR on the MH-3Es is usually used to check waypoints at night and spot people and vehicles on the ground.

When the pilots were flying over water, the NVGs allowed them to see two or three miles ahead, but the 4x magnification on the FLIR increased that drastically. However, neither piece of equipment could penetrate the smoke from the oil fires in Kuwait, and at least one crew flying in smoke was saved by the ability of the GPS to determine the position of the helicopter when the crew could not see one foot in front of the aircraft. By the time the unit returned home, on 21 March 1991, the 34 aircrew members had flown 251 combat and combat support missions.

CHAPTER 14

SPECIAL OPERATIONS TODAY, 1992–'94

THE GUARD

BASED AT HARRISBURG INTERNATIONAL Airport, the 193rd Special Operations Group, Pennsylvania Air National Guard is currently the only special ops unit in The Guard. In the 1960s things were somewhat different, with the 129th Air Resupply Squadron, California ANG; 135th ARS, Maryland ANG; 143rd ARS Rhode Island ANG and 130th ARS, West Virginia ANG all organised to infiltrate and exfiltrate special forces teams.*

*The 129th ARS flew the Curtiss C-46 Commando and Grumman SA-16 Albatross between 1955 and 1958, then became a troop carrier squadron until 1963 when they became an Air Commando squadron flying C-119s and U-1Os. After becoming a special operations squadron in 1968 the unit was transferred to MAC as an air rescue and recovery squadron in 1975 and re-equipped with HC-130H/Rs and HH-3Es. The 135th ARS had a similar beginning to the 129th ARS, but flew HU-16s, UbAs and U-10s as an Air Commando squadron. In 1967 the U-10s were replaced by 0-2As and the squadron became the 135th TASS in 1971. The 143rd ARS had a brief spell with the C 46D and SA-16A between 1955 and 1958 and became a troop carrier squadron until July 1963 when it became an Air Commando unit flying HU-16s, U-6As and U-10s. As a special operations squadron they flew the C-119G/L as well, becoming a C-130A-equipped Tactical Airlift Squadron in 1975. The 143rd is unique in that it flew float-equipped U-10s, the only ANG unit ever to do so. The 130th ARS followed the same path as the 143rd with virtually the same equipment, and became a MAC C-130E unit in 1975.

The 193rd Special Operations Group started out as the 193rd Tactical Electronic Warfare Squadron (TEWS), flying C-121Cs converted in 1968 to EC-121S configuration as airborne radio/television stations for the Coronet Solo mission. This was a result of the Dominican crisis in 1965, following which the air force determined that a broadcast ability was needed to break into civilian and military radio networks. For five months in 1970 the unit deployed two aircraft to Korat RTAFB for Operation Commando Buzz, flying missions over Cambodia. For eight months during 1977 the unit was redesignated 1st Special Operations Group and then back to 193rd TEWG. At the same time the C-121Cs were retired and C-130Es began to arrive for conversion to EC-130E(RR) "Rivet Rider" airborne radio/television stations for psychological warfare operations and the EC-130E(CL) "Comfy Levi" for "Senior Scout" electronic intelligence/electronic countermeasures (ELINT/ECM) operations on behalf of the USAF Electronic Security Command.

The first converted C-130 arrived in March 1979 to continue the Coronet Solo mission. The unit uses four EC-130E(RR) to broadcast psychological operation programmes in the standard AM/FM radio, television, short-wave and military communications bands. This system may also be used in a civil affairs and/or public affairs role, supporting disaster assistance efforts by broadcasting public information and instructions for evacuation operations, providing temporary replacement for existing transmitters during evacuation operations, or expanding their television broadcasting in its frequency ranges. Secondary missions are electronic countermeasures and intelligence collection.

In 1983 the 193rd moved to MAC as a special operations outfit, and the name of its classified mission was changed from Coronet Solo to Volant Solo. The primary crew complement is eleven crewmembers: aircraft commander, pilot, navigator, engineer, loadmaster, mission control chief and five electronic communications specialists. The aircraft were used during Urgent Fury, Just Cause and Desert Shield/Storm.

On 29 July 1992 the latest example of the EC-130E(RR) arrived. Its most prominent features are two underwing 23ft × 6ft pods mounted near the blade antennae, which house antennae dedicated to high-frequency television channels. In addition, four missile-like antennae protrude from either side of the fin. These are additional antennae dedicated to low-frequency television broadcasting. Combined with upgraded transmitters and formatting equipment, the entire modification program permits color television to be broadcast in any format, worldwide.

Other modifications include the addition of trailing-wire antennae. One is released from the ''beavertail'' below the fin and used for high-frequency broadcasts. A second antenna is lowered from beneath the aircraft, held in a vertical position by a 500lb weight and used for AM broadcasts. Other on-going enhancements include self-protection equipment such as chaff, flares, infrared countermeasures (IRCM) and radar homing and warning (RHAW). Eventually all four Rivet Rider aircraft will receive this modification for the Commando Solo mission; the nickname having changed from Volant Solo when the unit moved from MAC to AFSOC.

Four EC-130E(CL) Comfy Levi aircraft fly the Senior Scout mission, which is highly classified. The configuration consists of a palletised electronics suite which is installed before a mission. An antenna array on the main landing gear doors usually signifies that the equipment is on board. Two Senior Hunter C-130s, which support the Commando Solos, will be modified to EC-130Es by 1997 if funding is available, bringing the unit strength up to ten aircraft.

THE RESERVE

There are two squadrons in the Air Force Reserve, both belonging to the 919th Special Operations Wing at Eglin Air Force Base in Florida. The 711th SOS is located with the Group in Florida, the 71st SOS at Davis-Monthan Air Force Base near Tucson, Arizona.* The 711th flies the AC-130A

---

*The 71st is scheduled to lose its Special Operations Squadron designation in March 1994. when it becomes an Air Rescue Squadron. However, with a special ops lineage going back to the days of the AC-119G Shadow in Vietnam, the 71st has earned its place in this book.

Spectre gunship, the model that was used in Vietnam, although the squadron will inherit the AC-130H models from the 16th SOS when that unit converts to the new AC-130U.

The 71st SOS, whose motto is "Anywhere, anytime," inherited the aircraft and mission of the 302nd SOS at Luke Air Force Base near Phoenix in October 1987. Partly because of their drug-interdiction mission, the unit moved south to Tucson and settled in with their six CH-3E. In 1990 they received the rescue version HH-3E, with aerial refuelling capability and the special ops designation MH-3E. When the author visited the squadron in August 1993 they were in the process of converting to the MH-60G Pave Hawk. Four of their old MH-3Es were in storage at the boneyard on the base, still in desert camouflage. Another is preserved near the main gate as a memorial to the squadron commander, Lt.-Col. Larry Rolle, and his three crew, Major Don Thomas, M/Sgt. Malte Breitlow and T/Sgt. Bill Slaven, together with eleven men from the Army's 5th Special Forces Group, killed when "Pony 12" crashed during a training exercise on 12 March 1989.

Major Mike Shook gave the author a guided tour of the unit and commented that there are some drawbacks to the new aircraft. The old MH-3E had more than twice the cabin area than the MH-60G and could land on water, although the Pave Hawk has more modern mission equipment and generally better performance. The MH-60G is fitted with an extending air refuelling probe, FLIR, the GPS navigation aid, an inertial navigation system (INS) and other communication and navigation enhancements. The old H-3 could carry ten to twelve fully-equipped troops, but because the H-60 carries internal fuel tanks to give another three hours' flying time, it is limited to only four to six. However, the new helicopter is 30 percent cheaper to operate and requires only half the maintenance of the MH-3. The rotorhead of the H-3 had ten parts, and seals were always leaking; the H-60 has only one moving part and it is dry.

The $7.5 million Pave Hawk is armed with 0.50-calibre machine-guns, a 30mm machine-gun and state-of-the-art avionics for the special operations mission. It cruises 35 knots faster and can hover at 15,000ft, whereas the H-3 was limited to

6,000ft. The Pave Hawk can also handle a 40g crash-landing and have crewmembers survive it.

Apart from training exercises and drug interdiction work, the squadron flies local rescue missions as well, having 20 rescues to its credit since 1987. In August 1992 Captain Maxwell in "Pony 01" flew a successful rescue mission on night vision goggles to lift a badly injured hiker from a canyon ledge. The MH-3E dumped fuel to hover near the walls of the deep canyon, out of ground effect, at 7,500ft on a moonless night to pay out the full 240ft of hoist cable down to the rescue litter. With the walls of the canyon only between five and eight feet away from the rotor tips it was a hairy mission for the crew. The injured hiker was lucky that day; that area of the Huachuca Mountains had claimed fourteen lives over the last 30 years.

THE 16TH SPECIAL OPERATIONS WING, HURLBURT FIELD, FLORIDA

Based at Hurlburt Field, the wing comprises six squadrons; the 8th SOS with its MC-130Es, the 16th SOS with the AC-130H Spectre gunship and the 20th SOS with the MH-53J. In addition, a second Combat Talon squadron, the 15th SOS was activated at Hurlburt on 1 October 1992 to fly the Combat Talon II. The 55th SOS with its MH-60G Pave Hawk helicopters moved in from Eglin AFB in 1993 and will be followed by the 9th SOS with its HC-130P/N when room is available.

Three other units at Hurlburt that should be mentioned are the 720th STG, USAFSOS and SMOTEC. The 720th Special Tactics Group has units strategically located in the US, Europe and the Pacific. The group is comprised of special operations combat control teams and pararescue forces. Their missions include establishing air assault landing zones, air traffic control, providing control for close air support for strike aircraft and Spectre gunship missions, establishing casualty stations and providing trauma care for wounded and injured personnel.

The US Air Force Special Operations School (USAFSOS) provides special operations-related education to personnel from all branches of the Department of Defense, governmental agencies and allied nations. Subjects covered in the thirteen courses presented at the school range from regional affairs and cross cultural communications to anti-terrorism awareness, revolutionary warfare and psychological operations.

The Special Missions Operational Test and Evaluation Center (SMOTEC) provides expertise to improve the capabilities of special operations forces worldwide. The center conducts operational tests and evaluations for equipment, concepts, tactics and procedures for employment of special operations forces. Testing includes operational as well as maintenance suitability factors. Many of these tests are joint command and joint service projects.

Known until recently as the 1st Special Operations Wing*, the 16th has inherited a long and glorious history. Activated as the 1st Air Commando Group in March 1944 at Hailakandi, India, the unit won fame during World War II providing fighter cover, air strikes and airlift support for Wingate's Chindits in Burma. The Group was disbanded in 1948, but revived again in 1963 with the activation of the 1st Air Commando Wing at Hurlburt Field. In common with all other Air Commando units, the 1st ACW was renamed the 1st Special Operations Wing in 1968. In April 1980 the wing provided forces for the abortive Iranian hostage rescue attempt and participated in Operation Urgent Fury in Grenada in 1983 and Just Cause in Panama in 1989. The wing deployed to Saudi Arabia in

---

*Despite the protests of Air Commando veterans, the 1st SOW was renamed the 16th SOW on 1 October 1993. The decision was made by the Air Force Chief of Staff to preserve the lineage of some of its older units owing to the current downsizing of the Air Force. The Air Force had a 1st Fighter Wing and a 1st Special Operations Wing and the 16th Pursuit Group, one of the original thirteen Army Air Corps organisations, was about to disappear from the books. As the 1st Fighter Wing has a lineage going back to 1919, longer than that of the 1st SOW (1944), the powers that be decided to preserve the heritage of the 16th, at the expense of the 1st SOW. Perhaps if the Chief of Staff was made aware of the achievements of the 1st SOW, particularly during the Vietnam war, he may have made a different decision.

August 1990 and took part in Desert Storm, the liberation of Kûwait from Iraqi control.

The ''Green Hornets'' of the 20th SOS provide the heavy-lift helicopter capability for the 16th SOW, flying MH-53J Pave Low IIIE helicopters. The most technologically advanced helicopter in the world, its range is limited only by crew endurance and tanker availability. Equipped with armour plating and three guns, either 7.62mm miniguns or 0.50-calibre machine-guns, the MH-53J has a Pave Low terrain-following radar and navigation package which enables it to fly in mountainous terrain in adverse weather. With a crew of six; two pilots, two flight engineers and two gunners, it can transport 37 troops, and was used to infiltrate and exfiltrate and resupply special forces teams throughout Iraq and Kuwait during Desert Storm.

The squadron was reactivated in 1976, flying the UH-1N and CH-3, the latter being replaced by the HH-53H in 1980. Between 1983 and 1985 the UH-1Ns took part in Operation BAT (Bahamas, Antilles and Turks) as a part of the South Florida Drug Enforcement Task Force. In 1986 the first two MH-53H Pave Lows arrived, followed by the MH-53J in 1988. The newer model has better integrated avionics, enhanced cockpit controls and displays, and improved weapon systems.

The 16th SOS was the first AC-130 squadron, activated in October 1968 at Ubon Royal Thai Air Force Base in Thailand and flying the AC-130A Spectre. Flown nightly over the Ho Chi Minh Trail through Laos and Cambodia in the truck-killing role, the Spectre was the most deadly night-flying weapons system in Southeast Asia. By the time the unit was relocated to Hurlburt Field in 1975, 52 aircrew members had been killed in action.

The A model Spectre is currently used by the AFRES 711th SOS at Duke Field, Florida, while the 16th SOS uses the newer AC-130H model. AFSOC is in the process of procuring a dozen new ''U'' models, which will have an improved weapons suite, 360° field of view infrared and all-light-level strike radar. In addition, one trainable 25mm Gatling gun will replace two fixed 20mm Vulcan cannon, giving greater accuracy and increased stand-off range to improve aircraft survivability.

The E models, which arrived at Ubon just before the end of the Vietnam war, were eventually modified to become AC-130Hs. Their armament has now standardised at two 20mm Vulcan cannon, one 40mm Bofors cannon and a 105mm howitzer. The crew comprises five officers: pilot, copilot, navigator, fire control officer and electronic warfare officer, and nine enlisted crew: flight engineer, low-light-TV operator, infrared detection set operator, five aerial gunners and a loadmaster.

The 8th SOS can trace its lineage back to 1917, when it was the 8th Bombardment Squadron. Since then it has flown sixteen different types of aircraft, and currently flies the MC-130E Combat Talon. The mission of the 8th is unconventional warfare, continuing the work pioneered during the Vietnam War by the Combat Talons of Detachment 1, 314th Tactical Airlift Wing, which carried out covert/clandestine single-ship operations in Laos and North Vietnam. Since its activation as a Combat Talon squadron in March 1974, the unit has participated in the abortive Iranian hostage rescue attempt, losing five of its members; Operation Just Cause in Panama, securing the airfield at Rio Hato Air Base under fire and flying the dictator Manuel Noriega back to the US; and more recently in Desert Storm. These and other operations give the 8th SOS its motto, "With the Guts to try and the skills to succeed."

In June 1991 the first MC-130H Combat Talon II entered service, and 24 are on order. The author was shown around a Talon II of the newly activated 15th SOS, and the inside of the cockpit is impressive, to say the least. This model features a "glass cockpit" with highly automated controls and displays to reduce crew workload. The entire cockpit and cargo areas are compatible with night vision goggles, worn as a matter of course on the low-level night missions. The pilot and copilot and the navigator/electronic warfare officers who sit on the flightdeck each have video displays and keyboards at their stations. The integrated control and display subsystem combines basic aircraft flight data, tactical data and mission sensor data into a comprehensive set of display formats that enable each operator to perform his task efficiently. The navigator, for instance, uses radar ground map displays, FLIR displays, tabular mission management displays and equipment status information.

The other two squadrons moving to Hurlburt from Eglin are the 55th and 9th SOS. They were formed when the 55th Aerospace Rescue and Recovery Squadron, a joint UH-60 and HC-130 unit, became the 55th SOS in March 1988. The 55th remained a helicopter squadron, and now flies the MH-60G Pave Hawk, and its HC-130 Combat Shadow aircraft were used to equip the 9th SOS. Like many of its sister squadrons, the 9th served in Southeast Asia during the Vietnam War.

The HC-130P/N Combat Shadow is also a modified version of the C-130 Hercules transport aircraft. It was initially modified to conduct search and rescue missions, provide a command and control platform, air-refuel helicopters and carry supplemental fuel for extending range or for air refuelling. In the special operations role it now has improved navigation, communications and threat detection and countermeasures systems. The HC-130 flies clandestine single-or multi-ship low-level missions, usually in low visibility or darkness, intruding into politically sensitive or hostile territory to provide air refuelling for special operations helicopters. They were deployed to Saudi Arabia and Turkey in support of Desert Storm, and were used for air refuelling over friendly and hostile territory, psychological warfare operations and leaflet drops.

The 55th SOS flies the MH-60G Pave Hawk, the special operations version of the Black Hawk helicopter. Its primary wartime missions are infiltration, exfiltration and resupply of special forces in day, night or marginal weather conditions. Other missions include long-range armed escorts of special operations helicopters and combat search and rescue. The MH-60 can fly loaded for Bear, mounting two 19-shot rocket pods, two 20mm cannon pods and two 7.62mm miniguns fixed forward. There are also two crew-served 7.62mm miniguns mounted in the cabin windows, and two 0.50-calibre machineguns can be mounted in the cabin doors. Other munitions or fuel can be substituted as the mission dictates.

THE 352ND SPECIAL OPERATIONS GROUP, ENGLAND

Both of AFSOC's Groups are overseas. The 352nd Special Operations Group is at RAF Alconbury in the United Kingdom, and is designated the Air Force component for Special Operations Command Europe. It comprises the 7th SOS, flying the MC-130E/H Combat Talon; the ''Dust Devils'' of the 21st SOS, equipped with the MH-53J Pave Low; and the 67th SOS with the HC-130P/N Combat Shadow. It was redesignated from the 39th SOW in December 1992, and can trace its lineage back to the 2nd Air Commando Group of 1944. The latest news is that the Group will soon relocate to RAF Mildenhall.

Flying in peacetime can be risky, as Captain Keith Lambert, an HC-130 pilot with the 67th SOS, can testify. He will never forget his first flight as an aircraft commander. On 29 October 1992 he was ferrying his Combat Shadow from Alconbury to Eglin AFB in Florida when a series of major malfunctions occurred, almost causing his aeroplane to glide into the Atlantic. The Combat Shadow usually flies at night, on clandestine or low-visibility, single-or multi-ship missions, intruding politically sensitive or hostile areas to provide air refuelling for special operations aircraft. On this mission, apart from the two pilots, the crew comprised navigators Captain Daniel Sanchez and Captain Shaun Maynard, radio operator S/Sgt. Matthew J. Hromalik, flight engineer T/Sgt. William Jennings, loadmaster T/Sgt. Ed Franklin and crew chiefs SrAs Peter S. Delcotto and Texas Spicer.

The pilot and his crew were cruising along at 270 m.p.h. at 18,000ft, carrying 150,000lbs of fuel and cargo on a ten-hour flight to deliver aircraft 66-0220 to a unit at Eglin. Lambert later recalled: ''We were just sitting down for a long cruise, when about an hour into the flight we lost power to one of the four Allison turboprop engines. All of a sudden the electronics told the engine to go to idle power, which means there is no thrust.'' The aircraft was still capable of flying on three engines, and the crew started shutdown procedures. However, the one engine malfunction quickly compounded, causing all four engines to ''roll back''. The number one engine exhibited symptoms of a fire, and copilot Captain Walter Mulder began engine shutdown procedures, but was stopped by flight engineer T/Sgt. William Jennings, who saw the number three engine roll back. Just as quickly, engines two and four followed suit.

Keeping cool, the crew went through a five-stage emergency

checklist procedure as the aircraft began to descend towards the Atlantic waters. When the last switch on the last step was turned, the malfunction corrected itself and the engines whined back into life. Rather than risk a repeat performance whilst crossing the ocean, Lambert declared an inflight emergency and immediately returned to Alconbury. Once on the ground again, the crew had to wait five hours while maintenance replaced the synchro-phaser, a device that synchronises the propellers to produce thrust. Maintenance crews also made engine-check runs and performed an inspection on the high-frequency radio wire shielding, before certifying the aircraft fit to continue the mission to Eglin.

Crew rest requirements now led to a change in flight plans, so instead of flying for ten hours over the Atlantic to Halifax, Nova Scotia, Lambert's crew stopped in the Azores for a rest, then flew 66-0220 to Eglin the next day. Thankfully, the flight was uneventful.

THE 353RD SPECIAL OPERATIONS GROUP, JAPAN

The 353rd Special Operations Wing was activated at Kadena Air Base, Okinawa, on 6 April 1989 and assigned to 23rd Air Force. The designation of the 353rd SOW was derived from the old 3rd Air Commando Group, which served in the Southwest Pacific at the end of the Second World War and the 553rd Reconnaissance Wing. The 553rd was activated in February 1967, and flew electronic reconnaissance missions in EC-121R aircraft out of Korat Royal Thai Air Force Base. A detachment at NKP provided combat evaluation of the Beechcraft QU-22 drone aircraft and associated equipment. The Wing supported Task Force Alpha activities involving the Igloo White infiltration surveillance programme. Electronic sensors were air-dropped at various locations over the Ho Chi Minh Trail to detect movement of trucks and personnel. When the sensors were activated a transmission would be sent to the orbiting EC-121R, which relayed the data to the Infiltration Surveillance Centre at NKP. Air strikes would then be tasked to the locations where the sensors had detected enemy activity. Recently redesignated a Group, the 353rd SOG headquarters is still at Kadena Air Base, and is the Air Force component for Special Operations Command Pacific. Its squadrons are the 1st SOS, flying the MC-130E/H; the 31st SOS with the MH-53J; and the 17th SOS with the HC-130P/N. The 1st SOS is stationed at Kadena and the 17th and 31st SOS are at Osan Air Base, South Korea.

The 31st SOS are known as the "Black Knights" and became a Special Operations Squadron in April 1989. The Black Knight symbol originated with Air Force Systems Command Aeronautical Systems Division. Their Special Projects Division chose the symbol because their projects, such as Pave Low, worked best on the blackest of nights. Before 1989 the 31st was a rescue squadron, based at Clark Air Base in the Philippines. Based in an area of typhoons and earthquakes, the unit has participated in many humanitarian relief efforts, including the earthquake that hit Luzon in 1990. That same year they exchanged their CH/HH-3s for MH-53Js.

The 1st SOS is a Combat Talon unit with a long and distinguished history stretching back to the Skyraider days of 1963. In 1972 the 1st moved to Kadena Air Base and took over the aircraft previously used in South Vietnam by the 15th and 90th SOS. Since then, the unit has been used in support of conventional warfare exercises and operational missions as directed by Commander-in-Chief, Pacific. The squadron moved to Clark Air Base in January 1981, in an effort to facilitate training and co-locate with other C-130 units. On 1 March 1981, when MAC assumed responsibility for the management of Special Operation Forces, the 1st SOS was assigned to MAC's newly established 2nd Air Division, with headquarters at Hurlburt Field. When the 2nd AD was deactivated in February 1987, the 1st SOS came directly under 23rd Air Force at Hurlburt until its transfer to the 353rd SOW.

THE TALON OF THE 1990S

Today's Combat Talon is equipped with terrain-following/terrain-avoidance radar, so that missions may be flown down to 250ft AGL in darkness and reduced visibility. The INS, GPS, advanced Doppler radar and mapping radar provide the extremely accurate position data required by extremely low-level flight. The aft cargo ramp and door operating system has been modified to permit the airdropping of cargo at normal cruising speeds. This enables the aircrew to execute resupply airdrops without tell-tale speed reductions detectable by enemy radar or visual means. Electronic countermeasures equipment is installed to detect and defeat (if necessary for escape) enemy defences. Missions are normally flown in a passive mode to ensure covert flight.

Typically, an MC-130 mission into denied territory requires extremely detailed planning over several days. Copious amounts of intelligence data and an outstanding knowledge of aircraft capabilities and possible tactics will be required by the aircrew in order to select the best possible ingress and egress route. The aircrew works with the customer to select personnel drop zones. Terrain features, electronic order of battle, ground order of battle, air order of battle and naval order of battle will all be studied. Additionally, backup plans for aircraft equipment failures, airborne emergencies and aircrew escape and evasion will become integral parts of the overall mission plan.

When the aircrew is satisfied that their mission plan is feasible and will meet the customer's requirement for either covert or clandestine (deniable) operations, the final plan is briefed back to the air commander for approval. The commander and his "murder board" test the aircrew and their plan to ensure reasonableness and validity. If the mission is to parachute or air-land a customer, a face-to-face briefing will normally be held to ensure perfect co-ordination and understanding of all details. The mission is then ready for execution.

When directed by competent authority the mission will launch in order to make good the prearranged time over target (TOT) at the drop zone. Normally the first portion of the mission will be flown as high as possible, given the threats and aircraft weight, to conserve fuel. Aerial refuelling may also be conducted.

The aircraft will descend to low level (1,000ft AGL or lower) before reaching the range at which it could be detected by unfriendly radar. The 500ft or 250ft system "detents" are normally selected to keep the aircraft well below detection altitudes. The low-level portion will be flown in segments of perhaps 40 to 100 miles, which facilitates working around the highest terrain, permitting the aircraft to stay below radar detection altitudes. If the aircraft were to be detected by radar, segmenting the route also prevents ground agencies from forecasting the target area or ingress/egress points. The onboard navigation equipment will frequently be updated against prominent radar points, such as bridges or peaks, and cross-checked for accuracy. The electronic warfare officer will constantly monitor his equipment for unplanned detection and threats.

As the aircraft approaches the drop zone, the aircrew will prepare the customer for parachuting, or finish rigging the resupply bundles. For personnel drops, a slowdown to a safe personnel exit airspeed and a climb to a minimum safe personnel parachute altitude will be made only moments before the drop signal is given. For resupply drops, cruise airspeed and minimum altitude will be maintained. Once the load is clear of the aircraft the aircrew will accomplish escape procedures. The doors and ramp will be closed. For a resupply, the present heading might be continued to ensure the drop zone is not highlighted. For a personnel drop, the aircraft will accelerate to cruise airspeed and descend back to cruise altitude.

The egress portion of the mission is flown with the same degree of accuracy and respect for defences as the ingress portion. A mistake during this part of the mission would be just as deadly for the aircrew as if it occurred inbound, and could compromise the mission. Clear of threats, the aircraft will climb up to mid-or high altitudes to conserve fuel for the return to base.

SOMALIA: OPERATION CONTINUE HOPE

One of the last foreign policy decisions made by President George Bush, before his election defeat by Bill Clinton, was to send American troops to Somalia, under the auspicies of the United Nations. Located in the Horn of Africa, on the Indian Ocean, Somalia is a country suffering from famine and disease. Ruled by despotic warlords, the country was in dire need of outside help. The United Nations decided to step in and Operation Provide Relief was launched.

The multi-national security and airlift operation began in August 1992 and 78,000 tonnes of food had been delivered to Somalia by 1 November. However, the various warring factions were preventing the aid convoys from reaching the people who needed them most, so on 3 December the United Nations Security Council passed resolution 794, authorising members to "establish a secure environment" for humanitarian relief operations in Somalia." The same day, Operation Restore Hope began, with the arrival of ships from the 1st Marine Expeditionary Force off the coast of Somalia. Six days later the first of 16,000 Marines and 10,000 infantrymen came ashore and moved into the country to suppress the warlords. Troops from other countries such as France, Canada, Belgium and Italy were sent to Somalia as well.

Operation Restore Hope had been superceded by Operation Continue Hope when Spectre appeared on the scene on 11 June. Three AC-130Hs from the 16th SOS took part in the initial air strike in the United Nations Operations in Somalia (UNOSOM II) attack directed against Somali warlord General Mohammed Farah Aidid. The aircraft, using the call signs "Reach 67, 68 and 69" flew from the nearby Republic of Djibouti to Mogadishu, Somalia and refuelled there, taking off at 10,000lb above normal peacetime maximum allowable gross weight.

Reach 68's primary mission was to destroy "Radio Mogadishu," a Somalian radio station used by General Aidid to broadcast propaganda, while Reach 67 engaged targets to the North. Despite problems with the fire control system computers, the crew of Reach 68 did an outstanding job of manipulating the 50-pound 105mm rounds in the blacked-out cargo bay and arming the fuses as directed by the Fire Control Officer. The gunners would have the next round ready to fire as the preceding round was impacting the target. In total, 96 105mm high explosive rounds were delivered on the target, destroying the four power generators and the radio equipment and causing massive damage to the buildings in the complex.

Reach 69, which was tasked to destroy an armored tank compound, also suffered multiple mission computer malfunctions and the crew was forced to manually fire the 105mm gun using a hand-pulled lanyard. This rarely used procedure requires exceptional co-ordination between the pilot, fire control officer and gunners. To complicate matters, the aircraft received several infrared surface-to-air missile launch warnings, which required defensive manoeuvres, even though the signals were later determined to be false alarms. All three crews were eventually recommended for the Air Medal following the missions.

On 16 June, Reach 67 was in action again, attacking several weapons caches, General Aidid's compound and guardhouse. Ground personnel also directed attacks on several other targets, including roadblocks and "technical vehicles" before the aircraft headed for Magadishu to assist another gunship which experienced an in-flight emergency.

Reach 66 was the unlucky aircraft concerned. Taking-off from Mogadishu airport, again weighing 165,000lb, 10,000lb over normal maximum allowable peacetime gross weight, the aircraft had ascended to 100 feet above the ground when the number three "engine fire" light illuminated. The right scanner confirmed that flames were coming from the aft portion of the engine. The flight engineer began dumping fuel as the electronics warfare officer disarmed the automatic defensive flare dispensing system—a false alarm would have ejected flares into the clouds of fuel.

Because of the marginal aircraft climb performance, the crew kept the engine running until reaching 1,000 feet, then it was shut down and its fire extinguisher activated. Since no operational instrument approaches into Mogadishu airport existed, the navigator began giving vectors for an airborne radar approach (ARA). However, while the flight engineer was carrying out the post-engine shutdown procedures for the number three engine, the copilot discovered the throttle for the number four engine was stuck in the maximum power position. The marginal weather conditions and the problem with the number four engine precluded landing on the first ARA, and in addition, cockpit indications revealed an engine bleed air leak continuing to burn wire bundles in the right wing, despite the number three engine being shut down, the number four engine bleed air valve being closed and the flight engineer isolating the right wing from all bleed air sources.

The crew set up for a second ARA and at ten miles out they initiated shutdown of the number four engine. The copilot and flight engineer anticipated the possibility that the malfunction jamming the number four engine throttle cable could also affect the operation of the condition lever. The copilot placed his free hand on the fire handle as an electrical backup to the condition lever. When the condition lever would only go two thirds of the way to the "Feather" position, the copilot immediately continued the shutdown with the fire handle. Had the propeller failed to feather, the AC-130 would likely have crashed.

The crew prepared to perform a two-engine no-flap landing, with a 15 knot tailwind, and the pilot executed a flawless approach and touch-down. Due to the tailwind, and having no capability to use engine reversing, the aircraft experienced hot brakes, but nevertheless taxied back to the parking area to keep the runway clear for the other gunships still in the air. With the lives of 16 crewmembers and a $70 million aircraft at stake, the crew displayed exceptional teamwork and coordination to overcome an extremely dangerous aircraft malfunction in combat conditions.

Combat conditions on the ground in Mogadishu on the 3 and 4 October 1993, led to the award of two Silver Stars and an Air Force Cross to three NCOs from the 24th Special Tactics Squadron, based at Pope AFB, North Carolina. The squadron, composed of combat controllers and pararescuemen, were part of United Nations Operations in Somalia II/Task Force Ranger, a joint-service team sent into Mohammed Farah Aidid-controlled territory to capture militia leaders, blamed for attacks on US and UN troops. In the ensuing gun battle, 19 Americans were killed and 74 others wounded in what would become the longest firefight involving US troops in twenty years. Somali casualties were estimated at nearly 1,000. The American public would be shocked by reports of dead troopers being dragged through the streets of Mogadishu, while a captured helicopter pilot was displayed on television.

The battle took place in a maze of streets, alleys and multi-storey buildings; a soldier's nightmare. Pararescuemen TSgt. Timothy Wilkinson and MSgt. Scott C. Fales were part of a combat search and rescue team that fast-roped into downtown

Mogadishu after Somalis downed the first of two Blackhawk helicopters. Despite the small-arms fire coming at them from three directions, they worked their way to the downed helicopter to extract wounded and dead crewmembers. Fales was shot in the leg during the rescue, but disregarded his injuries to tend to his more seriously wounded comrades during the 18-hour ordeal, often throwing himself over the wounded during frequent grenade attacks. Crouched in the hull of the wrecked helicopter, Wilkinson worked frantically to free a trapped crewman as small-arms fire threw razor-sharp shrapnel in every direction. Metal fragments hit Wilkinson in the face and lower arm, but he continued until all the injured were removed to the casualty collection point.

Wilkinson then raced through a hail of small-arms fire across an open intersection to care for Rangers cut down while manoeuvring towards the helicopter crash site. He ran through a thick barrage of enemy fire to help pull the wounded, one by one, to safe cover. When his medical supplies ran out, he ran back across the deadly intersection to retrieve supplies from the wreckage. He rejoined the wounded Rangers to treat them throughout the night, despite continuous small-arms fire and two direct hits by rocket-propelled grenades in the defensive strongpoint.

Also in the same strongpoint was SSgt. Jeffrey W. Bray, who helped fend off advancing Somalis by directing helicopter gunship missions over the besieged area. Bray, a combat controller, called in "Danger Close" fire support missions that brought gunship rounds to within ten metres of his position. Eye witnesses spoke of his courage and coolness under fire, while directing precise helicopter gunfire to keep a determined enemy from over-running the team.

Wilkinson received the Air Force Cross and Fales and Bray the Silver Star on 31 January 1994, from Air Force Chief-of-Staff General Merrill A. McPeak. Wilkinson is the first enlisted man to earn the Air Force Cross in 19 years. Fales and Bray join nine enlisted men who earned Silver Stars during Desert Storm.*

*Eight other members of the 24th STS were awarded Bronze Stars with Valor or Bronze Stars, for their action during the firefight. They

On 14 March 1994 a 16th SOS AC-130H, call sign "Jockey 14" crash-landed 200 yards off the coast near the town of Malindi, Kenya. Eight of the 14 crewmen perished, following "a catastrophic malfunction" whilst on a UN support mission over Somalia. They were Captain David J. Mehlhop, navigator; Captain Anthony Stefanik, fire control officer; Captain Mark A. Quam, electronic warfare officer; SSgt. William C. Eyler, sensor operator; MSgt. Roy S. Duncan, loadmaster; TSgt. Robert L. Daniel, sensor operator; SSgt. Brian P. Barnes, aerial gunner; SSgt. Mike E. Moser, aerial gunner. A board of Air Force officers has been appointed to investigate the accident.

By the end of March, the three remaining AC-130Hs and the last United States combat troops had departed from Somalia.

THE FUTURE FOR SPECIAL OPERATIONS?

What does the future hold for AFSOC? It will be interesting, to say the least. Let us look, for example, at Spectre operations during 1993. Much of the details of gunship operations during the Gulf War are still classified, "due to the nature of some of the equipment used, sources and areas involved. Some of the sources are still in place and release of certain information would endanger their continued operation and existence." Those words were spoken by one of the special operators who may have to return to the Gulf to finish what the Allies started in 1991.

In June 1993 four Spectres were despatched to Djibouti to support US/UN operations in Somalia. They performed night reconnaissance and fired upon identified weapons caches and storage areas of the local warlords. They returned to the States on 14 July, and just three days later two aircraft and four crews were despatched to Brindisi, Italy, to support the UN mission

---

are MSgt. Jack J. McMullen, SSgt. Daniel G. Schilling, Sgt. Patrick C. Rogers, Lt.-Col. James L. Oeser, 24th STS Commander, SMSgt. Russell J. Tanner, MSgt. Robert G. Rankin, SSgt. Ray J. Benjamin and SSgt. John L. McGarry.

in the former Yugoslavia. Two weeks later another two aircraft joined them. The mission was to locate and identify locations of warring factions and to respond, if necessary, to support any UN forces which might be engaged by hostile forces. Although they did no shooting during those missions, they were fired upon by AAA and AA missiles on several occasions. They avoided the threats by the use of jammers, decoys and evasive manoeuvres.

As a result of the ambush of US forces in Somalia on 3 October, after which the bodies of dead troopers were dragged through the streets of Mogadishu, the Spectres were deployed to "a location in Africa" to provide support for US troops in Somalia if they were engaged again in hostile actions with the Somali gunmen. The Spectre is ideally suited for this mission, as it has the equipment to take out opposing forces while staying out of range of many of the ground-based weapons. In addition, the 40mm and 105mm guns are more accurate than helicopter-launched rockets and missiles, and cause less collateral damage. It is also a lot cheaper to use a 40 or 105mm gun than a TOW or AGM-114 Hellfire missile to take out a truck or building. The ability to engage targets from above is of advantage in a built-up area. Helicopters usually have to engage over a slant range, and enter the threat range of small-arms and RPGs. Moreover, the sensors allow Spectre to identify targets without their being aware that they have been spotted. At night, the first clue the enemy has that Spectre is in the area is the impact of incoming rounds.

A few modifications have taken place to enhance the survivability of Spectre in the Yugoslavian and African theatres. The 2kW searchlight has been panelled over, as it is too strong an IR target source for surface-to-air missiles when operating. The number one gun, a 20mm, has been removed, and a clear panel has been put in the gunport to accommodate an additional scanner. Despite the introduction of automatic threat identification and response systems, the Mark One eyeball tied to a brain trained to identify threats is still the most accurate system on board.

Current operations aside, a lot of money is being spent on modifying and upgrading aircraft and systems, even in these hard times. All 28 HC-130s are being modified with precision navigation systems and a limited electronic countermeasures capability, and an air-refuelling program is also under way for all Combat Shadow aircraft. Twenty-eight MH-53Js are in the AFSOC inventory, and 13 more are to be converted to the J-model configuration for a future total force of 41 Pave Low III helicopters. The AC-130U Spectre will have all-weather capability with the installation of the F-15 strike radar. The new fire control system can track multiple targets and shoot two different weapons at two different targets simultaneously. Thirteen should join the force between 1994 and 1996. Fourteen Combat Talon 1s are in service, nine fitted with the Fulton recovery system, and some are modified to conduct missions as penetrating tankers. All Combat Talon 1s are being retro-fitted with this helicopter air-refuelling capability. Soon, 24 Combat Talon II MC-130Hs will be in service, with one arriving every two months. In addition, as its organisation grows, AFSOC's 11,000 members will be joined by 2,100 more by 1996.

The weapons, systems and manpower are not cheap, but it may be money well spent. The world is still unstable; Yugoslavia is in turmoil with civil war, Iraq still has a war-mongering dictator running the country, and the newly dissolved USSR and its fledgling states are due for a long cold winter. It is also likely that former Soviet nuclear weapons have been sold to unstable countries such as Iran. The humanitarian relief efforts in Somalia finally deteriorated into a small guerrilla-type war, for which the Air Commandos were reactivated in the 1960s. Have we gone full circle, through total war to brushfire wars again? Perhaps the Special Operations Squadrons will be in action again sooner than we think.

APPENDIX 1

Tail codes of Air Commando and Special Operations aircraft during the Vietnam years

Aircraft code	Unit assigned	Base assigned	Aircraft type	Notes
AA	Det 1/1 SOW	Da Nang, RVN	C-123K, U-10A/B	
AB	Det 2/1 SOW	Pope AFB, NC	C-130E	
AB	318 SOS/1 SOW	Pope AFB, NC	C-130E	
AD	4407 CCTS/1 SOW/4410 CCTW	Hurlburt Field	A-1E/G/H, T-28D	After A-26A
AF	603 SOS/1 SOW	Hurlburt Field	A-37B	
AG	319 SOS/1 SOW	Hurlburt Field	C-123K	
AH	415 SOTS/1 SOW	Hurlburt Field	AC-119G/K, AC-130A	
AO	4408 CCTS/4410 CCTW/1 SOW	Hurlburt Field	C-123K	
AO	317 SOS/1 SOW	Hurlburt Field	UH-1N, U-10A/B, A-1E	
			C-123K, A-1E	
AP	4409 CCTS/4410 CCTW/1 SOW	Hurlburt Field	UH-1F/P	Became 549 TASTS
AP	549 TASTS/1 SOW	Hurlburt Field	UH-1F/P, OV-10A	
AQ	4410 CCTS/4410 CCTW/1 SOW	Hurlburt Field	UH-1F/P	Became 547 TASTS
AQ	547 TASTS/1 SOW	Hurlburt Field	O-1E, O-2A, UH-1F/P, U-10A	
CF	8 AS/3 TFW	Bien Hoa, RVN	A-37B	
CG	90 AS/14 SOW	Bien Hoa, RVN	A-37B	
CK	604 SOS/3 TFW	Bien Hoa, RVN	A-37A/B	
EA	16 SOS/8 TFW	Ubon, Thailand	AC-130A	Combat Dragon
EC	1 ACS/14 ACW	Pleiku, RVN	A-1E/G	Spectre
EF	17 SOS/14 SOW	Nha Trang, RVN	AC-119G	Hobos
EH	18 SOS/14 SOW	Nakhon Phanom, Thailand	AC-119K	Shadow
EK	8 SOS/14 SOW	Bien Hoa, RVN	A-37B	Stinger

Aircraft code	Unit assigned	Base assigned	Aircraft type	Notes
EL	3 SOS/14 SOW	Pleiku, RVN	AC-47D	Spooky
EN	4 SOS/14 SOW	Pleiku, RVN	AC-47D	Spooky
EO	5 SOS/14 SOW	Nha Trang, RVN	C-47D, U-108B/D	Psyops
ER	9 SOS/14 SOW	Nha Trang, RVN	C-47, O-2B	Psyops
ES	78 SOS/917 SOG/434 SOW	Barksdale AFB, LA	A-37B	Became 47 TFS
ET	6 SOS/633 SOW	Pleiku, RVN	A-1E/H	Spads
FT	16 SOS/8 TFW	Ubon, Thailand	AC-130A/E	Spectre
HO	17 SOS/930 SOG/434 SOW	Grissom AFB, Ind	A-37B	
HW	24 SOS/24 CW	Howard AFB, Panama	A-37, UH-1N	
IA	Det 1/1 SOW	Otis AFB, Mass	C-123K	
IB	Det 2/1 SOW	Pope AFB, NC	C-130E	
IC	71 SOS/4410 CCTS, 4410 SOTG	Lockbourne AFB, Pease AFB	AC-119G/AC-130A	
ID	317 SOS/4410 SOTG	England, AFB, LA	EC-47P/Q	1968-70
ID	72 SOS/931 SOG/434 SOW	Grissom AFB, Ind	A-37A	
IE	319 SOS/4410 SOTG	England AFB, LA	UC-123B, C-123K	
IE	4408 CCTS/4419 SOTG	England AFB, LA	C-123K	
IE	43 SOTS/4410 SSOTG	England AFB, LA	C-123K	
IF	603 SOS/4410 CCTW	England AFB, LA	A-26A	Big Eagle
IG	4412 CCTS/4410 SOTG	England AFB, LA	AC-47D	
IG	548 SOTS/4410 SOTG	England AFB, LA	AC-47D	
IH	4413 CCTS/4410 CCTW	Lockbourne AFB, OH	AC-119G/K, AC-130A	Became 415 SOTS in 1970
II	4532 CCTS/4410 CCTW	England AFB, LA	A-37A/B	
IJ	4406 CCTS/4410 CCTW	England AFB, LA	A-37B	Became 427 SOTS in 1970
IJ	427 SOTS/4410 SOTG	England AFB, LA	A-37B	
IK	6 SOS/4410 SOTG	England AFB, LA	A-37B	
IK	514 AS/4410 CCTW	England AFB, LA	A-37B	1969-70

Code	Unit	Location	Aircraft	AFRES 1974-87 / Notes
IY	757 SOS/910 SOG/434 SOW	Youngstown, OH	A-37B	AFRES 1974-87
LH	302 SOS/302 SOG	Luke AFB, AZ	CH-3E	
OB	40 TAS/317 TAW	Lockbourne AFB, OH	AC-130A	1969-70
OS	4 SOS/432 TRW	Udorn RTAFB, Thailand	AC-47D	Nimrods
TA	609 SOS/56 SOW	Nakhon Phanom RTAFB, Thailand	A-26A	Hobos
TC	1 SOS/56 SOW	Nakhon Phanom RTAFB, Thailand	A-1E,G/H/J C-123K	Candle Zorro
TO	606 SOS/56 SOW	Nakhon Phanom RTAFB, Thailand	T-28D	Zorro
TS	22 SOS/56 SOW	Nakhon Phanom RTAFB,	A-1E/G/H/J	
TT	602 SOS/56 SOW	Nakhon Phanom RTAFB,	A-1E/G/H/J	
VA	703 SOS/4463 TASG	Shaw AFB, SC	HH-3E	
WE	19 ACS/315 ACW	Tan Son Nhut, RVN	C-123B/K	To 315 TAW in Jan 1970
WH	309 ACS/315 ACW	Tan Son Nhut, RVN	C-123B/K	To 315 TAW in Jan 1970
WM	310 ACS/315 ACW	Nha Trang, RVN	C-123B/K	To 315 TAW in Jan 1970
WP	16 SOS/8 TFW	Ubon RTAFB, Thailand	AC-130H	1974
WV	311 ACS/315 ACW	Da Nang, RVN	C-123B/K	To 315 TAW in Jan 1970

No Tail Codes Assigned to Aircraft

Unit	Location	Aircraft	Notes
10 FS(C)/3 TFW	Bien Hoa, RVN	F-5A	Transferred its 18 aircraft to 522nd FS, VNAF, 17 April 1967
15 SOSs/14 SOW	Nha Trang, RVN	MC-130	
12 ACS/315 ACW	Bien Hoa, RVN	UC-123B/K	Ranch Hand
1st Flt det, SOG	Nha Trang, RVN	C-123	
20 SOS/14 SOW	Nha Trang, RVN	CH-3, UH-1	
21 SOS/14 SOW	NKP, RTAFB, Thailand	CH-3	

After 1978 tail codes were deleted from all Special Operations aircraft.
In 1968 24 PACAF Wings were allocated a letter code to be followed by another letter identifying the squadron. 14 SOW was E, 56 SOW was T, and 315 SOW was W.

APPENDIX 2

The F-4 Song
Composed by Paul "Hulk" Marshalk and Leon "Crazy" Poteet
whilst flying Nimrods out of NKP, this song was a result of their
frustration with the "fast movers" and the boredom of flying holding
patterns over the Trail during the wet season. It is sung to the tune
of "Freight Train, Freight Train," and is reproduced here with their
kind permission.

> The other night I worked with Nail,
> F-4 showed up without fail,
> Through the area without a word,
> Came so close I flipped him a bird.

> *Chorus*
>
> > F-4, F-4, fly so fast,
> > Can't see shit, can't hit your ass
> > Why the hell do you fly at night
> > And give us all a fright?

> The marks are out, the flares are lit,
> The trucks are down there to be hit
> As I rolled in for my first pass,
> Here came the F-4 out of gas.

> Says the Candle, "Sorry Nim,
> F-4's low, got to put him in,
> Pull off twenty miles and stay
> And I'll go thirty the other way."

> Then comes another F-4 flight,
> Straight from the tanker, fuel's all right.
> In they go, up comes the gun
> "Sorry Candle, we've got to run."

F-4s are there, they see their mark,
Cleared in hot they make their start,
Down the chute, one pass and go,
Candle tells them RNO.

Ten minutes later, back over the Trail
Candle looks, but no avail,
"Sorry Nim, but there's nothing to see,
all the trucks are in the trees."

Sometimes F-4s are okay
That is mostly in the day.
To get BDA at night,
Keep the bastards out of sight.

Appendix 3

ORGANIZATIONAL CHART

HQ AFSOC
Hurlburt Field, Fla.

16th SOW
Hurlburt Field, Fla.

16th OG
9th SOS
9th SOS*
16th EOS
18th FDS
20th SOS
55th SOS
16th OSS

16th SPTG
16th CRS
16th CES
16th EMS
16th LSS
16th COMS
16th SUPS

16th S/FTG
16th LG
16th M&S
16th SPS
16th MWR
ASS
16th OS

OLA**
OL A (Dam Neck, Va.)
OL B (Harrisburg, Pa.)
OL C (Duke Field, Fla.)

352nd SOG
RAF Alconbury, U.K.

7th SOS
21st SOS
67th SOS
352nd SOMS
352nd SOSS
321st STS
Det. 2. (RAF Mildenhall, U.K.)

353rd SOG
Kadena AB, Japan

1st SOS
17th SOS
31st SOS (Osan AB, Korea)
353rd SOMS
353rd SOSS
320th STS
OLA (Osan AB, Korea)

720th STG
Hurlburt Field, Fla.

23rd STS
24th STS (Pope AFB, N.C.)
OLA (Coronado NAB, Calif.)

* Located at Eglin AFB, Fla.
** Located at Ft. Campbell, Ky.

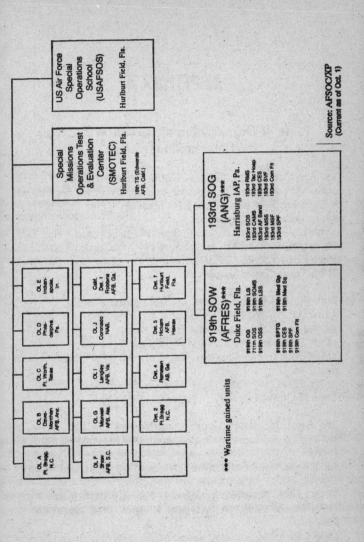

US Air Force Special Operations School (USAFSOS)

Hurlburt Field, Fla.

Special Missions Operations Test & Evaluation Center (SMOTEC)

Hurlburt Field, Fla.

18th TS (Edwards AFB, Calif.)

OL A Ft. Bragg, N.C.	OL B Davis-Monthan AFB, Ariz.	OL C Ft. Worth, Texas	OL D Phila- delphia, Pa.	OL E Indian- apolis, In.
OL F Shaw AFB, S.C.	OL G Maxwell AFB, Ala.	OL I Langley AFB, Va.	OL J Coronado NAB.	Calif. Det. 1 Robbins AFB, Ga.
	Det. 2 Ft. Bragg N.C.	Det. 4 Pennsacola AB, Ga.	Det. 5 Hickam AFB, Hawaii	Det. 7 Hurlburt Field, Fla.

919th SOW (AFRES)***

Duke Field, Fla.

919th OG
711th SOS
919th OSS

919th SFTO
919th CES
919th SPF
919th Com Flt

919th RMS
919th SOMS
919th LSS

919th Med Gp
919th Med Sq

193rd SOG (ANG)***

Harrisburg IAP, Pa.

193rd SOS
193rd CAMS
553rd AF Band
193rd MSS
193rd MSF
193rd SPF

193rd RMS
193rd Tac Hosp
193rd CES
193rd SVF
193rd Com Flt

*** Wartime gained units

Source: AFSOC/XP
(Current as of Oct. 1)

APPENDIX 4 ·

Table of Organisation of Second World War Commando Groups

1st Air Commando Group. China-Burma-India.

Initially Fighter Section, Bomber Section, Transport Section and Light Plane Section. In late 1944 became;

5th and 6th Fighter Squadrons.

164th Liaison Sqdn. Activated 1 Sept 1944. Inactivated 3 Nov 1945.

165th Liaison Sqdn. Activated 1 Sept 1944. Inactivated 3 Nov 1945.

166th Liaison Sqdn. Activated 1 Sept 1944. Inactivated 3 Nov 1945.

319th Troop Carrier Squadron.

2nd Air Commando Group. China-Burma-India.

Activated 25 April 1944

1st and 2nd Fighter Squadrons.

127th, 155th and 156th Liaison Squadrons.

317th Troop Carrier Squadron. Activated 1 May 1944, Inactivated 28 Feb 1946.

327th, 328th, 340th and 342nd Airdrome Squadrons.

236th Medical Dispensary (Aviation).

3rd Air Commando Group. South-West-Pacific.

3rd Fighter Squadron. Activated April 1944. Inactivated February 1946.

4th Fighter Squadron. Activated 1 May 1944. Inactivated February 1946.

157th Liaison Squadron. Activated 23 February 1944. Inactivated?

159th Liaison Squadron. Activated 1 March 1944. Inactivated 31 May 1946.

160th Liaison Squadron. Activated March 1944. Inactivated December 1945.

318th Troop Carrier Squadron. Activated 1 May 1944, Inactivated 25 March 1946.

334th Airdrome Squadron. Activated 1 May 1944. Inactivated 8 November 1945.

335th Airdrome Squadron. Activated 1 May 1944. Inactivated February 1946.

341st Airdrome Squadron. Activated 31 May 1944. Inactivated September 1945.

343rd Airdrome Squadron. Activated 1 May 1944. Inactivated 29 October 1945.

237th Medical Dispensary (Aviation). Activated 15 March 1944. Inactivated 31 December 1945.

BIBLIOGRAPHY

1st Air Commando Group, R. D. Van Wagner, Military History Series 86-1, USAF Air Command and Staff College, 1986.

Back to Mandalay, Lowell Thomas, Fredrick Muller, London, 1952. The best account of the 1st Air Commando Group in Burma.

Chindit, Richard Rhodes James, John Murray Ltd, 1980. Story of an officer in 111 Brigade.

The Unforgettable Army, Colonel Michael Hickey, Book Club Associates, 1992. Story of the British 14th Army in Burma.

Honored and Betrayed, Richard Second, John Wiley and Sons Inc, 1992.

The Guts To Try, Colonel James H. Kyle, Orion Books, 1990. Operation Eagle Claw.

Just Cause, Malcolm McConnell, St Martin's Press, 1991. The Invasion of Panama 1989.

Tragic Mountains, Jane Hamilton-Merritt, Indiana University Press, 1993. Story of the Hmong, the Americans and the secret war for Laos 1942–92.

The Raid, Benjamin F. Schemmer, Avon Books/Harper and Row, 1986. Story of the Son Tay Raid.

Beyond the Chindwin, Bernard Fergusson, Anthony Mott Ltd, 1983. Wingate's first Burma expedition in 1943.

Gunship; Spectre of Death, Henry Zeybel, Pan Books, 1987. First Hand "Fiction" from former Spectre Navigator.

A-37 "RAP" Combat and *What Happened to Me since Vietnam* stories. In-house book produced by A-37 Association. See address on page 9.

Air War Grenada, Stephen Harding, Pictorial Histories Publishing Co, Montana, 1984.

Commando Operations, Time-Life Books. Good account of Grenada and Panama operations.

Gunships, Larry Davis, Squadron/Signal Publications. Excellent pictorial guide to AC-47, AC-119G/K and AC-130.

Air Force Combat Wings; Lineage and Honors Histories 1947–77, Office of Air Force History, 1984. Includes lineage, dates, equipment of Air Commando Wings.

ABBREVIATIONS/
GLOSSARY OF TERMS

AAA	Anti-Aircraft Artillery
ACG	Air Commando Group
ACS	Air Commando Squadron
ACW	Air Commando Wing
AD	Air Division
AFSOC	Air Force Special Operations Command
AFSOF	Air Force Special Operations Force
AGL	Above Ground Level
ANG	Air National Guard
ARS	Air Resupply Squadron/Air Rescue Squadron
ARVN	Army of the Republic of Vietnam
BDA	Bomb Damage Assessment
Black Crow	Sensor for detecting emissions from truck engines
Black Spot	Fairchild AC/NC-123 gunship project
Blind Bat	Lockheed C-130 Hercules flareship
cal	calibre
Candlestick	Fairchild C-123B/K Provider flareship
CAS	Controlled American Source
CBU	Cluster Bomb Unit
CCTS	Combat Crew Training Squadron
CCTW	Combat Crew Training Wing
CIA	Central Intelligence Agency
CIDG	Civilian Irregular Defense Force
Combat Talon I	Lockheed MC-130E Hercules
Combat Talon II	Lockheed MC-130H Hercules
COSVN	Central Office for South Vietnam
DFC	Distinguished Flying Cross
DMZ	Demilitarized Zone
EOD	Explosive Ordnance Disposal
FAC	Forward Air Controller
FLIR	Forward-Looking Infra-red
FROG	Free Rocket Over Ground

FS	Fighter Squadron
Hooch	Hut/dwelling
H and I	Harrassment and Interdiction artillery fire
IFR	Instrument Flight Rules
IP	Instructor Pilot
IR	Infra-red
Klick	Short for Kilometer
Kt	Knots
LLLTV	Low Light Level Television
LS	Liaison Squadron
LZ	Landing Zone
MAAG	Military Assistance Advisory Group
MAC	Military Airlift Command
MACTHAI	Military Assistance Command Thailand
MACV	Military Assistance Command Vietnam
MSgt	Master Sergeant
NKP	Nakhon Phanom Royal Thai Air Force Base
NVA	North Vietnamese Army
NVG	Night Vision Goggles
Pave Low	Sikorsky MH-53H/J project
PJ	Para-Jumper/Para-Rescueman
POW	Prisoner of war
Prep	Preparation or pre-landing fire on an LZ
PZ	Pickup Zone
Raven	Callsign of USAF FACs assigned to General Vang Pao
rpm	Revolutions per minute
RTAFB	Royal Thai Air Force Base
SAM	Surface to air missile
SAS	Special Air Service
SATCOM	Satellite Communications
SEA	South-East Asia
SEALs	Sea-Air-Land Navy Commandos
SEATO	South-East Asia Treaty Organisation
Shadow	Fairchild AC-119G Flying Boxcar gunship
Slicks	Troop-carrying Hueys
SOF	Special Operations Forces
SOG	Special Operations Group
SOTS	Special Operations Training Squadron
SOS	Special Operations Squadron
SOW	Special Operations Wing
Spectre	Lockheed AC-130A/E/H Hercules gunship

Spooky	Douglas AC-47 gunship
Stinger	Fairchild AC-119K Flying Boxcar gunship
TAC	Tactical Air Command
TACAIR	Tactical Air Support
TAOR	Tactical Area of Operational Responsibility
TASS	Tactical Air Support Squadron
TIC	Troops in contact
Tropic Moon	Martin B-57G Night Intruder project
USARV	United States Army Vietnam
USMACV	United States Military Assistance Command, Vietnam
USSOCOM	United States Special Operations Command
VC	Viet Cong
VNAF	Vietnamese Air Force
VFR	Visual Flight Rules
Waterpump	Air Commando training detachment in Thailand

Associations

Mr. Kenneth E. Heller, 2nd and 3rd Air Commando Group Association, 3716 E. Smoke Rise, Hill Drive, Charlotte, NC 28226, USA.

Mr. Jim Boney and Dan d'Errico, Air Commando Association, PO Box 7, Mary Esther, Florida 32569, USA.

Mr. Ollie Maier, (604th ACS)

A-37 Association, 306 Village Oak Drive, San Marcos, Texas 78666, USA.

Mr. Reuben Ware,

Skyraider Association, 9411 Nona Kay Drive, San Antonio, Texas 78217, USA.

Mr. William Johnson, First Air Commando Association, Box 445, Destin, Florida 32541, USA.

Major Jack Spey, Ranch Hand Association, 850 Tarpon Drive, Fort Walton Beach, Florida 32548, USA.

The author would also like to thank the Commandant of the Air War College, Air University, Maxwell AFB, for his permission to quote from Lt.-Colonel Theodore M. Faurer's professional study Number 5588, ''The First and Last AC-47 Squadron—a personal perspective.''

Index